Association and Enlightenment

STUDIES IN EIGHTEENTH-CENTURY SCOTLAND

Series editor: Richard B. Sher, New Jersey Institute of Technology and Rutgers University

This series, sponsored by the Eighteenth-Century Scottish Studies Society, publishes interdisciplinary multiauthor volumes on particular themes that explore a wide variety of topics having to do with the thought and culture of eighteenth-century Scotland, including Scottish connections and relations with other parts of the world.

Titles in the series:

Mark C. Wallace and Jane Rendall, eds., *Association and Enlightenment: Scottish Clubs and Societies, 1700–1830* (2020)

Ralph McLean, Ronnie Young, and Kenneth Simpson, eds., *The Scottish Enlightenment and Literary Culture* (2016)

Stana Nenadic, ed., *Scots in London in the Eighteenth Century* (2010)

Deidre Dawson and Pierre Morère, eds., *Scotland and France in the Enlightenment* (2004)

Ned C. Landsman, ed., *Nation and Province in the First British Empire: Scotland and the Americas, 1600–1800* (2001)

Association and Enlightenment

Scottish Clubs and Societies, 1700–1830

EDITED BY
MARK C. WALLACE
JANE RENDALL

FOREWORD BY
CHRISTOPHER A. WHATLEY

Bucknell University | University Press
LEWISBURG, PENNSYLVANIA

Library of Congress Cataloging-in-Publication Data

Names: Wallace, Mark C., editor. | Rendall, Jane, 1945- editor. | Whatley, Christopher A., writer of foreword.
Title: Association and enlightenment: Scottish clubs and societies, 1700–1830 / edited by Mark C. Wallace and Jane Rendall; foreword by Christopher A. Whatley.
Description: Lewisburg, Pennsylvania: Bucknell University Press, [2020] |
Series: Studies in eighteenth-century Scotland | Includes bibliographical references and index.
Identifiers: LCCN 2020008407 | ISBN 9781684482665 (paperback) | ISBN 9781684482672 (hardcover) | ISBN 9781684482689 (epub) | ISBN 9781684482696 (mobi) | ISBN 9781684482702 (pdf)
Subjects: LCSH: Clubs—Scotland—History—18th century. | Clubs—Scotland—History—19th century. | Societies—Scotland—History—18th century. | Societies—Scotland—History—19th century.
Classification: LCC HS2515.G7 A87 2020 | DDC 367/.941109033—dc23
LC record available at https://lccn.loc.gov/2020008407

A British Cataloging-in-Publication record for this book is available from the British Library.

♾ The paper used in this publication meets the requirements of the American National Standard for Information Sciences—Permanence of Paper for Printed Library Materials, ANSI Z39.48-1992.

www.bucknelluniversitypress.org

Distributed worldwide by Rutgers University Press

Manufactured in the United States of America

THE STRATHMARTINE TRUST

The authors acknowledge the receipt of a grant toward production costs from the Strathmartine Trust.

Contents

Foreword by Christopher A. Whatley vii
Abbreviations ix

Introduction 1
Mark C. Wallace and Jane Rendall

PART I
The Theory and Practice of Associational Life

1 Politeness, Sociability, and the "Little Platoon": Associational Theory in the Scottish Enlightenment 33
David Allan

2 Buildings, Associations, and Culture in the Scottish Provincial Town, c. 1700–1830 49
Bob Harris

PART II
Professional Men and Their Societies

3 Medical Societies and the Scottish Enlightenment 69
Jacqueline Jenkinson

4 Professors, Merchants, and Ministers in the Clubs of Eighteenth-Century Glasgow 85
Ralph McLean

PART III
Clubs, Societies, and Literary Culture

5 "Soaping" and "Shaving" the Public Sphere: James Boswell's "Soaping Club" and Edinburgh Enlightenment Sociability 103
James J. Caudle

6 The "Bohemian Club": A Study of Edinburgh's Cape Club 127
Rhona Brown

7 "Caledonia's Bard, Brother Burns": Robert Burns and Scottish Freemasonry 143
Corey E. Andrews

8 Inventing the Public Sphere: Fictional Club Life in Ireland and Scotland 161
Martyn J. Powell

PART IV
Gender and Associational Culture

9 Achieving Manhood in Associational Culture: Student Societies and Masculinity in Enlightenment Edinburgh 191
Rosalind Carr

10 Women's Associations in Scotland, 1790–1830 206
Jane Rendall

Acknowledgments 229
Bibliography 231
Notes on Contributors 257
Index 261

Foreword

The appearance of this volume in print is something to celebrate. It has been a long time in gestation. The instigator of the project that has resulted in the book, Mark C. Wallace, is to be commended, not only for taking the initiative and recruiting an impressive team of authors to write individual chapters, but for sticking with the task. Book editing is a fraught, drawn-out, patience-testing process, often held up by just a single laggard contributor who, when agreeing to participate, may have taken on one job too many. But as the editor implores (gently so as not to cause offense and the possible loss of a key chapter), and awaits the promised material, those contributors who have met their deadlines on time complain and demand to know why the publication has been delayed. In the hot seat is the editor. Veritably, a thankless undertaking.

Association and Enlightenment: Scottish Clubs and Societies, 1700–1830 has, though, been well worth the wait. Clubs and societies and other forms of associational behavior have for a long time now been the subject of serious inquiry for historians of the early modern era. However, a step change in our appreciation of their numbers, and understanding of their provenance, characteristics, and significance, occurred with the publication in 2000 of Peter Clark's *British Clubs and Societies, 1580–1800: The Origins of an Associational World.* Yet Clark had little to say about Scotland. This may have owed something to the fact that other than a few eminent exceptions, including Roger L. Emerson (on the part certain societies played in sowing the seeds of the Scottish Enlightenment), John Dwyer (on sociability), Richard B. Sher (notably on the Glasgow clubs), and one or two others, Scottish historians had paid less attention to associational activity than its importance merited. The better-known clubs and societies found their rightful place in the literature on improvement and Enlightenment. In some cases, notably those in Edinburgh and Glasgow, they were investigated. But of the others, whether in Edinburgh or elsewhere, little was known. This is no longer so. Since the turn of the present century, both established scholars and younger historians have shed new light on and made much clearer the range and roles of the numerous Scottish clubs and societies that flourished after the first of these were founded in the later seventeenth century.

The editors' rich introduction reveals the vigor and depth of this recent research endeavor. Several of the "new wave" of luminaries in the field have contributed chapters to this volume. Albeit that sociability was a common denominator, what is revealed is the sheer variety of associational activity, ranging from the lewdness and excesses of James Boswell's Soaping Club, which seems to have had much in common with the Fife-founded Beggar's Benison, to those with a more serious, improving, and even moral purpose. While Edinburgh and Glasgow feature prominently, we are introduced to hitherto little-studied clubs and societies, such as Edinburgh's Cape Club. But enormously welcome are contributions that either directly address or include reference to associational activity in the provinces—places like Perth and Dundee. Female associations too are included. The hope is that this neglected aspect of the subject will inspire further research. The same can be said of Freemasonry in the eighteenth century, which also features here, but is still massively underresearched and poorly understood. This represents a major lacuna in Scottish historical studies, given the sheer ubiquity of Freemasonry in nineteenth-century Scotland.

Rightly, the editors—Jane Rendall along with Mark C. Wallace—and their contributors are concerned with the motivations that lay behind the foundation of Scotland's clubs and societies. Much is said about the distinctly Scottish concerns of many of them. Not all had such concerns, being Scottish equivalents of their counterparts south of the border. Yet they were often spaces that allowed for the discussion of issues such as national identity (which some societies consciously forged), Scottish culture, and Scotland's apparent "backwardness." Many nurtured patriotism—national of course, but also (perhaps surprisingly) provincial, or local. At the same time, they could also be intensely pragmatic when it came to debating and even tackling specific Scottish challenges—such as the need to hasten agricultural improvement and disseminate more widely the means by which this could be achieved. But to summarize like this is to risk making unwarranted generalizations, and ignore the varied and competing aims and ideologies of the various clubs and societies, as well as the vexed questions of exclusiveness, inclusiveness, and class—all of which find a place in this volume.

Association and Enlightenment is not the final word on Scottish associationalism. Nor does it claim to be. But by taking stock of where we are now, asking the right questions, and providing at least partial answers to some of them, this collection of fresh and fascinating contributions represents a major advance in our knowledge and comprehension of institutions that played what is often an overlooked part in the making of modern Scotland.

—Christopher A. Whatley

Abbreviations

The date following the first mention of any club or society in the text is the date of its foundation, given wherever known. Frequently cited works, archives, libraries, journals, and periodicals have been identified throughout by the following abbreviations.

For archives and libraries:

ECA	Edinburgh City Archives
EUL	Edinburgh University Library
NLS	National Library of Scotland
NRS	National Records of Scotland
PKCA	Perth and Kinross Council Archive

For journal, periodical, and serial titles:

AJ	*Aberdeen Journal*
BOEC	*Book of the Old Edinburgh Club*
Br J Hist of Sci	*British Journal for the History of Science*
CM	*Caledonian Mercury*
ECI	*Edinburgh Christian Instructor*
GH	*Glasgow Herald*
Hist Sci	*History of Science*
HJ	*Hibernian Journal*
J for 18th Cent Stud	*Journal for Eighteenth-Century Studies*
MM	*Missionary Magazine*
SM	*Scots Magazine*

SMPR	*Scottish Missionary and Philanthropic Register*
SVEC	*Studies on Voltaire and the Eighteenth Century*

For specific works:

Boswell Gen. Corr. 1757–1763	James Boswell. *The General Correspondence of James Boswell, 1757–1763*. Edited by David Hankins and James J. Caudle. Edinburgh: Edinburgh University Press; New Haven, CT: Yale University Press, 2006.
Carlyle	Alexander Carlyle. *Autobiography of the Rev. Dr. Alexander Carlyle, Minister of Inveresk*. 3rd ed. Edinburgh: William Blackwood and Sons, 1861.
Clark	Peter Clark. *British Clubs and Societies, 1580–1800: The Origins of an Associational World*. Oxford: Oxford University Press, 2000.
DSL	*DSL / Dictionary of the Scots Language*. Online ed., incorporating the *Scottish National Dictionary*. https://dsl.ac.uk.
E-B	James Boswell. *Letters between the Honourable Andrew Erskine, and James Boswell, Esq*. London: W. Flexney, 1763.
Harris and McKean	Bob Harris and Charles McKean. *The Scottish Town in the Age of the Enlightenment, 1740–1820*. Edinburgh: Edinburgh University Press, 2014.
Humphry Clinker	Tobias Smollett. *The Expedition of Humphry Clinker*. Edited by Louis M. Knapp. Revised by Paul-Gabriel Boucé. Oxford: Oxford University Press, 1998.
McElroy, 1952	Davis D. McElroy. "Literary Clubs and Societies of Eighteenth-Century Scotland." PhD diss., 2 vols., University of Edinburgh, 1952. Index, with Lucille McElroy, University of Edinburgh, 1955.
McElroy, 1969	Davis D. McElroy. *Scotland's Age of Improvement: A Survey of Eighteenth-Century Literary Clubs and Societies*. Pullman: Washington State University Press, 1969.
NSA	*The New Statistical Account of Scotland*. 15 vols. Edinburgh: William Blackwood and Sons, 1845.
ODNB	*Oxford Dictionary of National Biography*. Oxford University Press, 2004; online ed. https://www.oxforddnb.com.

OED Online	*Oxford English Dictionary Online.* https://www.oed.com.
"Sociability and Society"	John Dwyer and Richard B. Sher, eds. "Sociability and Society in Eighteenth-Century Scotland." Special issue, *Eighteenth-Century Life* 15, nos. 1–2 (1991).
Strang	John Strang. *Glasgow and Its Clubs: Or Glimpses of the Condition, Manners, Characters, and Oddities of the City, during the Past and Present Centuries.* 3rd ed. Glasgow: John Smith, 1864.

Association and Enlightenment

Introduction

Mark C. Wallace and Jane Rendall

In May 1712 the poet Allan Ramsay became one of the six founding members of the Easy Club in Edinburgh; its members "Resolved at somtimes to retire from all other Business and Company and Meet in a Society By Themselves in order that by a Mutual improvement in Conversation they may become more adapted for fellowship with the politer part of mankind." The name of the club was intended to check "all unruly and disturbing behaviour among their Members," of whom there were never more than twelve during its short life; it was dissolved in 1715.[1] Almost a century later, in February 1811 in the small town of Maybole in Ayrshire, the annual celebration of friendly societies took place. Eight male and two female friendly societies along with two Masonic lodges marched in procession, together with all the schoolchildren of the town and accompanied by the Ayrshire militia band, to church to hear a sermon; since the local Farmers' Society had its quarterly meeting that day, some of its members also attended. After the sermon, the procession visited the minister's house and then paraded through the town, still accompanied by music.[2] This was an associational world, and in Scotland, as elsewhere in Britain, the impulse to association manifested itself in many different ways in the course of the long eighteenth century. Clubs and societies appealed to people from most social classes, although they remained almost entirely male until around 1800, and largely urban, with some exceptions. There were philosophical, literary, and scientific societies, bawdy clubs, Masonic lodges, sporting societies, societies dedicated to economic improvement, horticultural clubs, clubs for students, regional societies, beekeeping clubs, musical societies, friendly societies, debating clubs, drinking clubs, religious, philanthropic, and missionary associations, and many more.

This volume focuses on the growth of these diverse social institutions in Scotland, from the end of the seventeenth century to the early nineteenth century. In Scotland as elsewhere there were elements of continuity with the urban corporate structures of the early modern period, as in artisans' friendly societies and their rituals. But eighteenth-century Scottish clubs and societies also had a particularly distinctive history that was inextricably linked to the growth of the Scottish Enlightenment. Inspired by the English model of urban growth, and encouraged by the expansion of print culture and the newspaper press, such clubs could be a significant and dynamic force, committed to improvement and national regeneration as well as to sociability. Their history, and especially the history of clubs and societies in Edinburgh and Glasgow between around 1730 and 1780, has tended to dominate the historiography. Yet Scottish clubs and societies were also part of the wider associational developments that stretched across England and Wales, Ireland, and the transatlantic world. By the late eighteenth century the vocabulary of sociability was everywhere shifting, as the use of the term "association" became more widespread. First employed in a political context, it came to be more widely adopted, and often implied a more serious purpose than the sociable or convivial "club," although the use of the term "voluntary association" was a nineteenth-century development.[3] This collection of essays is intended to contribute to a new framework for understanding clubs and societies in Scotland, one that brings together the inheritance of the Scottish past, the unique and cohesive polite culture of the eighteenth-century Enlightenment, and the broader context of associational patterns common to Britain, Ireland, and transatlantic areas of settlement.

Histories of Clubs and Societies

Eighteenth-century Scottish clubs and societies did attract some attention from antiquarians and historians of the nineteenth and early twentieth centuries. An anonymous survey of Edinburgh's eighteenth-century literary and philosophical societies in *Hogg's Instructor* in 1852 was followed by John Strang's celebratory *Glasgow and Its Clubs* (1856), in which the history of social clubs was viewed as "the vehicle through which the ever-changing manners and habits of Glasgow society might be popularly portrayed and chronicled."[4] Histories of individual clubs were often sponsored by the clubs themselves. The earliest was the *History of the Speculative Society of Edinburgh* (1845), later followed by histories of the Aberdeen Philosophical Society (1863), the Juridical Society (1875), the Highland and Agricultural Society of Scotland (1879), the Dialectic Society (1887), the Friday Club (1910), and the New Club (1938).[5]

The modern history of Scottish clubs and societies begins with the pioneering work of Davis D. McElroy, *Scotland's Age of Improvement* (1969), which built upon McElroy's PhD dissertation of 1952. This volume when it appeared was unique in the Anglophone world for its scope and attention to the cultural vitality of the eighteenth century. McElroy traced, for the first time, the growth of Scottish clubs and societies from 1700 onward, including those in which leading writers of the Scottish Enlightenment participated along with members of the aristocracy and gentry and prominent professional figures. He described all these societies as inspired by the Scottish drive toward improvement and encouraged by English precedents and examples; he surveyed literary, philosophical, and scientific societies, and discussed debating societies, student societies, and convivial clubs.[6] McElroy's thorough research provided a starting point for much subsequent work on Scottish clubs and societies and their relationship to the Scottish Enlightenment.

That Enlightenment still remained relatively unstudied in 1969.[7] The title of Nicholas Phillipson's first book, *Scotland in the Age of Improvement*, edited with Rosalind Mitchison, mirrored that of McElroy's work, and the clubs and societies that McElroy had traced were to be fundamental to Phillipson's influential reinterpretation of the Scottish Enlightenment.[8] Focusing on Edinburgh as a provincial capital, Phillipson reflected on the post-Union history of its landed elites and intellectuals, who came together to form a modern-minded and improving leadership, intent both on the improvement of agriculture and science and on the adoption of an anglicized polite culture. He suggested that "the characteristic institutions of Edinburgh's cultural life between the 1720s and the 1740s were the club and the college."[9] The Honourable the Society for Improvement in the Knowledge of Agriculture (1723), with its three hundred members by 1743, appealed to the aristocracy and gentry. But at the same time, smaller clubs grew quickly, attracting a wider mixture of men with intellectual interests in pursuing literature, philosophy, and science. In Phillipson's words, "Edinburgh became a city of para-parliamentary clubs and societies of patriotically-minded men devoted to the regeneration of the manners of a fallen nation and improving the virtue of its citizens."[10] The foundation of the Select Society in 1754, with David Hume and Adam Smith among its members, marked the gradual assumption of leadership by the literati, as the landed elite became increasingly more London-oriented. Though Edinburgh was undoubtedly at the center of his Enlightenment world, Phillipson did not neglect other Scottish cities, recognizing the importance of distinctive intellectual developments in Glasgow and Aberdeen, also strongly shaped by a culture of club life.

Phillipson had been able to make use of the work of Roger L. Emerson on the Select Society. For, simultaneously, Emerson had begun the work of recovering in depth many of the leading societies of Enlightenment Edinburgh, viewed as one of the many European cities in which the Enlightenment flourished.[11] He looked back to the late seventeenth century for the origins of Edinburgh's clubs and societies, identifying in particular the work of Sir Robert Sibbald, a member of several early clubs, and instrumental in establishing the Royal College of Physicians of Edinburgh (1681). Emerson emphasized the centrality of scientific learning and the influence of European institutions on the Scottish Enlightenment. He took a more pragmatic view than Phillipson of Enlightenment sociability, arguing that such organizations allowed debate, ensured social prominence and visibility, and provided academic learning and vocational skills. His detailed studies of a number of these societies, especially the Philosophical Society of Edinburgh (1737), have been of great value.[12]

Not all scholars, however, followed Emerson's stress on scientific initiatives. Phillipson's emphasis on the importance of civic humanism and polite stoicism to the sociable lives of the literati was refined further by others interested in the interactions of sociability and sentiment. In 1985 Richard B. Sher set the lives and work of the Moderate clergy of eighteenth-century Edinburgh in their intensely clubbable world, as they participated in the Select Society and the more informal Poker Club (1762), allegedly named for its role as a means of stirring up national pride over the denial of a militia to Scotland.[13] In *Virtuous Discourse* (1987), John Dwyer elaborated on the strategies used by the literati to call for a virtuous and moral community in daily life, with particular reference to the writings of Henry Mackenzie and the Mirror Club (1776).[14] And he and others continued to focus on the ways in which polite conversation and sociability provided the framework for the development of the moral philosophy of the Enlightenment, notably in the writing of Francis Hutcheson.[15]

In 2000 the publication of Peter Clark's magisterial *British Clubs and Societies, 1580–1800: The Origins of an Associational World* transformed the narrative history of British clubs and societies. Clark traced, for the first time, the emergence of associational activity across the four nations of the United Kingdom and British settlements abroad; he placed such activity within its European context, suggesting, however, that contemporaries did see the extent and pluralism of such an associational life as a distinctly British development. He considered the origins of such a movement in the years after the Civil War as lying in Britain's, or England's, early urbanization and expanding patterns of consumption and leisure; he questioned the balance between a progressive and modernizing vision of such patterns of sociability and an inheritance of traditional forms; and he asked whether the spread of such associational forms helped to integrate a wider British world, or whether, rather, they marked out the distinctiveness of its constituent nations. In discussing these questions, he addressed an exceptionally wide range of clubs and societies, appealing to the landed classes, to mercantile and professional groups, and to tradesmen and artisans, though rarely admitting the very poorest or laboring classes. He included in his subject matter not only convivial, literary, scientific, and philanthropic societies but also, among others, the influential and ever-expanding networks of Masonic lodges and the increasing numbers of benefit clubs and friendly societies founded by artisans and tradesmen.

Clark acknowledged that his book's coverage was better for England than for elsewhere in the British Isles, though he also referred to Georgian Edinburgh as "a brilliant centre of associational life" and took care to review the evidence for provincial Scotland as well as Ireland and Wales.[16] Although he did not produce a history of Scottish clubs and societies, the breadth of his social-historical perspective is certainly suggestive of the task that lies ahead, which is to construct an approach that both complicates the history of Enlightenment Scotland and acknowledges the importance of wider patterns of associationalism in the Anglophone world.

Such an approach must incorporate the legacies of the Scottish past, as well as recognize that the growth of eighteenth-century urban clubs and societies took place in a world dominated by a landed hierarchy, with very limited forms of political representation. Patronage remained the all-important mechanism for change and for individual advancement; rising standards of civility coexisted with military and imperial priorities, public violence, and the continuing practice of dueling.[17] Though clubs and societies might offer a rhetoric of sociability and improvement, an apparent opportunity to practice benevolence and fraternity, they also, as will become apparent in this collection, reflected social hierarchies and class differences. The most glaring inequality was gender difference. A new framework needs to incorporate the different masculinities that structured the appeal and identities of diverse clubs and societies. It also needs to explain the changing, and for the most part entirely marginal, relationship of women to associational life in this period. And, although "improvement" was a key word in the Scottish associational movement, space must also be left for alternative languages, which might include the appeal to Scottish history or legend, or ritual practices that drew on older customary lives but were also open to reconstruction in different circumstances. Such languages might also encompass the politicization of associations that took place from the 1790s, as the case for conservatism and reaction came to be opposed to that for reform and improvement.

In this volume it is assumed that what was taking place in Scotland on the broader front, beyond the central narrative of Enlightenment, paralleled what was happening elsewhere in the Anglophone world, though the chronology and the particularities of clubs and societies might vary. At the same time, we also seek to establish what was different in the theory and practice of Scottish sociability. In some cases, as with Freemasonry, it has been argued that Scotland led the way from the seventeenth century; in others, and especially in relation to evangelically based developments from the 1790s, London initiatives were rapidly followed in Scotland.

Some of the materials for a new approach already exist. Rosalind Carr has argued strongly that discourses of gender should be central to the study of Scottish Enlightenment discourse and practice; clubs and societies helped to construct appropriate forms of elite masculinity and femininity for a polite and improving sociability.[18] David Stevenson's research has played an important role in illustrating the significance of Scottish Freemasonry as shaping the form taken by the British movement in the eighteenth century.[19] Recent work on Scottish politics has greatly increased our knowledge of the political societies of the late eighteenth and early nineteenth centuries, reforming, radical, and loyalist.[20] And campaigning societies, including those established to campaign for the abolition of slavery and those set up to resist abolition, now have their historians.[21] But much more remains to be done in a number of areas. In particular, much work remains to be done on the history of friendly societies in Scotland, as Clark pointed out in 2000. Sandra Marwick's excellent micro-study of the St. Crispin societies of shoemakers in Edinburgh and elsewhere traced the survival of pre-Reformation devotions to St. Crispin in the shoemaking craft throughout the seventeenth and eighteenth centuries, and later growth, with the founding of the Royal St. Crispin Society of 1817 and its formalized rituals, regalia, and processions; she also notes the interaction of Crispin societies with the friendly society movement and with Freemasonry.[22] A much fuller picture of the complex public sociability of Scottish urban life in the late eighteenth and early nineteenth centuries can be found in Bob Harris and Charles McKean's fine work, *The Scottish Town in the Age of the Enlightenment, 1740–1820* (2014), which warns against too easy an acceptance of a progressive narrative of politeness and "civilization."[23] More recently, Murray Pittock has seen Edinburgh from 1660 to 1750 as a distinctively innovative or "smart" city, and the Enlightenment there in this period as already enabled by a particular set of intersecting conditions, including the strength of its associational life.[24] The essays in this collection offer further illustration of the complexity of the history of Scottish clubs and societies, viewed as part of a wider movement.

The Growth of Scottish Clubs and Societies

The earliest Scottish societies certainly drew on past Scottish traditions, some with a Jacobite element. Pittock describes the social club associated with the Trained Bands of Edinburgh, the Society of Captains, authorized by the Edinburgh Town Council in 1663, with a monthly convivial meeting from 1687.[25] The Royal Company of Archers was founded in 1676, initially by Jacobite sympathizers to encourage archery, but revived on Queen Anne's accession as an ostensibly Hanoverian bodyguard, though with a continuing Jacobite presence.[26] The Knights of the Horn club was established in 1705 by the third Earl of Selkirk in order to oppose the Union, though also with a convivial purpose.[27] Another important early initiative was the foundation in 1679–1680 by Sibbald of a medical club, which in 1681 became the Royal College of Physicians of Edinburgh. In 1701 he twice proposed the creation of a Royal Society of Scotland.[28]

But even in the years following 1689, the number of such societies outside Edinburgh was small. Trade-based corporations were formally structured by the constitution of their burgh, as part of the official urban community, but a few benefit societies outside such structures had a lengthy history, especially among the seafaring communities of Fifeshire and East Lothian. Such societies included, for instance, the Anstruther Easter Sea Box Society (1618), the United Fisherrow Fishermen's Friendly Society (1669) of Musselburgh, and the Aberdeen Society of Porters (1666).[29] It was among working stonemasons that new brotherhoods were to emerge, bound together by initiations, rituals, and secret modes of identification, organized in groups known as lodges. Though in their origins such lodges were formed by working stonemasons, David Stevenson has argued that in the course of the seventeenth century these "operative" members were joined by "non-operatives," gentlemen, tradesmen, or artisans. Stevenson has identified twenty-five such lodges founded on a permanent basis before 1710, sixteen of which had non-operative members; he has argued that in its essentials modern Freemasonry was Scottish rather than English.[30] Another network of societies, the Independent Order of Free Gardeners, had its origins in the Ancient Fraternity of Free Gardeners of East Lothian, founded in Haddington in 1676.[31]

Other societies derived from a wider movement for moral revival across Britain following the establishment of societies set up in London to prosecute and campaign against all forms of what was seen as vice and immorality. In 1699 a small group of Presbyterians established the Edinburgh-based Society for the Reformation of Manners in Scotland: it campaigned against all forms of dissolute behavior but also took an active interest in education. It aimed to correct what it perceived as the "gross Ignorance, Atheism, Popery and Impiety wherewith the Highlands and Islands of Scotland abounded."[32] By July there were up to thirteen such societies in Edinburgh, and meetings continued intermittently until the late 1740s.[33] In 1709 a small number of its leaders founded the Society in Scotland for Propagating Christian Knowledge (mirroring in structure and name the English Society for the Propagation of the Gospel). It proposed to "found schools 'where religion and virtue might be taught to young and old in the shape of reading, writing, arithmetic and religious instruction,'" in an effort to reform and improve Scottish culture, especially in the Highlands.[34] By 1713 the society had banned Gaelic reading in its schools.[35]

In the first decades of the eighteenth century, signs of that polite culture which was to characterize Enlightenment Scotland were appearing in Edinburgh, again influenced by developments in London but also with a strongly Jacobite element. That was true of the Easy Club, the formation of which in 1712 has already been mentioned. The London-based periodical *The Spectator*, produced by Joseph Addison and Richard Steele in 1711–1712, became, in David Allan's words, a "hugely seductive manifesto" for the power of polite and intelligent conversation, in settings that were conducive to mutual understanding and exchange, and to generating new ideas. As Allan has written, "Addison's message certainly struck a chord in Scotland in those early disorientating years immediately after the Union," as Scots became increasingly conscious of the need for economic, social, and intellectual improvement.[36] Newly established societies provided the space within which those needs could be explored. The Rankenian Club, founded in 1716 or 1717 and surviving until 1774, attracted some leading figures of the early Enlightenment, including the mathematician Colin MacLaurin, the theologian and educationalist George Turnbull, the rhetorician John Stevenson, and William Wishart, Presbyterian minister and later principal of Edinburgh University. There is evidence that these men were especially interested in the writings of Lord Shaftesbury, whose *Characteristicks of Men, Manners, Opinions, Times* (1711) provided a philosophical basis for the pursuit of virtue in a cultural environment characterized by sociability and the free exchange of opinions in a polite and gentlemanly setting.[37] Other early societies included the Associated Critics (1717), Thomas Ruddiman's club (1718), and the Athenian Society (1719).[38]

Yet the major expansion of clubs and societies in the leading Scottish cities, Edinburgh, Glasgow, and Aberdeen, took place from the 1720s to the 1770s and 1780s. In this period their history was distinctive, without parallel elsewhere in the United Kingdom. Clubs and societies drew for their members on academics from the Scottish universities and on the professional environments of the church and the legal profession. These were uniquely cohesive and homosocial worlds, closely linked to landed and urban elites; they were united not only by common experiences but by a drive to economic and cultural improvement inspired by the model of English development. Landowners from the aristocracy and gentry, especially those from the Lowlands, were actively engaged in agricultural innovation. The Honourable the Society for Improvement in the Knowledge of Agriculture in Scotland was founded in Edinburgh in 1723 with just such a membership, and was responsible for proposing to the government in 1726 the establishment of a Board of Trustees for Fisheries, Manufactures and Improvements in Scotland, set up the following year. Other societies, possibly ephemeral, followed at Ormiston (1737), Ayr (1748), Cupar (1759), and Buchan (1769), and more were to come.[39] In 1754 the Edinburgh-based Select Society rapidly expanded to draw in "the political class of decision makers, patrons and beneficiaries of the status quo," including merchants, bankers, and landowners: it had over 130 members in 1759.[40] Members debated a wide range of issues including literature, national improvement, politics, and farming. In 1755 the society established the subsidiary Edinburgh Society for Encouraging Arts, Sciences, Manufactures and Agriculture in Scotland, which sought to encourage new inventions and fine workmanship through the award of premiums, following similar societies in London and Dublin. It also promoted the Select Society for Promoting the Reading and Speaking of the English Language in Scotland (1761), as a part of its project of improvement.

Enlightened Scots were self-consciously committed to such sociability, and to creating their own form of polite culture. In his essay in this volume, David Allan traces the ways in which the ideas of Addison and Steele, and of Lord Shaftesbury, were taken up and thoughtfully developed in the influential works of

Francis Hutcheson, professor of moral philosophy at the University of Glasgow from 1730, who explicitly defended the growth of associations whether for the advancement of commerce and manufactures or for conviviality. After Hutcheson, David Hume also defended the advantages of "particular clubs and societies" whose growth he saw as indicating the progress of refinement and politeness in commercial societies.[41] The leading literati of Edinburgh were active in a series of societies. The Poker Club, whose members included William Robertson, Hugh Blair, Joseph Black, John Gregory, Adam Ferguson, David Hume, and Adam Smith, and country gentlemen who supported the idea of a Scottish militia, had seventy-eight members in 1768 and lasted until 1784. It clearly promoted conviviality, meeting regularly at a tavern near the High Street Cross. Though its activities in promoting the militia are less obvious, members did engage anonymously in pamphleteering, and in parliamentary lobbying.[42]

The Edinburgh Belles Lettres Society (1759), discussed below by Rosalind Carr, had an eclectic range of concerns, though its members made particular contributions to the discussion of rhetoric and literature. This was a student society, appealing especially to divinity students, though distinguished members of the literati were honorary members and attended regularly.[43] One member, William Lothian, a future minister, clearly viewed the society as in accordance with the ideas of Hutcheson and Hume: "This society was founded so that proper opportunities might not be wanting where gentlemen of taste might communicate their opinions to one another, and receive mutual improvement."[44] Lothian was also a member of the Theological Society at Edinburgh, which met regularly from 1759 to 1764, and described it as "not only a school of mental improvement but a nursery of brotherly love and kind affections."[45] Many former members of the Belles Lettres Society later joined another small literary society, the Feast of Tabernacles, founded 1770, from which the Mirror Club emerged in 1776. Under the leadership of the novelist Henry Mackenzie, club members included landowners and literary figures who shared a belief in a policy of improvement resting on a gentrified, landed, and domesticated form of sociability, expressed in the "virtuous discourse" described by John Dwyer.[46]

One particular scientific club had an extended life. The Philosophical Society of Edinburgh was founded in 1737, organized mainly by Colin MacLaurin, arising out of the interest of a group of Edinburgh astronomers in an annular solar eclipse visible on 18 February of that year. Its members, professional men and landowners, were committed to national improvement and interested in natural philosophy. The new society was set up "for the Improving of Natural Knowledge," including natural philosophy, mathematics, astronomy, chemistry, and medicine, modeled on the Royal Society of London and the provincial academies of Europe. The Philosophical Society gathered fifty-three members in its first decade and, while building an international reputation, succeeded in forging a new relationship between science and the improvement of Scotland.[47]

Emerson has traced the decline of the society by 1748 and its subsequent revival and later moments of crisis around 1760 and in the 1770s. By the early 1780s, however, recruitment was failing, and political differences were appearing. The society was challenged by the appearance of two rivals, first the Newtonian Club (1778) and then the Society of Antiquaries of Scotland (1780), which applied for a royal charter. Both were Whiggish and opposed Henry Dundas, the government manager of Scotland, and the leaders of the Philosophical Society. The latter now applied for a charter for a new Royal Society of Edinburgh, to replace the Philosophical Society and to cover all fields of learning. Both applications were granted, but the movement toward incorporation of the Royal Society of Edinburgh (1783) now reflected the conservatism of the intellectual establishment rather than the dynamism of the original founders of 1737.[48]

Much research on eighteenth-century clubs and societies has been focused on Edinburgh. Yet each of the major Scottish cities had its own character, reflected in the associational world of those cities. In Glasgow academics united with clergymen, and with the merchants of the city's expanding trade; Ralph McLean discusses in his chapter in this volume four societies founded between 1743 and 1752, the Political Economy Club (c. 1743), the Anderston Club (c. 1745), the Hodge Podge Club (1750), and the Glasgow Literary Society (1752).[49] In Aberdeen ephemeral societies were in existence from 1736, when the philosopher Thomas Reid was involved in a philosophical club at Marischal College, though it probably lasted for no more than a year; a theological club met in the 1740s, and a medical club in July 1750. More important than any of these was the Aberdeen Philosophical Society (1758), also known as the Wise Club. All but one of the original nine members held university posts; they included Thomas Reid, George Campbell, and John Gregory. The society's meetings were convivial but also addressed serious intellectual issues, developing a critical perspective on the philosophical writings of David Hume. Members also debated educational reform, political economy, and contemporary political issues. Another more practical Aberdeen society was the Gordon Mill's Farming Club (1758), to which Reid and Gregory also belonged, but this was more narrowly focused on agricultural improvement, involving tenant farmers as well as landlords.[50]

Learned bodies such as the Medical Society (1731), discussed by Jacqueline Jenkinson in her chapter in this collection, the Philosophical Society of Edinburgh, and its successor, the Royal Society of Edinburgh, published large volumes of their own essays or transactions. But other Scottish clubs and societies also made enormous contributions to the print culture of the Scottish Enlightenment.[51] The Mirror Club evolved into a dedicated vehicle for producing two anonymous periodicals, *The Mirror* (1779–1780), and *The Lounger* (1785–1786), with essays written in the spirit of *The Spectator* and *The Tatler*, discussed by Martyn J. Powell in his chapter in this volume.[52] Learned societies that did not publish their papers, such as the Aberdeen Philosophical Society and the Glasgow

Literary Society, provided forums for men of letters to exchange ideas that often found their way into print. For example, large portions of Thomas Reid's three major philosophical works derived from discourses originally presented and discussed at meetings of those two societies.

The publications of the Scottish Enlightenment also benefited from opportunities for interaction among authors, and between authors and their patrons and publishers, in societies that were not specifically directed toward literary or scientific pursuits. At Masonic lodges, notably, Henry Mackenzie, Dugald Stewart, Dr. Alexander Monro secundus, Lord Hailes, Lord Monboddo, and many other leading literary and scientific figures mixed freely with each other and with prominent booksellers and highborn literary patrons. When the Edinburgh bookseller William Creech organized the important 1787 subscription edition of *Poems, Chiefly in the Scottish Dialect* by the still little-known Ayrshire farmer and freemason Robert Burns, he drew upon the Masonic members of the town's most prestigious lodge, Canongate Kilwinning No. 2, including the fourteenth Earl of Glencairn, who had introduced Creech (his former tutor) to Burns and would subsequently secure large numbers of subscriptions, and Alexander Nasmyth and John Buego, painter and engraver, respectively, of the author's likeness that formed the book's frontispiece. In 1793 Creech would spearhead the establishment of Scotland's first professional association of booksellers, the Society of Booksellers and Stationers of Edinburgh, or Edinburgh Booksellers' Society, which sought to bring order—as well as control over the book trade by elite booksellers—to the sometimes chaotic world of Scottish printing and reprinting.[53]

Across Edinburgh and Glasgow, there were many societies appealing to students, some highly specialized. The Royal Medical Society of Edinburgh, considered by Jenkinson in her chapter, was founded in 1737. The Speculative Society, discussed by Carr, was founded in 1764, with its members aiming to devote themselves to "Improvement in Literary Composition and Public Speaking." Membership came to be seen as effective training for successful future careers in politics and the law.[54] Both these societies are still in existence. In Glasgow student clubs were already a source of anxiety to university authorities by 1720, when the principal, with the professors of moral philosophy and divinity, considered abolishing all student clubs. In 1768 two societies, the General Society and the Parliament of Oceana, again set the students at odds with the university authorities. By 1776 three societies, the Eclectic, the Dialectic, and the Academic, had better relations with the university.[55] Such societies were an important part of the training of professional men and many more developed in the last twenty years of the eighteenth century.

Other developments in the major cities of Scotland paralleled the growth of the institutions of a polite culture elsewhere, as in England and Ireland. Following an earlier Musick Club (1695), the Edinburgh Musical Society, founded in

1728, survived until 1798; though its membership was male, it often attracted more women than men to its concerts.[56] The Aberdeen Musical Society was established in 1748, the Dundee Musical Society in 1757.[57] A few debating societies signaled that debating had become a popular amusement. The Pantheon Society in Edinburgh (1773) emerged from the earlier Robinhood Society, the name perhaps adopted from an earlier London society, and included from one to three hundred spectators. The Dundee Speculative Society (fl. 1772) was the first to admit women as visitors, a precedent followed by the Pantheon Society.[58]

Convivial tavern-based societies also flourished. The Cape Club, founded in Edinburgh in 1764, with a branch in Glasgow from 1771, and the Soaping Club, also in Edinburgh and probably in existence from 1760 to 1765, are discussed in the chapters by Rhona Brown and James J. Caudle, with reference to the membership of Robert Burns and James Boswell. Other Edinburgh clubs, among many, included the Wig Club (1775), the Crochallan Fencibles (1778), and the Oyster Club (c. 1778).[59] In Glasgow John Strang mentions the Morning and Evening Club (1779), My Lord Ross's Club (1780), named for the landlord of the tavern, and the Accidental Club (1780), among many others.[60] The spread of such drinking clubs was less marked in provincial towns; one exception is the Beggar's Benison (1732), a bawdy club in the East Neuk of Fife with branches in Edinburgh (1752) and Glasgow (1765).[61]

Even in smaller towns, the period also saw the expansion of some new societies, as subscription libraries, book clubs, and reading societies were founded. The first subscription library was established in 1741 by relatively well-paid lead miners, and clerks employed at the mines, at Leadhills. It was followed by Kelso (1750), Hawick and Ayr (both 1762), and Duns (1768).[62] Mark Towsey has suggested that fifteen such libraries existed by 1790.[63] These libraries were fundamentally private clubs, in which members paid an entrance fee and a subscription every quarter, accumulating a permanent stock, though nonmembers could also borrow books. Book clubs and reading societies tended to be smaller, sometimes selling books off to fund the purchase of new ones.

There was continuity and expansion also for societies founded in an earlier period. Mark C. Wallace has noted that "Scottish Freemasonry between the years 1740 and 1790 experienced a period of marked growth and development."[64] In 1736, when the Grand Lodge of Scotland was founded, Scotland had 49 lodges; by 1765, 168; and by 1785, 267.[65] Freemasonry was spreading right across Scotland. The authority of the Grand Lodge was, however, still disputed, in that the lodge that claimed the greatest antiquity, Lodge Mother Kilwinning, demanded precedence and continued to grant charters. Well-known freemasons included not only James Boswell and Robert Burns but Robert Adam, Lord Monboddo, Henry Mackenzie, and Dugald Stewart, all of whom attended Masonic lodges as well as the clubs described above.[66] Wallace has characterized Scottish Freemasonry in the early eighteenth century as an "improvement society," oriented toward

Enlightenment goals and sharing many of the characteristics of other clubs and societies.[67] Although like many other associations it had its secret rites and ceremonies, it operated in public alongside other societies, with lodges marching in processions at important civic events, committed to practical philanthropy as well as providing spaces for convivial sociability.

The movement for moral reform and regeneration in Scotland, and especially the Highlands, was by no means dead. The Society in Scotland for Propagating Christian Knowledge continued its campaign to provide schools in the Highlands to counter Jacobitism, Catholicism, and the use of Gaelic. From 25 schools in 1715, their number rose steadily to 152 in 1783.[68] But the ending of the Jacobite threat and the pressure that schools were under in Gaelic-speaking areas led the society to relax its language policy to some extent; having commissioned a translation, in 1767 it began the distribution of Gaelic New Testaments.[69]

The same period also saw a steady growth in benefit clubs and friendly societies. In Glasgow in 1779 eighty-three such societies, claiming over twelve thousand members, signed a petition against the repeal of penal legislation against Roman Catholics, and there was a similar growth in Edinburgh and Aberdeen.[70] *The Statistical Account of Scotland* provides some evidence that friendly societies extended well beyond the cities, recording for instance that in 1770 the weavers of Crieff came together to form their own corporation for mutual support, and later to build their own hall and take part in annual processions.[71] Nevertheless, both Harris and Clark stress the limited nature of the growth of clubs and societies in smaller towns before the 1770s.[72] And, apart from Inverness, the Highlands were affected very little by this associational culture, except insofar as they were the object of missionary impulses.

Expansion and Complexity

From the late eighteenth century onward, in Scotland as elsewhere in Britain, clubs and societies were developed in far greater variety, in provincial towns and villages as well as in the major cities. For Edinburgh, Andrew J. Dalgleish has identified eighty-seven new associations founded from 1780 to 1829, a list compiled from printed sources that does not claim to be exhaustive.[73] The societies founded between 1780 and 1810 include the Society for Relief of the Destitute Sick (1785), the Dialectic Society (1787), the Society for Effecting Abolition of the African Slave Trade (1790), the Society for Relief of the Indigent Blind (1792), the Edinburgh Association for the Support of the Constitution (1792), the Duddingston Curling Society (1795), the Canongate Friendly Society (1798), the Select Subscription Library (1800), the Friday Club (1803), the Bible Society (1809), and the Lancastrian School Society and the Society for the Support of Gaelic Schools (both 1810).[74] Harris and McKean illustrate the same range of societies in selected provincial towns, listing twenty-two founded in Dundee between 1744 and 1819, though only four before the 1790s. Montrose saw eleven new societies between 1760 and 1819, though only one before 1799, and Inverness twelve between 1800 and 1822.[75]

Societies founded in this period included many which looked very much like those that had preceded them, in that they were small, exclusive, and convivial, as was for instance the Friday Club, which attracted many of the literati from the late Scottish Enlightenment, notably Sir Walter Scott.[76] Yet from the 1780s onward many were organized on different lines; they were open to larger numbers, with a membership based on subscriptions, and held relatively infrequent general meetings. Women's subscriptions were normally also welcome. The growth of such associations was certainly stimulated by the late eighteenth-century evangelical revival, and some, like the Bible societies founded across Scotland from 1809, were part of a much wider British network.[77] Scottish missionary societies, founded in 1796 in Edinburgh and Glasgow, and later elsewhere, initially had more in common with English missionary societies than they did with the official outlook of the Church of Scotland, which rejected such activity until 1824.[78] The revival was to invigorate the movement for the evangelization of the Highlands, as first the Society for Propagating the Gospel at Home (1797) and then, more successfully, the nondenominational Society for the Support of Gaelic Schools spread knowledge of evangelical Protestantism along with literacy in Gaelic.[79]

Other societies founded for philanthropic and charitable purposes might also emerge from a similar evangelical impulse, and draw inspiration from English models. They might have a quasi-administrative function, as they came to establish a wide variety of institutions for poor relief, and schools to supplement the weaknesses of the parochial system, in towns, cities, and rural areas. Lancastrian School Societies were set up in 1810 in Edinburgh and Glasgow, with others across Scotland, to develop the monitorial methods of teaching that Joseph Lancaster had developed in his Southwark school.[80] The Edinburgh Society for the Suppression of Beggars, founded in January 1813 and modeled on similar societies in England, aimed not only to suppress begging on Edinburgh streets but also to relieve "the Industrious and Destitute Poor," with the support of the Edinburgh Town Council.[81] The Dundee Orphan Institution, set up in 1815, was established as a result of a public subscription and planned at a meeting of subscribers; its directors included both men and women.[82] At the same time, many philanthropic initiatives—benevolent societies, educational societies, and clothing and lying-in societies—were small, inspired by local needs and organized by local patrons and elites, both men and women.

Subscription libraries and reading societies continued to expand: a further 37 libraries were founded in the 1790s and 203 between 1800 and 1830.[83] Such libraries encouraged the circulation of specialized works of importance to particular communities, such as, in the Selkirk Subscription Library (1772), works on agricultural improvement, but more generally Enlightenment texts, novels, and polite literature of all kinds. They provided spaces for polite sociability since in some, though not all, libraries women could participate and borrow books.[84] Towsey makes a compelling case for subscription libraries offering their members "the chance to engage in the cultural imperatives of the age, the patriotic improvement of Scottish society through association, intellectual interaction, critical consumption and the pursuit of polite learning."[85] But they were also sustained by the expansion in this period of religious publishing, and especially of sermons, by both Moderate clergy and their evangelical opponents.[86] Alexander Dick has recently reminded us that practices of devotional reading derived from Calvinist theology continued to coexist in such clubs with the sermons of Moderate ministers and more improvement-oriented works. The tension between the two was noted by Robert Burns, who, as one of the founders of a book club, the Monkland Friendly Society (1789), wrote with irritation of the insistence of members that he order Calvinist theological works for the club.[87]

Another developing form of association was the antiquarian society. The Perth Antiquarian Society, founded in 1784 but renamed the Perth Literary and Antiquarian Society in 1786, declared that antiquarian collecting was central to its purpose, but also sought to retain an interest in natural history. Like the Society of Antiquaries in Edinburgh and especially its combative leader, David Steuart Erskine, Earl of Buchan, the members of the Perth society saw themselves as promoting and re-editing authentically Scottish literary works, in opposition to what they saw as the more specialized, and anglicized, claims to dominance of the Royal Society of Edinburgh. The Perth society published only one volume of transactions, in 1827.[88] In 1823 Walter Scott, with several associates, founded the Bannatyne Club, partly in imitation of the English Roxburghe Club (1812), which had already begun to publish important literary and historical manuscripts. The Bannatyne Club sought to publish works that would illustrate the history, literature, and antiquities of Scotland, in the spirit of the interest in Scottish history inspired by Scott.[89] The Northern Institution for the Promotion of Science and Literature, with a particular interest in the Highlands, was founded in Inverness in 1825.[90]

Societies and associations were subject to government intervention in these decades. The formation of friendly societies and benefit clubs was encouraged by the Friendly Societies Act of 1793, which for the first time prescribed a form for friendly societies and encouraged them to register with local justices of the peace to give them legal status. Besides arising from working-class initiatives, they also came to be seen as part of a range of philanthropic measures for addressing local poverty and encouraging independence and self-help.[91] By 1800 just under 400 friendly societies were registered, and in 1831 a total of 2,111.[92] The largest single category on which male societies were based was that of occupation, sometimes defined further by neighborhood, as, for example, for the United

Society of Weavers in and about the West Port in Dundee (1797).[93] Others, including female friendly societies, were simply rooted in a neighborhood or street, or by adjectives denoting fraternity, benevolence, and social union, as in the Beith Humane Society (1800) and the Closeburn Associate Sisterly Society (1811).[94] Many societies were founded in an emphasis on Scottish identity, especially after the royal visit of 1822. The Lonach Highland and Friendly Society, of Strathdon, was set up in 1825 to support the Highland dress and Gaelic language and to act as a philanthropic organization.[95] The best-known society in this category, the Braemar Wrights Society, founded in 1816, became the Braemar Highland Society in 1826, and is now the Braemar Royal Highland Society.[96]

Heated political divisions after the French Revolution of 1789 saw campaigning political societies set up across the country at all social levels. In the early stages these included, for instance, the Whig Club of Dundee (1789), founded in support of the French National Assembly. There was a very sudden rise in support for organized radicalism in the second half of 1792, when links were developed with the London-based Society for Constitutional Information (1780) and the London Corresponding Society (1792), both of which had Scottish members.[97] Before September 1792 there had been only two or three reform societies in Scotland; by the end of that year, in a remarkably rapid growth, there were between eighty and a hundred, with general conventions held in Edinburgh in December 1792 and April 1793.[98] The severity of government responses, notably in the treason trials and sentences of transportation passed in the summer of 1793 and in 1794, and in the suppression of the convention in December 1793, meant that numbers fell away rapidly from mid-1793 onward. Further extensions of government repression included the suspension of habeas corpus in 1794, the Seditious Meetings and Treasonable Practices Acts (1795), the Unlawful Oaths Act (1797), and the Secret Societies Act (1799). Nevertheless, in 1797 the secret Society of United Scotsmen was founded in resistance, partly directly inspired by delegates from the Society of United Irishmen (1791); twenty-six individual societies, with particular strengths among the weavers of textile towns, have been identified.[99] Outlawed by government in 1799, it finally failed in 1802. Also in 1797, a number of reading societies were founded among the laboring population of west and southwest Scotland, possibly linked to radical activity.[100] After the end of the Napoleonic Wars, from 1816 to 1820 artisan radicals again campaigned, especially in southwestern Scotland, in a movement culminating in the failed armed rising of 1820. Again, one form of organization was through Union societies, ostensibly reading societies for self-improvement and self-education, as advised by English radicals.[101]

On the other side, only three or four loyalist associations in Scotland have been identified in the 1790s, compared to what were clearly hundreds in England; these included the Edinburgh Association for the Support of the Constitution (1792). Harris has surmised that loyalism in Scotland was mainly led from above, by the propertied classes and ministers of the Kirk, and that they were reluctant to encourage further associations.[102] In the late 1790s, after the foundation of the Orange Order in County Armagh in September 1795, the first Scottish Orange lodges appeared. Between March and May 1798 soldiers from the Breadalbane Fencibles and the Argyll Fencibles, after serving in Ireland, established the first Scottish Orange lodges within their regiments. The first civilian Orange lodge was established in Maybole, Ayrshire, in 1808, and by the 1820s there were at least forty Scottish Orange lodges across central and southwestern Scotland.[103]

Freemasonry fell under government suspicion. By the 1790s most freemasons found it necessary to assert their patriotism and loyalty to the Crown, although some lodges may well have been associated with radical societies; certainly some individual freemasons were. Freemasonry was affected most seriously by the Secret Societies Act, which required that all initiation ceremonies should be public. During the committee stage of the bill, the Grand Lodge of Scotland was exempted, but it still lost its charter-granting powers. It was agreed that all lodges should be required to submit their place of meeting and list of members to magistrates, to ensure constant monitoring. These difficulties tended to strengthen the powers of the Grand Lodge, so that Freemasonry became more effectively "an authoritative, federal organization."[104] But internal conflicts and the Whiggish outlook of the Grand Lodge meant that this was a period of some decline. Although Wallace has noted that there were three hundred lodges in Scotland by 1800, the pace at which new lodges grew was slowing down, with only twelve new ones appearing between 1795 and 1808.[105] Other comparable networks, later to be described as the affiliated orders, were also growing. Eighty-two Free Gardeners' societies were recorded as friendly societies across Scotland before 1830.[106] Eight lodges of Oddfellows, linked to the Independent Order of Oddfellows founded in Manchester in 1810, have been identified in Scotland before 1830, the first being the Brechin Benevolent Society of Oddfellows (1812).[107]

Membership and Organization

The limitations placed on membership are a useful indication of the extent to which clubs and societies encouraged a genuinely egalitarian and fraternal practice. One fundamental qualification for admission to the great majority of eighteenth-century Scottish clubs was gender: clubs were based upon the professional, occupational, and convivial lives of men, and women were almost entirely excluded before 1800. In 1720 a pamphlet, *An Account of the Fair Intellectual-Club in Edinburgh: In a Letter to a Honourable Member of the Athenian Society*, gave a sympathetic account of a club of young, intellectually engaged women; it is represented as similar to many male clubs, in that there was an initiation ritual, a membership fee, and a membership limited to nine, with members' names kept secret. The pamphlet suggests that women too might participate in the culture of improvement, and reproduces two members' initiation speeches, which defend women's intellectual aspirations and achievements, seeing them as linked to the pursuit of female virtue. It remains unclear, however, whether the club existed or was a literary fiction, designed to present an argument for women's inclusion in Scottish literary sociability.[108]

Women were, as in London, admitted to the mixed debating societies in Edinburgh and Dundee, but only on highly gendered terms, and there were no all-female debating societies as in London. In Edinburgh and Dundee, unlike London, they did not contribute to debates. In the Pantheon Society of Edinburgh, women, admitted after 1775 on "ladies' tickets," were treated to an orange rather than the customary glass of rum for men. They were, however, allowed to vote, which they did with enthusiasm, and they made up somewhere between less than a third to almost half the crowded audience.[109] Small numbers of women were also admitted to some, though by no means all, subscription libraries, including those at Ayr, Wigtown (1790), and Hamilton (1808); the six women heads of household listed in Wigtown's original subscription list, all presumably widowed, included five active borrowers.[110] Very unusually, in 1805, the Ayr Library Society appointed a female librarian.[111] At a higher social level, the second founding member of the Highland Society of Edinburgh (1784) was Elizabeth, Countess of Sutherland, followed by six other landowning women before 1830.[112] Only by the late 1790s, rather later than in England, did women come to form all-female philanthropic societies and friendly societies, as described by Jane Rendall in this volume. In the following decades they were also to play a part in mixed societies with philanthropic, religious, and educational objectives, but always in ways limited by gender. They were unlikely to speak in any mixed gatherings but could nevertheless play significant organizational and fund-raising roles. There appears to be no evidence for purely convivial or sociable societies among Scottish women in this period.

Individuals joined societies for many different reasons, but most sought a sense of belonging through the attainment of fraternity, harmony, and sociability; to secure such goals, societies had their own sometimes demanding admission procedures. These procedures might involve a daunting combination of nomination, entry fees, election, initiation rituals, and regular annual dues, normally laid down in a written, sometimes printed, constitution. There could be tensions between the expectations of applicants and the exclusivity, and sometimes the hierarchies, of societies, as the chapter by Corey E. Andrews in this volume shows was the case for Robert Burns and Masonic lodges. Many clubs limited their numbers, though the limits could change under pressure for entrance. The Select Society of Edinburgh initially set its numbers at fifty in 1754, raising them to a hundred in 1755, and it excluded sixty-two applicants over its ten-year life.[113] Some societies appealed to elites, or were intended for a professional or student membership. Some conditions for admission could be more specialized. Membership of the Glasgow Highland Society (1727), established to provide a fund for the education and training of boys from the Highlands, was limited to those from a Highland background. The Gaelic Club of Glasgow (1780) required that in addition to a Highland background members be able to converse in Gaelic.[114] Friendly societies imposed conditions for membership that might include age, place of residence, occupation, and moral character. Some friendly societies, especially philanthropic ones, were dependent on patronage and introduced two different classes of membership, for the ordinary and the honorary, or wealthier, members. Larger philanthropic or religious societies, especially from the later eighteenth century onward, aimed to attract the largest possible number of subscribers, and had no limits.

Many clubs, especially convivial ones, had requirements for initiation that involved some kind of ordeal, ritual, or secret oath, as did many trade organizations. The best known of these were the ceremonies of Freemasonry. In some respects these followed the rites of initiation found in many trades, but they also incorporated layers of Renaissance symbolism relevant to the concerns of operative freemasons. The applicant, or apprentice, was blindfolded, and had to take part in a catechism and be introduced to the secret Masonic Word, before being welcomed into the lodge to make further progress through the levels of Freemasonry.[115] Masonic lodges developed increasingly elaborate regalia for such ceremonies and for public processions.[116] These ceremonies may well have influenced other organizations. The Independent Order of Free Gardeners had its own rituals and symbols, based on the gardeners' trade but undoubtedly influenced by Masonic practice.[117] Members of the Cape Club in Edinburgh went through an elaborate ritual, reflecting their playful assumption of the roles of Knights of the Cape, with each member taking a knightly name. Rhona Brown describes the ritual in detail in her chapter in this volume, in relation to the admission of the poet Robert Fergusson. The three degrees, initiation ceremonies, regalia, and elaborate processions of the Royal St. Crispin's Society were clearly derivative in some respects of Freemasonry.[118] But some initiations were less ritualistic: members of the Pantheon Society had to qualify by speaking on "three different questions proposed by the society."[119]

Every society had its rules, embedded in its constitution. These prescribed not only the regulations for admission but the entry fees, the selection of officers, the conduct of business, and fines for poor or immoral behavior. The officers of Scottish clubs and societies characteristically included the preses (or president), treasurer, boxmaster, and clerk. Their procedures might be formal or informal, but they would normally be regulated by rules determining appropriate behavior, enforced by fines. In the Aberdeen Philosophical Society, the rules prescribed that at meetings members would first listen to, and then discuss, a discourse read by one of them and would finish with a debate on a question proposed to them.[120] The students of the Belles Lettres Society of Edinburgh followed a similar pattern, with the discourse required to be between twelve and twenty-five minutes long, and members enjoined "to study a perspicuous brevity in their discourses."[121] Members were fined sixpence for every night's absence. In the Tarbolton Bachelors Club, founded by Robert Burns and his brother Gilbert in 1780, any interruption of a speaker, swearing, and "all obscene and indecent conversation" were banned, on pain of a reprimand, and paying a double or treble share of the bill.[122]

Not all societies were so focused on literary and intellectual activity, and many convivial clubs were formed for evenings of drinking, eating, and conversation. The Pig Club of Glasgow (1798) served a roasted suckling pig at every club dinner, to a membership composed of the mainly Tory merchants dominating the sugar trade.[123] The most common meeting place for all these societies was a tavern, though some student societies were able to use university rooms. In 1769–1770 the University of Edinburgh helped to build an apartment in the university for the Speculative Society, and in 1819 rehoused it within Robert Adam–designed premises in the new (now Old) College.[124] Harris's chapter in this volume explores the appearance of new cultural buildings in the urban context, and the more diverse spaces that they provided for associational meetings from the late eighteenth century onward.

The voluntary associations founded from the 1780s, which appealed to a wider public for support, with an open membership, tended to have meetings of a more formal kind, with an agenda devoted to financial and administrative matters, including fund-raising, the running of institutions, and charitable visiting; larger associations would often have a list of distinguished patrons and a clear committee structure.[125] Women could normally attend regular meetings of these societies but did not play any part in their formal direction, though female committees might be formed for particular purposes. In Edinburgh, Dalgleish found that of the thirty-seven societies founded between 1780 and 1810, two-thirds were of this type.[126] They were increasingly sensitive to the sanction of public opinion, and held themselves accountable through the publication of annual reports and financial statements, with accounts of their meetings frequently published in the press. Such societies saw themselves as dedicated to improvement, whether of their community, city, or country, and, although they might draw on English models, they also deliberately appealed to Scottish national identity. The Lancastrian School Society chose to rename itself the Edinburgh Education Society in 1814.[127] The Society for the Support of Gaelic Schools, founded in Edinburgh, rapidly developed a network of branches across Scotland.[128]

Invented and Imagined Clubs and Societies

As the editors of *The Scottish Enlightenment and Literary Culture* have recently pointed out, arbitrary distinctions between the philosophical and scientific concerns of the Scottish Enlightenment and imaginative literature are anachronistic, in that the academic study of literature was institutionalized only in the nineteenth century. Such distinctions fail to reflect the realities of eighteenth-century culture.[129] It will already be apparent that key literary figures of the period, including James Boswell, Henry Mackenzie, and Robert Burns, actively participated in the associational world described here, and were involved in the founding of a number of clubs. And the consideration of fictitious clubs and societies allows us to understand more clearly how contemporaries perceived and criticized that world. McElroy first pointed out, in 1952, the range and variety of these fictitious societies, and it has already been suggested that the Fair Intellectual Club may have been one of them. McElroy identified three categories: the societies that appeared in periodical publications, those that were deliberate inventions, and those in works of imaginative literature. Martyn J. Powell argues in his chapter in this volume that we should add to the first group clubs and societies appearing in newspapers, whose representation served a similar purpose to those in periodicals.

Most fictitious societies in Scotland, following the proliferation of invented societies in *The Tatler* and *The Spectator*, were engaged in satirizing the associational world. In June 1745 the *Scots Magazine* imagined a Society of Pinchers, who campaigned for the reformation of manners by pinching their fellow members. It asked "whether it is not proposed that this order, like the *Free Masons*, *Gregorians*, and *Ubiquarians*, should branch itself out into numerous *lodges*, *chapters*, or *senates*, to be held in different parts, not only of this *metropolis*, but of the whole kingdom."[130] In 1773 the *Weekly Magazine, or Edinburgh Amusement* mocked the world of clubs and societies as made by men fleeing their crabbed and quarreling wives, while implausibly uniting heavy drinking and serious schemes for the improvement of their country.[131] Another deliberately invented reason for creating a fictitious society was to give authority to a publication that was in practice by an individual. So in 1771 the title page of the *Encyclopaedia Britannica* attributed it to "A Society of Gentlemen in Scotland," when in fact it was compiled by William Smellie, a founding member of the Newtonian Club, the Crochallan Fencibles, and the Society of Antiquaries of Scotland.[132] Smellie also printed Andrew Duncan senior's *Medical and Philosophical Commentaries* (1773–1795), which employed the same tactic.[133]

The associational culture was also explored through imaginative writing, notably by Tobias Smollett, Walter Scott, and John Galt. Smollett left a portrait of the society of cawdies at Leith race course giving a ball to members of the nobility and gentry and "all the celebrated ladies of pleasure," with drink circulating freely and a whole series of toasts, including one to the "beggar's benison"; Powell's chapter in this volume discusses this and other references in Smollett's works.[134] Scott, himself a member of the Speculative Society, the Friday Club, and other Edinburgh societies, reflected his experiences through the different clubs represented in novels from *Waverley* (1814) onward.[135] Clubs help define the world of *The Antiquary* (1816); Scott was familiar with the rivalries of antiquarian societies. Jonathan Oldbuck of Monkbarns, the antiquary of the title, was "a member of various antiquarian societies," and we are told of the existence of two contemporary political clubs, one loyalist, the Royal True Blues, and one connected with the Friends of the People.[136] In *St Ronan's Well* (1823) the history of the Cleikum Inn is related through its clubs. Once, before the decay of the village, "a set of feuars and bonnet-lairds" had drunk there under the name of the Chirupping Club, though at the time of the novel it was regularly visited by young Edinburgh hell-raisers, members of the Helter-Skelter Club or the Wildfire Club.[137] At the Friday Club, held regularly at Fortune's Tavern in Princes Street, Scott had met regularly with leading Scottish literati, including Dugald Stewart and Henry Mackenzie, since 1803. In 1822 *Blackwood's Edinburgh Magazine* began to publish the successful series known as "Noctes Ambrosianae," quasi-satirical parodies of just such clubs of the literati, in the form of imaginary, convivial, whisky-fueled dialogues at Ambrose's Tavern. Some participants were real, under pseudonyms, including John Wilson ("Christopher North") and James Hogg ("The Ettrick Shepherd"), some fictional.[138] The satire and the sharp wit of these dialogues expressed a Tory and romantic nationalism directed against Whig competitors such as the *Edinburgh Review*. Ian Duncan has termed these conversations "a sentimental apotheosis of the clubs and societies that incubated masculine literacy of all classes . . . in Enlightenment Scotland."[139] Drawing on the model of the "Noctes Ambrosianae," the novelist and journalist Christian Isobel Johnstone recreated the Cleikum Inn in *The Cook and Housewife's Manual; . . . by Mrs Margaret Dods* (1826), in which she represented some of Scott's characters, together with others from Susan Ferrier's novel *Marriage* (1818), as members of the Cleikum Club, engaged in lengthy conversations about food both before and after their meal.[140] John Galt referred to both an imaginary club, the Yarn Club, and a real one, the Anderston Club, in his *The Entail* (1823).[141] Such fictional playfulness suggests an audience familiar with and receptive to the tropes surrounding club life.

Conclusion

This volume seeks to explore both the distinctiveness of Scottish clubs and societies and their relationship to a wider associational history. Part I offers some new insights into the broader theory and practice of associations. David Allan explores the ways in which writers of the Scottish Enlightenment conceptualized associationalism, through discussion of the innate human capacity for sociability. Writers including Hutcheson, Hume, and John Millar were eager to defend the role of Edmund Burke's "little platoon," but were also aware of the dangers of factionalism and sectarianism. Bob Harris discusses the locations in which clubs, societies, and associations met, in Scottish towns rather than the major cities. He traces the interaction of old and new patterns of sociability and notes the emergence of new kinds of buildings, with particular reference to reading rooms, inns, and taverns.

Part II of the book explores the participation of professional men in the clubs and societies of Edinburgh, Glasgow, and Aberdeen. Jacqueline Jenkinson focuses especially on the medical societies, which for physicians, surgeons, and medical students were an important part of their professional careers and training. She stresses that increasingly such societies challenged the authority of older medical corporations, which originated in the sixteenth and seventeenth centuries. Ralph McLean investigates the interactions among merchants, academics, and ministers in four important Glasgow societies, and suggests that the coexistence of the University of Glasgow with the prosperous mercantile community of the city made the Glasgow experience distinctive.

The connections between literary worlds and Scottish clubs and societies are considered in part III. James J. Caudle considers James Boswell's engagement with the roistering Soaping Club, devoted to the shaving of members' pretensions and foibles; though Boswell tried to cast off the habits of a raucous and sometimes cruel Edinburgh sociability, he found himself unable to do so. Rhona Brown examines the Cape Club through her work on the poet Robert Fergusson and finds that, contrary to earlier representations, the club was by no means purely convivial but was also a literary, social, and support network, and one that became increasingly politically aware. Corey E. Andrews looks at the involvement of Robert Burns with Freemasonry in Tarbolton and Edinburgh and concludes that he came to be disillusioned with its failure to practice the fraternity that was part of its ideals, and with its political conservatism. The interaction of fictitious and real societies is discussed by Martyn J. Powell in a comparative study of Irish and Scottish clubs. He finds that although the Irish press was generally not critical of clubs, in Scotland there was condemnation of excessive drinking, gluttony, swearing, and obscenity and emphasis on the desirability of the pursuit of a politer culture.

Part IV, the final part of the book, explores issues of gender. Rosalind Carr discusses the shaping of masculinity through the student societies of Enlightenment Scotland, suggesting that such societies provided both a transition to the familiarity with polite culture required for professional and married life and an avenue toward a tavern-based libertine masculinity. Jane Rendall traces the participation of women in societies in Scotland from the late 1790s, examining their role in philanthropic, charitable, and religious associations, and the restrictions placed upon them.

The importance of the social and cultural history of the associational movement should not be underestimated. This volume attempts to broaden our understanding of this movement beyond the gatherings of the literati in Scotland's main cities, important though those were: it is notable that the literati provided a theoretical appreciation of the role which clubs and societies might play in an aspiring, modernizing, and progressive society. Chapters have looked at the ways in which societies were structured by class, profession, and gender, and at the expanding spaces that they occupied across the urban communities of Scotland. The appeal of such societies was wide-ranging and evident in imaginative literature, although they could also be exclusive, limiting, and nostalgic in their practice and their rituals. In the course of this period, clubs and societies were politicized, and found new missions and new roles in a changing civil society. After 1800 women too might participate, to a very limited extent, in this movement. This collection is intended as a contribution toward a much-needed history of the complex development of clubs and societies in eighteenth- and early nineteenth-century Scotland, within the associational expansion of the wider Anglophone world.

NOTES

1. Allan Ramsay, "Journal of the Easy Club," in *The Works of Allan Ramsay*, vol. 5, ed. Alexander M. Kinghorn and Alexander Law (Edinburgh: William Blackwood and Sons, 1972), 5.

2. *Air* [*Ayr*] *Advertiser*, 4 Mar. 1811.

3. Clark, 11.

4. "Literary and Philosophical Societies of Edinburgh during the Eighteenth Century," *Hogg's Instructor* 8 (1852): 44–46; Strang, "Preface to First Edition," unpaginated.

5. *History of the Speculative Society of Edinburgh, from Its Institution in 1764* (Edinburgh: printed for the Society, 1845); James Valentine, "A Society of Aberdeen Philosophers One Hundred Years Ago," *Macmillan's Magazine* 8 (1863): 436–444; [William Reid], *History of the Juridical Society of Edinburgh* (Edinburgh: printed for the Society, 1875); Alexander Ramsay, *History of the Highland and Agricultural Society of Scotland* (Edinburgh: William Blackwood and Sons, 1879); *History of the Dialectic Society* (Edinburgh: printed for the Society, 1887); Harry A. Cockburn, "An Account of the Friday Club," *BOEC* 3 (1910): 157–158; Harry A. Cockburn, *History of the New Club, Edinburgh, 1787–1937* (Edinburgh: W. and R. Chambers, 1938).

6. McElroy, 1969, 9.

7. Exceptions include Gladys Bryson, *Man and Society: The Scottish Inquiry of the Eighteenth Century* (Princeton, NJ: Princeton University Press, 1945); Duncan Forbes, "'Scientific Whiggism': Adam Smith and John Millar," *Cambridge Journal* 9 (1953–1954): 643–670; John Clive and Bernard Bailyn, "England's Cultural Provinces: Scotland and America," *William and Mary Quarterly*, 3rd ser., 11 (1954): 163–179; David Daiches, *The Paradox of Scottish Culture: The Eighteenth-Century Experience* (London: Oxford University Press, 1964); H. R. Trevor-Roper, "The Scottish Enlightenment," *SVEC* 58 (1967): 1635–1658.

8. Colin Kidd, "The Phillipsonian Enlightenment," *Modern Intellectual History* 11 (2014): 175–190.

9. Nicholas Phillipson, "Towards a Definition of the Scottish Enlightenment," in *City and Society in the Eighteenth Century*, ed. Paul Fritz and David Williams (Toronto: Hakkert, 1973), 133; see also Nicholas Phillipson, "Culture and Society in the Eighteenth-Century Province: The Case of Edinburgh and the Scottish Enlightenment," in *The University in Society*, ed. Lawrence Stone (Princeton, NJ: Princeton University Press, 1975), 2:407–448.

10. Nicholas Phillipson, "Hume as Moralist: A Social Historian's Perspective," in *Philosophers of the Enlightenment*, ed. S. C. Brown (Brighton: Harvester Press, 1979), 144.

11. Phillipson, "Towards a Definition," 139; Roger L. Emerson, "The Enlightenment and Social Structures," in Fritz and Williams, *City and Society*, 99–124; Roger L. Emerson, "The Social Composition of Enlightened Scotland: The Select Society of Edinburgh, 1754–1764," *SVEC* 114 (1973): 291–329; Roger L. Emerson, "Select Society (*act.* 1754–1764)," in *ODNB*, https://doi:10.1093/ref:odnb/73614.

12. Roger L. Emerson, "The Philosophical Society of Edinburgh, 1737–1747," *Br J Hist of Sci* 12 (1979): 154–191; "The Philosophical Society of Edinburgh, 1747–1768," *Br J Hist of Sci* 14 (1981): 133–176; "The Philosophical Society of Edinburgh, 1768–1783," *Br J Hist of Sci* 18 (1985): 255–303; "The Scottish Enlightenment and the End of the Philosophical Society of Edinburgh," *Br J Hist of Sci* 21 (1988): 33–66. See also Roger L. Emerson, "The Edinburgh Society for the Importation of Foreign Seeds and Plants, 1764–1773," *Eighteenth-Century Life* 7 (1982): 73–95; Roger L. Emerson and Jennifer Macleod, "The Musick Club and the Edinburgh Musical Society," *BOEC* 10 (2014): 45–62; Roger L. Emerson, *Neglected Scots: Eighteenth Century Glaswegians and Women* (Edinburgh: Humming Earth, 2015), chap. 2.

13. Richard B. Sher, *Church and University in the Scottish Enlightenment: The Moderate Literati of Edinburgh* (Edinburgh: Edinburgh University Press; Princeton, NJ: Princeton University Press, 1985).

14. John Dwyer, *Virtuous Discourse: Sensibility and Community in Late Eighteenth-Century Scotland* (Edinburgh: John Donald, 1987); see also John Dwyer, "Mirror Club (*act.* 1776–1787)," in *ODNB*, https://doi:10.1093/ref:odnb/73612.

15. See Susan M. Purviance, "Intersubjectivity and Sociable Relations in the Philosophy of Francis Hutcheson," in "Sociability and Society," 23–80; Kathleen Holcomb, "A Dance in the Mind: The Provincial Scottish Philosophical Societies," *Studies in Eighteenth-Century Culture* 21 (1991): 89–100; Mark Kingwell, "Politics and the Polite Society in the Scottish Enlightenment," *Historical Reflections / Réflexions Historiques* 19 (1993): 370; Kathleen Holcomb, "Thomas Reid in the Glasgow Literary Society," in *The Glasgow Enlightenment*, ed. Andrew Hook and Richard B. Sher (East Linton: Tuckwell Press, 1995), 95–110; Paul Bator, "The University of Edinburgh Belles Lettres Society (1759–64) and the Rhetoric of the Novel," *Rhetoric Review* 14 (1996): 280–298.

16. Clark, 2 passim.

17. Rosalind Carr, *Gender and Enlightenment Culture in Eighteenth-Century Scotland* (Edinburgh: Edinburgh University Press, 2014), 142–174.

18. Ibid.

19. David Stevenson, *The Origins of Freemasonry: Scotland's Century, 1590–1710* (Cambridge: Cambridge University Press, 1988).

20. J. D. Brims, "The Scottish Democratic Movement in the Age of the French Revolution" (PhD diss., University of Edinburgh, 1983); J. D. Brims, "From Reformers to 'Jacobins': The Scottish Association of the Friends of the People," in *Conflict and Stability in Scottish Society, 1700–1850*, ed. T. M. Devine (Edinburgh: John Donald, 1990), 31–50; Bob Harris, *The Scottish People and the French Revolution* (London: Routledge, 2008); Atle L. Wold, *Scotland and the French Revolutionary War, 1792–1802* (Edinburgh: Edinburgh University Press, 2015).

21. Iain Whyte, *Scotland and the Abolition of Black Slavery, 1756–1838* (Edinburgh: Edinburgh University Press, 2006), 185–190.

22. Sandra Marwick, *Sons of Crispin: The St Crispin Lodges of Edinburgh and Scotland* (Newcastle upon Tyne: Cambridge Scholars Publishing, 2014).

23. Harris and McKean, 492.

24. Murray Pittock, *Enlightenment in a Smart City: Edinburgh's Civic Development, 1660–1750* (Edinburgh: Edinburgh University Press, 2019), 22–24.

25. Ibid., 197.

26. Ibid., 199–201; James Balfour Paul, *The History of the Royal Company of Archers, the Queen's Bodyguard for Scotland* (Edinburgh: William Blackwood and Sons, 1875), chaps. 1–2.

27. Pittock, *Enlightenment in a Smart City*, 197–198.

28. Roger L. Emerson, "Sir Robert Sibbald, Kt, the Royal Society of Scotland and the Origins of the Scottish Enlightenment," *Annals of Science* 45 (1988): 41–72.

29. Clark, 352; *NSA*, 9:302–303, 628; Minute-books, 1669–1889, of the Incorporation of Sailors of Fisherrow and Musselburgh, or Fisherrow Sailor's Society, NLS, MS 1995–1996; William Kennedy, *Annals of Aberdeen* (London: A. Brown, 1818), 2:174.

30. Stevenson, *Origins of Freemasonry*, chap. 8 and 234–235. See also Margaret C. Jacob, *Living the Enlightenment: Freemasonry and Politics in Eighteenth-Century Europe* (New York: Oxford University Press, 1991), 38–46; Lisa Kahler, "Scottish Definitions and Transitions," in *Freemasonry in Context: History, Ritual, Controversy*, ed. Arturo de Hoyos and S. Brent Morris (Lanham, MD: Lexington Books, 2004), 3–18.

31. Ian MacDougall, ed., *A Catalogue of Some Labour Records in Scotland and Some Scots Records outside Scotland* (Edinburgh: Scottish Labour History Society, 1978), 9; Victoria Solt Dennis, *Discovering Friendly and Fraternal Societies: Their Badges and Regalia* (Princes Risborough: Shire, 2005), 81–89.

32. William Maitland, *The History of Edinburgh, from its Foundation to the Present Time* (Edinburgh: printed by Hamilton, Balfour and Neill, for the author, 1753), 471; see also Victor Edward Durkacz, *The Decline of the Celtic Languages* (Edinburgh: John Donald, 1983), 26.

33. Nathan Gray, ed., "Sir David Hume, Lord Crossrig, 'A Narrative of the Rise, Progress and Success of the Societies of Edinburgh for Reformation of Manners,' 1701," *Miscellany of the Scottish History Society*, 6th ser., vol. 4, miscellany XIV (2013): 120–122.

34. T. C. Smout, *A History of the Scottish People, 1560–1830* (London: Fontana, 1998), 434.

35. Durkacz, *Decline of the Celtic Languages*, 26–30.

36. David Allan, *Scotland in the Eighteenth Century: Union and Enlightenment* (Harlow: Longman, 2002), 130–131. Murray Pittock has argued strongly for the importance of Jacobite politics in the Easy Club; see Pittock, *Enlightenment in a Smart City*, 201–205.

37. Lawrence E. Klein, *Shaftesbury and the Culture of Politeness: Moral Discourse and Cultural Politics in Early Eighteenth-Century England* (Cambridge: Cambridge University Press, 1994).

38. McElroy, 1969, 19–25.

39. McElroy, 1952, 1:21–22.

40. Emerson, "Social Composition"; Emerson, "Select Society."

41. David Hume, "Of Refinement in the Arts," in *Essays Moral, Political, and Literary*, ed. Eugene F. Miller (Indianapolis: Liberty Classics, 1987), 271.

42. Richard B. Sher, "Poker Club (*act.* 1762–1784)," in *ODNB*, https://doi:10.1093/ref:odnb/73613.

43. Jeng-Guo S. Chen, "William Lothian and the Belles Lettres Society of Edinburgh: Learning to Be a Luminary in Scotland," *J for 18th Cent Stud* 27 (2004): 173–187; see also Bator, "Edinburgh Belles Lettres Society."

44. William Lothian, "Note and Speech," NLS, Adv. MS 22.3.8, fols. 46–47, quoted in Chen, "William Lothian," 177.

45. Quoted in McElroy, 1952, 2:205–207.

46. Dwyer, *Virtuous Discourse*; Corey E. Andrews, "The Mirror Club: Periodicals as Tastemakers in Eighteenth-Century Scotland," in *The Scottish Enlightenment and Literary Culture*, ed. Ralph McLean, Ronnie Young, and Kenneth Simpson (Lewisburg, PA: Bucknell University Press, 2016), 171–184.

47. Emerson, "Philosophical Society of Edinburgh, 1737–1747": 161.

48. Emerson, "Philosophical Society of Edinburgh, 1747–1768"; "Philosophical Society of Edinburgh, 1768–1783"; "Scottish Enlightenment and the End of the Philosophical Society

of Edinburgh." On the founding of the Royal Society of Edinburgh, see also Steven Shapin, "Property, Patronage, and the Politics of Science: The Founding of the Royal Society of Edinburgh," *Br J Hist of Sci* 7 (1974): 1–41.

49. See also Richard B. Sher and Andrew Hook, "Introduction: Glasgow and the Enlightenment," in Hook and Sher, *Glasgow Enlightenment*, 1–17; Holcomb, "Thomas Reid in the Glasgow Literary Society"; Emerson, *Neglected Scots*, chap. 2.

50. Paul Wood, "Aberdeen Philosophical Society [Wise Club] (*act.* 1758–1773)," in *ODNB*, https://doi:10.1093/ref:odnb/95092; Stephen A. Conrad, *Citizenship and Common Sense: The Problem of Authority in the Social Background and Social Philosophy of the Wise Club of Aberdeen* (New York: Garland, 1987); H. Lewis Ulman, ed., *The Minutes of the Aberdeen Philosophical Society, 1758–1773* (Aberdeen: Aberdeen University Press, 1990), 15–17 passim.

51. This paragraph and the next rely principally on Richard B. Sher, *The Enlightenment and the Book: Scottish Authors and Their Publishers in Eighteenth-Century Britain, Ireland, and America* (Chicago: University of Chicago Press, 2006), esp. 106–114, 181.

52. For a further discussion of the relationship between late eighteenth-century periodicals and club culture, see Jon Mee, "The Buzz about the *Bee*: Policing the Conversation of Culture in the 1790s," in *Before Blackwood's: Scottish Journalism in the Age of Enlightenment*, ed. Alex Benchimol, Rhona Brown, and David Shuttleton (London: Routledge, 2015), 63–74.

53. Richard B. Sher, "Corporatism and Consensus in the Late Eighteenth-Century Book Trade: The Edinburgh Booksellers' Society in Comparative Perspective," *Book History* 1 (1998): 32–90.

54. McElroy, 1969, 111–114; *History of the Speculative Society of Edinburgh*, 16–31.

55. McElroy, 1969, 120–122.

56. Emerson and Macleod, "The Musick Club and the Edinburgh Musical Society."

57. Ulman, *Minutes of the Aberdeen Philosophical Society*, 15; Harris and McKean, 410.

58. McElroy, 1969, 87; Carr, *Gender and Enlightenment Culture*, 82–85.

59. Carr, *Gender and Enlightenment Culture*, 145–169; David Stevenson, *The Beggar's Benison: Sex Clubs of Enlightenment Scotland and Their Rituals* (East Linton: Tuckwell Press, 2001), chap. 9; Cockburn, "Account of the Friday Club," 135–178.

60. Strang, 91–95, 101–105, 181–186.

61. Stevenson, *Beggar's Benison*, 156, 158–159.

62. K. A. Manley, *Books, Borrowers, and Shareholders: Scottish Circulating and Subscription Libraries before 1825; A Survey and Listing* (Edinburgh: Edinburgh Bibliographical Society in association with the National Library of Scotland, 2012), 17–21.

63. Mark Towsey, *Reading the Scottish Enlightenment: Books and Their Readers in Provincial Scotland, 1750–1820* (Leiden: Brill, 2010), 58.

64. Mark C. Wallace, *The Great Transformation: Scottish Freemasonry, 1725–1810* (Washington, DC: Westphalia Press, 2018), 56.

65. Ibid, 329.

66. Lisa Kahler, "Freemasonry in Edinburgh, 1721–1746: Institutions and Context" (PhD diss., University of St. Andrews, 1998), abstract.

67. Wallace, *Great Transformation*, 44.

68. Durkacz, *Decline of the Celtic Languages*, 47.

69. Ibid., 48–67.

70. Clark, 350; NRS, RH2/4/383, fols. 757–758.

71. Sir John Sinclair, ed., *The Statistical Account of Scotland* (Edinburgh: W. Creech, 1793), 9:589–590.

72. Bob Harris, "The Enlightenment, Towns and Urban Society in Scotland, c. 1760–1820," *English Historical Review* 126 (2011): 1103, 1132–1133; Clark, 91.

73. Andrew J. Dalgleish, "Voluntary Associations and the Middle Class in Edinburgh, 1780–1820" (PhD diss., University of Edinburgh 1992), 2.

74. Ibid., 61–63.

75. Harris and McKean, 410–412.

76. McElroy, 1969, 114–116, 161.

77. For these societies, see Leslie Howsam, *Cheap Bibles: Nineteenth-Century Publishing and the British and Foreign Bible Society* (Cambridge: Cambridge University Press, 1991); and Jane Rendall's chapter in this volume.

78. William Law Mathieson, *Church and Reform in Scotland: A History from 1797 to 1843* (Glasgow: James MacLehose and Sons, 1916), 77–87; Esther Breitenbach, *Empire and Scottish Society: The Impact of Foreign Missions at Home, c. 1790 to c. 1914* (Edinburgh: Edinburgh University Press, 2009), 55.

79. Durkacz, *Decline of the Celtic Languages*, 101–102, 111–113.

80. *Observations upon the Propriety of Establishing a Lancastrian School in Edinburgh* (Edinburgh, 1811); James Cleland, *Annals of Glasgow, Comprising an Account of the Public Buildings, Charities, and the Rise and Progress of the City* (Glasgow: printed by James Hedderwick, 1816), 2:258.

81. *Society for the Suppression of Beggars, for the Relief of Occasional Distress, and the Encouragement of Industry among the Poor, within the City and Environs of Edinburgh* (Edinburgh: Alex. Lawrie, 1813), 11–17; see also R. J. Morris, "Voluntary Societies and British Urban Elites, 1780–1850: An Analysis," *Historical Journal* 26 (1983): 98.

82. Alexander Abbot, *Dundee Directory for 1818* (Dundee: printed by A. Colville, [1818]), 178–180.

83. Towsey, *Reading the Scottish Enlightenment*, chap. 2.

84. Mark Towsey, "'Store their Minds with Much Valuable Knowledge': Agricultural Improvement at the Selkirk Subscription Library, 1799–1814," *J for 18th Cent Stud* 38 (2015): 569–584; Manley, *Books, Borrowers, and Shareholders*, 33–34.

85. Towsey, *Reading the Scottish Enlightenment*, 90.

86. Ann Matheson, "Religion," in *The Edinburgh History of the Book in Scotland*, vol. 2, *Enlightenment and Expansion, 1707–1800*, ed. Stephen W. Brown and Warren McDougall (Edinburgh: Edinburgh University Press, 2012), 459–470.

87. Alexander Dick, "'A good deal of trash': Reading Societies, Religious Controversy and Networks of Improvement in Eighteenth-Century Scotland," *J for 18th Cent Stud* 38 (2015): 585–598; Robert Burns, *Commonplace Books, Tour Journals, and Miscellaneous Prose*, ed. Nigel Leask, vol. 1 of The Oxford Edition of the Works of Robert Burns (Oxford: Oxford University Press, 2014), 17–33, 160–170, esp. 166.

88. David Allan, "The Scottish Enlightenment and the Politics of Provincial Culture: The Perth Literary and Antiquarian Society, ca. 1784–1790," *Eighteenth-Century Life* 27 (2003): 1–30; Charles Sanford Terry, *A Catalogue of the Publications of Scottish Historical and Kindred Clubs and Societies . . . 1780–1908* (Glasgow: James MacLehose and Sons, 1909), 135.

89. Alasdair Ross, "The Bannatyne Club and the Publication of Scottish Ecclesiastical Cartularies," *Scottish Historical Review* 85 (2006): 202–233.

90. Terry, *Catalogue of the Publications*, 100, 131.

91. Simon Cordery, *British Friendly Societies, 1750–1914* (Basingstoke: Palgrave Macmillan, 2003), 5, 45–47.

92. *Parliamentary Papers*, 1831–1832 (90), XXVI.291, Return of the Number of Friendly Societies filed by Clerks of the Peace of each County, etc, since 1 January 1793, 35–44.

93. The following discussion is based on Jane Rendall, "'The Principle of Mutual Support': Female Friendly Societies in Scotland, c. 1789–1830," *Journal of Scottish Historical Studies* 40 (2020): 17–39.

94. *Articles of the Beith Humane Society, Constituted 27th March 1800* (Dalry: printed by J. Gemmill, 1801); Sederunt Book of the Justices of the Peace for the County of Dumfriesshire, 1779–1815, registered 27 Oct. 1812, Ewart Library, Dumfries, EGD 046/2, fol. 164.

95. *NSA*, 12:556.

96. Ibid., 12:653; Braemar Royal Highland Society, "The Braemar Gathering," https://www.braemargathering.org (accessed 17 June 2020).

97. Harris, *Scottish People and the French Revolution*, 97–98.

98. Ibid., 77.

99. Ibid., 157–166; Michael T. Davis, "United Scotsmen (*act.* 1797–1802)," in *ODNB*, https://doi:10.1093/ref:odnb/95551.

100. Harris, *Scottish People and the French Revolution*, 165–166, 284n129.

101. Gordon Pentland, *The Spirit of the Union: Popular Politics in Scotland, 1815–1820* (London: Pickering and Chatto, 2011), 66–68.

102. Harris, *Scottish People and the French Revolution*, 125–145; see also Wold, *Scotland and the French Revolutionary War*, 137–139.

103. R. Michael Booker, "Orange Alba: The Civil Religion of Loyalism in the Southwestern Lowlands of Scotland since 1798" (PhD diss., University of Tennessee, Knoxville, 2010), 33–35; see also Elaine McFarland, *Ireland and Scotland in the Age of Revolution: Planting the Green Bough* (Edinburgh: Edinburgh University Press, 1994), 210.

104. Wallace, *Great Transformation*, 141.

105. Ibid., chaps. 5–6 and 329.

106. Rendall, "'The Principle of Mutual Support.'"

107. Ibid.; MacDougall, *Catalogue of Some Labour Records*, 4; Daniel Weinbren, *The Oddfellows, 1810–2010: 200 Years of Making Friends and Helping People* (Lancaster: Carnegie Publishing, 2010). Weinbren is mistaken in stating (28) that the first Oddfellows' lodge in Scotland was founded in 1837.

108. Carr, *Gender and Enlightenment Culture*, 76–82; see also Derya Gurses Tarbuck, "Exercises in Women's Intellectual Sociability in the Eighteenth Century: The Fair Intellectual Club," *History of European Ideas* 41 (2015): 375–386; McElroy, 1969, 20–21.

109. Carr, *Gender and Enlightenment Culture*, 82–92; for London societies, see Mary Thale, "Women in London Debating Societies in the 1780s," *Gender and History* 7 (1995): 5–24.

110. Mark Towsey, "First Steps in Associational Reading: Book Use and Sociability at the Wigtown Subscription Library, 1795–9," *Papers of the Bibliographical Society of America* 103 (2009): 455–495.

111. Towsey, *Reading the Scottish Enlightenment*, 64–65.

112. Ramsay, *Highland and Agricultural Society*, 46–47; The Highland Society of Edinburgh (1784) later became the Highland Society of Scotland at Edinburgh (1787), the Highland and Agricultural Society of Scotland (1834), and finally the Royal Highland and Agricultural Society of Scotland (1948).

113. Emerson, "Social Composition," 300; Emerson, "Select Society."

114. Strang, 106–108; Charles W. J. Withers, "Kirk, Club and Culture Change: Gaelic Chapels, Highland Societies and the Urban Gaelic Subculture in Eighteenth-Century Scotland," *Social History* 10 (1985): 188–191.

115. Stevenson, *Origins of Freemasonry*, chap. 6; Clark, 334–335.

116. Dennis, *Discovering Friendly and Fraternal Societies*, 57.

117. Ibid., 81–89; Marwick, *Sons of Crispin*, 72.

118. Marwick, *Sons of Crispin*, 69–70, 86 passim.

119. McElroy, 1969, 92.

120. Ibid., 45–46.

121. Ibid, 106–109.

122. Burns, *Commonplace Books, Tour Journals, and Miscellaneous Prose*, 22–23.

123. Strang, 262–269.

124. *History of the Speculative Society of Edinburgh*, 20–21, 43–44.

125. See, on these associations, Morris, "Voluntary Societies."

126. Dalgleish, "Voluntary Associations and the Middle Class," 68.

127. *Report of the Committee of Directors of the Edinburgh Education Society, to the General Meeting of the Society . . . on November 28, 1814* (Edinburgh: Alex. Lawrie, 1814).

128. *Annual Reports of the Society for the Support of Gaelic Schools* (Edinburgh: printed for the Society, 1811–1830).

129. McLean, Young, and Simpson, introduction to *Scottish Enlightenment and Literary Culture*, 1–4.

130. McElroy, 1952, 2:450–451.

131. Ibid., 2:454–458.

132. Ibid., 2:470; Stephen W. Brown, "Smellie, William (1740–1795)," in *ODNB*, https://doi:10.1093/ref:odnb/25753.

133. McElroy, 1952, 2:471–472; see also Jacqueline Jenkinson's chapter in this volume.

134. *Humphry Clinker*, 226–228.

135. McElroy, 1952, 2:478; see also Arthur Melville Clark, "The Background," in *History of the Speculative Society*, bicentenary ed. (Edinburgh: printed for the Society by T. and A. Constable, 1968), 32.

136. Walter Scott, *The Antiquary*, ed. David Hewitt, vol. 3 of The Edinburgh Edition of the Waverley Novels (Edinburgh: Edinburgh University Press, 1995), 27, 35; McElroy, 1952, 2:484–485.

137. Walter Scott, *Saint Ronan's Well*, ed. Mark Weinstein, vol. 16 of The Edinburgh Edition of the Waverley Novels (Edinburgh: Edinburgh University Press, 1995), 7, 10; McElroy, 1952, 2:485–486.

138. Charles Snodgrass, "*Blackwood's* Subversive Scottishness," in *Print Culture and the Blackwood Tradition, 1805–1930*, ed. David Finkelstein (Toronto: Toronto University Press, 2006), 90–116.

139. Ian Duncan, *Scott's Shadow: The Novel in Romantic Edinburgh* (Princeton, NJ: Princeton University Press, 2007), 42–43.

140. Ibid., 288–289; Christian Isobel Johnstone, *The Cook and Housewife's Manual; . . . by Mrs Margaret Dods* (Edinburgh: printed for the author, 1826); for the "Final Sederunt of the Cleikum Club," see Johnstone, 2nd ed. (Edinburgh: Oliver and Boyd, 1827), 513–525; Pam Perkins "A Taste for Scottish Fiction: Christian Johnstone's *Cook and Housewife's Manual*," *European Romantic Review* 11 (2000): 248–258.

141. John Galt, *The Entail, or The Lairds of Grippy*, new ed., ed. Ian A. Gordon (1823; London: Oxford University Press, 1970), 189–191.

PART I

The Theory and Practice of Associational Life

CHAPTER 1

Politeness, Sociability, and the "Little Platoon"

ASSOCIATIONAL THEORY IN THE SCOTTISH ENLIGHTENMENT

David Allan

It is clear that the Scottish Enlightenment formed an integral part of what Peter Clark has described in the subtitle of his *British Clubs and Societies, 1580–1800* (2000) as "an Associational World." Indeed, in the wake of Davis D. McElroy's pathbreaking survey in his PhD dissertation more than sixty-five years ago, followed by the shorter work he later published from it, the importance of clubs and societies in eighteenth-century Scotland now appears beyond dispute.[1] The significance of this development, however, was appreciated even at the time. John Ramsay of Ochtertyre, for example, the advocate and Stirlingshire laird who lived through the second half of the century, argued that what he called "literary societies" had actually been one of the period's most salient features: "Soon after the extinction of the rebellion of 1715, a number of promising young men began to distinguish themselves in science or polite literature. In order to improve themselves and counteract conceit, which is never more apt to spring up than in rich minds unaccustomed to contradiction, societies were instituted wherein at stated times, literary subjects were canvassed with freedom and impartiality: ingenious paradoxes were started and assailed with equal ingenuity."[2] Another articulate witness, the lawyer Henry Cockburn, likewise recalled the extraordinary enthusiasm for membership of extracurricular debating societies that had gripped his fellow Edinburgh undergraduates toward the close of the century—even labeling the entire era, as a consequence, "a discussing age."[3] In just one of those organizations, the Academical Society (1796), Cockburn added wistfully, "There were more essays read, and more speeches delivered, by ambitious lads, in that little shabby place, than in all Scotland."

The striking cultural phenomenon recalled so fondly by both Ramsay and Cockburn evidently not only was prevalent in eighteenth-century Scotland but also ranged in ostensible focus across the full spectrum of contemporary endeavors, from the unashamedly recreational, like the Nine Tumbler Club at St. Andrews, to the ambitiously educative, such as the Edinburgh students' Newtonian Club (1778)—to say nothing of prestigious intellectual institutions in the capital, patronized and promoted by the intelligentsia and the social elite, such as the Select Society (1754) and the Philosophical Society (1737).[4] It should therefore be no surprise that when radical politics erupted in Scotland in the 1780s, associationalism was again a crucial mechanism for mediating ideological energies. Edmund Burke certainly noticed this development in *Reflections upon the Revolution in France* (1790), quipping that the French revolutionaries would be heartened by the support they had received from one voluntary institution in particular:

> Let them rejoice in the applauses of the club at Dundee, for their wisdom and patriotism in having thus applied the plunder of the citizens to the service of the state. I hear of no address upon this subject from the directors of the Bank of England; though their approbation would be of a *little* more weight in the scale of credit than that of the club at Dundee. But, to do justice to the club, I believe the gentlemen who compose it to be wiser than they appear; that they will be less liberal of their money than of their addresses; and that they would not give a dog's-ear of their most rumpled and ragged Scotch paper for twenty of your fairest assignats.[5]

The target of Burke's invective was the Whig Club of Dundee, which, founded in 1789 by George Dempster, the local MP, had issued a congratulatory address to the French National Assembly on 4 June 1790.[6] Yet this organization was not alone in embodying eager Scottish clubbishness in this most assertively political of forms. By the last two decades of the century there were voluntary membership-based organizations aplenty active in the cause of constitutional change—associational bodies like the numerous corresponding societies, the Association for the Abolition of Patronage and a Repeal of the Test and Corporation Statutes (c. 1791–1792), the Society of the Friends of the People (1792), and eventually, at the revolutionary end of the spectrum, the secretive and insurrectionary Society of United Scotsmen (1797).[7]

Addison and the Associational Imperative

Involvement in clubs, then, was impressively broad as well as deep in eighteenth-century Scotland: a rich and diverse "associational world" clearly prospered north of the border. But when had this habit first emerged among the Scots and for what reasons? On this too we have the shrewd testimony of Ramsay of Ochtertyre. As we have already seen, he thought it had probably begun with the "literary societies" that had emerged in the early years after the Union. His analysis, however, went somewhat further, portraying the rise of organized sociability as part of a broader cultural revolution underway after 1707, a process traceable in his view to new intellectual influences entering the country from the south. In particular, Ramsay considered it crucial that "the 'Tatlers,' 'Spectators,' and 'Guardians' made their appearance in the reign of Queen Anne. These periodical papers had a prodigious run all over the three kingdoms, having done more to diffuse true taste than all the writers, sprightly or serious, that had gone before them. Nothing, indeed, could be better calculated to please the fancy, inform the judgment, and mend the hearts of readers of all descriptions. . . . Those admirable papers prepared the minds of our countrymen for the study of the best English authors, without a competent knowledge of which no man was accounted a polite scholar."[8] In other words, it was the rapid absorption of polite literature, epitomized by Joseph Addison and Richard Steele's *The Spectator* in 1711–1712, that had initially been critical. For Addison's writing more than anything else had promoted the benefits of associationalism in Scotland, popularizing a cultural practice that simultaneously gave vent to eternal human impulses and helped manufacture a new kind of personality—emollient, sociable, rational, tolerant—best suited to existence in a modern society defined increasingly (or so progressive Whigs like Addison earnestly hoped) by its greater political stability, its growing material prosperity, and its expanding individual freedom.

Importantly, Addison's manifesto for associationalism as a mechanism for achieving modernization both for the individual and for wider society was nested within a coherent Lockean account of human nature as by instinct and aptitude fundamentally social. As the ninth number of *The Spectator* formulated this classic Addisonian dictum, "Man is said to be a Sociable Animal, and, as an Instance of it, we may observe, that we take all Occasions and Pretences of forming ourselves into those little Nocturnal Assemblies, which are commonly known by the name of *Clubs*."[9] Addison's analysis also displayed a keen understanding of how such institutions were suited to a considerable variety of outlooks and personalities, accommodating and even celebrating diversity rather than allowing it to become an impediment to fruitful interpersonal engagement: "Our Modern celebrated Clubs are founded upon Eating and Drinking, which are Points wherein most Men agree, and in which the Learned and Illiterate, the Dull and the Airy, the Philosopher and the Buffoon, can all of them bear a Part. The *Kit-Cat* itself is said to have taken its Original from a Mutton-Pye. *The Beef-Steak* and *October* Clubs, are neither of them averse to Eating and Drinking, if we may form a Judgment of them from their respective Titles."[10] It followed for Addison that the gregarious inclusivity—indeed the boisterous excess—which characterized the internal life of so many clubs and societies also served recognizably ideological purposes. For it forged bonds of amity and mutual understanding that bound people together. It leveled out potential obstacles to peace between disparate individuals which might otherwise have triggered disagreement and provoked open hostility in the community at large. As Addison asserted, "When Men are thus knit together, by Love of Society, not a Spirit of Faction, and don't meet to censure or annoy those that are absent, but to enjoy one another; When they are thus combined for their own Improvement, or for the Good of others, or at least to relax themselves from the Business of the Day, by an innocent and chearful Conversation, there may be something very useful in these little Institutions and Establishments."[11] According to Addison, then, the reinforcement of people's inherent sociable tendencies through voluntary participation in social organizations was essential precisely because it held out the promise of successfully narrowing political divisions and creating greater cohesion throughout society.

These were the much broader purposes for associationalism, which, promoted shortly after the turn of the eighteenth century and in the wake of a turbulent hundred years of religious argument and revolutionary upheaval across the British Isles, appeared so utterly beguiling to so many of Addison's contemporaries. As he later said elsewhere, in the pages of *The Freeholder* (1715–1716), a publication that reinforced many of the trademark arguments for clubbability first aired in *The Spectator*, "It would therefore be for the Benefit of every Society, that is disturbed by contending Factions, to encourage such innocent Amusements as may thus disembitter the Minds of Men, and make them mutually rejoice in the same agreeable Satisfactions. When People are accustomed to sit together with Pleasure, it is a Step towards Reconciliation."[12] It was disembitterment—to adapt Addison's apt neologism—that sociability, cultivated through willing engagement in clubs, seemed best placed to facilitate. This would finally teach people, particularly those Britons most eager to turn their backs on the disagreement and turmoil of the previous century, how to live together in relative tranquility. Ultimately, it would help prevent a repetition of the chronic disturbances that differences of opinion and diversity of belief, when allowed to manifest themselves only in partisanship and intolerance, had so recently engendered.

We do not, of course, need to take Ramsay's word that Addison's prescription for pacifying and civilizing modern people in this way was quickly embraced and assimilated in post-Union Scotland. His namesake, the poet and wigmaker Allan Ramsay, was actually himself among the first Scots to feel this newfound enthusiasm for associational activities in the years immediately after 1707, combining deep attachment to *The Spectator* with ardent involvement in a membership-based organization. For Ramsay's immersion in the Easy Club, formed by a group of like-minded young men in Edinburgh in 1712, was transparently about seeking self-improvement through institutionalized social interaction of just the sort that Addison in London was even then propounding. As the club's secretary recorded, "The Gentlemen who Compose this Society Considering how much ye unmaturity of years want of knowing ye world and Experience of living therein Exposes them to ye Danger of being Drawn away by Unprofitable Company to the waste of the most valuable part of their time Have Resolved at sometimes to Retire from all other Business and Company and Meet in a Society By Themselves in order that by a Mutual improvement in Conversation they may become more adapted for fellowship with the politer part of mankind."[13] Addison's influential journalism, according to the members, remained at the forefront of their minds whenever they met: "ye better to acquaint Us with fine Thoughts," they related, "we have Observ'd as one of our fundamentall Laws that one or two of ye Spectators shall be Read at every Meeting That in Case any passage or Sentence occur we have any Scruples or Doubts about everyone may give his thoughts on't And thus (by ye Rubbing two hard bodies together will smooth Both) we have all been Satisfied about ye thing each of us our Selves could not be Convinced of."[14] The Easy Club's choice of an evocative physical metaphor for the benefits of institutionalized conversation—suggesting the smoothing effects of regular contact on hard bodies, like pebbles on the foreshore, losing their sharp edges over time through constant movement and close interaction—was revealing.

Indeed, it further underlines the powerful English influence over early eighteenth-century Scottish ways of conceptualizing the ramifications of associational activity, clearly echoing a claim for the positive effects of structured sociability very recently offered by Addison's friend Anthony Ashley Cooper, third Earl of Shaftesbury, who in the tract *Sensus Communis, an Essay on the Freedom of Wit and Humour* (1709) had insisted that "all politeness is owing to liberty. We polish one another and rub off our corners and rough sides by a sort of amicable collision."[15] That the Easy Club's members thought themselves engaged in something very much like "amicable collision" seems undeniable. Nor was theirs the only Edinburgh institution in the post-Union years to be so resolutely committed to this agenda: the Rankenian Club, founded in 1716 or 1717, whose members included the young mathematician Colin MacLaurin and the future Aberdeen professor George Turnbull, avowed remarkably similar aspirations, seeking (as the *Scots Magazine* later glossed the Rankenian's purpose, in strikingly Addisonian vocabulary), "mutual improvement by liberal conversation and rational inquiry."[16] Evidently polite sociability, as Ramsay of Ochtertyre later suggested, had indeed soon come to matter greatly to a growing number of Scots in the early decades of the eighteenth century. This was because they had accepted that it was a congenial and effective method for cultivating a more tolerant and enlightened disposition, to the considerable advantage not only of themselves but also of Scottish society as a whole. We need now, however, to ask how this convincing intellectual case for associationalism, demonstrably rooted at first in the receptiveness of some Scots to English journalism and to English philosophical discourse, developed further within Scotland as the Enlightenment unfolded.

The Scottish Philosophy of Sociability

The arguments for associationalism that evolved in Scotland from the 1720s onward in fact had one vital conceptual foundation which tied them in to wider Enlightenment philosophical discussion: the innate human capacity for sociability—of exactly the sort allegedly on display whenever people participated freely in membership-based organizations. As Glasgow's professor of moral philosophy, the Ulsterman Francis Hutcheson, explained in *An Essay on the Nature and Conduct of the Passions* (1728), "There is something like to this in the Desire of *Society*, or the Company of our fellow Creatures. Our Nature is so much formed for this, that altho the *Absence* of *Company* is not immediately painful, yet if it be long, and the Person be not employed in something which tends to *Society* at last, or which is designed to fit him for Society, an uneasy *Fretfulness*, *Sullenness*, and *Discontent*, will grow upon him by degrees, which Company alone can remove."[17] That social interaction was not only natural, as Hutcheson suggested, but also necessary for people to become properly human was certainly central to David Hume's understanding of the implications of clubbish avocations. For example, in the essay "Of National Characters," first published in 1748, Hume emphasized that sociability came automatically to men and women but added that many of their other manners and mores also appeared to have their origins in the resulting proximity to other people: "The human mind is of a very imitative nature; nor is it possible for any set of men to converse often together, without acquiring a similitude of manners, and communicating to each other their vices as well as virtues. The propensity to company and society is strong in all rational creatures; and the same disposition, which gives us this propensity, makes us enter deeply into each other's sentiments, and causes like passions and inclinations to run, as it were, by contagion, through the whole club or knot of companions."[18] Small wonder, then, that Hume, persuaded that satisfying a natural yearning for sociability in a "club or knot of companions" was a recognizable Lockean experience through which a person's own feelings and dispositions might be constructed, was himself such an inveterate attender of such institutions in enlightened Edinburgh—at the Select Society, the Poker Club (1762), the Philosophical Society, and elsewhere.

Yet precisely because polite sociability was potentially so useful both to personal development and to broader social cohesion, it was clear to some in Scotland that it also needed to be sharply differentiated from participative activities of the kind represented in their country's chaotic recent past by various forms of religious and political sectarianism. Indeed, to eighteenth-century Scots still wracked by the memory of the conventicle movement and the Killing Time of the 1680s, it seemed crucial to distinguish genuinely beneficial sociability from damaging factionalism, the constructive club from the destructive cabal. This alertness to the dangers of what was essentially the wrong type of associationalism—conceived as the proximate cause of dangerous political division rather than as its most effective antidote—was again first exhibited by Hutcheson himself in *An Inquiry into the Original of Our Ideas of Beauty and Virtue* (1725). In fact, in parts this treatise can be interpreted as an astute criticism of the excessively simplistic generalizations about the advantages of voluntarism that had recently been influentially disseminated by polite sociability's more sanguine English advocates. If anything, Hutcheson's conclusion appears to have been that Shaftesbury in particular had not done enough to highlight the specific problems posed by sectarian groupings or to make plain the grave threat that this all-too-real phenomenon posed to the unity and stability of communities or nations as a whole. To a philosopher whose priorities were still very obviously shaped by the legacy of the low-intensity civil war that had scarred the relatively recent era of the Cameronians and later Covenanters and in both Scotland and Ireland had seen pitched battles fought between sizable Jacobite forces and their ideological opponents, "faction," as it was often termed by contemporaries, seemed a far greater danger than the London-based author of *Sensus Communis* could ever have appreciated:

> A late ingenious Author justly observes, "That the various Sects, Partys, Factions, Cabals of Mankind in larger Societys, are all influenc'd by a publick Spirit: That some generous Notions of publick Good, some strong friendly Dispositions, raise them at first, and excite Men of the same Faction or Cabal to the most disinterested mutual Succour and Aid: That all the Contentions of the different Factions, and even the fiercest Wars against each other, are influenc'd by a sociable publick Spirit in a limited System." But certain it is, that Men are little oblig'd to those, who often artfully raise and foment this Party Spirit; or cantonize them into several Sects for the Defence of very trifling Causes.[19]

In other words, the natural tendency toward forming groups and cliques was in fact an important basis for sectarianism and political and religious conflict and therefore deeply problematic for society in ways that Shaftesbury's optimistic analysis simply had not adequately acknowledged.

In Hutcheson's rather different view, the coalescence of "Associations" for the most blameless purposes was indeed beneficial, as he recognized by including a knowing allusion to the early Enlightenment environment of Addisonian sociability and politeness in which Scotland was becoming increasingly involved even as he was writing: "Associations for innocent Commerce, or Manufactures; Cabals for Defence of Liberty against a Tyrant; or even lower Clubs for Pleasantry, or

Improvement by Conversation," he conceded, "are very amiable and good." They were also profoundly pernicious, however, when formed in order to assert particular beliefs at the expense of others. As he continued:

> But when Mens heads are filled with some trifling Opinions; when designing Men raise in their Minds some unaccountable Notion of Sanctity, and Religion, in Tenets or Practices, which neither increase our Love to God, or our own Species; when the several Factions are taught to look upon each other as Odious, Contemptible, Profane, because of their different Tenets, or Opinions; even when these Tenets, whether true or false, are perhaps perfectly useless to the publick Good; when the keenest Passions are rais'd about such Trifles, and Men begin to hate each other for what, of it self, has no Evil in it; and to love the Zealots of their own Sect for what is no way valuable; nay, even for their Fury, Rage, and Malice against opposite Sects; (which is what all Partys commonly call Zeal) 'tis then no wonder if our moral Sense be much impair'd, and our natural Notions of Good and Evil almost lost; when our Admiration, and Love, or Contempt, and Hatred, are thus perverted from their natural Objects.[20]

On this reading it was especially important to avoid encouraging membership of any organizations that promoted exclusivity rather than inclusiveness and that generated mutual intolerance instead of greater understanding. Hutcheson's palpable fear of "designing Men" co-opting the immense formative power of participatory institutions for malign ends, stoking "Fury, Rage, and Malice against opposite Sects," and spreading their bile to the detriment of society at large, speaks eloquently of the reasons why so much was understood to rest on the proper and responsible use of associationalism. It also explains the striking claim subsequently made many years later by Hutcheson's most distinguished pupil: "Of all the corrupters of moral sentiments," Adam Smith insisted, laying down an *obiter dictum* that would perhaps have made most sense to readers who appreciated the peculiarly challenging historical background in Scotland, "faction and fanaticism have always been by far the greatest."[21]

The wider social and political implications of people freely associating together in small groups were also of concern because of the tendency of such gatherings to generate debate and disputation—which, as Cockburn's later recollections remind us, were the stock-in-trade of the clubs and societies that grew up around the eighteenth-century Scottish universities in particular. Thus it was that Hugh Blair, the professor of rhetoric at Edinburgh during the 1760s, 1770s, and early 1780s, fretted that institutionalized discussion by its nature was as liable to encourage pointless displays of argumentative prowess by rival participants engaged in aggressive competition as it was to stimulate that amity and concord between individuals which clubbishness was ideally meant to nurture. This fear was what lay behind Blair's warning in *Lectures on Rhetoric and Belles Lettres*

(1783) that only those "academical associations" for men intending to enter the traditional professions, or at least debating societies structured and constrained by their having properly polite or formal educational purposes, could be considered desirable:

> As for those public and promiscuous Societies, in which multitudes are brought together, who are often of low stations and occupations, who are joined by no common bond of union, except an absurd rage for Public Speaking, and have no other object in view, but to make a show of their supposed talents, they are institutions not merely of an useless, but of an hurtful nature. They are in great hazard of proving seminaries of licentiousness, petulance, faction, and folly. They mislead those who, in their own callings, might be useful members of society, into fantastic plans of making a figure on subjects, which divert their attention from their proper business, and are widely remote from their sphere in life.[22]

In other words, the frenzy of interest in debating societies, as Blair's patronizing comments about those of "low stations and occupations" make clear, increasingly seemed to be encouraging ordinary people not only to engage in heated disputes but even to challenge the established order—indeed, as we have already seen, they would emerge as an important focus for the radicalized Scottish politics of the final quarter of the century. In Blair's view, then, the injudicious speechifying and fiery rhetoric into which certain types of associationalism could evidently tempt their participants, giving conversation and dialogue a distinctly subversive edge, actually rendered them a threat to civility and to social stability.[23]

Nature, History, and the Politics of Clubbishness

Given their own country's difficult recent history of sectarian extremism (and the evident concern later in the century that this troubling dimension to participatory voluntarism was re-emerging in a new guise), it should perhaps not be surprising that some Scottish theorists favored a more nuanced account of associationalism's potential political implications. Yet discussion of membership-based organizations during the Scottish Enlightenment also yielded a deeper appreciation of their origins and evolution in the progressive emergence of civil society. Here again it was Hume who best captured the growing sense that associational activity, exemplified in what he called the "particular clubs and societies" of present-day Britain, was in fact a historical construction to be understood as inextricably intertwined with other important aspects of incipient modernity. In a much-quoted passage in the 1752 essay "Of Refinement in the Arts," in which he sketched out the very essence of an emerging age of Enlightenment, Hume made this point forcefully:

> The more these refined arts advance, the more sociable men become: nor is it possible, that, when enriched with science, and possessed of a fund of conversation, they should be contented to remain in solitude, or live with their fellow-citizens in that distant manner, which is peculiar to ignorant and barbarous nations. They flock into cities; love to receive and communicate knowledge; to show their wit or their breeding; their taste in conversation or living, in clothes or furniture. Curiosity allures the wise; vanity the foolish; and pleasure both. Particular clubs and societies are everywhere formed: Both sexes meet in an easy and sociable manner: and the tempers of men, as well as their behaviour, refine apace. So that, beside the improvements which they receive from knowledge and the liberal arts, it is impossible but they must feel an encrease of humanity, from the very habit of conversing together, and contributing to each other's pleasure and entertainment. Thus *industry*, *knowledge*, and *humanity*, are linked together by an indissoluble chain, and are found, from experience as well as reason, to be peculiar to the more polished, and, what are commonly denominated, the more luxurious ages.[24]

Hume's opinion here was once again fully alive to the ideological aspects of associationalism, since the recent proliferation of institutions where people mingled "in an easy and sociable manner" and engaged in "conversing together," exploiting the unprecedented levels of freedom of association available in places like Hanoverian Scotland, was presented as a defining feature of an increasingly advanced and liberal society. Nor was this all. Hume also saw strong similarities between the ways in which membership in a smaller voluntary association and membership in the wider political community each rewarded the participant. As he argued elsewhere: "No enjoyment is sincere, without some reference to company and society; so no society can be agreeable, or even tolerable, where a man feels his presence unwelcome, and discovers all around him symptoms of disgust and aversion. But why, in the greater society or confederacy of mankind, should not the case be the same as in particular clubs and companies?"[25] Human society, in other words, functioned in an important sense as but a club rendered on a vastly larger scale. As Hume suggested, it conferred exactly the same psychological benefits—which is to say, the reassurance and affirmation of one's acceptability that comes from the manifest approval of one's immediate fellows.

Henry Home, Lord Kames, the philosopher, judge, and friend of Hume who was such an important figure in the Scottish Enlightenment as well as in its club life, recognized that the human propensity for associating together not only was expressed in ways that were profoundly shaped by historical context but also had significant implications for a better understanding of how political society as a whole had evolved. In *Sketches of the History of Man* (1774), Kames claimed that what he called the "social appetite," while undoubtedly universal in its application to a person's relations with other human beings, nevertheless exerted particularly forceful influence when animated by membership of small-scale organizational units: "The next question is, Whether the appetite be limited, as among other animals, to a society of moderate extent; or whether it prompt an association with the whole species. That the appetite is limited, will be evident from history. Men, as far back as they can be traced, have been divided into small tribes or societies."[26] For Kames, recreational societies of the kind with which he was personally familiar in contemporary Edinburgh, with their intimate and face-to-face character, were especially useful in drawing out and giving expression to men's sociable instincts. But equally, the much more extensive eighteenth-century nation-state, almost as large a social formation as had ever existed in history, was for exactly the same reason not at all well molded to the distinctive contours of human nature:

> We find now, after an accurate scrutiny, that the social appetite in man comprehends not the whole species, but a part only; and commonly a small part, precisely as in other animals. Here another final cause starts up, no less remarkable than that explain'd above. An appetite to associate with the whole species, would form states so unwieldy by numbers, as to be incapable of any government. Our appetite is wisely confined within such limits as to form states of moderate extent, which of all are the best fitted for good government: and we shall see afterward, that they are also the best fitted for improving the human powers, and for envigorating every manly virtue.[27]

Kames's subtle analysis of the disparate settings in which natural sociability led human association to occur clearly entailed a slightly uncomfortable political conclusion for modern Britons: "Patriotism is vigorous in small states," he insisted, "and the hatred to neighbouring states not less so: both vanish in a great monarchy."[28] Even more importantly, he added, "Small states, however corrupted, are not liable to despotism."[29] As a result, an understanding very close to that later adduced by Burke in *Reflections*, when hailing the superiority of social units of limited size in generating loyalty and conferring identity, was strongly implicit in Kames's argument. To him there seemed to be a vital relationship between how the sociable impetus for association actually functioned in practice and the forms of political organization that were consequently most in accordance with human nature. This was a connection, moreover, that favored not the modern state, with its far-flung boundaries and remote locus of authority, but rather what Burke would subsequently immortalize as the "little platoon we belong to in society"—the small-scale social entity inherently better adapted to the needs and instincts of its members, which, as he would controversially propose in 1790, was nothing less than "the first principle (the germ as it were) of public affections."[30]

The professor of civil law at Glasgow, John Millar, Smith's pupil, was no less fascinated than Kames by the potential political consequences of men's demonstrable preference for associating freely in relatively small groups. This is probably why parts of his *Observations Concerning the Distinction of Ranks in Society* (1771) read like a serious attempt at a history of communal organization as such, rooting the emergence of political society in particular in the concatenation of pre-existing social constructs, themselves formed originally on the natural principle of association and with discrete antecedents that long remained discernible. As Millar says of the political formations found in the earlier periods of European history, "Every kingdom was composed of a great variety of parts, loosely combined together, and for several centuries may be regarded as a collection of small independent societies, rather than as one great political community. The slow advances which were afterwards made by the people towards a more complete union, appear to have been productive of that feudal subordination which has been the subject of so much investigation and controversy."[31] Intriguingly, this argument, revolving around what Millar conceived as the much smaller social and political communities of the remote past, before the emergence of what he described pejoratively as "feudal subordination," was something to which he seems to have paid particularly close attention when revising the original text of *The Distinction of Ranks* to reflect the subsequent evolution of his own social theory and to fill out a more complete conjectural history of early society.

By the time the third edition appeared in 1779—with revisions on this point perhaps colored by the intervening publication of Kames's somewhat similar account—Millar had provided a fully worked-out explanation of the relationship between the horizontal fusion of natural small-scale associations and the emergence of an increasingly stratified society structured along vertical lines, in which political authority had steadily gravitated toward the top. Initially, Millar thought, this development had advanced the sectional interests of the feudal magnates:

> These observations may serve to show the general aspect and complexion of that political constitution which results from the first union of rude tribes, or small independent societies. The government resulting from that union is apt to be of a mixed nature, in which there is a nobility distinguished from the people, and a king exalted above the nobles. But though, according to that system, the peculiar situation of different nations may have produced some variety in the powers belonging to these different orders, yet, unless in very poor states, the influence acquired by the nobles has commonly been such as to occasion a remarkable prevalence of aristocracy.[32]

This, however, was not the end of the process. The historical coalescence of ever-larger social organizations out of more limited groupings had inexorably brought about further concentrations of political power, until what resulted was merely an autocracy or absolute monarchy of the kind familiar across eighteenth-century Europe: "The continued union of rude tribes, or small societies, has a tendency to produce a great alteration in the political system of a people," Millar wrote. "The same circumstances, by which, in a single tribe, a chief is gradually advanced over the different heads of families, contribute, in a kingdom, to exalt the sovereign above the chiefs, and to extend his authority throughout the whole of his dominions."[33]

Like Alexis de Tocqueville, then, Burke's great French disciple, who would famously denounce the eighteenth-century ancien régime for having suppressed voluntary associationalism of any kind—arguing, indeed, that the repressive state had prevented "the formation of any free society. It could brook no association but such as it had arbitrarily formed, and over which it presided"[34]—Millar concluded that feudalism and the gradual convergence of all effective authority, first within a social elite of aristocrats and finally under a single absolute ruler, had inevitably cramped and curtailed participatory voluntarism. In short, freedom of association, conceived by both Millar and Tocqueville as a necessity before people could express their natural sociable instincts, had been among the most striking casualties of the rise of increasingly hierarchical and oppressive forms of political organization.

Nor was Millar, a convinced Whig and supporter of parliamentary reform, unaware that this same conjectural account of the historical loss of primitive associationalism had significant consequences for an understanding of Britain's own political evolution. In *An Historical View of the English Government* (1787), he confirmed that the people of what eventually became England had in earlier times lived in communities of remarkably limited extent. As "strangers to agriculture," they were "divided into small independent tribes," Millar maintained, "under their several chiefs, as commonly happens in that early state of mankind." The problem, however, was that "these little societies being much addicted to plunder, and for that reason frequently engaged in hostilities, a regard to mutual defence had occasionally produced alliances among some of them from which a variety of petty princes, or kings, had arisen in different parts of the country."[35] Once again, as in *The Distinction of Ranks*, the development of something recognizably like centralized political authority appeared to be attributable to the fusion of much smaller previous human associations. For Millar, this was a critical feature of the long, slow, painful unfolding of the constitutional arrangements of his own day, and it meant that the British people had gradually secured the peace and prosperity which they now enjoyed only by abandoning their more intimate and more satisfying forms of communal organization. They had purchased greater stability and order, certainly, but at what in Millar's view needed to be recognized, as it would later be in Tocqueville's critique of absolute monarchy, as the very significant price of the rights of free association for which their nature properly fitted them.

Conclusion

On 10 April 1784, during a trip to Scotland that saw him installed as Lord Rector of the University of Glasgow, Burke took breakfast with Smith and Millar at the Saracen's Head in Glasgow.[36] This meeting further deepened an acquaintance with the Scottish philosophical community that had earlier seen him engage closely with the writings of Hutcheson, Hume, Kames, and Adam Ferguson and enter into correspondence with several of the major Scottish theorists. If his early rejection of the French Revolution would soon open up substantial distance with at least some of them (Millar especially), there remain grounds for seeing Burke's valorization of the "little platoon" as closely linked to a familiar theme that had over the previous decades been elaborated by several of his friends in Scotland, concerned as they too had long been with the political ramifications of associationalism. For wider questions raised by active membership of social organizations had exercised particular fascination among the eighteenth-century Scottish intelligentsia. Enthusiastic about its modernizing and improving potential as propagandized by Addison and Shaftesbury, which seemed peculiarly relevant to their own national predicament following the Union, they had also been alert to the danger, again highlighted by Scotland's own stormy recent history, that what was ordinarily presented as the definitive modern answer to factionalism and fanaticism might actually promote them further. Equally, that various forms of associational activity had actually waxed and waned historically, and that small-scale organizations in particular seemed best adapted to human nature and human appetites, had also been seen by some of Burke's Scottish friends, though the latter clearly differed among themselves as to when those voluntary institutions had most flourished, just as they were also divided as to whether the contemporary state, especially in Britain, protected or actually jeopardized the freedom to associate. The result was a richly textured analysis of associationalism in the Scottish Enlightenment, positive but also questioning—aware of its potential advantages in a political context but by no means uncritical about the risks and the problems involved. When Burke set his mind to working through the ideological implications of the same fascinating feature of human social and political organization some years later, in the wake of the French Revolution, it turned out that he could not have been keeping better company.

NOTES

1. McElroy, 1952; McElroy, 1969.

2. John Ramsay, *Scotland and Scotsmen in the Eighteenth Century*, ed. Alexander Allardyce (Edinburgh: William Blackwood and Sons, 1888), 1:8. "Rise of literary societies" is the page heading.

3. Henry Cockburn, *Memorials of His Time*, new ed., ed. Harry A. Cockburn (1856; Edinburgh: T. N. Foulis, 1909), 24–25.

4. McElroy, 1952, 1:211–212, 2:360; Roger L. Emerson, "The Philosophical Society of Edinburgh, 1737–1747," *Br J Hist of Sci* 12 (1979): 154–191; Roger L. Emerson, "The Social Composition of Enlightened Scotland: The Select Society of Edinburgh, 1754–1764," *SVEC* 114 (1973): 291–329.

5. Edmund Burke, *Revolutionary Writings*, ed. Iain Hampsher-Monk (Cambridge: Cambridge University Press, 2014), 242.

6. J. D. Brims, "The Scottish Democratic Movement in the Age of the French Revolution" (PhD diss., University of Edinburgh, 1983), 64–65. Burke has been taken by some scholars as addressing these comments to the Dundee branch of the Friends of Liberty; e.g., *The Writings and Speeches of Edmund Burke*, vol. 8, *The French Revolution, 1790–1794*, ed. L. G. Mitchell (Oxford: Clarendon Press, 1989), 285n. In fact the Friends of Liberty, a more radical and also less well-heeled organization, did not emerge until 1792. The Dundonian address to the French revolutionaries appears in *SM* 52 (1790): 457–459.

7. Brims, "Scottish Democratic Movement," 46–47, 133–134, 205–206.

8. Ramsay, *Scotland and Scotsmen*, 1:6–7.

9. *The Spectator* (London) 9 (1712): 48–49.

10. Ibid., 51.

11. Ibid., 51.

12. *The Freeholder* 34 (1716): 203.

13. Allan Ramsay, "Journal of the Easy Club," in *The Works of Allan Ramsay*, vol. 5, ed. Alexander M. Kinghorn and Alexander Law (Edinburgh: William Blackwood and Sons, 1972), 5.

14. Ibid., 8.

15. Anthony Ashley Cooper, third Earl of Shaftesbury, *Characteristicks of Men, Manners, Opinions, Times*, ed. Lawrence E. Klein (Cambridge: Cambridge University Press, 1999), 31.

16. Quoted in McElroy, 1969, 62–70.

17. Francis Hutcheson, *An Essay on the Nature and Conduct of the Passions and Affections, with Illustrations on the Moral Sense*, ed. Aaron Garrett (Indianapolis: Liberty Fund, 2002), 67.

18. David Hume, "Of National Characters," in *Essays Moral, Political, and Literary*, ed. Eugene F. Miller (Indianapolis: Liberty Classics, 1987), 202.

19. Francis Hutcheson, *An Inquiry into the Original of Our Ideas of Beauty and Virtue*, ed. Wolfgang Leidhold (Indianapolis: Liberty Fund, 2004), 142.

20. Ibid., 142–143.

21. Adam Smith, *The Theory of Moral Sentiments*, ed. D. D. Raphael and A. L. Macfie, The Glasgow Edition of the Works and Correspondence of Adam Smith (1976; rev. repr., Indianapolis: Liberty Fund, 1982), 156.

22. Hugh Blair, *Lectures on Rhetoric and Belles Lettres* (London: W. Strahan and T. Cadell; Edinburgh: W. Creech, 1783), 2:240–241.

23. Smith made a similar point about the foibles of certain associations, arguing that the "prudent man" would not seek "the favour of those little clubs and cabals, who, in the superior arts and sciences, so often erect themselves into the supreme judges of merit." Smith, *Theory of Moral Sentiments*, 213.

24. David Hume, "Of Refinement in the Arts," in *Essays Moral, Political, and Literary*, 271.

25. David Hume, *Enquiries concerning Human Understanding and concerning the Principles of Morals*, ed. L. A. Selby-Bigge, 3rd ed., rev. Peter H. Nidditch (Oxford: Oxford University Press, 1975), 280–281.

26. Henry Home, Lord Kames, *Sketches of the History of Man* (Edinburgh: W. Creech; London: W. Strahan and T. Cadell, 1774), 1:365.

27. Ibid., 1:366.

28. Ibid., 1:416.

29. Ibid.

30. Burke, *Revolutionary Writings*, 47.

31. John Millar, *The Origin of the Distinction of Ranks*, ed. Aaron Garrett (4th ed., 1806; repr., Indianapolis: Liberty Fund, 2006), 216.

32. Ibid., 212.

33. Ibid., 213. For another possible influence on Millar's evolving analysis, see Adam Ferguson's curious discussion of "states of small extent" in *Institutes of Moral Philosophy* (Edinburgh: A. Kincaid and J. Bell, 1769), 293. Naturally, because Ferguson, politically more conservative, had a strong aversion to outright citizen democracy, he was disinclined to imply any criticism of the British constitution when praising the participatory citizenship of antiquity.

34. Alexis de Tocqueville, *The Old Regime and the Revolution*, trans. John Bonner (New York: Harper and Brothers, 1856), 86, http://oll.libertyfund.org/titles/tocqueville-the-old-regime-and-the-revolution-1856 (accessed 10 May 2018).

35. John Millar, *An Historical View of the English Government* (London: A. Strahan and T. Cadell, and J. Murray, 1787), bk. 1:9–10. This account may echo Ferguson's intriguing translation of Julius Caesar's observation that the island's pre-Roman inhabitants had been "associated into small clubs or fraternities, of ten or a dozen in number." Adam Ferguson, *The History of the Progress and Termination of the Roman Republic* (London: W. Strahan and T. Cadell; Edinburgh: W. Creech, 1783), 2:262.

36. Michael Brown, "The Meal at the Saracen's Head: Edmund Burke and the Scottish Literati," *Studies in Burke and His Time* 22 (2011): 13–44.

CHAPTER 2

Buildings, Associations, and Culture in the Scottish Provincial Town, c. 1700–1830

Bob Harris

This chapter starts from the wrong end of a particular question: What happened to patterns of sociability and associational habits in provincial Scottish urban society between the beginning of the eighteenth century and circa 1830? This issue is explored in what follows, primarily through the evidence of changes to the built environment. The focus is thus as much on *locale* as on activity.

Why Space and Place?

Current views of associational habits and practices in urban Scotland in this period are skewed heavily toward Edinburgh and Glasgow; of most burghs, especially the smaller ones—the majority in Scotland—we know surprisingly little.[1] This partly reflects a lack of evidence. Hints in the sources about new clubs and societies are usually just that, and much is hidden from view. Thus, for example, excepting Masonic lodges and subscription libraries, which have left quite plentiful records, minutes survive for only a handful of clubs established in towns other than the two big cities during the Enlightenment.[2] The surviving records of the Dundee Speculative Society (fl. 1772) comprise a list of members from 1782 and a single letter published in a periodical a decade earlier.[3] Even with the rise of new sources in the early nineteenth century, such as, most importantly, an expanding provincial newspaper press, the silences can be resounding. A short-lived Kilmarnock literary periodical from the later 1810s contains a letter from "Prudentia" from the Ayrshire industrial village of Catrine, bemoaning her husband's devotion to debating societies and calling on the editor to warn of the follies of tradesmen neglecting their businesses to engage in "abstract disquisitions."[4]

Perhaps these were similar to the literary clubs occasionally mentioned in the journals of contemporaries, such as the one referred to in the autobiography of the Dunbar bookseller and printer George Miller.[5] While this assumption seems highly plausible, hard evidence is lacking, as it is for the tavern cultures that flourished in burghs and smaller settlements throughout this period, which may have become even more closely identified primarily with tradesmen and artisans. Moreover, it is very easy to be misled by nomenclature. When I first came across a reference to the Dundee Scientific Society, I assumed it was, as the title suggests, a club devoted to the pursuit of scientific knowledge. It later emerged, however, that it was a friendly society established in 1799.[6]

Given such gaps, exploring changing associational habits and practices from the perspective of urban renewal and building starts to make sense. There is, however, another, stronger reason for taking this approach. From the 1730s, or a little earlier in several burghs, increasing numbers of Scottish townscapes were subject to a process of renewal and improvement that steadily gathered pace, until accelerating and broadening significantly in incidence in the 1790s.[7] In the course of this development, the centers of many burghs were restructured in pursuit of enhanced amenity and efficiency. At the same time, new cultural pretensions were registered in new attitudes toward the nature of the street, the clearer delineation of different spaces and activities within the town, and the rise of new types of civic and public building, which reflected these changed understandings and the transformed social and cultural relationships and expectations that underpinned them. So closely linked were these developments that they enable us to read the changing form of the town precisely in terms of such shifts in mentalities. It is, in short, the legibility of changes to townscape that make them a helpful lens through which to make sense of wider patterns of social and cultural change in urban life.

The chapter begins, therefore, by describing briefly some of the main patterns discernable in this period in relation to the construction of new buildings that had a major cultural or social purpose. It then turns to examine in greater depth several types of building or space that assumed crucial roles in the cultural lives of Scottish townsfolk in the Georgian era—the reading room, inn, and tavern. The chapter concludes with some reflections on what this evidence can tell us about patterns of change and continuity in respect to sociability and associational habits within provincial Scots burghs.

Cultural Buildings

A "cultural building" is defined here as a building that served an important cultural or social purpose. Some cultural buildings were long-standing features of the Scottish townscape, most obviously schools (although they were often undistinguished structures or spaces). Other cultural buildings represented an evolution or redesign of an existing civic building, as the townhouse developed from the tollbooth. As we will see, this represented rather more than simply a change in name. A series of new types of buildings arose in the Georgian period: theaters, reading rooms, libraries, assembly rooms, Masonic lodges, and large inns. Many of these buildings were funded either by subscription or by private capital, whereas others, notably schools and townhouses, were funded through either burgh revenues or borrowing, or some combination of these, along with subscription. In practice, things were often not quite so neat, and quite a few buildings defy ready or simple categorization. This might be because their use changed over time, or because they had multiple functions, as Scottish burghs had relatively few single-purpose civic or public buildings during this period.

Although churches and religious buildings are excluded from this chapter because of its secular focus, we must keep in mind the very considerable amount of capital and energy invested in church building during this period. In a good many burghs the only example—or certainly one of a small number—of new civic buildings was the parish kirk. One crude measure of the importance of religious institutions during this period is the amount of church building, including the rebuilding of many parish kirks, the division of large urban parishes, and construction of new kirks (as in Dumfries in 1727, Paisley in 1733, and Perth in 1807). From the end of the eighteenth century this trend included the building of new churches and chapels to house proliferating religious denominations and groups, which became a marked feature of the burghs from the 1790s, especially in the larger towns, such as Greenock and Paisley, but also in medium-sized ones, for example, Dunfermline, which had ten churches, chapels, or meetinghouses by 1801.[8] The legalization of Roman Catholic worship in 1793 led to the construction of Catholic chapels, while more architecturally distinctive Episcopalian meetinghouses or chapels began to appear from the final decades of the eighteenth century.

There is one other type of building or space that requires brief notice at this point: the shop. This period saw the rise of retail shops as an important aspect of revitalized civic centers and the evolution of certain streets into new parades.[9] The rise of the shop was a very widespread phenomenon by the end of the eighteenth century, although there was wide variation among towns in respect to their number and range. In 1800 a visitor to Kirkcaldy, certainly not the best endowed Scots burgh in the Georgian period (and one marked by little change to its townscape before the passage of a local improvement act in 1811), remarked on the "many new and even elegant shops" then appearing.[10] Among the tradesmen who rented these shops were a good number of booksellers, quite a few of whom operated circulating libraries, and in a number of cases, such as George Miller in Dunbar, some kind of a reading room.[11]

Although generalizing about building patterns across what was a very diverse urban order is clearly a dangerous exercise, a number of basic observations can be made. First, as already noted, single-purpose cultural buildings were relatively uncommon. Dedicated theaters, assembly rooms, or reading rooms and libraries appeared in only a small number of towns. Stirling was unusual in boasting the Athenaeum (1817), built specifically to house a reading room and library on its two main floors, although quite when and how the plan took shape is unclear.[12] Separate assembly rooms were to be found in Ayr, Dumfries, and Peterhead; Inverness had its grand Northern Meeting Rooms erected in 1790 to house the annual meetings of the regional Highland gentry in the form of the Northern Meeting Club (1788), which converged on the town for two weeks in the autumn.[13] Ayr's assembly room before the early nineteenth century was also called the town hall—which suggests that it may well have been another multipurpose space—and was located near the Cross at the heart of old Ayr. There were evidently plans in the early 1800s for a much grander set of rooms, designed by John Patterson, Robert Adam's factotum, to be funded by means of a tontine.[14] The scheme was aborted, perhaps in favor of a more modest one built to a design by John Robertson.[15] Much more impressive was the imposing suite of rooms that formed most of the second floor of Thomas Hamilton's assembly rooms and spire, built in 1827.[16] Greenock's Exchange Buildings (1814), possibly an early commission from William Burn and completed at a cost of seven thousand pounds, housed two major assembly rooms.[17] In Kirkcaldy, Hawick, and Dunbar, assembly rooms were built by subscription in 1818, 1821, and 1822, respectively, probably because there were no other suitable venues for assemblies in these towns by this period.[18] Small theaters were built in Dumfries (1792), Greenock (1808), Dundee (1810), Montrose (1814), Arbroath (1815), Ayr (1815), and Perth (1820).

How can this pattern be explained? Perhaps it is not that surprising, given the small size of many of the Scots burghs. Comparing like with like, the pattern may not be so dissimilar from what was occurring in England. Only towns of a certain size or character could produce the scale and continuity of demand that warranted investment in specialist facilities. Therefore, throughout the British Isles such investment was typically greatest in large, rapidly growing manufacturing towns or in specialist resort or spa towns.[19] There were relatively few of both types in Scotland, although the early nineteenth century did see the rise of a small number of sea-bathing locations to join Moffat and Peterhead as resorts.[20]

However, the rarity of such buildings may also be something of an illusion, insofar as the functions they performed tended often to be distributed around other buildings, notably inns, but also townhouses or even other multipurpose buildings, including Masonic lodges. This, in fact, was typical in most Scottish burghs. Before the construction of the Tontine Hotel in Greenock (which opened in 1805) and the Exchange Buildings, the main meeting places and cultural venues in this rapidly expanding port were the town's main inns: the Masons' Lodge (later known as the Masons' Arms Hotel), the Buck's Head, the White Hart, the town hall (completed in 1766), and the Gardeners' Hall.[21] Assemblies, reading rooms, and even theaters often found sites in the new townhouses. The meeting halls of the growing number of Masonic lodges—there were at least four in Dunfermline by 1813, for example—were readily turned over to use for exhibitions, concerts or assemblies, and dances. In Stirling, Cowan's Hospital hosted assemblies, meetings, and classes by dancing masters, and also served as the Guildry.[22] In Dundee, annual subscription assemblies were held in the town hall, although a complaint was made about the quality of the venue in 1810,[23] while the Sailors' Hall on Yeaman Shore, built in 1790, was frequently used for balls, concerts, and lectures. Subscription libraries were to be found in a variety of sites, especially townhouses. Sometimes a room was specially created for them in the new school buildings, as happened, for example, in Greenock in the early 1800s and in Kirkcudbright when it built its new academy in 1818. The Cupar library was housed in the town's new county buildings before being somewhat controversially evicted in 1818 by the Fife county commissioners of supply.[24]

Townhouses, which were built in a wide range of burghs in this period, had an inherent flexibility of function. To some extent this attribute was inherited from their direct predecessors, the tollbooths, but it also signified how established and newer needs were combined in their construction and use, often in ways that were very largely circumstantial. Take, for example, Montrose's townhouse, built in the early 1760s and enlarged by a further story and extended in 1819: the proposal for this building first emerged when local gentry suggested to the burgh council that a subscription should be raised for an assembly room. The council did not appear very interested until the idea was linked to provision of a merchants' exchange.[25] From the later eighteenth century, county communities and government increasingly sought meeting places and courtrooms in the county towns, and quite a few of the later townhouses were, strictly speaking, town *and* county houses. This was true, for example, of the Forfar Town Hall, designed by James Playfair and built in the later 1780s. It is not coincidental that its construction was overseen by George Dempster of Dunnichen, then provost of the burgh, and supported financially by the local gentry.[26] Conversely, many county buildings of a slightly later period—as, for example, in Ayr (1821) and Paisley (1818)[27]—contained several rooms reserved specifically for burgh use.

More broadly, the imperatives of economy lent an unassailable logic to combining functions in single buildings. When the flourishing but still rather modest-sized port and manufacturing town of Arbroath decided to construct a new townhouse as part of a wider program of redeveloping its main street, the old tollbooth was sold to the guildry for use as a guild hall and reading room (as well as to house the local subscription library), instead of being demolished.

Scots burgh authorities typically inherited an urban fabric in a sorry, even parlous, condition, the consequence of the sharp and protracted economic downturn that lasted from the 1690s into the 1730s, and well beyond in the case of some less fortunate burghs, particularly many of those on the Fife coast. Much of their time was thus taken up simply with maintenance and repair. Between 1753 and 1787, the Forfar Town Council, for example, was forced to spend around sixteen hundred pounds on repairs to the kirk, manse, and school, and the local heritors spent a similar sum again.[28]

There were, moreover, pressing demands on councils' attention and money other than pursuit of architectural aggrandizement, however desirable that might have been. The principal of these was ensuring the prosperity of the burgh, meeting basic needs and amenity (maintenance, improvement and cleaning of streets, lighting, water supply, etc.), and making the burgh fit for commerce and manufacturing. In many coastal burghs, the harbor was a nearly constant and very heavy drain on funds. While some financial support was available through the Convention of Royal Burghs, the outlays could be very significant indeed. For places such as Arbroath, Banff, or Greenock, maintaining and improving the harbor and its facilities accounted for by far the bulk of building expenditures. That the councils were essentially reactive and opportunistic when it came to most building projects is much more readily comprehensible against this background.

Maintaining and—increasingly from the later eighteenth century—enhancing provision of education and school accommodation were part of the same set of impulses and conditions. Education brought people and money to burghs; it also played a crucial part in maintaining civic reputation among the Scots burghs. The rash of academy construction from the later eighteenth century was driven by the importance that the burghs traditionally placed on provision of learning, but this goal was re-energized by a strengthening impulse toward modernization of the curriculum that can be traced back to at least the end of the previous century, although it gained new strength after about 1760. Part of it was simply about civic rivalry: there was keen recognition that schools rose and declined in reputation and in their capacity to attract pupils, sometimes from considerable distances. Underpinning it, however, was also (and crucially) a new ability to raise funds for this purpose from local gentry and communities of Scots who had found prosperity within Britain's expanding empire, in America, the West Indies, and India.[29] Had the academies relied on the financial capacity of local communities and burgh revenues alone, far fewer of them would have been built.

Other factors also help to explain the relative rarity of single-purpose cultural buildings. Theater struggled in many burghs, not only as a result of continuing religious hostility but also because of unstable demand, set against a background of sharply fluctuating economic fortunes from the early 1790s.[30] Suspicion of the arts may sometimes have been a feature of Scottish urban society, although these kinds of tensions were equally present in English commercial and manufacturing towns. Libraries, which fitted well with the culture of improvement as it took shape in Scottish urban society in this period, spread rapidly, but encouragement of a wider vision of culture was altogether a harder proposition. Early nineteenth-century Greenock flirted with successive initiatives to promote literary and scientific debate, but none was enduring. When the Society for the Encouragement of Arts and Sciences in Greenock was established in 1808, it evidently was met with a significant degree of suspicion, part of which was a perception that it was devoted only to the arts.[31] Provision of assembly rooms often seems to have depended on the patronage of neighboring gentry and their demand for urban meeting places.

In some respects, therefore, it is what did not happen that is most striking. The most visible increases in new cultural buildings were concentrated in a small, select group of burghs before 1820. What distinguished these burghs was either their roles as places of gentry resort or, as with Greenock or to a lesser extent Dundee, their size and prosperity. Moreover, even where such buildings did appear, it was usually quite late in the period, after about 1800. Perth, for example, was, for a town of its size, growing in prosperity and ambition, seriously deficient in new public buildings of any kind by 1800. That its traditional rival Dundee had furnished itself with three kinds of public buildings by 1800 (Town Hall in 1734, Trades' Hall in 1778, and English Chapel in 1785), and four if we include the St. Andrew's Trades' Kirk (1772), can only have made this shortcoming harder to bear. In Perth at the end of the eighteenth century, the main assemblies in the town were held in the Glovers' Hall, erected on the new George Street in the 1780s.[32] Faced with this deficiency, and benefiting from the patronage of Perth Hunt meetings from 1784, the town from the 1790s began to unfold plans for a grand new redesigned civic center, the main focus on which was to be a new riverside parade, which later became Tay Street. However, relatively little of what was planned (including a new assembly room and coffee room) actually emerged, although the grand new county buildings (1821) did result.[33] Stirling and Dumfries, two medium-sized burghs which were also places of gentry resort, were hardly notable for their public buildings in this period. This was even more the case with respect to many of the smaller burghs, for example, Hawick, Dunbar, or Forres, to take a fairly random selection. As two English female visitors to another such burgh, Linlithgow, complained in 1824, "the Town-house and fountain opposite it are worth looking at & nothing else as the town is very beggarly."[34]

Yet this is only part of the story. For if new buildings were in some respects quite limited in range and number, especially those for cultural purposes, the extent and scope of change within the heart of many a townscape in this period is easily underestimated. However piecemeal and episodic, the centers of an ever-growing number of towns underwent increasingly systematic improvement, which, while driven for the most part by a concern for utility and efficiency as well as amenity, was serving to recast the street and spaces within and just off it as sites for new kinds of sociability and social performance. Improvement might mean in some cases a wholesale reorientation of the townscape as, for example, in Ayr, where the Sandgate was recreated as the "principal street," following the construction of the new Ayr bridge in 1787, and genteel Ayr spread onto the Low Green. Another fine example is Kilmarnock, which saw wholesale redevelopment of the area around the Cross from 1802, as the town sought to escape the constraints and the stain of its old narrow streets.[35] Moreover, as already noted, new activities did not always require new buildings, but rather often found a home in multipurpose buildings. It is a pattern that will come into clearer focus as we consider several specific types of buildings or spaces: reading rooms, inns, and taverns.

Reading Rooms

The rise of the reading room as a distinctive space within the Scottish (and indeed British) townscape was a product of the final decades of the eighteenth century. Its roots can be traced back to the later seventeenth century and the rise of the coffee room, although the end product was quite different. Coffee rooms in the Scots burghs tended to be supported by the burgh council, and they in turn emerged from earlier sets of arrangements through which the councils had furnished themselves with newsletters and later newspapers, which often involved local postmasters.[36] By the mid-eighteenth century, however, the relationship between burgh councils and coffee rooms was breaking down,[37] presumably in large part because newspapers were becoming much more widely available. At this point, coffee rooms started to fade from the historical record.

The Scottish model for the "reading room" was Glasgow's majestic reading room within its Tontine Hotel, completed in 1781. Membership in reading rooms was by subscription, and one feature distinguishing them from the earlier coffee rooms was the abundance of newsprint and periodicals available by the later Georgian period. Reading rooms were stocked with London, English provincial, Scottish, and international newspapers, as well as a variety of periodicals.[38] Furthermore, the reading room very rapidly became a key site of male sociability among the commercial and professional elites. In this, it partly replaced the Exchange, less a building than a space in Scots burghs, a site of congregation usually located on the main street, and, to a lesser extent, the Cross, another common meeting place. In Dundee and several other burghs, the merchants' walk, the habitual place of congregation of the town's merchants, was close to the harbor. The emergence of reading rooms marked a key moment in the reshaping of this stratum of society, as well as spaces of difference within the townscape.

In 1792 the travel writer John Lettice claimed, correctly, that all "great towns of North Britain" boasted a subscription coffee or reading room.[39] Paisley's first reading room was created in 1784 by converting one of the shops on the lower floor of the Public Inn (later known as the Saracen's Head) on the High Street.[40] Dunfermline had two reading rooms by the later 1820s, one of which was found under the new Guildhall linked to the Spire Inn.[41] Dumfries also had two subscription reading rooms by that date.[42] Stranraer's enterprising townspeople solicited their local innkeeper to create a coffee room in his inn, which they supported by subscriptions.[43] Equally noteworthy in the present context was their high visibility within the new townscapes. Dundee's reading room, to cite one example, had its home from 1799 in the Trades' Hall at one end of the marketplace, before migrating in 1828 to the imposing new Exchange Coffee House, designed by the Edinburgh architect George Angus and located on Dock Street, overlooking the town's two new enclosed docks.[44]

If the subscription reading rooms were frequently accorded prominent sites within the restructured townscapes of the early nineteenth century, they were quickly assimilated into the lives of male members of the urban elites. This partly reflected the importance of news and information for commercial and business life. Reading rooms were both symptomatic and symbolic of the shrinkage of time and space in the rapidly commercializing and modernizing society of later Georgian Scotland and Britain. They also, however, registered more subtle changes within urban society, the rise of new modes of inclusion (and exclusion) and new types of collective identity. This new world may have grown out of the old one in important ways, and the break between them may well have been uneven and partial—hence the identification of the Arbroath guildry and the reading room, and the sense of the reading room as a "civic" space. But a new kind of public was taking shape, one that basically organized itself outside the structures of the traditional burgh community. The reading room was a recreational and commercial space, and it was also necessarily a political one, since membership defined in a significant way the boundaries of the urban commercial and professional elite. It is not coincidental in this context that when in 1819 the Paisley Town Council agreed to produce a printed balance sheet detailing the town's income and expenditure, as well as having it published in the *Glasgow Courier*, with copies sent to councillors, the town's hospital, commissioners of police, and the deacons of the trades, and six copies left at the "Coffee Room."[45] Dundee's reading room hosted a series of important meetings on public matters of great moment to the town's mercantile classes in the early nineteenth century.[46]

Inns and Taverns

If the reading room was a multipurpose space, this was of course equally true of inns and taverns. In contrast to its English counterpart,[47] the history of the Georgian Scottish inn has yet to be written. Nevertheless, it is reasonably clear that the combined effects of growing commercial prosperity and the rise of commercial and recreational travel led to the emergence of much larger, more imposing inns in many Scots burghs by the later eighteenth century. As the editor of the *Greenock Advertiser* declared in 1813, "Inns are of great importance in the system of internal communication, and nothing affords so striking a proof of the state of trade in the country, as the condition of these houses, and the treatment which travellers experience in them."[48] Paisley's three-story Public Inn—later called the Saracen's Head—was built by the burgh council in 1750–1751, and enlarged in 1791 with a new building at the back that housed an assembly room on the first floor and bedrooms above.[49] In many smaller settlements, in planned villages and new towns, and in the Highlands, landowners were behind their construction—partly to provide accommodation for visitors to their estates, partly as key aspects of wider programs of improvement. The New Inn in Paisley, completed in 1782, was funded by the Earl of Abercorn, who owned the Abbey lands on which Paisley's new town was laid out from 1788. Designed by the London architect George Stewart, the inn boasted thirty rooms with hearths, one of which was 34′ × 18′ × 16′; a large coffee room at one end; and stables for twenty-eight horses and six carriages.[50] The initiative for the redevelopment of the Hamilton Arms Inn in 1784 (which included construction of a grand assembly room) appears to have come from the Duchess of Hamilton, who wished to create a ballroom in the town, which, in turn, seems to have been closely linked to the emergence of the Hamilton races in the later 1770s.[51] Similar examples could be cited.

Local gentry were important sponsors of quite a few of the new larger inns of the later eighteenth century. This was true of the New Inn in Forfar, which provided a meeting place for the summer assemblies of the Angus gentry. Another example is the Peebles Tontine Inn, built in 1808 at the cost of almost three thousand pounds; it was the initiative of the Peebles Shooting Club (1790), which before its construction had held its annual ball in the townhouse.[52] Early nineteenth-century leases on the Grapes Inn in Selkirk (sometimes known as the County Inn) were even negotiated by a committee appointed from local commissioners of supply.[53]

However, the point that really needs underlining is how much investment there seems to have been in building new and redeveloping older inns from the final third of the eighteenth century. The full extent of this investment is unknown, since we are largely reliant on stray records and impressionistic comment. Take the Cross Keys Inn in Kelso, said by one (admittedly probably partial) commentator in the later eighteenth century to be the finest inn between Newcastle and Edinburgh.[54] It was built in the early 1770s by Admiral William Dickson, who also had Sydenham House constructed slightly earlier as his home in the town; the stables at least were rebuilt and enlarged at the end of the eighteenth century.[55] The Tower Inn in Hawick was evidently refitted at the beginning of the nineteenth century.[56] Similarly, the George Inn in Perth, which stands on George Street, was begun in 1783 and extensively remodeled sometime in the mid-1820s.[57] This was probably partly in response to the refurbishment of the Salutation Inn, the town's other main inn, around 1800, which included the fitting up of a ballroom.[58] This in turn points to a further crucial dynamic underpinning these developments: intensifying commercial rivalry. Time and again, the improvement of one inn in a town led to the remodeling of its main competitor(s). This evidently happened, for example, in the case of Dundee's two main inns in the early 1800s, Gordon's and Morren's, while construction of Greenock's Tontine Inn appears to have stimulated improvements to the Buck's Head and the White Hart.[59]

These new and redeveloped inns typically housed ballrooms, assembly rooms, or large dining and public rooms. The ballroom was a prominent feature of Kelso's Cross Keys Inn from the time it was first built, and notices in the press in the early 1780s about assemblies held in the Kelso assembly room were almost certainly referring to this space.[60] About twenty years later, the Cross Keys had been joined by the George Inn on Bridge Street, which had an "extensive" dining room, and at least one further inn with similar facilities.[61] Forfar's New or County Inn boasted a dining room (40′×20′), drawing room (25′×20′), two parlors (19′×20′), as well as fourteen bedrooms and various other rooms and offices. By the early nineteenth century, if not rather earlier, such facilities seem to have been available in inns in many small burghs. This was, for example, true of many inns in the borders, such as the Black Bull and the White Swan in Duns, the Black Bull in Lauder, the Spread Eagle in Jedburgh, and even inns in places such as Castleton in the extreme south.[62]

Thus, various impulses lay behind the growth of larger, more commodious inns in many Scots burghs. They were symptomatic of a society characterized by ever-increasing and faster circulation of goods and people and the growing demands for meeting places in the burghs from parts of rural society, particularly landowners but also the growing ranks of prosperous tenant farmers, and their wives and daughters. From the later eighteenth century, the inns played host to the proliferating clubs and associations that derived most of their membership from neighboring rural society—hunts, sporting clubs, agricultural improvement societies, and farmers' clubs. The New Club, for example, formed in 1810 from the principal members of the landed gentry in East Lothian, held its four annual meetings in the George Inn in Haddington, while the Jed-Foresters met in the Spread Eagle in Jedburgh, and the Forest Club in Minto's in Selkirk.[63] As the example of the Hamilton Arms Inn cited earlier highlights, the rise from the 1770s and 1780s of annual hunts and race meetings also extended regular landed patronage of the main inns in a growing number of burghs, such as Kelso, Hamilton, Ayr, Perth, Cupar, Stirling, and Linlithgow.

However, a good number of the clubs that met in these premises had their origins much more firmly in urban society, or they served to link urban and rural elites. Examples include the Pitt and Fox Clubs, Burns clubs, patriotic societies, and the Paisley Bachelors or Baron's Club, to name one that is better documented than most. Formed in 1794 by "a number of influential . . . and successful men of business," the Paisley Bachelors met in one of the card rooms of the Saracen's Head, with a membership that fluctuated between the high 50s and around 120.[64] The Kilmarnock Thistle Club (fl. 1818), which convened on the anniversary of the Battle of Bannockburn, met in the town's Star Inn, while the relatively short-lived Philological Society of Dumfries (1802) held its anniversary dinners in the Globe.[65] Dundee's Morren's Inn or Hotel played host to, among others, the Camperdown Club (1806?), which met on the anniversary of the battle; the Centre Bowmen (fl. early 1800s), a sporting club; the Dundee Highland Society (1814/1815), essentially a charitable foundation; the Valentine Club (1816), which organized socially exclusive assemblies; as well as Pitt and Fox Clubs.[66] Exactly who comprised the members of these clubs is usually hidden from the historian's scrutiny, but they were almost certainly drawn mainly from the mercantile, manufacturing, and professional elites. The dinner on the anniversary of William Pitt the Younger's birth in 1811, held in Gordon's Inn (as it was then called), was said to have attracted a "numerous attendance of the mercantile and manufacturing interest of Dundee."[67] In this context, "numerous" probably meant between about fifty and one hundred. Semiformal public dining was becoming much more prominent by the early nineteenth century as an aspect of urban and public life, a development given powerful further impetus by the burgeoning practice of patriotic celebration and commemoration associated with the French Revolutionary and Napoleonic Wars.[68]

If large, commodious inns were, therefore, increasingly visible and influential elements in the dynamic provincial urbanism of Scotland in the later Georgian era, they did not so much replace as augment older drinking establishments. For taverns also multiplied in this period. By 1820, the Ayrshire burgh of Irvine had not only two "head inns," both of which had "large rooms for public meetings," but also a further fifty-three "houses of entertainment."[69] In 1825 Arbroath had two inns—the George and the Town's Arms (also known as the White Hart)—and thirty-eight taverns or public houses. By the same date, Dundee had three "hotels" and well over a hundred "vintners."[70]

Unfortunately, even less is known about these places than about the inns and, as is evident, the nomenclature was in flux. Some of these establishments were apparently little more than rooms in tenements, parts of a shadowy economy of makeshifts very strongly associated in the minds of the urban elites with disorder and immorality. James Hackston's tavern in Perth, for example, was described in 1799 as "a house of the most disorderly kind and of exceeding bad fame."[71] A list drawn up of Perth houses of "bad fame" in 1819 included several in South Street, and seven others distributed around the town, including three in the Skinnergate.[72] Others, however, were more substantial affairs, and in the first half of the eighteenth century taverns were evidently patronized by members of the middling sort and the elites, as well as the laboring sort. When the Earl of Strathmore was killed in an affray on the streets of Forfar in 1720, he had been drinking in a tavern with several others of the local gentry after attending a funeral in the town.[73] In 1799 "Philetus," the pseudonymous author of a series of letters in the short-lived *Dundee Magazine*, sketched a world that had passed, in which merchants spent their evenings at their tavern "club"; by the end of the century it was the drawing room and not the tavern that claimed them of an evening, or so the same writer contended. Others, such as George Penny, the early historian of Perth, hinted at something very similar, although change was no doubt uneven, colored by generational differences and even counter-trends in the opening decade or so of the nineteenth century.[74]

Consequently, the tavern seems in this period to have become increasingly a site of sociability mainly for tradesmen, artisans, and others among the laboring classes. Nor was it purely a male province, since women seem to have been regularly present. Dances were commonplace, but more spontaneous in form than those given the title "assemblies." Following events such as processions, members of trades incorporations and societies typically met in the evening for dinners and balls, usually in inns and taverns, but also (where they existed) in trades halls.[75] Card playing was common, but not the "card clubs" that tended to meet in inns.[76] Taverns were also the sites of meetings of friendly societies, which grew very significantly in number from the later eighteenth century.[77] Other types of tradesmen's clubs also met there, for example, clothing, debating, and political clubs. This was where much politics at this level of society was discussed and transacted. But these gatherings were informal, on a small scale, and inherently fluid, as well as increasingly distant from those of the elites, and perhaps for these reasons they have left few traces in the records for this period.

Conclusion

By the early nineteenth century, then, patterns of sociability and association within the Scots towns were becoming increasingly diverse and multilayered. There was an important spatial dimension to these developments, and buildings and spaces were increasingly differentiated by location and character. Major inns tended to cluster in streets that had been systematically modernized, a process that included provision of lighting and pavements. There was almost certainly a very powerful association between clubs and their place of meeting; the identity of the "club room" was part of the experience of membership. Quite a lot of this history remains subterranean, partly because of the nature of the Scots townscape, in which new activities did not necessarily produce new buildings, and multipurpose spaces remained the norm, and partly because of the paucity of the sources. Formal, elite associations and clubs have left the most records; they required advertisement precisely because they met relatively infrequently or drew on support from beyond as well as inside the town. The changes we have been examining were, moreover, aspects of a much wider process of transforming the townscape, as boundaries were becoming ever more clearly delineated, an impulse that was increasingly pervasive after about 1800, even though the results were usually uneven and selective. Rates of change in relation to habits and mentalities varied significantly between different levels of society and different types of towns, and older habits of association and sociability—such as those focused on the churches or guilds and incorporations—were not quickly marginalized. Rather, old and new often interacted in quite complex ways. If a world of new associational behavior was taking shape, therefore, it was a world that seems to have taken strongest root among a small male elite. Even then, just as within other social strata, it may be a story as much about adaptation as about transformation.

NOTES

1. But see Bob Harris, "Cultural Change in Provincial Scottish Towns, c. 1700–1820," *Historical Journal* 54 (2011): 105–141.

2. Most notably, the Stirling Port Club (1782), NLS, Acc. 7862, no. 3; the Perth Literary and Antiquarian Society (1784), Perth Museum and Art Gallery, MSS 6–7; the Paisley Philosophical Institution (1808), Paisley Central Library (although the minutes are currently missing); Banff Literary Society (1818), Aberdeenshire and Aberdeen City Archives (although the minute book for 1818–1866 is in too fragile a condition for consultation).

3. *The Dundee Register of Merchants and Trades, With All the Public Offices, &c for M,DD, LXXXIII*, ed. A. C. Lamb (1782; repr., Dundee: A. C. Lamb, 1879), 41–42; "Extract of a letter from Dundee, 1772," *Gentleman and Lady's Weekly Magazine* (Edinburgh, printed by William Auld) 1 (1774): 30. Stray newspaper references are also the only evidence for the existence of two later Enlightenment societies in Dundee: see *Dundee, Perth and Cupar Advertiser*, 12 Aug. 1814, for the Dundee Botanical and Horticultural Club, and 5 July 1816, for the New Reading Club.

4. *Ayrshire Miscellany, or Kilmarnock Literary Expositor* 6 (1818): 19–22.

5. W. J. Couper, *The Millers of Haddington, Dunbar and Dunfermline: A Record of Scottish Bookselling* (London: T. F. Unwin, 1914), 71.

6. Rules of the Scientific Society of Dundee, 21 Oct. 1816, NRS, GD1/369/227.

7. Harris and McKean, chap. 2.

8. Ebenezer Henderson, *The Annals of Dunfermline and Vicinity from the Earliest Authentic Period to the Present Time, A.D. 1069–1878* (Glasgow: J. Tweed, 1879), 548; A. Mercer, *The History of Dunfermline, from the Earliest Period Down to the Present Time* (Dunfermline: John Miller, 1828), 126–134.

9. It also reflected an important development in the specialization of retailing in the burghs, since at the beginning of the period there was much less differentiation between merchants and tradesmen, with the former frequently operating out of premises that sold a very wide array of goods. The rise of shopping in this period has attracted much attention from historians of England, but there is as yet no similar scholarship for Scotland.

10. *Notes of a Tour through the Shires of Fife, Forfar, Perth, and Stirling in 1800* (Dundee: printed for private circulation, 1898), 7.

11. See the handbill advertising Miller's "Agricultural, Commercial, Military Intelligence, News & Reading Room" and library, which were to be found immediately above his shop on the town's High Street: NLS, MS 5409, fol. 160r.

12. It began life as a proposal by the local gentry for a ballroom in 1804, but seems quickly to have metamorphosed into something quite different.

13. The Northern Meeting Club held its initial meetings in the town hall. The Northern Meeting Rooms were erected on the site of a large inn that had burnt down in 1779 (*Memorabilia of Inverness* [Inverness, 1912], 63). Of the Dumfries assembly rooms, the Reverend William Burnside wrote in 1791, "We have an Elegant assembly room in town 48′ by 24′, with card & tea rooms in proportion—subscription assemblies are held once a fortnight in the winter season. During our circuits in spring & autumn, the rooms will often exhibit 150 or 200 people, as genteel & fashionable as are to be seen in any provincial town whatever" (William Burnside, MS History of Dumfries, 1791, Ewart Library, Dumfries, strongroom 058, fol. 72). A further new set of assembly rooms in Dumfries was built in 1825.

14. Copies of the plans for this building, from the Culzean Castle drawings, are held by the Royal Commission for Ancient and Historical Monuments for Scotland, AYD/79/1–3. The Ayr Town Council minutes refer to a scheme for a tontine inn, but it seems very likely that they were one and the same.

15. John Robertson, architectural plan for building a new assembly room, 7 Apr. 1802, NRS, RHP2563. See also Ayr Town Council Minutes, esp. 4 Apr. 1803, Carnegie Library, Ayr.

16. Plan of the Principal Story of the Assembly Rooms, Spire &c for the Town of Ayr, 1827, Ayrshire Archives, Auchincruive, Ayr, which shows the main assembly room of 47.6′ × 24.6′ and a joining card room of 29.2′ × 19.0.′

17. Daniel Weir, *History of the Town of Greenock* (Greenock: Daniel Weir; Glasgow: Robertson and Atkinson; Edinburgh: John Boyd; London: Whittaker, 1829), 36.

18. Robert Wilson, *History of Hawick*, 2nd ed. (Hawick: printed by R. Armstrong, 1841), 92; James Miller, *The History of Dunbar: From the Earliest Records to the Present Period* (Dunbar: W. Miller, 1830), 233; David Brewster, ed., *The Edinburgh Encyclopaedia* (Edinburgh: William Blackwood, 1830), 12:463–464.

19. C. W. Chalkin, "Capital Expenditure on Building for Cultural Purposes in Provincial England, 1730–1830," *Business History* 22 (1980): 51–70.

20. They included, on the Clyde, Largs, Helensburgh, and Ardrossan and, on the east coast, St. Andrews and Broughty Ferry.

21. Based on notices published in the *Greenock Advertiser* from 1802. All continued as important venues after completion of the Tontine Hotel and Exchange Buildings.

22. *A General History of Stirling* (Stirling: printed by C. Randall, 1794), 101.

23. *Dundee, Perth and Cupar Advertiser*, 19 Jan. 1810. The paper's correspondent complained that the room in the town hall was not in keeping with the "wealth, refinement, and luxury" now found in the town, and even fifty years earlier would have been thought "incommodious."

24. Brewster, *Edinburgh Encyclopaedia*, 12:464–466; *Dundee, Perth and Cupar Advertiser*, 10 Apr. 1818, 30 Oct. 1818; Weir, *History of the Town of Greenock*, 25.

25. Magistrates of Montrose v. James Scott, 1762, NRS, Court of Session Papers, CS235/M3/9.

26. For details, see Papers relating to the new townhouse of Forfar, Angus Archives, Hunter Library, Restenneth Priory, Forfar, F/5/181 (1–13).

27. Minutes and reports of general meetings of the county, of the committee on the public buildings, and of the town council of Ayr, relating to the new public buildings, with some correspondences, 1805–1816, Ayrshire Archives, CO3/7/1; Renfrewshire commissioners of supply minute books, 1812–1819, 24 Dec. 1812, 30 Apr. 1813, 26 Oct. 1813, 25 Oct. 1814, Glasgow City Archives, CO2/1/1/4.

28. Forfar Heritors Records, 1717–1795, entry for 11 Apr. 1788, NRS, HR415/3/1.

29. On this point in regard to Inverness Academy, see Douglas J. Hamilton, *Scotland, the Caribbean and the Atlantic World, 1750–1820* (Manchester: Manchester University Press, 2005), 204–211.

30. Harris and McKean, chap. 6.

31. Society for the Encouragement of Arts and Sciences, Greenock, *Observations on the Best Mode of Promoting the Society Instituted for the Encouragement of Arts and Sciences, in Greenock* (Glasgow: Mennons, 1814).

32. See, e.g., Agreement between the Perth Glover Incorporation and the County of Perth regarding the use of their new hall for meetings and during the races, 1793, PKCA, B59/29/132. The building later housed a theater and then the reading room.

33. Developments in Perth are discussed in detail in Harris and McKean, chap. 5.

34. Mrs. and Miss Beecroft, "Journal of a tour to Scotland in the summer of 1824," NLS, MS 29500, fol. 68.

35. See the discussion of developments in Ayr in Charles McKean, "Was There a British Georgian Town? A Comparison between Selected Scottish Burghs and English Towns," *Historical Research* 86 (2013): 253–291.

36. In Banff in the early eighteenth century, the "weeklie news letters" were rouped to the highest bidder, who had the right to charge one penny per sight of them (William Cramond, *Annals of Banff* [Aberdeen: New Spalding Club, 1891], 1:173).

37. See Dumfries Council Minutes, 28 July 1755, Dumfries Archive Center, Ewart Library, A2/16. Dumfries burgh council sold its coffeehouse in 1755, having previously supplied it with newspapers.

38. Perth's reading room made available to its subscribers at least eight London and two Edinburgh newspapers, while Dundee's offered ten London, three Edinburgh, and five provincial papers (*Perth Courier*, 10 May 1810; *Dundee, Perth and Cupar Advertiser*, 25 Apr. 1817). Newspapers and "magazines" from the previous year were sold to subscribers to Dundee's Exchange Coffee Room at their annual general meeting (*Dundee, Perth and Cupar Advertiser*, 26 Apr. 1816).

39. John Lettice, *Letters on a Tour through Various Parts of Scotland, in the Year 1792* (London: T. Cadell, 1794), 454.

40. David Semple, *Paisley Town's House, Public Inn, or Saracen's Head Inn: Its History* (Paisley, 1870), 15. In 1814 Paisley's reading room moved to the bottom two floors of a four-story tenement on the corner of Moss Street. Its construction was financed by subscription to 160 shares each worth five pounds.

41. Brewster, *Edinburgh Encyclopaedia*, 8:199–200.

42. *Short Account of the Town of Dumfries* (Dumfries, 1828), 3.

43. Robert Heron, *Observations Made in a Journey through the Western Counties of Scotland in the Autumn of 1792*, 2nd ed. (Perth: R. Morison and Son; Edinburgh: Bell and Bradfute; London: Vernor and Hood, 1799), 2:285–286.

44. See *Dundee Magazine, and Journal of the Times* (1799), 692, for the initial agreement to convert the main hall on the first floor of the Trades Hall into a reading room and exchange.

45. Paisley Town Council Minutes, 22 Jan. 1819, Paisley Central Library.

46. See *Dundee, Perth and Cupar Advertiser*, 4 Feb. 1814, 27 May 1814, 4 June 1815, 15 Sept. 1820. The room was also used for auctions and sales of notable properties in the town, as well as being commonly used for collecting subscriptions to various funds.

47. Peter Clark, *The English Alehouse: A Social History, 1200–1830* (London: Longman, 1983).

48. *Greenock Advertiser*, 8 Feb. 1813.

49. Semple, *Paisley Town's House*, 15–16.

50. George Crawfurd and William Semple, *The History of the Shire of Renfrew* (Paisley: printed by Alex. Weir, 1782), 290.

51. I am grateful to Sharon Paton, museums officer for South Lanarkshire, for communication of her researches on this topic based on accounts for building work and repairs on the inn from the Hamilton estate papers.

52. See notice for letting of "a new inn in Forfar" in *Edinburgh Courant*, 23 Jan. 1792, which refers to a "representation by some of the principal gentlemen of the County of Forfar, that there was no sufficient accommodation at the inns at Forfar for the reception of the Company of Assemblies or Public Meetings of the County." The initial lease on the Peebles Tontine Inn, dating from 1808, specified that the ballroom and supper room were to be used as "public rooms of the county" and to be reserved for the use of subscribers "at pleasure" (NRS, Conditions of lease of Peebles Tontine Inn, 1808, GD293/1/1).

53. Papers relative to the Selkirk Arms Inn, 1807–1828, NRS, Buccleuch Papers, GD224 /1126/299.

54. *Kelso Records* (Kelso, 1789), 147.

55. John Gilkie to Admiral Dickson, specification and estimate to rebuild the Crosskeys for Admiral Dickson of Sydenham, 21 May 1796, Borders Regional Archives, Hawick, Kelso Collection 5, box 1. The rooms, including the ball or assembly room, were also repainted at fairly regular intervals.

56. Third Viscount Palmerston, "Journal of a tour from London to Edinburgh . . . and an excursion . . . to the highlands . . . begun Friday October 1800," University of Southampton, special collections, Broadlands Papers, BRA23A/1, fol. 59.

57. PKCA, PE/51, bundle 470. See also Charles Abbott, "Journal of a tour to Scotland, July–Aug, Sept 1827," NLS, MS 9816, fol. 34, where Abbott notes: "The George Inn—newly built & finished is good." In 1810, when it was advertised for sale at forty-five hundred pounds, the inn comprised four stories, including in the third of these two large dining rooms, while its stables had capacity for fifty-seven horses. There was also a coach house and two complete granaries (*Perth Courier*, 10 May 1810). The George hosted the town's Jubilee ball in 1809.

58. Copy of tack betwixt Robert Miller and his spouse and James McCulloch, 1810, PKCA, PE/16, bundle 17/15.

59. The lease on Gordon's Inn in the High Street, the largest inn in Dundee, was taken over by Alexander Morren in 1811, when it took the name Morren's Hotel. In 1813 the lease on Morren's previous inn, in Castle Street, was assumed by Alexander Merchant, and this became the Castle Street Inn and Hotel. Both establishments were almost certainly refitted at around this time. On Greenock's Tontine Inn, see *Greenock Advertiser*, 20 July 1802, 26 June 1805. The White Hart appears to have further remodeled in 1811 (*Greenock Advertiser*, 14 June 1811).

60. See notices for balls in the "assembly room" in the *Kelso Chronicle*, 28 May 1784, 4 June 1784.

61. *Kelso Mail*, 24 May 1802 (notice for George Inn), 13 Mar. 1815 (notice for subscription assembly in Swan Inn).

62. *Kelso Mail*, 15 Mar. 1802, 16 Jan. 1802, 30 Oct. 1809.

63. James Miller, *The Lamp of Lothian; or, The History of Haddington* (Haddington: Allan, 1844), 526; *Kelso Mail*, 18 Apr. 1805, 1 May 1805.

64. Semple, *Paisley Town's House*, 17–19.

65. *Ayrshire Miscellany*, 3 July 1818; *Apostle to Burns: The Diaries of William Grierson*, ed. John Davies (Edinburgh: William Blackwood, 1981), 137, 160.

66. Information derived from notices and items published in the *Dundee, Perth and Cupar Advertiser*.

67. *Dundee, Perth and Cupar Advertiser*, 31 May 1811.

68. The connection between patriotism and the rise of the public dinner was especially evident in the role of volunteer companies in organizing dinners and balls in the early 1800s.

69. George Robertson, *Topographical Description of Ayrshire; More Particularly of Cunninghame* (Irvine: Cunninghame Press, 1820), 414.

70. J. Pigot, *Pigot & Co.'s New Commercial Directory of Scotland, for 1825–6* (London: J. Pigot, 1825), 377–378, 390–394.

71. Process ag[ainst] James Hackston for keeping a house of bad fame, 1798, PKCA, PE/51, bundle 121, item 153; bundle 312.

72. A list of houses of bad fame and harboring vagabonds in Perth, 1819, PKCA, PE/15, bundle 312.

73. Hugo Arnot, ed., *A Collection and Abridgement of Celebrated Criminal Trials in Scotland. From A.D. 1536 to 1784. With Historical and Critical Remarks* (Glasgow: printed by A. Napier, 1812), 199–215.

74. *Dundee Magazine, and Journal of the Times*, 1799, 181–188, 361–370; George Penny, *Traditions of Perth, containing Sketches of the Manners and Customs of the Inhabitants, and Notices of Public Occurrences, during the Last Century* (Perth: Dewar, Sidey, Morison, Peat, and Drummond, 1836), 117–118.

75. New trades halls were built in Dundee (1778), Dumfries (1804), and Kirriemuir (1815) in this period.

76. For card clubs, see Strang, 212–219, 466.

77. Female friendly societies seem to have met mostly in parish schoolrooms and dissenting chapels. I am grateful to Jane Rendall for information on this point.

PART II

Professional Men and Their Societies

CHAPTER 3

Medical Societies and the Scottish Enlightenment

Jacqueline Jenkinson

The formation of clubs and societies was an integral part of the development of the medical profession in the Scottish Enlightenment. Medical associations and societies were formed for varied reasons. As well as advancing medical knowledge, they also provided forums for further education, opportunities to progress the profession, and chances for networking through regular meetings. In addition, the more "social" medical clubs that are discussed in this chapter provided a convivial atmosphere in which physicians and surgeons could cooperate rather than compete.

The earliest forms of professional association were the Scottish medical corporations: the Incorporation of Surgeons and Barbers of Edinburgh (1505), which became the College of Surgeons in 1726; the Faculty of Physicians and Surgeons in Glasgow (1599); and the College of Physicians of Edinburgh (1681). Thus Scotland did not mirror the tripartite division of medicine in England—divided into the Royal College of Physicians (1518), the Company of Surgeons (1540, associated with barbers until 1745), and the Society of Apothecaries (1617)—and an apparently more cohesive medical profession emerged earlier in Scotland. Physicians and surgeons belonged to the same medical faculty in Glasgow from the late sixteenth century, while in Edinburgh the fusion of apothecaries' and surgeons' duties was completed by 1656.[1]

In the course of the eighteenth century, the hierarchical, elitist structure of the corporations was challenged from within the developing associational movement. Edinburgh was the focus of Scottish medical education and professional development for much of the century, as Christopher J. Lawrence, Steven Shapin, and contributors to W. F. Bynum and Roy Porter's edited volume have all shown.[2] However, as medical societies achieved a wider geographical spread around the country by the early nineteenth century, the emphasis came to be placed on providing an alternative to the exclusive hierarchy and high fellowship costs of the medical corporations. According to A. M. Carr-Saunders and P. A. Wilson, newly formed medical associations quickly targeted the "fossilized corporations" as being in desperate need of reform.[3] The divisions, costs, and restricted jurisdiction of the Scottish medical corporations meant that although they were based on a broader system of medical instruction and examination than was the case in England, their traditional preeminent position, enjoyed since the sixteenth century, was gradually undermined. The challenge came from the rise of professional associations outside the rigid, divisive confines of the medical corporations, coupled with an increasingly university-based system of medical education, initially focused in Edinburgh, but in evidence in Aberdeen and Glasgow before the end of the eighteenth century.

The starting point for the medical and scientific advances during this period was the establishment of the medical faculty of the University of Edinburgh in 1726, closely followed by the emergence of student teaching facilities in the first voluntary hospital in Scotland, opened in 1729 as the Edinburgh Hospital for the Sick Poor and renamed the Royal Infirmary seven years later. A common intellectual purpose lay behind the extended provision of medical education in Edinburgh and the formation of the early medical societies. Often those involved in the creation of associations were also significant figures in Scottish medicine and had links with Edinburgh and its university for major parts of their career. The focus on Edinburgh for much of the discussion of developments in eighteenth-century Scottish medicine is justified because a unique set of circumstances enabled that city to lead the way in medical education and medical science. Other cities—particularly Glasgow and Aberdeen—witnessed medical and scientific advance and society-formation, but to a lesser extent.

Eighteenth-Century Medical Societies and the Spread of Medical Knowledge

In his exploration of the history of British professional associations and clubs from 1580 to 1800, Peter Clark declares that "clubs and societies became one of the most distinctive social and cultural institutions of Georgian Britain."[4] The activities of associations in eighteenth-century Edinburgh in particular have attracted attention from a range of scholars. Davis D. McElroy pioneered this research in 1952, with an emphasis on the literary publications produced by Edinburgh societies.[5] Later, J. B. Morrell approached this subject with a focus on developments in the history of science.[6] Most relevant for this analysis, Roger L. Emerson has placed Scottish medical advance (in which societies played a central part) in the wider framework of the Scottish Enlightenment.[7] However, within these studies exploring the British history of associations and Scottish—particularly Edinburgh—medicine, the creation and concerns of medical clubs and societies have generally been neglected.[8] This is surprising, since the founding of formal associations by medical practitioners signaled a desire for further education. It is also crucial to look deeper than simply naming societies and clubs that were formed in this period; the purpose of their activities must also be considered.

The elevation of Edinburgh medicine onto a worldwide stage was an essential element of the Scottish Enlightenment. The transactions published by the early medical societies aided this process. The earliest medical society for which documentation exists in Scotland is the Medical Society, dating from 1731. The Medical Society followed the creation of more modest medical societies and other, broader-based scientific clubs in Edinburgh in the late seventeenth and early eighteenth centuries. Emerson refers to at least five unnamed science clubs that had "some existence" between circa 1684 and circa 1712.[9] A key difference between these earlier medical and scientific clubs and the Medical Society was their intended purpose: unlike its predecessors, the Medical Society was expressly formed to produce a publication devoted to the furtherance of medical knowledge. Since the society was established several years after the revival of the medical faculty and opening of the infirmary, it was able to harness local expertise and opportunities for case studies.

Dr. Alexander Monro primus was instrumental in establishing the Medical Society. Monro, a surgeon, had played an integral part in the formation of the medical faculty at Edinburgh University and was appointed the first professor of anatomy.[10] He became the Medical Society's secretary and dominant figure and also edited and made extensive contributions to the five published volumes of *Medical Essays and Observations*. Monro included three of his papers in the first volume, including "An Essay on the Art of Injecting the Vessels of Animals."[11]

The creation of the new Edinburgh infirmary, although initially a modest construction with only four beds, provided the dynamic for the new society. As noted in an advertisement in the *Edinburgh Magazine and Review*, the society's published transactions included frequent contributions from the professoriate of the recently created medical faculty, drawn from patient studies: "When patients were received into the infirmary, and a regular register kept of all their cases, it was reasonably expected that many histories worth publishing might be extracted from that register, and might assist to form volumes of medical observations or essays, which it was proposed should be published from time to time."[12] Hence the Medical Society was established with the intention of improving medical knowledge via published transactions, consisting of papers that had been heard by, or communicated to, the society. The five volumes of *Medical Essays and Observations* (1733–1744), the first such collection of medical proceedings to be published in Britain, included 217 papers.[13] Of these, 88 (41 percent) were case histories. Two instances from the first volume of *Medical Essays and*

Observations give a flavor of the instructive case histories included: "Two Examples of Children born with preternatural Conformities of the Gut, by Mr. James Calder Junr., Surgeon at Glasgow" and "An Ulcer in the Lungs piercing through the Diaphragm into the Liver, by Dr. Edward Barry, Physician at Cork in Ireland."[14] Aside from case histories, broader investigations were reported, such as "An Account of the Virtues and Use of the Mineral Waters near Moffat, by Mr. George Milligen, Surgeon at Moffat."[15]

The Medical Society's network of correspondents stretched across Scotland, around Britain, and overseas. The five volumes attracted contributions from outside the British Isles and included essays by European and colonial medical practitioners. *Medical Essays and Observations* received a wide readership; four editions were published by 1752, and French translations began appearing in 1733. The influence of *Medical Essays and Observations* reached the whole continent of Europe, making an impact at a time when knowledge of available books on medical topics was by no means widespread. The section in each of the volumes containing a list of recently published books on medical matters therefore provided a notable service. By including this list, *Medical Essays and Observations* further fulfilled the stated purpose of the society to disseminate medical knowledge beyond its membership. Fiona Macdonald describes it as "a groundbreaking periodical that conveyed Scottish learning to Europe."[16]

Using evidence from a contemporary manuscript, most likely by Monro himself (which may account for the emphasis on Monro's role as facilitator of the organization and its outputs), Emerson found that the society rapidly became a one-person production. Members attended the society's monthly meetings during its first year, hearing and commenting on papers read before it. However, following the publication of the first volume of *Medical Essays and Observations*, active membership declined, and Monro as secretary received and filtered individual contributions "without any other member seeing any of the papers except what some of them were authors of, till after they were printed."[17] Monro primus saw the first four of the five volumes through the press in the years 1733–1737. The two parts of the fifth and final volume were later published by the Philosophical Society of Edinburgh in 1742 and 1744.

While Emerson has emphasized the dominant position of Monro primus, the emergence of the Medical Society in the 1730s was also due to broader educational, political, and economic circumstances then prevailing in Edinburgh. Scottish Enlightenment historians have identified the crucial role of the town council in the creation and expansion of the medical faculty at Edinburgh.[18] The town council's support re-invigorated medical teaching at the university, creating an ideal environment for the Medical Society. Edinburgh's town council was unique in Scotland in its control over the local university, and the merchant and trading guilds that dominated it saw the provision of medical education as essential to the financial health of the city. Shapin has described how the town council supported the expansion of the medical faculty for local economic considerations; in turn, this circumstance ensured enthusiastic Scottish attendance and attracted other British as well as overseas students to the city.[19]

Local factors stressed by Shapin in the development of university medical education also help to explain why Edinburgh—rather than Glasgow or Aberdeen—witnessed the origin, and later the proliferation, of medical societies in the eighteenth century. However, both Glasgow and Aberdeen had some influence on the development of medical thought and education during the century. For example, the still flourishing Aberdeen Medico-Chirurgical Society was established in 1789. Meanwhile, papers from Glasgow physician Peter Paton and Glasgow surgeon James Calder junior were included in the first volume of *Medical Essays and Observations*, while John Paisley, another Glasgow surgeon, had papers in all the subsequent volumes, and he was later a founding member of the Philosophical Society of Edinburgh in 1737, along with John Johnston, the titular professor of medicine at Glasgow University.[20] Paisley lectured extramurally in Glasgow on anatomy; however, Johnston's tenure as professor of medicine coincided with a period of inactivity in medical teaching at Glasgow University, and it is unlikely that he delivered any lectures there.[21] The slow progress of university-based medical education in Glasgow, unsupported by external motivating agencies such as the town council, and without an infirmary for student instruction until 1794, also helps to explain why it lagged behind Edinburgh in the development of medical and other scientific societies.

An article by Morrell argues that the difference between Glasgow and Edinburgh in the fifty years between 1780 and 1830 with respect to scientific development was that in Glasgow business people (merchants and manufacturers) outnumbered professionals, while the position was reversed in Edinburgh. The article illustrates this difference by contrasting the membership of the Glasgow Philosophical Society (established in 1802) with that of the Royal Society of Edinburgh (established in 1783). Merchants, manufacturers, and skilled workers made up the majority of the former, while the latter contained a cross-section of the Edinburgh elite: mainly professors, medical practitioners, lawyers, and gentry.[22]

This distinction was not absolute. Emerson has noted that Glasgow possessed an elite association for wide-ranging intellectual debate in the mid-eighteenth century in the shape of the Glasgow Literary Society, formed in 1752, which discussed scientific topics, including medical subjects alongside moral philosophy, fine arts, and government.[23] In Aberdeen, two of the six founding members of the city's Philosophical Society established in 1758 were medical practitioners, and there were a number of medical contributions to the society's proceedings. This society remained a small group and, as with the Glasgow Literary Society, lacked the sustained impetus toward educational enterprise and professional cooperation provided by the faculty of medicine at Edinburgh.[24]

The influence and importance of the Medical Society stretched beyond its relatively short life span from 1731 to 1737. Although it had ceased to be, in any practical sense, a society after a year, the new association marked the beginning of a trend in medical cooperation in which the correspondent of a medical society and its published transactions benefited from a regular engagement with like-minded others for medical debate and mutual education. Indeed, the more general role of the written communication to a society was increasingly significant for providing a network of contacts far exceeding the geographical limits of a society's regular attendance, at a time when organized transport around the country, even between cities, was haphazard and hazardous. The significance of association went beyond the simple act of attending meetings or corresponding with a society. Clark has convincingly shown that clubs and societies in this period "may have served as a vector for new ideas, new values, new kinds of social alignment, and forms of national, regional, and local identity."[25]

The Medical Society's *Medical Essays and Observations* was continued by the Philosophical Society of Edinburgh, which published the fifth volume (in two parts) in 1742 and 1744, and also issued corrected second and revised editions of the first four volumes.[26] The preface to volume 5, part 1, noted that there had been a disruption in publication due to the transition from one society to another: "Members of our society being adopted into this new one, the design of publishing more Volumes of Medical Papers was dropt some Time ago. It is now at the Desire of the Gentlemen of this new society that we cause the fifth volume to be printed, which is so much enlarged by the Papers which they generously furnished us from their Repository, that we are obliged to divide it into two Parts."[27]

This new society, the Philosophical Society, despite its title and avowed original intention to improve the level of knowledge in both arts and science, was heavily influenced by its medical members throughout its close to fifty-year existence (1737–1783). Sixteen of its forty-eight members in 1739 were medical practitioners.[28] By the time of the publication of the final volume of the Philosophical Society's own transactions, *Essays and Observations: Physical and Literary* in 1771, the majority of members were medical practitioners.[29] The published *Essays and Observations* stretched across three volumes in 1754, 1756, and 1771. The majority of papers were clinical observations (including a small number on individual cases) and research-based medical reports. Typical papers include "A description of the American Yellow Fever, in a letter from John Lining, Physician at Charles-Town, to Robert Whytt, Professor of Medicine in the University of Edinburgh" and "Answer to an Objection against Inoculation, by Ebenezer Gilchrist, Physician at Dumfries."[30] There were also a large number of papers on anatomical and obstetrical subjects, most written by Alexander Monro primus and his son Alexander Monro secundus.[31] A key difference between the Medical and Philosophical Societies was the presence in the ranks of the latter of the nonmedical elite: enlightened patrons of the arts and sciences who added prestige to the society. As expected, given the wider remit of the Philosophical Society, there were some papers on entirely nonmedical themes (3 percent), but almost one in five papers (17 percent) were on medical-related scientific subjects. As Arthur Herman has indicated in his book on the global influence of the Scottish Enlightenment, "Science and medicine were probably more closely linked in Scotland than in any other European country."[32]

Ironically, the decline in fortunes of the Philosophical Society by the third quarter of the eighteenth century was linked to the success of another periodical publication: *Medical and Philosophical Commentaries*—edited by Andrew Duncan senior—first published in 1773.[33] The regular volumes of this medical review journal (twenty were published between 1773 and 1795) provided a more successful alternative to the intermittent volumes of the Philosophical Society's *Essays and Observations*. This was partly because of the astute commercial management of the London-based publisher John Murray, who commissioned William Smellie as printer of the *Commentaries* and managed publication from 1773 to 1780 and again from 1782 to 1786, after which it was taken over by Murray's son-in-law, Charles Elliot.[34] Moreover, in the *Commentaries* medical practitioners around Scotland and beyond were presented with a more comprehensive range of medical papers than featured in *Essays and Observations*. The success of the *Commentaries* contrasts with the fate of the Philosophical Society, which in 1783 was replaced by the broader, scientifically based Royal Society of Edinburgh—a society that still flourishes today.

The successful tradition of society transactions epitomized by the Medical Society and the Philosophical Society became the standard for demonstrating scientific or cultural merit during the Scottish Enlightenment. This point is illustrated by Duncan's creation of a fictitious publishing society to which he attributed the reviews of the medical works in his *Medical and Philosophical Commentaries*. The title page of the *Commentaries* announced they were the proceedings of a "Society in Edinburgh." "This 'Society' however, never existed . . . only one man was really responsible . . . Andrew Duncan."[35] With this fiction, Duncan sought to emulate the society transactions produced by the Medical Society and the Philosophical Society. The *Commentaries* were the precursor of the long-lived *Edinburgh Medical Journal* (originally the *Edinburgh Medical and Surgical Journal*), which gave much prominence to the activities of medical associations. Following the model of the Medical Society and its successor, the Philosophical Society, later eighteenth-century Scottish medical societies were initiated chiefly for the purposes of medical education for the members and the profession as a whole through the publication of transactions. The transactions often appeared in translation on the Continent, enabling Scottish societies and their discussions to reach an international medical community. Other objectives, such as the development of intra-professional cooperation, also prompted the founding of Scottish medical societies and clubs. Unsurprisingly, most of these early societies were based in Edinburgh, which Clark has accurately described as "a brilliant centre of associational life."[36]

Educational improvement achieved through association and publication was important in the development of the medical profession in Enlightenment Scotland because it fostered the notion of a medical community. This sense of community was further developed by the creation of social groupings for medical practitioners. Between 1760 and 1800 at least six elite social medical clubs were established in Edinburgh in which membership was limited, application for new membership was by recommendation, and admission required the approval of at least three-quarters of existing members. The most prominent were the Aesculapian Club (1773) and the Harveian Society (1782), both of which remain in existence today. The Gymnastic Society (1786–1807) was the Aesculapian Club's short-lived sporting offshoot. The others were the Dissipation Club (before 1782), the Galenian Society, and the Celsian Society.[37] The Harveian Society was a largely fraternal club established to celebrate renowned medical figures at an annual festival. The Harveian Society—named after the famed seventeenth-century physician who first described the systematic circulation of blood—was also formed to take over the burden of running the Aesculapian Club's five-guinea prize medical essay competition, which was proving too expensive for the limited membership of the older club to maintain.[38] The annual medical essay prize shows that even among convivial associations collaborative medical education remained important. Glasgow had a similar exclusive club—the Glasgow Medical Club. It was formed in 1798 by leading medical figures who were also directors of the newly established Glasgow Royal Infirmary (opened in 1794), including Robert Freer, professor of medicine at Glasgow University, but it was dissolved within fifteen years.[39]

Unlike the Medical Society, these groups were chiefly convivial. In addition to his interest in the publication of medical periodicals previously mentioned, Duncan senior was the leading figure behind the creation of the Harveian Society, the Aesculapian Club, and the Gymnastic Society.[40] These associations were intended to bring physicians and surgeons together in an atmosphere of fraternity, and therefore aid in overcoming self-interested professional divisions. Despite the longevity of these groups and the later formation of the educational Edinburgh Medico-Chirurgical Society in 1821 (also still in existence), with Duncan senior as their guiding light, Duncan's club-forming habit drew criticism from Henry Cockburn, who wrote: "He was the promoter and the president of more innocent and foolish clubs and societies than perhaps any man in the world."[41] This comment contained an element of truth. John Chalmers has noted that Duncan was an "inveterate joiner" who was a member of at least seventeen clubs.[42] Yet the social aspect dominant in several of these fraternal organizations remained important in many medical associations formed after the late eighteenth century. Duncan's Aesculapian Club provided an early example of the role of medical societies and clubs in creating a focus for developing professional relationships, since it was from its inception open to equal numbers of physicians and surgeons. The club's first regulation states: "The Club shall consist of twenty-two members, chosen from among the Fellows of the Colleges of Physicians and Surgeons."[43]

The Challenge of Societies and Clubs to the Medical Corporations

Professional cooperation between physicians and surgeons was an early objective for medical associations. Comments in the preface to the first volume of the Medical Society's *Medical Essays and Observations* in 1733 underlined this intention: "Where two or more physicians or surgeons are employed in treating the same patient, or in making the same experiment, it is to be wished they would write the case or account of the experiment conjunctly, or at least that he who relates it would do it with all fairness and ingenuity, without discovering partiality for his own opinion, or disputing against the sentiments of others."[44] The attempt to acknowledge the merits of both physicians and surgeons within the profession was further evidenced in the list of contributors to the Medical Society's *Medical Essays and Observations*. Two of the five volumes contained the same number of papers by physicians and surgeons. The other three volumes contained more essays submitted by surgeons. The final volume contained thirteen papers contributed by physicians and twenty-six by surgeons—an imbalance caused by the editor, Alexander Monro primus, including ten of his own papers.

The creation and intentions of the Medical Society did not remove status-based divisions between physicians and surgeons. The 1739 membership list of its successor, the Philosophical Society of Edinburgh, shows that there were eight physicians to four surgeons in the ranks of this elite society.[45] While the efforts of the Medical Society made little long-term impression, further attempts to overcome the divisions between Edinburgh's physicians and surgeons can be found in the social medical clubs, most notably in the formation by Duncan senior of the Aesculapian Club in 1773. However, as Douglas Guthrie has shown, membership of the Aesculapian Club was strictly limited, as potential new members were balloted for and two black balls were sufficient for rejection.[46]

The establishment of convivial societies for Edinburgh physicians and surgeons in the late eighteenth century acted as a counterweight to the ongoing power struggle between the two rival medical corporations in the city. Until the beginning of the nineteenth century, the physicians successfully opposed the institution of a chair in surgery at the university, and surgeons were further alienated after 1785 by their exclusion from the nominations for honorary appointments in the Royal Infirmary. In the late 1780s many prominent surgeons in the city resigned in protest from their Royal Infirmary duties, and by the turn of the century only four of the twenty-three senior surgeons on the roll of the Royal College of Surgeons remained attached to the Royal Infirmary.[47] This dispute indicates division among physicians and surgeons within the elite of the Scottish medical profession. The focus on expanding medical knowledge and furthering scientific investigation evident in the publications of the Medical Society and the fraternal atmosphere of later eighteenth-century clubs sought to overcome such professional and status-based disputes.

The creation of fraternal clubs such as the Aesculapian Club and the Harveian Society was part of a trend toward regulating intra-professional relationships in order to create unity and cooperation within the group. This model had more enduring success than the efforts of the Medical Society in this respect. In the course of the late eighteenth and early nineteenth centuries, local medical clubs and societies were increasingly formed by medical practitioners to further conviviality and for professional self-regulation.

Edinburgh Medical Students and the Creation of the Royal Medical Society

The institution of the Royal Medical Society owed much to the example of the Medical Society and was also closely linked to the rapid rise of the medical faculty of the University of Edinburgh. The society originated in informal meetings held by six students in 1734 to discuss medical papers they had written. By 1737 a formal society had been established, and it remains a thriving institution for Edinburgh medical students to this day.[48] The Edinburgh student body was a powerful independent institution due to the distinctive structure of the Edinburgh medical school, which permitted students to choose many of their classes. The medical professoriate and extramural lecturers derived a substantial amount of their income from student fees, ultimately giving Edinburgh medical students confidence in their own opinions and a sense of independence.[49] This influence led a former member of the Royal Medical Society, John Gregory, professor of medicine at Edinburgh University and a pioneer of medical ethics, to warn that the "freedom of spirit" of eighteenth-century Edinburgh student medical societies sometimes led to an absence of "decency and regularity." However, he praised those he felt were well ordered: "The medical societies of students which have been conducted with decency and regularity, have in this, as well as in other respects, produced the best effects. In these, they have been taught to feel and exercise their own powers, to arrange their ideas, and to express them with facility."[50]

The diarist Sylas Neville left a record of his experiences in the Royal Medical Society. At his first visit, in January 1772, aged thirty, he complained of papers full of "undigested matter," and few well-dressed men. Nevertheless, a year later he petitioned for membership because of the "advantage and probability of increasing my knowledge in Medicine," in spite of the "many low ignorant and illiberal men" who were members.[51] After 1773 there are frequent entries in his diary on the labors involved in his regular papers and commentaries for the society, as, for example:

> *Jan. 1 Sunday.* [1775.] Had little comfort this New Year's day. Spent the whole of it till very late in writing this *Question* or last exercise for the Society. . . .
>
> *Mon. Jan. 2.* Got up early & finished my *Question* before breakfast. Read it over to Mr John Browne who pointed out some objections, which I obviated or corrected &c before sending it away to circulate.[52]

In December 1775, having graduated, he was elected one of the annual presidents of the society and in that capacity helped to preside over the opening of its new hall in George Street, at a celebration attended by almost all the Edinburgh professors of medicine.[53]

By 1792 there were at least nine student medical societies in Edinburgh whose main focus was essay presentation on a range of medical, scientific, and philosophical subjects, with a significant degree of cross-membership.[54] James Mackintosh, the future political radical, was a medical student in Edinburgh from 1784 to 1787. He joined both the Royal Medical Society and the Natural History Society (1782) in early 1785, becoming president of both in December 1786; he was also a member of the Royal Physical Society (1771).[55] He wrote retrospectively, within three months of his arrival in Edinburgh, "I discussed with the utmost fluency and confidence the most difficult questions in the science of medicine."[56] At the same time, in 1785 he helped to lead a group known as the "Associated Students," which defended the rights of medical students against the managers of the Royal Infirmary, and was also a very active participant in the Speculative Society (1764), the lively debating club discussed by Rosalind Carr in this volume.[57]

The formation of the Royal Medical Society is fundamentally important to understanding the significance of eighteenth-century medical societies within the Scottish Enlightenment. Key figures in Scottish medicine, science, and philosophy (including Gregory) were among its early members. For much of the eighteenth century at least, those "students" who made up the majority of the membership of the Royal Medical Society were often already graduates in other subjects. Some had also already engaged in medical practice and had come to study medicine in Edinburgh to further their education. As the reputation of Edinburgh University's medical faculty rose, it attracted those who wished to augment their medical knowledge and increase their prestige, not necessarily immediately sitting for their MD degree. A case in point is the early career of William Cullen, future professor of medicine and chemistry at Edinburgh University, physician to King George III, and leading Scottish Enlightenment figure. Cullen had five years of medical experience before he proceeded to Edinburgh University to study medicine in 1734. This included a two-year apprenticeship to Glasgow surgeon John Paisley, a contributor to *Medical Essays and Observations*. Cullen then served as a ship's surgeon on a voyage to the West Indies and spent a year in practice in London. In 1735 he moved to Edinburgh to enhance his medical study and joined the nascent student medical society that became the Royal Medical Society two years later. In 1736 he left the university to set up a new practice in Hamilton. He eventually took his MD degree in 1740 at Glasgow University, where he became a pioneering lecturer in chemistry before his return to Edinburgh.[58]

The pattern of Cullen's career indicates that it would be inaccurate to categorize the Royal Medical Society as a "student society" at a time when the achievement of an MD degree was not the first priority of a medical practitioner. This point is further highlighted in the case of Alexander Monro secundus, who, at age twenty-one, became conjoint professor of anatomy and surgery with his father, Alexander Monro primus, in 1754, when he had no formal medical qualifications (although he had previously studied mathematics and philosophy at Edinburgh University).[59] There were also a number of practitioners who remained active in the society after qualification; four, including Andrew Duncan senior, are referred to in the society's minute book for 1780.[60] Moreover, five of the twelve contributors to a surviving bound manuscript volume of papers read before the society in 1779–1780 were already in medical practice.[61]

Later eighteenth-century student medical societies echoed the formation and characteristics of both the Medical Society and the Royal Medical Society. The Royal Medical Society in particular acted as a template for eighteenth-century Scottish student medical societies, 83 percent of which were based in Edinburgh.[62] The general numerical and geographical supremacy of Edinburgh, in both senior and student medical societies, was belatedly challenged at the end of the eighteenth century by the creation of an influential medical society in Aberdeen. The new society was initially a student association but later became a senior society, which is still in existence today. The establishment of the Aberdeen Medical (later Medico-Chirurgical) Society in 1789 demonstrates how strong an influence was exerted by the example of the Edinburgh student societies. John Craig has noted that the founders of the Aberdeen society, James McGrigor and James Robertson, following completion of their studies at Aberdeen University's Marischal College, had proceeded to Edinburgh to study under Monro secundus. While in Edinburgh they attended meetings of unnamed student societies.[63] From this example it is clear that the influence of Edinburgh medicine, and its medical associations in particular, remained strong in Enlightenment Scotland.

Conclusion

The intellectual advance of Scottish medicine during the Enlightenment contributed to the expansion of medicine as a more scientifically based discipline in and beyond Scotland. For most of the eighteenth century, Scottish medical developments were led by the medical profession in Edinburgh due to a unique combination of circumstances, including the interventionist support of the town council and the emergence of forceful figures such as Monro primus and Duncan senior. Their influence was felt across the whole spectrum of medical activity: from the creation of the medical faculty of the University of Edinburgh to the opening of the Royal Infirmary, and from the founding of medical periodicals to the formation of medical clubs and societies. Although these activities may have been at first chiefly confined to the elite of the profession in Scotland's capital, they were not exclusively bound to the geographical limits of Edinburgh owing to the influence of, and contributions to, the variety of printed transactions discussed in this chapter.

For much of the eighteenth century, medical improvement and teaching in Scotland, particularly in Edinburgh, led the way in Europe. The Medical Society and the Royal Medical Society became role models for the formation, regulation, and conduct of future medical associations. Moreover, their role in furthering medical education achieved international esteem, as indicated by the numerous published editions and the rapid translation into French of the Medical Society's *Medical Essays and Observations*.

Although the Medical Society was short-lived, it provided a template for later, more enduring associations. As noted, several of these eighteenth-century institutions survive to the present day, including the Royal Medical Society, the Aberdeen and Edinburgh Medico-Chirurgical Societies, and the convivial Aesculapian Club and Harveian Society. Such medical associations quickly formed an integral part of Scottish medicine. They also contributed to professional cooperation and regulation and, in the nineteenth century, became a focus for medico-political debate. In these ways, the discussions, activities, and publications of medical clubs and associations provided a bridge between emerging ideas in culture, philosophy, and literature and new scientific developments. Medical societies epitomized the desire for the advancement of knowledge during, and beyond, the Scottish Enlightenment.

NOTES

1. John D. Comrie, *History of Scottish Medicine to 1860* (London: Wellcome Historical Medical Museum, 1927), 183.

2. Christopher J. Lawrence, "Medicine as Culture: Edinburgh and the Scottish Enlightenment" (PhD diss., University of London, 1984); Steven Shapin, "The Audience for Science in Eighteenth-Century Edinburgh," *Hist Sci* 12 (1974): 95–121; W. F. Bynum and Roy

Porter, eds., *William Hunter and the Eighteenth-Century Medical World* (Cambridge: Cambridge University Press, 1985).

3. A. M. Carr-Saunders and P. A. Wilson, *The Professions* (Oxford: Clarendon Press, 1933), 300.

4. Clark, 2.

5. McElroy, 1952. See also McElroy, 1969.

6. J. B. Morrell, "The University of Edinburgh in the Late Eighteenth Century: Its Scientific Eminence and Academic Structure," *Isis* 62 (1971): 158–171; Morrell, "Reflections on the History of Scottish Science," *Hist Sci* 12 (1974): 81–94.

7. This coverage was begun in Roger L. Emerson's series of articles: "The Philosophical Society of Edinburgh, 1737–1747," *Br J Hist of Sci* 12 (1979): 154–191; "The Philosophical Society of Edinburgh, 1747–1768," *Br J Hist of Sci* 14 (1981): 133–176; "The Philosophical Society of Edinburgh, 1768–1783," *Br J Hist of Sci* 18 (1985): 255–303; and "The Scottish Enlightenment and the End of the Philosophical Society of Edinburgh," *Br J Hist of Sci* 21 (1988): 33–66. See also Emerson, "Science and the Origins and Concerns of the Scottish Enlightenment," *Hist Sci* 26 (1988): 333–366, and his more recent works, including *Academic Patronage in the Scottish Enlightenment: Glasgow, Edinburgh and St Andrews Universities* (Oxford: Oxford University Press, 2008) and *Essays on David Hume, Medical Men and the Scottish Enlightenment: Industry, Knowledge and Humanity* (Farnham: Ashgate, 2009).

8. See Jacqueline Jenkinson, *Scottish Medical Societies, 1731–1939: Their History and Records* (Edinburgh: Edinburgh University Press, 1993).

9. Emerson, "Science and the Origins," 353.

10. See Anita Guerrini, "Monro, Alexander, Primus (1697–1767)," in *ODNB*, https://doi:10.1093/ref:odnb/18964.

11. Medical Society [of Edinburgh], *Medical Essays and Observations*, 4th ed. (Edinburgh: Hamilton, Balfour and Neill, 1752), 1:70–79.

12. *Edinburgh Magazine and Review* 1 (1774): 339.

13. Fiona Macdonald, "Medicine," in *The Edinburgh History of the Book in Scotland*, vol. 2, *Enlightenment and Expansion, 1707–1800*, ed. Stephen W. Brown and Warren McDougall (Edinburgh: Edinburgh University Press, 2012), 499.

14. Medical Society [of Edinburgh], *Medical Essays and Observations*, 1:165–167, 219–220.

15. Ibid., 1:54–68.

16. Macdonald, "Medicine," 500.

17. Emerson, "Science and the Origins," 353.

18. Anand C. Chitnis, "Provost Drummond and the Origins of Edinburgh Medicine," in *The Origins and Nature of the Scottish Enlightenment*, ed. Roy Hutcheson Campbell and Andrew S. Skinner (Edinburgh: John Donald, 1982), 91.

19. Shapin, "Audience for Science," 97.

20. On the society's membership, see regulations in Philosophical Society of Edinburgh, *Essays and Observations: Physical and Literary* (Edinburgh: G. Hamilton and J. Balfour, 1754), 1:14.

21. Comrie, *History of Scottish Medicine*, 357–359.

22. Morrell, "Reflections," 81.

23. Emerson, "Science and the Origins," 365. See also Ralph McLean, "Rhetoric and Literary Criticism in the Early Scottish Enlightenment" (PhD diss., University of Glasgow, 2009); and McLean's chapter in this volume.

24. H. Lewis Ulman, ed., *The Minutes of the Aberdeen Philosophical Society, 1758–1773* (Aberdeen: Aberdeen University Press, 1990), 21.

25. Clark, ix.

26. The revised and corrected first and subsequent volumes of *Medical Essays and Observations* were printed by a range of publishers, including T. and W. Ruddiman in Edinburgh, resulting in an edited and corrected edition of volume 1 in 1737 and volume 5, part 1, pub-

lished under the auspices of the Philosophical Society of Edinburgh in 1742. Volume 5, part 2 was published in 1744.

27. Medical Society [of Edinburgh], preface to *Medical Essays and Observations* (Edinburgh, 1742), 5, pt. 1, iii.

28. Philosophical Society of Edinburgh, *Essays and Observations*, 1:13–14.

29. Emerson, "Philosophical Society of Edinburgh, 1768–1783," 266–267.

30. Philosophical Society of Edinburgh, *Essays and Observations*, 2:370–395, 396–402.

31. Of the thirteen papers on anatomical and obstetrical subjects in *Essays and Observations*, nine were written by the two Monros. See Philosophical Society of Edinburgh, *Essays and Observations*, vols. 1–3.

32. Arthur Herman, *The Scottish Enlightenment: The Scots' Invention of the Modern World* (London: Fourth Estate, 2001), 309.

33. Duncan at this time was an extramural lecturer in medicine in Edinburgh. From 1789 he was professor of the institutes of medicine at Edinburgh University. He also served as president of the Royal College of Physicians in 1790. For further biographical details, see George Thomas Bettany, "Duncan, Andrew, the Elder (1744–1828)," rev. Lisa Rosner, in *ODNB*, https://doi:10.1093/ref:odnb/8212.

34. William Zachs, *The First John Murray and the Late Eighteenth-Century Book Trade* (Oxford: Oxford University Press, 1998), 179–180. For Smellie's role, see Stephen W. Brown, "William Smellie and Natural History: Dissent and Dissemination," in *Science and Medicine in the Scottish Enlightenment*, ed. Charles W. J. Withers and Paul Wood (East Linton: Tuckwell Press, 2002), 191–214.

35. McElroy, 1952, 2:471.

36. Clark, 2.

37. The histories of the Dissipation Club (established sometime before 1782, with no known end date), the Galenian Society, and the Celsian Society are less well-documented than the three clubs discussed in this chapter. For the Dissipation Club, see Jenkinson, *Scottish Medical Societies*, 131–132; for brief information on the latter two clubs, see McElroy, 1952, 1:312–313.

38. James Innes, "The Harveians of Edinburgh: Their First Two Hundred Years," *Scottish Medical Journal* 28 (1983): 285–289.

39. Jenkinson, *Scottish Medical Societies*, 159.

40. John Chalmers, "Medical Clubs and Societies Founded by Andrew Duncan," in *Andrew Duncan Senior: Physician of the Enlightenment*, ed. John Chalmers (Edinburgh: National Museums Scotland, 2010), 115–122.

41. Henry Cockburn, *Memorials of His Time* (1856), new ed., ed. Harry A. Cockburn (Edinburgh: T. N. Foulis, 1909), 273.

42. Chalmers, "Medical Clubs and Societies," 115.

43. Douglas Guthrie, "The Aesculapian Club of Edinburgh," *Edinburgh University Journal* 23 (1968): 245.

44. Medical Society [of Edinburgh], *Medical Essays and Observations*, 1:xix–xx.

45. On the society's membership, see regulations in Philosophical Society of Edinburgh, *Essays and Observations*, 1:13–14.

46. Guthrie, "Aesculapian Club," 246.

47. Guenter B. Risse, *Hospital Life in Enlightenment Scotland: Care and Teaching at the Royal Infirmary of Edinburgh* (Cambridge: Cambridge University Press, 1986), 65.

48. James Gray, *History of the Royal Medical Society of Edinburgh, 1737–1937* (Edinburgh: Edinburgh University Press, 1952), 2.

49. Lawrence, "Medicine as Culture," 196.

50. John Gregory, *Lectures on the Duties and Qualifications of a Physician* (London: W. Strahan and T. Cadell, 1772), 7.

51. *The Diary of Sylas Neville, 1767–1788*, ed. Basil Cozens-Hardy (London: Oxford University Press, 1950), 147, 200.

52. Ibid., 213.

53. Ibid., 241.

54. Lisa Rosner, *Medical Education in the Age of Improvement: Edinburgh Students and Apprentices, 1760–1826* (Edinburgh: Edinburgh University Press, 1991), 121. In addition to the Royal Medical Society, the following student medical and scientific societies were active in 1792: the Royal Physical, the Chirurgo-Physical (1788), the American Medical (before 1792), the American Physical (before 1790), the Hibernian Medical (before 1790), the Hibernian Physical (before 1792), the Chirurgo-Obstetrical (1786), and the Natural History Society. For an annotated list of student medical societies in Edinburgh and elsewhere in Scotland, see Jenkinson, *Scottish Medical Societies*, app. 2, 205–221.

55. *Memoirs of the Life of the Right Honourable Sir James Mackintosh*, ed. Robert James Mackintosh, 2nd ed. (London: Edward Moxon, 1836), 1:21–40; Natural History Society of Edinburgh, *Laws of the Society Constituted at Edinburgh MDCCLXXXII for the Investigation of Natural History* (Edinburgh: C. Stewart, 1803), 27, 33.

56. Mackintosh, *Memoirs*, 1:26.

57. Ibid., 1:26–28; Gray, *History of the Royal Medical Society*, 77–79.

58. Comrie, *History of Scottish Medicine*, 311.

59. Rex E. Wright-St. Clair, *Doctors Monro: A Medical Saga* (London: Wellcome Historical Medical Library, 1964), 70. See also Lisa Rosner, "Monro, Alexander, Secundus (1733–1817)," in *ODNB*, https://doi:10.1093/ref:odnb/18965.

60. Royal Medical Society Minute Book, 1780, Royal Medical Society Library, University of Edinburgh.

61. Royal Medical Society, Papers Read to the Society, 1779–1780, Royal College of Physicians of Edinburgh Library.

62. Jenkinson, *Scottish Medical Societies*, 205–221.

63. John Craig, "The Aberdeen Medico-Chirurgical Society," *Medical Press and Circular* 195 (1968): 302–305.

CHAPTER 4

Professors, Merchants, and Ministers in the Clubs of Eighteenth-Century Glasgow

Ralph McLean

Writing about Tobias Smollett's early years in the city of Glasgow, Dr. John Moore remarked that "the chief objects that occupied the minds of the citizens were commerce and religion; the chief means of acquiring importance among them were, wealth and piety."[1] As Peter Clark has argued, "The origin of clubs and societies is not simply a point of historical genealogy." Rather, it is that the particular pressures and conditions of the early modern period molded the distinctive character of British, and Scottish, clubs and societies, and consequently their role in modern society.[2] In Glasgow, from the 1740s onward, the university came to play a significant role in an associational life that drew together professors, merchants, and ministers. Most of the students who passed through the University of Glasgow in the 1740s came from mercantile backgrounds, and some 60 percent of them entered the business world. Rather than celebrate the cohabitation of the mercantile and the religious, though, some contemporary commentators viewed it as irreparably damaging to the commercial development of the city. Rev. William Thom of Govan saw this trend as endemic throughout Scotland, but especially pronounced in Glasgow. He observed that "the Universities of *Scotland* in general, and particularly this of *Glasgow*, have been founded and designed purely or chiefly for the sake of that Theology which was in vogue two or three hundred years ago, some of the Classes bear evident Marks of this original Design, being either totally or in part calculated for the Disputes and Wranglings of Divines, and of little Use to the Lawyer or Physician, and still less to the Merchant or Gentleman."[3] Thom had studied at the University of Glasgow under the great moral philosopher Francis Hutcheson, and was active in a literary club in the 1740s. Alexander Carlyle described him as "a learned man, of a very particular but ingenious turn of mind."[4]

Despite the skepticism of men like Thom, David Hume recognized that the civilizing effects of trade and commerce could help to create ideal conditions for clubs and societies. The establishment of an urbane and socially engaged "middling rank" who wished to communicate knowledge, and to demonstrate their taste in areas as diverse as conversation, fashion, and furniture, led to a proliferation of such groups. According to Hume, "Particular clubs and societies are every where formed: Both sexes meet in an easy and sociable manner; and the tempers of men, as well as their behaviour, refine apace."[5] Similarly, Adam Ferguson identified the need for a strong civil society founded on the bedrock of the rule of law, private property, robust commerce, and the encouragement of both the arts and manufactures.[6] Rather than liberty being maintained by "concurring zeal," Ferguson argued that it was most effectively sustained by "continued differences and oppositions." This could be achieved through informed debate in public assemblies or, in other words, through discussion in clubs and societies.[7] As Paul Elliott has noted, thanks to the rise of print culture and other forms of urban sociability, an extremely vigorous associational life with literary and scientific clubs emerged in all the major centers.[8] Like its fellow Scottish cities Edinburgh and Aberdeen, Glasgow developed a bustling club scene in the second half of the eighteenth century that combined both literary investigations and scientific and economic inquiry. This chapter investigates four prominent clubs and societies in the center of Glasgow, all founded within a decade of each other: the Political Economy Club (c. 1743), the Anderston Club (c. 1745), the Hodge Podge Club (1750), and the Glasgow Literary Society (1752). All will be viewed through the prism of three prominent Glaswegian social groupings: the professors, the ministers, and the merchants, in order to assess how they interacted with each other and the extent to which they influenced the Enlightenment in Glasgow.

The Political Economy Club

A good place to start in identifying mercantile and professorial interactions in Glasgow's social institutions is the Political Economy Club. The most famous of its members was Adam Smith (1723–1790), whose groundbreaking work *The Wealth of Nations* (1776) elucidated how nations accumulated and generated income. Given that membership in the club was almost exclusively composed of merchants, and that the records of the society have been lost, it is tempting to imagine a scenario in which erudite and economically engaged traders offered practical refinements to Smith's philosophical principles. While this interpretation would be an exaggeration, the club was certainly compatible with Smith's ultimate aims in *The Wealth of Nations*. Founded in the early 1740s, possibly in

1743, the remit of the club was to inquire "into the nature and principles of trade in all its branches, and to communicate their knowledge and views on that subject to each other."[9] The breadth of such educational opportunities may have been greater in Glasgow than elsewhere in the British Isles. According to W. M. Mathew, English merchants were put into counting houses at an early age and expected to serve a long apprenticeship, where they encountered little to refine their characters.[10] In Bristol, for example, R. I. James reports that merchants were "uncouth, and apart from the minimum requirements of business substantially illiterate."[11]

The guiding light of the Glasgow group was Provost Andrew Cochrane, one of the city's most prominent tobacco lords.[12] Indeed, the club was often referred to as the Cochrane Club. It appears to have lain dormant during the Jacobite threat to the city in 1745–1746 but was reactivated shortly before 1750.[13] Cochrane's tightrope-walking efforts as provost to appease the invading Jacobites while maintaining loyalty to the ruling Whig establishment contributed to this hiatus.[14] Although no extant list of club members has survived, David Murray managed to extrapolate the identity of several members through analysis of contemporary sources. In addition to Cochrane, the club also boasted men such as Alexander Speirs, who imported one-twelfth of the total import of tobacco to Europe, and John Glassford, who had a turnover of over half a million pounds sterling per year. William Cunninghame, who ran the tobacco firm Cunninghame and Company, and James Ritchie—another successful merchant operating in Virginia, and a friend of Smith—were also likely members.[15] Although primarily merchants conversing with merchants, there were later two professorial admissions of which we are aware: Smith and Rev. William Wight.[16] Wight was a Church of Scotland minister who secured the chair of ecclesiastical history in 1762, and the chair of divinity in 1778, in addition to playing a central role in the Glasgow Literary Society. In his Glasgow class, Wight devoted a number of lectures to the state of commerce, ranging from classical Greece to the expanding British Empire. Wight also adapted his courses in order to incorporate more specific investigations into British commercial interests. In 1767 he advertised a series of lectures that concluded with a lecture on the "wealth, power and influence of Britain comparatively with other nations."[17] By 1772 he had altered this lecture to include details on the "navigation, commerce, and consequent wealth and power of the British empire compared with the other trading nations in Europe," with a focus on the "remarkable laws for the encouragement of trade and shipping."[18]

For Smith, the opportunity to listen to such debates among the mercantile class must have germinated ideas that would eventually bear such spectacular fruit in *The Wealth of Nations*. Smith's contemporary Alexander Carlyle noted that the Glasgow professor openly acknowledged his debts to the members of the club—in particular to Cochrane, who secured his admission as an honorary burgess of the city, and who had aided him when he was collecting materials for *The Wealth of Nations.*[19] However, as Nicholas Phillipson has noted, when musing on Smith's description of the "wretched spirit of monopoly" that afflicted even the most literate of merchants, "It is hard not to think that he was reflecting in part on thirteen years of conversations heard in Glasgow."[20] This would seem to be reinforced by the actions of the merchants themselves. For example, in 1756, when the Glasgow merchants succeeded in securing the abolition of the duty on foreign linen yarns, they were not doing so under the banner of free trade. They had no intention of abolishing the export bounty on homemade linen or of repealing a law from 1748 that prohibited the import of foreign linen; merchants even fined men who let their wives wear it.[21] Richard B. Sher goes further, arguing that in Smith's view the actions of the mercantile class sometimes went beyond the realm of self-interest, into the territory of deception and oppression.[22] As an example of this type of behavior, he cites Smith's letter to the Duc de La Rochefoucauld of 1 November 1785, where he laments that "the regulations of Commerce are commonly dictated by those who are most interested to deceive and impose upon the Public."[23] This attitude of the city's commercial elite—at best self-interest, at worst oppressive dishonesty—qualifies Davis D. McElroy's assumption that Smith's activities in the Political Economy Club led Glasgow merchants to a more liberal attitude toward trade restrictions.[24] Nonetheless, Dugald Stewart cautiously acknowledged Smith's potential influence in Glasgow when he referenced James Ritchie's assessment that "before he quitted his situation in the University," Smith was able to "rank some very eminent merchants in the number of his proselytes."[25] Smith's biographer W. R. Scott noted that in 1751 the Foulis Press had advertised a number of books relating to mercantile interests, including such works as *On Money and Trade*, *Trade and Navigation*, and *Proposals for a Council of Trade in Scotland.*[26] The publication and dissemination of these materials demonstrate that there was an appetite, as well as a market, for works relating to commercial interests, which Smith understood and articulated more effectively than anyone else.

It is also to Dugald Stewart that we owe our knowledge of a paper given to the Cochrane Club that has become known as the "Lecture of 1755." The lecture itself remains elusive, as it was neither published nor preserved in manuscript form. According to Stewart, the purpose of the paper was to enumerate "certain leading principles, both political and literary, to which [Smith] was anxious to establish his exclusive right."[27] Stewart notes that many of the important opinions in *The Wealth of Nations* were contained in this lecture, but he offers only a glimpse of its contents, seeking to demonstrate Smith's ownership of the ideas rather than to elucidate Smith's theories.[28] That Smith expounded his ideas on political economy at this club is further hinted at by his correspondence with club member and prominent merchant John Glassford. In a letter to Smith dated 5 November 1764, Glassford wrote: "I hope that your Time passes agreeably and that you are bringing forward at your Leisure Hours the usefull work that was so well advanced here. It would be a Pity to want it longer than you find necessary to finish it to your own liking, as it may then very safely make its appearance."[29] Ernest Campbell Mossner and Ian Simpson Ross follow Smith's biographer John Rae in interpreting this passage as a reference to Smith's activities in the Political Economy Club, whose members would have heard firsthand his views on economics.[30]

The Anderston Club

Robert Simson, professor of mathematics at the University of Glasgow, was the driving force behind one of the earliest literary clubs in the city. The club met in the Anderston District, and is therefore sometimes referred to as the Anderston Club, although it was also known as the Friday Club. No records of the club have survived. However, we know that it operated from around the early 1740s until 1768 and that members attended meetings on Fridays—as the alternative title of the club would suggest. Carlyle, who was studying in the city at this time, was one of the students admitted to the group in 1744. From him we know that despite the mathematical disposition of Simson and his "greatest favourite" Matthew Stewart (the future professor of mathematics at Edinburgh and father of Dugald Stewart), the club discussed both philosophical and literary matters.[31] Even the instrument maker of Glasgow University, James Watt, who would go on to achieve international renown for his improvement of the Newcomen steam engine, was a member. Watt, in similar fashion to Carlyle, noted that the arts dominated the group's discussions. He recalled that "our conversations . . . besides the usual subjects with young men, turned principally on literary topics, religion, belles lettres &c; and to those conversations my mind owed its first bias to such subjects, I never having attended a college, and being then but a mechanic."[32]

Simson appears to have kept the club a select affair, choosing only favorites to partake in the debates. These included a number of significant figures, such as Hercules Lindsay, teacher of Law; James Moor, professor of Greek; William Cullen, professor of the practice of medicine; Thomas Hamilton, professor of anatomy and botany; and Alexander Ross, professor of humanity, in addition to younger men such as Carlyle, Smith, and Robert and Andrew Foulis.[33] As Dugald Stewart recounted in his biography of Smith, Smith's main interests while a university student were mathematics and natural philosophy.[34] This assertion has led J. C. Bryce to surmise that it was from Simson that Smith learned his idea of a "system," which was initially set out by the mathematician over his views on astronomy. There is a good case for this argument, as Smith endeavored to build his rhetorical system upon a solid foundation of Newtonian empiricism.[35]

In the club itself, however, science sometimes took a back seat to conviviality, and among the more lighthearted distractions were Simson's efforts to sing Greek odes set to modern music.[36] The Glasgow journalist John Strang envisioned an environment in which the criticism of Greek and Latin texts would give way to discussion of modern works such as Tobias Smollett's novels *Roderick Random* (1748) and *The Adventures of Peregrine Pickle* (1751), which were published during the heyday of the club.[37] Although this hypothesis is pure conjecture, it is not outside the realm of possibility that Smollett's works would have been discussed, particularly because, as a former student of the university, he included in his novels caricatures of some of the faculty members, which would have provided members with direct local references.[38] The club continued to meet regularly until the death of its founding member in 1768. Although we can only guess what literary discussions occurred in it, the very existence of the club demonstrates that there was an interest in belles lettres that was met both inside and outside the university.

Carlyle spoke of two other clubs to which he belonged during his stay in Glasgow from 1743 to 1744. The first was entirely a literary society, which met at the porter's lodge in the college, where the assembled members criticized books and wrote abridgments of them with critical essays. In this respect, the activities of this group were not altogether removed from the literary practices of Francis Hutcheson, who would often make his students provide abridged versions of literary works in order to demonstrate that they understood what they had read. This club also appears to have served a function as an intermediary between students and the university, because the discourses delivered to fellow members were also given before the Divinity Hall when appointed by the professor.[39] Carlyle viewed these discourses as a vital component of a rounded education. Although he praised the divinity professor William Leechman's theological teachings, he remarked that "if there was any defect, it was in the small number of exercises prescribed to the students, for one discourse in a session was by no means sufficient to produce a habit of composition: our literary clubs, in some degree, supplied that defect."[40] Despite this minor criticism, Hutcheson himself believed that the appointment of Leechman as professor of divinity would "put a new face upon Theology in Scotland."[41] Having secured the position following a fierce battle with his evangelical opponent John MacLaurin, Carlyle certainly concurred with Hutcheson's assessment, stating that thanks to both Hutcheson and Leechman "a better taste and greater liberality of sentiment were introduced among the clergy in the western provinces of Scotland."[42] Many of these students would go on to become members of the Moderate party in the Church of Scotland in the decades that would follow.

The other club to which Carlyle belonged met every week in a tavern near Glasgow Cross owned by a Mr. Dugald, and accommodated members who were not intended for the study of theology. According to Carlyle, it drew in members from the next generation of merchants, such as Robin Bogle (who happened to be related to Carlyle), James and George Anderson, William Sellers, and Robin Craig. Among its members who did go on to become ministers was John Bradfute, the minister of Dunsyre and an intimate friend of Sir James Clerk of Penicuik, who accompanied Clerk on many of his tours through England and Scotland.[43] Future minsters also included James Leslie of Kilmarnock, John Robertson of Dunblane, James Hamilton of Paisley, and Robert Lawson of London Wall. The topics for discussion were almost entirely literary but appeared to be of such local reputation that even some of the local ministers frequented the club.[44] Lawson was nearly prevented from attending the club following a suggestion to his uncle, Robert Paton, the minister of Renfrew, that the conversations and discussions held at the club were not appropriate for their future profession. Carlyle noted that although Paton was a man of "liberal sentiments," he was also "too much a man of worth and principle not to be offended by licentious manners in students of divinity."[45] The incident was smoothed over with the help of Carlyle, and Lawson continued to attend the club. Paton, who was described as the "bosom friend" of Hutcheson, remained supportive to Lawson when he took up his position at London Wall.[46] In a warm tribute to Lawson's abilities, Paton remarked that his "education was in the sound principles of our church, in his father's family, and afterwards, for a course of years, when he pursued the studies of philosophy and divinity, at the College of Glasgow."[47]

The Hodge Podge Club

Another Glasgow club with literary pretensions, at least initially, was the Hodge Podge Club. It was founded in 1750, although official records were not taken until 1752.[48] The club has enjoyed enormous longevity and is still active in the city. Initially, meetings were held fortnightly, but as time passed attendance dwindled. By 1822 the members resolved to meet once a month, which was further reduced to five meetings a year in 1839.

The club—which primarily drew its membership from the city's merchants—started as a literary society with the same aspirations that the Edinburgh-based Select Society (1754) was to develop: to improve the public speaking of its members as well as their political and literary compositions.[49] Of the original nine members, six were merchants: James Luke, James Simson, Peter Blackburn, John Dunlop, Thomas Wright, and William Anderson.[50] Although the names of those who founded the society were not as renowned as those who attended Robert Simson's club, it did count as one of its members John Moore, the biographer of Tobias Smollett and the author of the novel *Zeluco* (1789). As Henry L. Fulton has noted, the club became the "chief social club of the young merchants and professionals in Glasgow" and formed the nucleus of Moore's early friendships in the city.[51] His son, General Sir John Moore, who rose to prominence in the

British army and achieved national recognition for his defense of Corunna against the French, was elected an honorary member in 1806. Moore senior appears to have provided a poetic work that attempted to depict the characters of those who attended.[52] From the tone of the poem it is clear that the Hodge Podge was a convivial club as much as it was a literary one. At the very first meeting, the first paper delivered asked, "What is Taste? Is it natural or acquired?"[53] However, as the club developed, food and drink became ever more important elements. This point is reinforced by the first extant set of rules and regulations, which can be traced to 1783. Rather than fines for failure to deliver discourses and engage in debates, members were more concerned with access to alcohol. For example, the first rule of the club established the election of a preses, "whose power must be considered as absolute, with this single exception—that he shall compel no member to drink more liquor than that member may chuse, but the Preses may order any member to abstain from drinking. However, in order that the power above mentioned may not be abused, every member who may think himself injured by the conduct of a Preses may, upon depositing twopence, appeal to the next Club for a redress of his grievances."[54]

Even the literary debates descended from the academic to the convivial.[55] The minute book for the club recorded that on 30 January 1788, Mr. Robert Scot wagered a bottle of rum with Dr. Alexander Stevenson (also a member of the Glasgow Literary Society) that *Tom Jones* was published before *Roderick Random*.[56] The club also decided from its inception to toast female members. These women were not allowed to attend meetings, however, and their only engagement with the club appears to have been as the subjects of the toasts. Agnes McLehose, who would go on to enjoy a literary correspondence with Robert Burns as the Clarinda to his Sylvander, was toasted by the Hodge Podge Club at the age of fifteen.[57] The club did, however, create a network of mercantile interests. According to Douglas J. Hamilton, as merchants began to diversify in the aftermath of American independence and spread into the Caribbean, it became a bastion of the sugar aristocracy. William Mure, William McDowall, Robert Houston Rae, Henry Glassford, Andrew Buchanan, the Grenadian planter John Graham of Dougalston, and the Jamaica merchant and planter Charles Stirling were all members.[58] Although not ostensibly political, they nevertheless promoted patronage connections between individuals, which in turn allowed interconnectivity with broader networks in Britain and the West Indies.

The Glasgow Literary Society

Although Glasgow had a number of clubs in this period, the most significant club in the city was the Literary Society, founded in January 1752.[59] McElroy went as far as to say that "because of its long life, the talents of its members, and the quality and quantity of their work, this was one of the most important societies of the century."[60] Part of the reason for this, according to McElroy, was that membership was open to the merchants of the town.[61] However, in Glasgow, merchants frequently attended clubs, so this was not a unique feature of the Glasgow Literary Society. In fact its core membership was far more professorial than mercantile. Between 1752 and 1753 almost half of the members taught at the college, but the club also included the Glasgow merchants Robert Bogle and William Crawfurd as original members, as well as local Presbyterian clergy such as Rev. William Craig of St. Andrews Church, and the lawyers Sir John Dalrymple and Walter Stewart. Others listed as members for the first year include Moor, Leechman, Thomas Hamilton, Cullen, Robert Simson, David Hume, Robert Foulis, John Anderson, and Hercules Lindsay.[62] In the 1760s Joseph Black and, after he had taken over the chair of moral philosophy from Adam Smith, Thomas Reid—who had done so much to establish the Aberdeen Philosophical Society in 1758—also attended the club.[63] The members, Hume excepted, were religious, but wore that religion lightly. According to Roger L. Emerson they believed that Christianity had to become simpler and plainer, and ought to be conveyed in a language that was more polite. In this regard they were at odds with their evangelical counterparts in the city who focused their attention more closely on the creed.[64]

As civil society became more complex, the establishment and enforcement of rules and regulations helped to construct a sense of identity for members of clubs. The Glasgow Literary Society established its own rules at its first meeting in 1752 when its founding members set in motion the procedures that would be followed for decades to come. For the first three weeks book reviews were conducted, presumably to allow members the time to compose discourses. The first regular meeting took place on 7 February, when James Moor delivered a paper titled "On Historical Composition." This was an auspicious start, as the paper was later published by fellow members Robert and Andrew Foulis in a collection of Moor's papers titled *Essays; Read to a Literary Society; at Their Weekly Meetings, Within the College at Glasgow* (1759).

The rules and regulations of the Glasgow Literary Society were similar to those of contemporaneous organizations. The Aberdeen Philosophical Society, or Wise Club, also imposed fines for nonattendance and requested that each of its members provide a "discourse" ("dissertation" in the parlance of the Glasgow Literary Society), in order to generate discussion. The Edinburgh Belles Lettres Society (1759) established parameters for the presentation and subsequent debate of discourses, including an appropriate duration for each talk. A series of fines were also implemented, with those missing meetings without due cause fined "sixpence sterling" for every night's absence.[65]

The extent to which rules ought to be enforced caused something of a rift among members of the Glasgow Literary Society in the late 1770s, when the club decided to adjourn its meeting set for 1 January 1779. Archibald Arthur, assistant to Thomas Reid in moral philosophy, proposed to read a discourse on the dispersion at Babel. However, the majority of members decided against this, and opted to reconvene on 8 January. Arthur remained resolute and announced that he would read his paper regardless of who would be in attendance; Reid, William Irvine, and John Anderson supported Arthur, who duly read his paper on New Year's Day. The following week a dispute arose over the club rule which stated that the previous speaker should become the chair, which William Richardson believed to be his privilege. Arthur challenged this on the grounds that he was the last to provide a discourse, and consequently he was the rightful chair. Although voted down by the majority of the members, Arthur protested vehemently, stating that it was "contrary to the clear and express Laws of the Literary Society." Furthermore, he raged, it would be "better to dissolve a Society which tramples upon its own Laws and therefore disgraces the name of Literary than for Britons to subject themselves to a Despotism unknown in Barbarous Countries."[66] Arthur's condemnation illustrates how seriously members took their club rules, and how far they were prepared to go to defend them.

The eclectic membership shows that just as Robert Simson's club did not confine itself to the scientific realm, neither did the Literary Society focus exclusively on belles lettres.[67] Alexander Wilson, the Glasgow University professor of astronomy and the typesetter for the Foulis brothers, achieved European renown when the discourse he delivered to the society in December 1769, "On the Solar Spots," was awarded a gold medal by the Royal Society of Sciences of Copenhagen in 1772 for the best paper on sunspots.[68] Just as in the Political Economy Club, commerce was on Smith's mind when he made his debut at the Glasgow Literary Society on 23 January 1752, reading an account of Hume's commercial essays from his recently published *Political Discourses* (1752).[69] Smith appears to have been an avid debater in the Literary Society. John Strang recounted an anecdote in which Smith, having spoken at great length against the whole of the assembly, and losing the point to an overwhelming majority, was overheard muttering to himself, "Convicted, but not convinced."[70]

Although the Literary Society concerned itself less with trade than Cochrane's club did, it was not only Smith who was captivated with commercial matters. Dalrymple, who wrote *An Essay towards a General History of Feudal Property in Great Britain* (1757), was greatly interested in the factors that promoted or diminished the development of trade. Reid was also a prolific contributor to the society's discussions, and frequently devoted his discourses to economic issues. On 1 May 1767 he asked, "Whether Paper Credit is beneficial or hurtful to a trading nation?" On 20 March 1778 he inquired, "Whether it is proper that the interest of money should be regulated by law in cases where the parties have contracted?" And on 7 May 1779 he returned to Hume's essay "Of the Original Contract" when he considered, "Wherein consists the nature of a contract and does it involve contradictions as Mr Hume asserts?"[71] As a member of the Glasgow Literary Society, Hume also contributed to the ongoing debates. However, his distance from Glasgow appears to have proved problematic in getting to the city. In a letter to Smith he wrote, "I beg you to make my Compliments to the Society, and to take the Fault on Yourself. If I have not executed my Duty, and sent them this time my Anniversary Paper. Had I got a Week's warning, I shou'd have been able to have supply'd them."[72] The distance from Edinburgh in the eighteenth century would have been prohibitive to Hume's regular attendance, but the society was keen to hear papers from those outside Glasgow. Dugald Stewart sent a letter to the secretary, recorded in the minutes of 7 March 1777, offering to read to the society "Some Observations on the state of the Mind in Sleep and the Phenomena of Dreaming."[73] This was eagerly accepted by the society, to whom Stewart delivered his discourse the following week.

The Literary Society was a forum where research papers were delivered, and where questions were debated on subjects proposed by the society's members. As James Buchanan—who became a member in the late 1750s—related in a letter to future member David Steuart Erskine, Earl of Buchan, "There are no restrictions as to the scope of our Papers, and Essays are sometimes sent to us by correspondents at a distance."[74] Unfortunately, a large section of the club's minutes—almost two-thirds of their entire records—are missing.[75] Despite this, from the records that do survive we can build a picture of a society responding critically to numerous investigations across a diverse range of scholarly interests. The wide variety of papers that the Foulis brothers read before the society illustrates this point. Robert Foulis gave papers titled "Memoir on the Discovery and Culture of Genius" (1764), "From what reasons founded in nature do the Imitative Arts of Music, Painting, and Poetry proceed" (1767), and "Whether Learning, Arts, Sciences, and Manners in Europe are upon the whole on the Advance or Decline" (1769), as well as on nonliterary subjects such as "Observations on the Knowledge or Science necessary to a Commercial Town or State" (1766) and "On the improvement of Agriculture and at the same time diminishing the expence" (1771). With regard to Robert Foulis's interaction with the Literary Society, William Richardson—professor of humanity at Glasgow—noted that "the first feature . . . that particularly struck me, was the great liking he showed to converse on literary topics, and even with persons much younger than himself. This disposition appeared not only in occasional interviews, but in his choosing to associate with them, and become a member of their Literary Clubs and Societies.[76] Andrew Foulis was just as prolific a contributor as his elder brother, and provided papers titled "On the Advancement of Learning" (1765) and "A Discourse concerning Literary Property" (1766), as well as on Egyptian papyrus and the libraries among the ancients.[77]

Merchants, professors, and clergymen mingled in the Literary Society. Rev. William Craig was the son of the merchant Andrew Craig, and was educated at the university, where he formed a bond of friendship with the newly established professor of moral philosophy, Francis Hutcheson. Through his wife, Jean Anderson,

Craig married into another wealthy merchant family, and his son John followed the path of his relatives when he likewise became a merchant.[78] Another son, also named William, would become the judge Lord Craig and keep up close ties with the literary interests of his father; he became a member of the Edinburgh convivial society known as the Feast of Tabernacles (1770), the precursor of the Mirror Club (1776). Like Hutcheson, Rev. William Craig rejected the rigidly orthodox approach to theology, playing his part in securing a more moderate brand of religious instruction at the university. Craig was originally in competition with his friend and future Literary Society member William Leechman for the divinity chair, but he decided to withdraw his candidacy due to lack of support. Thanks to his backing, Leechman was able to defeat his orthodox opponent John MacLaurin in a closely fought contest, and then to usher in a more moderate brand of theology among Glasgow's divinity students. Craig was listed as one of the original members of the Literary Society in 1752, but no records relating to his talks at the society have survived. Nevertheless, Craig's background demonstrates the social factors that contributed to Georgian Glasgow's Enlightenment.

Conclusion

As we have seen, historians have previously made the claim that the links between the university and the emerging business community in Glasgow led to a far better educated mercantile class in the town than could be found in comparable British cities. T. M. Devine has argued that the liberal education which some merchants received allowed them to sustain a "vigorous urban culture" during the second half of the eighteenth century.[79] This view would appear to have had some currency within the merchant class itself. An unidentified member of the Bogle trading dynasty believed that "all the Merchants in Glasgow (excepting those who deal in Exchange) are quite idle for one half or two thirds of the year which may be one reason why the frequent keeping of company does prevail so much and in Glasgow more than in any place in the world."[80] However, as W. M. Mathew reminds us, the numbers involved in university education were very small, and for those who did receive an education, the duration could often be short.[81] Carlyle noted that during his time in Glasgow "it was usual for the sons of merchants to attend the College for one or two years, and a few of them completed their academical education."[82] Some even held the presence of the university to be a hindrance. An ironical pamphlet from the mid-1780s opined that among the merchants of Glasgow, the most ignorant had gone on to enjoy the most success. Therefore it would be more efficient to abolish the University of Glasgow and transfer all the funds to "the Chamber of Commerce, that late most admirable institution, which . . . already promises the most beneficial effects in Scotland in general and to the city of Glasgow in particular."[83] Nevertheless,

Glasgow's position as an emerging industrial powerhouse, coupled with the attendance of students who were more disposed to enter the world of commerce after attending the university, placed the city in a position to harness talent and direct it into powering mercantile and industrial growth. The emergence of so many clubs during this period provided conduits for intellectual exchange, opportunities for networking and patronage, and convivial retreats for those wishing to escape from everyday business. It was the blending of the clerical, the mercantile, and the professorial that made this experience uniquely Glaswegian.

NOTES

1. John Moore, "The Life of T. Smollett," in *The Works of Tobias Smollett, M.D.* (London: B. Law et al., 1797), 1:cxi.

2. Clark, viii.

3. [William Thom], *The Defects of an University Education, and Its Unsuitableness to a Commercial People* (London: E. Dilly, 1762), 3.

4. Carlyle, 100. For Hutcheson's interest in, and defense of, clubs and associations, see David Allan's chapter in this volume.

5. David Hume, "Of Refinement in the Arts" (1742), in *Essays Moral, Political, and Literary*, ed. Eugene F. Miller (Indianapolis: Liberty Classics, 1987), 271. For further examples of Hume's observations on clubbability, see Allan's chapter in this volume.

6. R. J. Morris, "Civil Society and the Nature of Urbanism: Britain, 1750–1850," *Urban History* 25 (1998): 290–291.

7. Adam Ferguson, *An Essay on the History of Civil Society*, ed. Fania Oz-Salzberger (Cambridge: Cambridge University Press, 1995), 124–125.

8. Paul Elliott, "The Origins of the 'Creative Class': Provincial Urban Society, Scientific Culture and Socio-political Marginality in Britain in the Eighteenth and Nineteenth Centuries," *Social History* 28 (2003): 383. See also Anand C. Chitnis, *The Scottish Enlightenment: A Social History* (London: Croom Helm, 1976).

9. Carlyle, 73.

10. W. M. Mathew, "The Origins and Occupations of Glasgow Students, 1740–1839," *Past and Present* 33 (1966): 87.

11. R. I. James, "Bristol Society in the Eighteenth Century," in *Bristol and Its Adjoining Counties*, ed. C. M. MacInnes and W. F. Whittard (Bristol: British Association for the Advancement of Science, 1955), 231.

12. Speaking through the words of Matthew Bramble, Smollett labeled him "one of the sages of this kingdom" (*Humphry Clinker*, 246).

13. J. F. Bell, "Adam Smith, Clubman," in *Adam Smith: Critical Assessments*, ed. John Cunningham Wood (London: Routledge, 1983), 1:95.

14. *The Cochrane Correspondence regarding the Affairs of Glasgow, 1745–46*, ed. James Dennistoun (Glasgow: Maitland Club, 1836).

15. David Murray, *Early Burgh Organisation in Scotland* (Glasgow: MacLehose, Jackson, 1924), 1:446–450.

16. Carlyle, 73.

17. William Wight, *Heads of a Course of Lectures on Civil History* (Glasgow: printed by Robert and Andrew Foulis, 1767), 20.

18. William Wight, *Heads of a Course of Lectures on Civil History* (Glasgow: printed by Robert and Andrew Foulis, 1772), 20.

19. W. R. Scott, *Adam Smith as Student and Professor* (Glasgow: Jackson and Son, 1937), 81–82; Carlyle, 73–74.

20. Nicholas Phillipson, *Adam Smith: An Enlightened Life* (London: Allen Lane, 2010), 129.

21. John Rae, *The Life of Adam Smith* (1895; repr., Cosimo: New York, 2006), 272.

22. Richard B. Sher, "Commerce, Religion and the Enlightenment in Eighteenth-Century Glasgow," in *Glasgow*, vol. 1, *Beginnings to 1830*, ed. T. M. Devine and Gordon Jackson (Manchester: Manchester University Press, 1995), 315–316.

23. *Correspondence of Adam Smith*, ed. Ernest Campbell Mossner and Ian Simpson Ross, rev. ed., The Glasgow Edition of the Works and Correspondence of Adam Smith (1987; repr., Indianapolis: Liberty Fund, 1987), 286.

24. McElroy, 1969, 41.

25. Dugald Stewart, "Account of the Life and Writings of Adam Smith, LL.D.," in *Essays on Philosophical Subjects*, ed. W.P.D. Wightman and J. C. Bryce, The Glasgow Edition of the Works and Correspondence of Adam Smith (1980; repr., Indianapolis: Liberty Fund, 1982), 300.

26. *Glasgow Courant*, 25 Mar. 1751; Scott, *Adam Smith as Student and Professor*, 82.

27. Stewart, "Life and Writings of Adam Smith," 321.

28. Ibid., 322–323.

29. *Correspondence of Adam Smith*, 104.

30. Rae, *Adam Smith*, 90–91.

31. Carlyle, 81.

32. James Watt, quoted in Robert E. Schofield, *The Lunar Society of Birmingham* (London: University of London Press, 1963), 62.

33. Strang, 22.

34. Stewart, "Life and Writings of Adam Smith," 270–271.

35. Of the system he was trying to create, Smith stated: "In the same way in Nat<urall> Phil<osophy> or any other Science of that Sort we may either like Aristotle go over the Different branches in the order they happen to cast up to us, giving a principle commonly a new one for every phaenomenon; or in the manner of Sir Isaac Newton we may lay down certain principles known or proved in the beginning, from whence we account for the severall Phenomena, connecting all together by the same Chain." Adam Smith, *Lectures on Rhetoric and Belles Lettres*, ed. J. C. Bryce, The Glasgow Edition of the Works and Correspondence of Adam Smith (1983; repr., Indianapolis: Liberty Fund, 1985), 145–146.

36. James Coutts, *A History of the University of Glasgow, from Its Foundation in 1451 to 1909* (Glasgow: James MacLehose and Sons, 1909), 227.

37. Strang, 26–27.

38. John Johnston, who held the chair of medicine at Glasgow from 1714 to 1751, is often cited as a prototype for Launcelot Crab, the underhanded surgeon to whom the eponymous hero is apprenticed. John Ramsay agreed with this assessment (*Scotland and Scotsmen in the Eighteenth Century*, ed. Alexander Allardyce [Edinburgh: William Blackwood and Sons, 1888], 1:277–278). However, there is an alternative version of the story which claims that one of the surgeons who taught Smollett, Thomas Crawford, was a more likely candidate. For this version, see *The Emmet; A Selection of Original Essays, Tales, Anecdotes, Bon Mots, Choice Sayings, &c.* (Glasgow: Purvis and Aitken, 1824), 1:5.

39. Carlyle, 76.

40. Ibid., 85.

41. Francis Hutcheson to Thomas Drennan, n.d., Glasgow University Library, MS Gen.1018/15.

42. Carlyle, 68.

43. *Memoirs of the Life of Sir John Clerk of Penicuik*, ed. John M. Gray (Edinburgh: Scottish History Society, 1892), 135n4.

44. Carlyle, 77.

45. Ibid.

46. James Moore, "Evangelical Calvinists versus the Hutcheson Circle: Debating the Faith in Scotland, 1738–1739," in *Debating the Faith: Religion and Letter Writing in Great*

Britain, 1550–1800, ed. Anne Dunan-Page and Clotilde Prunier (Dordrecht: Springer, 2013), 189.

47. Robert Paton, quoted in Walter Wilson, *The History and Antiquities of Dissenting Churches and Meeting Houses in London, Westminster, and Southwark* (London, 1808), 2:499.

48. T. F. Donald, *The Hodge Podge Club, 1752–1900* (Glasgow: James MacLehose and Sons, 1900).

49. Strang, 30–55.

50. The other two members were Robert Maltman, one of the masters of the grammar school, and Thomas Hamilton, a surgeon. See Donald, *Hodge Podge Club*, 4.

51. Henry L. Fulton, *Dr. John Moore, 1729–1802: A Life in Medicine, Travel, and Revolution* (London: Rowman and Littlefield, 2015), 106.

52. There appear to be two different versions of this poem: a manuscript copy, "Verses On the Hotch Potch Club at Glasgow By the late Dr. Moore" (NLS, MS 5003, fol. 107), and an expanded version, in Strang, 41–43.

53. Donald, *Hodge Podge Club*, 21.

54. Ibid., 14–15.

55. George Stewart, *Curiosities of Glasgow Citizenship* (Glasgow: James MacLehose, 1881), 143.

56. Donald, *Hodge Podge Club*, 50.

57. James Mackay, *RB: A Biography of Robert Burns* (Edinburgh: Mainstream Publishing, 1992), 369.

58. Douglas J. Hamilton, *Scotland, the Caribbean and the Atlantic World, 1750–1820* (Manchester: Manchester University Press, 2005), 187.

59. On the club within a British context, see Clark, 91–92.

60. McElroy, 1969, 43.

61. Ibid.

62. Strang, 21–22.

63. For Reid's activities in the club, see Kathleen Holcomb, "Thomas Reid in the Glasgow Literary Society," in *The Glasgow Enlightenment*, ed. Andrew Hook and Richard B. Sher (East Linton: Tuckwell Press, 1997), 95–110.

64. Roger L. Emerson, *Neglected Scots: Eighteenth Century Glaswegians and Women* (Edinburgh: Humming Earth, 2015), 22.

65. "Proceedings of the Belles Lettres Society," NLS, Adv. MS 23.3.4; Paul Bator, "The University of Edinburgh Belles Lettres Society (1759–64) and the Rhetoric of the Novel," *Rhetoric Review* 14 (1996): 280–298.

66. "Laws of the Literary Society in Glasgow College," Glasgow University Library, MS Murray 505, 78–79.

67. On the Glasgow Literary Society as a vehicle for the promotion of science and medicine, see Roger L. Emerson and Paul Wood, "Science and Enlightenment in Glasgow, 1690–1802," in *Science and Medicine in the Scottish Enlightenment*, ed. Charles W. J. Withers and Paul Wood (East Linton: Tuckwell Press, 2002), 101–109.

68. *Glasgow Courant*, 28 May 1772; "Laws of the Literary Society," 37.

69. William James Duncan, ed., *Notices and Documents Illustrative of the Literary History of Glasgow* (Glasgow: Maitland Club, 1831), 133. The *Scots Magazine* for January 1752 noted that the *Political Discourses* had recently been published (56).

70. Strang, 314.

71. "Laws of the Literary Society," 22, 67, 86.

72. *Correspondence of Adam Smith*, 17–18.

73. "Laws of the Literary Society," 49.

74. Buchanan to Lord Cardross [Earl of Buchan], 22 Feb. 1758, quoted in David Murray, *Robert and Andrew Foulis and the Glasgow Press* (Glasgow: James MacLehose and Sons, 1913), 37.

75. There are no minutes from 10 Jan. 1752 to May 1764, from 22 Nov. 1771 to Jan. 1773, from 11 Feb. 1773 to May 1776, and from May 1779 to Apr./May 1794.

76. Duncan, *Notices and Documents*, 41.

77. Ibid., 134–135.

78. Hew Scott, *Fasti Ecclesiae Scoticanae: The Succession of Ministers in the Church of Scotland from the Reformation*, vol. 3, *Synod of Glasgow and Ayr* (Edinburgh: Oliver and Boyd, 1920), 433.

79. T. M. Devine, *The Tobacco Lords: A Study of the Tobacco Merchants of Glasgow and Their Trading Activities, c. 1740–90* (Edinburgh: Edinburgh University Press, 1975), 9.

80. Bogle to Robert Bogle, 5 Mar. 1726, "George Bogle's Letterbook," Bogle MSS, Mitchell Library, Glasgow.

81. Mathew, "Origins and Occupations of Glasgow Students," 90.

82. Carlyle, 74.

83. Quoted in David Murray, *Memories of the Old College of Glasgow* (Glasgow: Jackson and Wylie, 1927), 383–384.

PART III

Clubs, Societies, and Literary Culture

CHAPTER 5

"Soaping" and "Shaving" the Public Sphere

JAMES BOSWELL'S "SOAPING CLUB" AND EDINBURGH ENLIGHTENMENT SOCIABILITY

James J. Caudle

Recent scholarship on sociability in eighteenth-century Scotland has often focused on how it was both described and promoted by the flowering of Enlightenment political theory, coupled with a cult of urbane civility and civic humanism.[1] Another, closely related historiographical agenda has been the investigation (or reification) of what academic jargon calls the "bourgeois public sphere," as created by "a polite and commercial people." More than a half century ago, Jürgen Habermas described eighteenth-century Britain as seeing the rise of a social space of *Öffentlichkeit* ("openness" and, by extension, "public-ness"), which his translators somewhat maladroitly rendered as "bourgeois public sphere." The rise of openness was indicative of an age of rising *bürgerlichen Gesellschaft* (a more individualistic middle-class civil society succeeding the older corporate/feudal *Gemeinschaft*), characterized by "social intercourse that . . . disregarded status," the "domain of common concern," and "a more inclusive public" engaging in serious debates about the direction of the state and society in coffeehouses and salons.[2] Georgian British politeness, another supposed key component in this cultural complex, was well defined by Lawrence E. Klein as "attentiveness to form, sociability, improvement, worldliness, and gentility."[3] Mark Kingwell, in his "Politics and the Polite Society in the Scottish Enlightenment," has argued that "politeness provides a useful keynote for much of Scotland's Enlightenment period . . . an indispensable quality of civilized human life, the foundation of progress . . . thought to be available to many strata of society."[4] K. Tawny Paul has questioned the degree to which the influential "polite and commercial" trope used by Paul Langford in discussing England in the period 1727–1783 is applicable to Scotland during the same century.[5] Nonetheless, the analysis of the rise of politeness and civility remains a common heuristic for discussing Scottish culture in this period, especially that of Lowland and urban Scotland, as well as governing most analyses of English associational culture in this period.

Doubtless, the doctrines of social progress through decorum, gentility, politeness, and refinement professed by David Hume, William Robertson, and others were at the heart of the Scottish Enlightenment. The picture of Scottish civility as eager to outdo the English in genteel and mannered gatherings and to shed the supposedly grosser aspects of the Scottish past is certainly present, and vociferously advocated, in Scottish high culture in this period.[6] Refined groups conforming or at least seeming to conform to this model, such as the Poker Club (1762), the Feast of Tabernacles / Mirror Club (1770/1776), which created the iconic Edinburgh essay series in *The Mirror* (1779–1780) and *The Lounger* (1785–1787), and the Select Society (1754) and its junior branch the Belles Lettres Society (1759), have deserved their corporate biographies added to the digital *Oxford Dictionary of National Biography*.[7] James Boswell (1740–1795) was very proud of his membership in the iconic Select Society, and noted in an anonymous autobiographical account in 1791 that "having an uncommon desire for the company of men distinguished for talents and literature, he was fortunate enough to get himself received into that of those who were considerably his superiors in age . . . and was admitted a member of the *Select Society* of Edinburgh."[8] Yet this Enlightenment-centric view of what clubs were and did runs the risk of ignoring the large number of clubs that were not dedicated to increasing knowledge or polishing manners, and whose goals were chiefly ludic, or even consciously pointless.[9]

This distinction between "high" and "low" forms of clubbability cannot be explained by recourse to a simple dichotomy between patrician society and plebeian culture, as defined by E. P. Thompson, or by a distinction between what two farces staged by David Garrick—Boswell's clubfellow in the Johnsonian Literary Club—would term "high life" and "low life."[10] Some of the lowest and crudest clubs to which Boswell belonged in his adult lifetime had members from the gentry and aristocracy, who also simultaneously held memberships in worthier and usually duller organizations such as the Select Society. Corey E. Andrews has capably discussed this Jekyll-Hyde duality of the more respectable clubs versus the more disreputable ones, and remarks that "an intriguing historical feature of the Scottish Enlightenment is the blend of philosophical and drinking clubs to which leading thinkers . . . belonged."[11] Andrews contrasts two serious clubs, the somewhat stuffy Select Society and the somewhat raucous Poker Club, mentioned above. He cautions that "many social histories tend to collapse all clubs from the mid-century into a single overriding example of 'improvement' through civic association; unfortunately, this approach obscures core differences that separated and distinguished clubs like the Poker and the Select Society."[12]

This divide between high and low modalities of sociability has been remarked upon with specific reference to Boswell. Rosalind Carr writes that "Boswell was active in what can be defined as the Habermasian public sphere" and that the "interrelationship of organized sociability and the free atmosphere of the tavern is a theme repeated throughout the journals [of Boswell]."[13] Peter Martin has observed that the fact that Boswell "could feel at ease both in the roistering Soaping Club and in the elegant company of scholars, writers, and philosophers in the Select Society was not unique in Edinburgh. . . . Social lines were not as clearly drawn in Edinburgh as in London."[14] Yet even in "Enlightenment" London in the 1760s, as Jason M. Kelly has reminded us, the circle of young Boswell's new friend John Wilkes, which included the frivolous "Medmenham Monks," overlapped with the membership of "the Dilettanti, who were attempting to establish cultural and scientific credentials in the Enlightenment public sphere." As Kelly observes, "In an age in which 'public utility' and 'service to the public good' were supposed to be the modus operandi of respectable societies," a club could be "associate[d] with ribald excess." Kelly concludes that "inherent to the associational world of the eighteenth century was the tension between the masculine libertinism of aristocratic individuals and the 'polite sociability' of their publicly recognized communities."[15] And so it remained into the year of Boswell's death in 1795.

We might choose to interpret the chaotic activities of such clubs as a continuation of the older forms of raucous masculine camaraderie. Much of what the Brother Soapers sang and said while in their cups would have been familiar in the medieval world in which the Goliard songsters had performed their drunken and mock-amorous carmina. Alternatively, one might elect to describe these clubs as distinctively modern—as being a deliberate reactionary revolt against the emerging culture of politeness, genteel sociability, and a closer integration of the masculine and feminine spheres by the cultures of the tea table, the assembly room, and the salon. Simon Dickie's research has reminded scholars dazzled by the lure of theories of the rise of an age of sentiment of the presence of an "*unsentimental* eighteenth century." In Dickie's opinion, much of even elevated and patrician literary culture's humor in the Georgian period depended on the practice of what modern critical theory of comedy would call "punching down," or rather ruthlessly aiming their mockery at all levels of society, high or low.[16]

The view that clubs and other aspects of the "associational world" were most typically engines of refinement and uplifting also ignores contemporary criticisms of low clubs by exponents of the Scottish Enlightenment such as Adam Smith and Henry Home, Lord Kames. Boswell's quondam professor Smith strongly criticized such clubs. In a passage in *The Theory of Moral Sentiments* (1759) that could have been applied to Boswell's less elevated clubs, Smith notes that "the prudent man . . . though capable of friendship . . . is not always much disposed to general sociality. He rarely frequents, and more rarely figures in those convivial societies which are distinguished for the jollity and gaiety of their conversation. Their way of life might too often interfere with the regularity of his temperance, might interrupt the steadiness of his industry, or break in upon the strictness of his frugality."[17] Boswell's mentor Lord Kames—a polymathic jurist, historian, educationalist, and literary theorist—personally admonished his wayward charge on the perils of low sociability in a conversation in mid-October 1762: "He told me that my greatest disadvantage was a too great avidity of pleasure, by which he understood elevation of spirits and high relish of company, which rendered me idle and made me unhappy in a calm situation. Just as a man who is accustomed to fine-seasoned dishes has no taste of plain and wholesome food."[18] Even a dissipated fellow Soaper, Andrew Erskine, could see the danger in other raffish clubs, even if he ignored the dangers of their own: "Erskine said he thought me in great danger of getting in with blackguard geniuses in London; bucks and choice spirits, under-players and fellows who write droll songs, who would admire my humour, make me king of the company, and allow me to pay the bill. I owned it; and determined to be upon my guard."[19]

Davis D. McElroy and Lucille McElroy in their index to "Literary Clubs and Societies of Eighteenth-Century Scotland" created a taxonomy that divided the clubs under examination into thirty-nine "convivial clubs," twelve "student's clubs," six "literary clubs," three "debating clubs," and ten "unclassified clubs," as well as twenty-one "fictitious clubs."[20] Even after deleting from their list the entries for clubs not located in Scotland, the abundance of "convivial clubs" is striking. Peter Clark estimated that in Edinburgh alone there were "200 or more societies functioning in the late eighteenth century, and at least forty different varieties."[21]

Andrews highlights "core differences" between what one might term Apollonian clubs with lofty improving purposes and fairly strict rules of order, often referred to as "societies," and bacchic or convivial clubs that might undertake serious discussions, but devoted themselves to pleasure and leisure, usually through drinking alcohol. He observes in his parallel lives of two useful clubs that "the Poker's valuation of convivial sociability . . . instigated and sustained by alcohol consumption" set it apart from "the Select Society's admitted elitism" and "highly regulated and formal" constitution.[22] Yet it is nonetheless possible to push beyond the boundaries set by Andrews's dyad of case studies, given that the Select Society (which Andrews locates in the "rational world") and the Poker Club (which Andrews locates in the rival world of "drinking and thinking") both had serious cultural or political goals, and could both be located within the Enlightenment culture of systemic improvement. Though the Select was rule-bound, refined, sober, and smooth, while the Poker admitted the potential for informality and free flow of talk and claret, they were from their origins designed to be good for something in terms of helping Scotland advance. But what about the clubs that were "good-for-nothing," a phrase with which Lord Kames jokingly admonished young Boswell in 1761 when he told his young friend, "You are a good, good-for-nothing fellow"?[23] Boswell's Soaping Club (c. 1760), a genteel club of rude and foolishly juvenile drunken behavior, was one of the frivolous low clubs, "good-for-nothing," and is the focus of this essay.

Boswell's Sociability and the Soaping Club

Boswell was fond of sociability and conviviality, and was a member of many clubs during his life, some in Edinburgh and some in London. In Edinburgh, where he resided for most of 1766–1785, his clubs were the University of Edinburgh Belles Lettres Society (1759), the Soaping Club, the Select Society, David Stewart Moncrieffe's "Tavern" (*fl.* 1775), and the Pantheon Society (1773). In London, to which he journeyed as a visitor on various occasions of varying durations in 1760–1785, and in which he resided in 1786–1795, his clubs were the Club of Honest Whigs (c. 1763), Friends Round the Globe (*fl.* 1783), the Royal Academy Club (c. 1769), the Essex Head Club (1783), the Ayrshire Club (*fl.* 1790), the Free and Easy Club at the Thatched House (*fl.* 1793), the Royal Humane Society for the Recovery of Persons Apparently Drowned (1774), the Eumelian (honorary member) (1789), and, most famously, the Literary Club or simply "the Club" (1764), whose best-known member was Samuel Johnson. He was usually a joiner of clubs which already existed, but he founded a brief-lived club in London in 1768 to celebrate the birthday of Corsican patriot leader Pasquale di Paoli. Boswell belonged to national clubs such as the anti-Jacobin Crown and Anchor Association (1792) and the international confraternity of the freemasons.[24] Even a small circle of four friends in the 1790s that included Boswell could take on some of the attributes of a club, and even have bestowed upon it a name, "the Gang"—though the question of whether we should categorize that circle of friends as a true club brings up some deeper hermeneutic questions about what level of membership, constitutional structure, and duration through the years was deemed necessary to constitute a club.[25]

Boswell was something of a scapegrace in his later teens and early twenties, and one of his mentors, Lord Kames, described him to his face in such terms: "Lord Kaims told me tonight that I was a Tom Jones. Mark that!—how must such a Comparrison flash upon my romantic brain!"[26] One of the more intriguing aspects of Boswell's "good-for-nothing" youth was his membership in the Soaping Club, which met on Tuesdays at Thom's Tavern in Edinburgh.

There were probably no more than ten members of the Soaping Club, and possibly just more than a handful. A ringleader in the club was the Church of England priest who was then serving at a "qualified" Anglican-liturgy chapel, the Reverend Edward "Ned" Colquitt (bap. 1716; d. 1777 or 1765?), who apparently also held a benefice as a rector in Leicestershire from 1754. The member besides Boswell who achieved the greatest fame was the then medical student and future American diplomat Arthur Lee (1740–1792), a younger son of the Stratford Lees of Virginia who had been sent over to England for schooling in 1751. Boswell's best friend in the lot was Andrew Erskine (1740–1793), the younger brother of an impoverished Scottish earl who shared Boswell's passion for poetry and achieved a minor distinction as an author of verses and songs. There were also two individuals known only to posterity as "Barclay" and "Bainbridge," one of whom may well be the man referred to as "my old brother soaper Dr. Berkeley" whom Boswell met in 1769.[27] The precise date of Boswell's joining the group is in doubt.

From the surviving evidence, the club seems to have existed from about 1760 to about 1765. The period of its greatest activity was probably in 1761–1762, since the members went their separate ways from 1762 onward. Erskine could have joined only after he met Boswell in May 1761. Boswell headed south to seek his fortune in London in November 1762, and would not return to Scotland until early 1766. Colquitt resigned his Edinburgh ministry in 1762 and was certainly gone from Edinburgh by October 1764. Lee completed the Edinburgh phase of his long education in 1764, returned to North America, where he began his career as a political pamphleteer, and did not return to Britain until 1768.[28]

Boswell's closest friends in the club seem to have been Erskine and Colquitt. Erskine and Boswell revised the bantering correspondence that they had exchanged in 1761–1762 and published it in London in 1763, to minimal acclaim.[29] In his autobiographical "Memoirs" of 1791, Boswell wrote that "he was very intimate with the Reverend Edward Colquet, one of the ministers of the Church of England Chapel at Edinburgh, a man who had lived much in the world, and, with other qualities, was eminent for gay sociality."[30] Most of the Soapers were twenty-somethings born around 1740, and Colquitt, then in his middle forties, was presumably an avuncular figure, more than two decades older than his brethren rather than "a raffish young priest."[31]

Frederick A. Pottle pointed out the affinities of the Soapers with the literary Nonsense Club of London (c. 1750), which, like the later Mirror Club of Edinburgh, produced an essay series that was a "collaborative effort of the group": *The Connoisseur* papers published in 1754–1756. Yet given the lack of similar literary luminosity of the Soaping Club, Pottle's comparison seems like wishful thinking to elevate Boswell's club's purposes above raucous jesting, singing, and drinking.[32] They appear to have done little else. It was not a club for mutual improvement, such as Edinburgh's Select Society for Promoting the Reading and Speaking of the English Language in Scotland (1761), which had Boswell's father and Boswell's friend George Dempster among its directors.[33] Despite the American/Virginian patriot Arthur Lee's claim in 1768 that a "true Soaper" was "a true friend to Freedom," the Soaping Club does not seem ever to have ascended above the facetious into politics or literature, at least not intentionally.[34] It was not connected in membership or outlook to the many Whig Clubs, Revolution Clubs, Militia Clubs, or Jacobite Clubs, whose members held strong political opinions and encouraged them in others.

Nor does it seem to have been founded on a religious principle, either of orthodox churchmanship or heterodox freethinking, despite Sir David Dalrymple's concerns that it was Boswell's gateway into Episcopalianism, since a high proportion of the known members were members of the Church of England or its community of adherents in Edinburgh.[35] Yet Dalrymple did not see the Soaping Club's possible role as a society for the propagation of the Church of England in Edinburgh as its main danger. His letter rebuking Boswell for dissipation appears to denounce it as one of the consociations of "the idle and dissipated, who depend for their pleasure upon every trifling amusement and upon every companion as idle and dissipated as themselves and as trifling as their amusements."[36]

The Theory and Practice of Soaping and Shaving

Having set the scene for the meetings of the Brother Soapers, we can now comprehend why the concepts of "soaping" and "shaving" became the basis of the club. A large part of club life, high or low, was the creation of extravagant and group-specific slang.[37] Had Boswell never sought to explain the motto of his club, the rationale for choosing the term "soaper" to describe the members of the band and the term "soaping" to describe what they did would be even more mysterious than it now is. A soaper normally meant someone who either manufactured or sold soap. However, unlike the freemasons, who divided their membership between operative and speculative masons, the Soapers had no soap-makers among their membership; there was never any connection between the Brother Soapers and the soapmaking trade, or any between soapers and the barbers who generously soaped their customers before shaving them.[38]

In his unpublished verse epistle to "Miss [Jean] Home" (1761 or earlier), Boswell added a footnote to the phrase "I let the Soaper have his way," explicating the word "Soaper" with the Soaping Club motto, "Every man soap his own Beard."[39] In the printed version of his "B[oswell]. A Song," published in 1762 in the second volume of Alexander Donaldson's poetry collection, Boswell added a clearer footnote to the first line, "B[oswell], of Soapers the King." The new note read, "Who has not heard of *Every man soap his own beard*—the reigning phrase for Every man in his humour?" (He added, "Upon this foundation B—— instituted a jovial society, called the Soaping Club.")[40] He revised this definition a year later for a London market in *Letters between the Honourable Andrew Erskine, and James Boswell, Esq.*: "The Soaping-Club—a Club in Edinburgh, the motto of which was, 'Every Man soap his own Beard; or, Every Man indulge his own Humour.'"[41] The allusion in both cases is presumably to Ben Jonson's play *Every Man in His Humour* (1598).[42]

The expression "Every man soap his own beard" is proverbial, but Boswell's use of it is eccentric. The Victorian catalogers of proverbs, William Carew Hazlitt and William Harrison, thought it meant that one must do for oneself, or, as Harrison noted, "that every man should be independent of his neighbor." Whereas a man of wealth could afford to have a professional barber come to soap and shave his face clean, the poor had to do for themselves, and soap their own beards. Hazlitt identified the phrase as being identical to the sentiment "Let every tub stand on its own bottom" and "Let every pedlar carry his own burden," although Hazlitt's wording in introducing the soaping phrase, "Some say," suggests its obscurity by the 1860s.[43]

Boswell and his fellow Soapers took a meaning opposite to the dour maxim of independence from one's neighbor later recorded by Hazlitt. They altered it into a jubilant motto of social Rabelaisian liberation, making it into a maxim that one should seek one's favorite pleasures without fear. As every individual had a different humor or temperament, so each would be pleased by different things. As Boswell stated in late September 1762 while on his Harvest Jaunt, "I have discovered that a man may just do as he pleases if he will firmly resolve and practise following his humour. It is often said, 'I could not do otherwise. They insisted upon my staying.' 'They insisted upon my drinking.' I was once of the same mind, but I have found by agreeable experience that this is a false maxim, and that the hypothesis so often acceded to is merely imaginary. For I am sure that if I am not overpowered by the strength of numbers, that I can and will *soap my own beard*."[44] In this case, soaping his own beard meant rejecting country house hospitality. It could also mean baffled acceptance of others following their own peculiar wishes. Boswell ventriloquized his friend Erskine as baffled by Boswell's going his own way, suggesting, perhaps, "You have been sunk into a frigid state of listless Indifference, and gone whistling up and down the room upon a Fife, and murmuring at Intervals while you took breath 'Let him do as he likes, let him please himself, yes yes let him soap his own Beard.'"[45]

More typically, soaping one's own beard meant seeking one's own pleasure rather than avoiding someone else's offer of it. Boswell wrote of London that "there a man may indeed soap his own beard, and enjoy whatever is to be had in this transitory state of things."[46] Edinburgh taverns or even Glasgow inns offered similar delights. Erskine wrote, "The New-Tarbat chaise will arrive at Glasgow. . . . Captain Andrew's slim personage will slip out, he will enquire for James Boswell, Esq; he will be shewn into the room where he is sitting before a large fire, the evening being cold, raptures and poetry will ensue, and every man will soap his own beard . . . ," "every man" here being a reflexive quotation of the club motto to describe a tête-à-tête.[47] Even an otherwise dull country house could offer such unrestricted delight of beard soaping. Boswell wrote of a jaunt to the New Tarbet House and his friends the Erskines of Kellie,

Then with the circle once again well met,
To whom for hours of bliss I'm drown'd in debt;
I chearfully shall live away at ease,
And *soap my beard* as freely as I please.[48]

Even under his father's shadow at the family's ancestral seat of Auchinleck House in Ayrshire, in a peaceful moment when the rest of the inhabitants of the country house were asleep, he could find ease and bliss rather than confinement: "I am just now (at three o'clock in the morning) sitting over the poor pale remnant of a once glorious blazing fire, and feasting upon it, till I am all in a *Lather*."[49] Though the term was part of the Soaping Club's secret language, he used this expression to others who were not, as far as we know, club members. As he wrote to John Johnston of Grange, "You shall just soap your own beard and shall see som<e fine pro>ductions of your fr<iend>."[50]

The ideal of soaping as following one's bliss lived on into Boswell's "Grand Tour" period. On 27 February 1764, when visiting Voltaire at Ferney, Boswell wrote that "after dinner we returned to the drawing room, where (if I may revive an old phrase) *every man soaped his own beard*. Some sat snug by the fire, Some chatted, some sung, some played the guitar, some played at Shuttlecock. All was full. The Canvas was covered."[51] This version of soap your own beard seems to connect to more modern archaisms, such as "Do your own thing," "Follow your bliss," and "You do you." However, that focus on individual ego-gratification over responsibilities in family and society galled Sir David Dalrymple. Dalrymple heaped scorn on Boswell's notion that his father ought to grant him a "*ménage à part*," funding a separate household for him as well as continuing to pay his parental allowance, while he was still a bachelor. This eccentric "plan of separate family" in bachelor lodgings, Dalrymple observed, would "in a few weeks be irksome to yourself." "It will be very fine," he noted with sarcasm, "to see you soaping your own beard tête-à-tête with yourself."[52] Radical individualism, for Dalrymple, was not the road to confraternal bliss; it was rather the road to loneliness.

Beyond Boswell's own definition of the term "soaper" as one who guiltlessly seeks his own pleasure and follows his whims, there are additional reasons for the name. Samuel Johnson's *Dictionary* (1755) defined the verb "to soak" as "to drink gluttonously and intemperately," citing John Locke. Locke, in *An Essay concerning Human Understanding* (1690), had written scornfully of "a drunkard" addicted to "companions," "his cups," and "the tavern," who indulges in "the tickling of his palate with a glass of wine, or the idle chat of a soaking club."[53] The self-styled "wits" and "geniuses" of mid-eighteenth-century Britain were fond of plays on words. Boswell's youthful circle, in particular, adored puns. With this in mind, the idea that the "Soaping Club" punned on the old concept of a "Soaking Club," as a club for unrepentant drunkards, is quite plausible.

"Soaping," in those cases where it was used as an expression of "soaping someone else," was also frequently the preliminary, in the invented argot of Boswell's friends, to "shaving" them. Certainly by the nineteenth century, the cant term to "soap" someone meant "to address with smooth or flattering words; to flatter," with connotations of duping, and this turn of phrase survived in the phrase to "soft-soap" someone.[54] The mildly derogatory phrase lived on into the nineteenth century, when Samuel Wilberforce (1805–1873) acquired the name "Soapy Sam" for his smooth and persuasive loquacity, and Robert Smith Surtees created the memorable equestrian con artist Soapey Sponge in his satirical novel *Mr. Sponge's Sporting Tour* (1853). "Soaper," in the slang of Boswell's Edinburgh circle, never won inclusion in the *Oxford English Dictionary.*

The inevitable result of the frothing of the soap by the shaving brush was the lather being raised. In his fragment at Lewes in 1792, Boswell recorded this usage, describing "a steady man who was all in a lather in the act of being shaved."[55] Boswell employed the club's slang to Erskine in the aforementioned letter where he noted he was "all in a *Lather.*"[56] In their rebuke to an absent Boswell, the club's "The lather is rais'd" also puns on the angry Brother Soapers being "in a lather" at Boswell's absence.[57]

The images of soaping and lathering beards in preparation for shaving them connects soaping to the eighteenth-century meaning of the expression to "shave" someone: meaning to dupe or cheat them.[58] The lexicographer of the underworld, Francis Grose, defined "shaver" in 1785 as "a cunning shaver, a subtle fellow, one who trims close, an acute cheat," and in his entry on "cunning shaver" described such a man as "a sharp fellow, one that trims close, i.e. cheats ingeniously."[59] The *Dictionary of the Scots Language* (or *DSL*), which digitally updates the older printed *Scottish National Dictionary*, noted that in Scots, a "shavie" was "a trick, practical joke, prank, an imposition or swindle," taking the etymology from "dim[inutive] form of colloq[uial] Eng. *shave*, a swindle, *to shave*, to cheat, fleece."[60] The metaphorical connection between a barber who shaves the beards and stubble from men and a sheep shearer who shaves the fleece from rams and ewes was palpable—the shaver was a cunning fleecer of men.

The razor-sharp blades used by barbers in shaving connoted slashing sarcasm. Patrons of eighteenth-century barbers in prints are sometimes shown in anxiety or horror as the razor approaches their necks. The razor was generally acknowledged as a symbol of sarcastic wit. Boswell's original journal of his tour in 1773 quoted Samuel Johnson as saying, "One mind is a vice, and holds fast; there's a good memory. Another is a file, and he is a disputant, a controversialist. Another is a razor, and he is sarcastical."[61] This more general use of the term "razor" was employed in criticism of Boswell's pranks by a nonmember, William McQuhae, who informed Boswell that "Mrs. Reid was always fond of you but was under some restraint in your Company for fear of the razor."[62] In a verse epistle, Boswell compared the sharpened razor to its duller cousins, and to blunter and cruder instruments:

> And why for this of weapons should I vaunt,
> Which like the razor keenest sharpness want;
> When to confound and stupify the skull,
> Sufficient weight will serve, tho' ne'er so dull?[63]

He linked the arts of razor making and soaping. "He who a shaving instrument can make, / Should somewhat of the soaper's praise partake."[64] That the members were explicitly thought to ply such razors of wit was made clear by Erskine, writing to Boswell of one of his odes in December 1761: "An Ode to Tragedy by a gentleman of Scotland, and dedicated to you! . . . May G—d d—n me, as Lord Peter says, if the edge of my appetite to know what it can be about, is not as keen as the best razor ever used by a member of the Soaping-Club."[65]

Allied to this fear of the razor was the respect for its wielder, the barber. Francis Grose's *Classical Dictionary of the Vulgar Tongue* (1785) noted that "the Barber," or "that's the barber," was a "ridiculous and unmeaning phrase, in the mouths of the common people about the year 1760, signifying their approbation of any action, measure, or thing."[66] In July 1763 Boswell sent a copy of the broadside "The Barber. A New Song" to his friend John Johnston, explaining its popularity in the streets. "I send you an excellent new song called *The Barber* with which the Streets of this great City are at present loudly resounding."[67] Boswell so liked the new slang and the song that he wrote his own song of two stanzas to the same tune as that of the broadside (i.e., "Nancy Dawson") with the incipit, or first words, "Bob Temple has at Sarum been." Boswell's fascination with the barber as rogue carried into his secret life. On the night of 4 June he dressed as a "compleat blackguard" in dirty and mismatched clothes, picked up "a low brimstone" who agreed to have outdoor sex with him in a public park for sixpence, and "called [him]self a barber."[68]

Thus, whereas the argot of soaping connoted seeking one's own pleasure or humor, or at worst, self-reliance, the slang of shaving and being a barber was far more nefarious. A barber was a clever man, but unafraid to cut and slice up his enemies and even the innocent. Although the urban legends of murderous tonsorialists such as "[Lewis] Joddrel, the Barber" (1844) and Sweeney Todd (*The String of Pearls*, 1846) were only to appear eighty years later, their roots were in the 1780s.[69]

The whole elaborated cant and code of soaping, shaving, wash balls, and basin used by Boswell exhausted Sir David Dalrymple. He condemned soaping and shaving, in a Latin curse that translated to "Death to the man who first thought up that concept of 'soaping one's own beard!'" He conjectured that "some *independent* evil spirit" must have invented the mind-set and the customs. "I wish the beard and the basin and the wash-balls had gone along with him into the vast profound. I am afraid that this will be the ruin of our poor friend the Baron"—by which he meant the future "*young laird*" of Auchinleck, James Boswell—through its encouragement of "every trifling amusement."[70]

Soaping and Shaving was a young man's crime even before "punked" and "pwned" entered the twenty-first-century lexicon.[71] Young Boswell had been addicted to shaving in the late 1750s and first two years of the 1760s. In his Harvest Jaunt journal of autumn 1762, he noted, "The showman came near me, so I thought proper to shave him a little. 'This, Sir,' says I (with a most important countenance), 'was very entertaining.' 'Ay, Sir,' said he, I always give some such thing as this for the encouragement of the place that I am in.' This I very gravely acquiesced in."[72]

However, as the time neared for his departure to London in November 1762 and his sought-after (though never realized) new life as an officer in the Guards, both shaving and the mimicry that often accompanied it were to be put away as childish things. When he and his fellow Soaper Andrew Erskine met with the "ladies" and their friends George Dempster and William Nairne at an inn, he fell into his old ways. "The story of my amazing bed made the whole house shake. I questioned both the waiter and the chambermaid gravely about it, and made excellent sport. We were merry and jovial this night. I shaved a good deal." However, on this occasion, the friends were not as accepting as the Soaping Club. Indeed, "They were very angry at me, and said it was the only fault I had. But it was a great one, as they were kept in continual apprehension and never knew whether to take me in earnest or not. They owned that I shaved inimitably well; but as I had now attained to perfection in the art, they thought I might lay it aside." Boswell added, "In reality it is a bad practice, for people cannot talk to one with seriousness and openness when they imagine that they are all the time making themselves perfectly ridiculous in the eyes of him to whom they are speaking. When I get into the Guards and am in real life, I shall give it over."[73]

Boswell was relapsing into old pranks just a few days before he left Edinburgh. "I took off whole groups of characters and was very great in mimicry. Yet I resolved to lay it aside with shaving when I get into the Guards."[74] By the time he got into the carriage for London, he appears to have been tempted to soap and shave his traveling companion, "a jolly honest plain fellow." Yet as he noted, "I set out with a determined resolution against *shaving*, that is to say, playing upon people; and therefore I talked sensibly and roughly."[75]

The pranks of soaping and shaving tapped into a contemporary Scottish culture of sarcasm in which even one's best friends were apt to cut their companions down to size through ridicule and practical jokes. Readers of Tobias Smollett's novels will be familiar with these sorts of bantering pranks and put-downs. When Boswell's indiscreet *Letters between the Honourable Andrew Erskine, and James Boswell, Esq.* was published in 1763, his father reported: "The Gentlemen at Jedburgh imagined and endeavoured to persuade me that it had been somebody who put in that article in the news by way of jest for they could not suspect the letter to be genuine. At the same time they said it was a cruel jest as it was exposing you." Lord Auchinleck may not have had the heart to tell these gentlemen that in this case, young Boswell was the author of his own cruel jest on himself. However, his son's seemingly incessant "mimicry, journals and publications" grated, as they were deemed unworthy of a young gentleman trying to establish a reputation as a laird's heir and a young lawyer in training.[76]

Boswell's propensity for these jokes made him feared by friends. Mrs. Reid was presumably not the only acquaintance who was, in the words of a friend in late 1762, "always fond of you but was under some restraint in your Company for fear of the razor."[77] In a poem of September 1761, Boswell's unattainable love interest Lady Elizabeth Macfarlane is portrayed as attempting, without success, to convince her admirer, Boswell, to give up his wicked ways: "In vain shall she, or pleas'd or angry, hope, / To make me yield my razors and my soap."[78]

This sort of mockery was often done by mimicry, or "taking off" their tics of speech and manner by impersonation.[79] A critique of Samuel Foote's farce *The Minor* (1760), published in 1761, now provisionally attributed to Boswell, admitted his love of mimicry: "I must confess that I am very fond of mimicry . . . —are you a mimic, Mr. Genius?—Am I a m[i]mic? ay, and a good one too, let me tell you.—I never was with a man in my life, who had got any thing odd about him, but I could take him off in a trice:—I can, I assure you; and I often find great benefit from it."[80] His father, Lord Auchinleck, knew of his son's mimicry, and detested the practice. In a letter written to his son, just arrived in London, he counseled Boswell to cease "mimickry of others," which he denounced as "the last Shift of Witlings at least the immediat preceding step to the Gin Shop."[81] Lord Auchinleck's critique of his son's behavior among the Soapers is very close to Dalrymple's criticism. Namely, that a man devoted to mimicry and becoming a witling has "no fund for rational Entertainment," "no manly pursuit," so his "time must ly heavy on him[;] he must wish to murther it any how and think it a great point to banish reflection," probably through excessive drinking (hence the mention of the gin shop); "in Short," Lord Auchinleck warned, "the sum of his wish is to be in the State of a Beaste."[82]

In a later letter, written near the end of his son's fateful residence in London 1762–1763, Lord Auchinleck was again condemning his son's "mimickry" during his Harvest Jaunt of autumn 1762. During that expedition, he had "taken off, as you called it" several Scottish notables "at different times & places." Auchinleck warned, "To make a mock of others is not praiseworthy; besides such things are seldom concealed." Through shaving mimicry, "You create enemies to yourself and even to your friends, it being the way of the world to resent such impertinences against all who show any countenance to the person guilty of them. To all which I add that mimickry has been justly considered as the lowest and meanest kind of wit."[83] If young James wanted to become like his mentor Sir David Dalrymple, his former elocution master Thomas Sheridan, or his newest hero Samuel Johnson, or even the "London Geniuses" of the Nonsense Club, he would need to rise above bibulous mimicry and improvisational comedy. The men worthy of impressing, in Lord Auchinleck's mind, would have been those whom Boswell mentioned in his later "Memoirs" of 1791, when he wrote of feeling in the early 1760s "an uncommon desire for the company of men distinguished for talents and literature," many of them luminaries of the Scottish Enlightenment. The names he recollected thirty years on were the type of rational and polite gentlemen drawn to "the *Select Society* of Edinburgh" into which young Boswell had been enrolled as a member during the same years in which he was carousing with the Soaping Club.[84]

For a man of feeling such as Boswell, the veneer of soaping and shaving ultimately barred a merry "companion" from being a "friend" who would accept him even when he was dull and depressed—his balls of soap used up and his razor dull. As Boswell observed to his Brother Soaper, Andrew Erskine, "If I were to fall into misfortune and become void of mirth and lively conversation, . . . Dempster and Erskine would probably have their jokes, and say, 'Poor brute, he is turned an arrant idiot now.'" Their presumed ability to mock his depression or "hypochondriack" moods, as he described them, meant that he only felt confident in seeing them when he was in high spirits. "I joked and said that if I was going to be married, . . . when the wedding was over and festivity was going on, then I would send for Dempster and Erskine, and we would be jolly and hearty and laugh and talk and make sport."[85] The possibility of having trusted companions among the Soapers and their ilk was put into doubt by their constant jesting and banter, mocking themselves, each other, and the world. How could professions of friendship be believed when everything was played for a laugh? In "B——. A Song," Boswell states of Edward Colquitt, "And he swears that he is not in jest, / When he calls this same C[olquit]t his friend."[86] Ordinarily, professions of friendship did not have to be guaranteed to be genuine rather than cruel hoaxes.

The merry Brothers of the Soaping Club expected to be entertained by rattling jokes and laughter at each other's foibles. And they expected to shave each other's overgrown grandiosity and pretensions down to the stubble, even if they nicked and cut their friends in the process. Boswell acknowledged this tendency for the Soapers to laugh at their Brothers in his "B——. A Song," when he noted, "So not a bent sixpence cares he, / Whether *with* him or *at* him you laugh."[87] Would that his claim of his own uncaring had indeed been the case. It may well have been in 1760 or even 1762, but by 1763, Boswell was tired of his making himself a laughingstock. He lamented to his journal (and its first audience, his university chum John Johnston), "Another shocking fault which I have is my sacrificing almost anything to a laugh, even myself; in so much that it is possible if one of these my companions should come in this moment, I might show them as matter of jocularity the preceding three or four pages, which contain the most sincere sentiments of my heart; and at these would we laugh most immoderately." "This" propensity to protect himself by making a joke of even his serious reflections, he added, "is indeed a fault in the highest degree to be lamented and to be guarded against." So he would change this bad habit, in tandem with other resolutions for self-improvement—and for becoming more like certain role models—which he made during the "London" residence. "I am firmly resolved to amend it. I shall be most particularly wary. I shall rather err on the other, which is the safer, side."[88] From henceforth, he might accidentally be shaved, but he must under no circumstances voluntarily leap into the chair and expose his throat to such demonic barbers as Erskine and Dempster.

Even the canniest Soaper always ran the risk of being shaved by his friends, of becoming their dupe or gull. The journal for 16–17 February 1763 records a prank ("a trick upon me") in which Brother Soaper Erskine and Dempster convinced Boswell that David Hume wished for him to meet an odious little man named Fletcher, "a cousin of Dempster's," for whom Boswell had "a very great antipathy." Boswell's friends "forged a letter from David Hume to me containing some genteel compliments and recommending Fletcher to me, who was come up to go out to the East Indies." (Such letters of recommendation were common courtesies, and Boswell would avail himself of such letters during his European travels.) Boswell, "suspecting no deceit," was "vastly pleased" to be seen as a mentor to a youth, even a deplorable "being" who was "very odious." Erskine and Dempster's practical joke depended on Boswell being "much distressed at having a being so disagreeable recommended to me," but his "great . . . vanity" led to him reading the letter with "exceeding good humour." A day later, they revealed "the artifice," at which Boswell was "really vexed," so much so that his mask of good humor disappeared and he "could not dissemble [his] resentment of it." "I told them it was what I would not have done to them, and that I did not think it genteel in them to give such a miscreant as Fletcher an opportunity of laughing at me as much as themselves." He was "quite chagrined," and warned Erskine that he would from this point consider him and Dempster "not in the light of friends." He did find it "surprising" that "such a thing" as Erskine and Dempster's Fletcher prank had caused him "so much pain."[89]

Was this sort of literary prank not their triumvirate's stock in trade, though? The trio of jokers had only recently combined forces to hiss the premiere of the drama *Elvira* written by fellow Scot David Mallet, whom they demeaned as "Malloch." When their gratuitous plot to damn the play (from pure spite, since none of them had read the script in advance) failed on 19 January, the trio had spent much of 20–21 January writing a pamphlet. The "too abusive" first draft of their anonymous *Critical Strictures on the New Tragedy of Elvira* (1763) contained "less cleverness than scurrility." Even the "more genteel" version, revised "without souring our own good-humour," was still vicious and scathingly "very severe on Malloch."[90]

Yet his having been gullible enough to "be made the sport of [Dempster and Erskine] and their emissary" was "very galling," and "sadly balked" his much-beloved "vanity" in being the perpetrator of antics rather than the butt of them. He confessed to his journal (and to Johnston), "I dare say if I was to talk in this way to the gentlemen I have mentioned, they would laugh most heartily; and what is more, their ridicule would not only silence but in some measure convince me."[91]

Boswell's agony at having been deceived was such that he seriously considered breaking off his friendships with Erskine and Dempster. He eventually relented, and kept the two as friends, mainly through correspondence, but the three would never again enjoy the opportunities for easy intimacy of those days in London in 1763, and Boswell came to fear that they only were merry companions and not true friends. Although Boswell would send both his "amiable and pleasant friend" Dempster and Erskine copies of some of his published works during his final decade of life, for old times' sake, their literary triumvirate was visibly damaged by that prank, and they were never to be as close to Boswell as they were in the early 1760s.[92]

In July 1763, when his stay in London was nearly finished, and he was contemplating with horror and resignation his imminent departure to the dull duty of legal education at a Dutch university, he deprecated the "roasting" and "licking" and "lash[ing]" of his most elegantly libertine older mentor, Alexander Montgomerie, tenth Earl of Eglinton, who founded Ayrshire's first agricultural improvement society, but also spent his spare hours at the Catch Club (1761) and the Jockey Club (1750). When Boswell fled from Glasgow to London in spring 1760, Eglinton had taken the runaway Boswell up, and according to Boswell's 1791 autobiography, "introduced him into the circles of the great, the gay, and the ingenious." Boswell's comment of disgust with Eglinton's jests in 1763 employed the metaphor of knife or razor. "The same genius and temper that qualifies a man to cut others make him sensible of being cut himself. Indeed, I think the less cutting which is used in a society, so much the happier will it be."[93]

During the same months of revising his method of living, Boswell's mentor Sir David Dalrymple wrote to him on 30 May 1763 with a severe censure of his young friend's wild Edinburgh days: "Let me deal freely with you," he began, "the *soaping Club* has confounded your ideas." There was, Dalrymple observed, "no maxim more absurd and at ye same time more dull than that implyed in ye phrase *every man soap his own beard*." That kind of reckless individualism verging into deliberate eccentricity tempted men "to forget their sociable nature & embrace that ingenious system." Were the entire world, and not just its dissipated young rakes, bucks, witlings, and lairds' heirs, ever to embrace that sort of ludic selfishness, Dalrymple warned, "ye world would not be worth ye living in," since "it would be a world of man's making[,] not that well ordered & connected state which ye good Creator formed." Taking on the tone and diction of a Moderate Church of Scotland preacher explaining his sermon's structure, he told Boswell, "I will put you upon a way of seeing ye danger & absurdity of ye Maxim, write a discourse upon ye text, explain its meaning, & shew its consequences, and I will answer for it, that you shall be convinced of ye truth of what I say." Young Boswell, he averred, lacked a goal, "an object," a purpose in life beyond carousing. Until he could find "some [worthwhile] object be it what you will," he would merely "hang on, like a young laird, upon every trifling amusement." In Dalrymple's opinion, the ancient Greek counsel to always strive for excellence was "an older and wiser maxim than *every man soap his own beard*."[94]

It should be noted that Dalrymple was no puritanical enemy to sociability, nor was he what Sir John Hawkins would later be described as, "unclubable."[95] Hume noted of Dalrymple's participation in the Select Society in 1754, "Sir David's zeal entertains."[96] However, the press of business eventually took Dalrymple from face-to-face sociable life: "In a general way after he became a judge [as Lord Hailes, in 1766] Hailes dropped the clubs and the personal contacts he had built up in favour of maintaining friendship by correspondence."[97] Lord Hailes knew the value of useful life in Edinburgh society, to young lairds and other gentlemen striving for advancement, "whether as a lawyer or in any other profession . . . studious or employed in improving himself in usefull knowledge."[98] He also knew better than to let the joviality of youth, especially that of young barristers and heirs to estates, get in the way of steady application to the dry business of a legal career.

In addition, two decades after the Soaping Club lived and died, a rising tide of moral reform polemic in the 1780s and 1790s had challenged the roistering clubs. In gentle but telling mockery, the fictional "Timothy Corncraik[,] Clerk," reporting the results of a "Meeting of Citizens, Edin. Jan. 15, 1783," made the following recommendation for reform of soaking clubs: "4*thly*, THAT all private persons and clubs, who drink more than is *necessary*, should be watched with a sharp eye, and assessed in particular sums, according to their opulence or *love of liquor*; and therefore that a strict attention should be paid to several clubs in this city. . . . Also that an officer should be appointed to take notice of all *dram drinkers*."[99]

The thirteen clubs blacklisted by "Corncraik" as being "clubs, who drink more than is *necessary*" and recommended to be "assessed in particular sums, according to their opulence or *love of liquor*" were all notable rowdy clubs. Several of these clubs advertised their heavy drinking by using the names of types of alcohol (Capillaire, a flavoring concoction made of maidenhair fern and orange flower water, often strengthened with brandy); making reference to large measures of wine (Jeroboam, or Joram, a huge bottle of wine, and Borachio, in the sense of "a large leather bottle or bag [*borracha*] used in Spain for wine or other liquors" [Italian, *boraccia*]); drawing allusions to terms for drunkards (Borachio, from the Spanish *borracho*); and employing terms for heavy drafts of wine or beer ("the Blast and Quaff," perhaps "the Ocean"). A few suggested that smoking was a major pastime of the club ("the Pipe," though this may also be a drinking reference, since a pipe is also a wine measure).[100] One club seems to have been made up of famous gourmets or chefs ("Apician," after the Roman gourmet and cookbook author Apicius). Some names of clubs suggested that the conversation was stirring up fiery emotions (the "Poker"). Others suggested, as did the name of P. G. Wodehouse's Drones Club, that the conversation was less than scintillating (the "Humdrum").[101]

The customs of soaping and shaving also had an effect on Boswell's writing style, particularly in his early verses. Boswell was extremely sensitive to ridicule coming disguised as praise, since that was precisely what he and his friends did in their "soaping" and "shaving" of unsuspecting victims. When Boswell published his serious poems *An Elegy on the Death of an Amiable Young Lady. With an Epistle from Menalcas to Lycidas* (1761), he "prefixed" "*Three Critical Recommendatory Letters*," advertised on the pamphlet's title page. Boswell wrote both poems but only two of the four accompanying critical letters. The other two were by George Dempster and Brother Soaper Andrew Erskine. Both his friends sarcastically lampooned Boswell's poem by using bombastic mock-praise. Erskine's letter smirked "that the bard, of whom we have all this time been talking, discovers here and there a noble negligence of grammar and spelling," and gushed that "the epistle after the elegy seems to be much in the style of Pliny; there is nothing like it in our language. Easy and pathetic, sublime and natural . . . it is really a capital piece." Boswell's own letter repaid their soaping and shaving in the same rhetoric. His retort—"The exquisite entertainment which I have received from the perusal of the inclosed poems, is rather to be conceived than expressed . . . such a poet! and such critics!"—matched and exceeded the spoof begun by his fellow triumvirs, and he ludicrously praised himself as "a Brobdingnagian genius" and "a giant of Parnassus."[102]

When he later decided to publish his juvenile correspondence of 1761–1762 with Erskine, a salmagundi of prose and verse, Boswell was aware that the enterprise (two years' worth of the lives of obscure young men) would be mocked as self-important. The entire volume of *Letters between the Honourable Andrew Erskine, and James Boswell, Esq.* (1763), as edited, rewritten, and in parts perhaps even ghostwritten by Boswell, therefore protected itself from critics by deploying the Soaping Club manner of pre-emptively self-deflating burlesque. Boswell prefaced the *Letters* with the words, "They have made ourselves laugh; we hope they will have the same effect upon other people."[103]

Indeed, much of Boswell's tendency to encode his earliest published works of verse and prose in spoof or burlesque seems to have stemmed from a view that by depicting his efforts as a poet and letter writer as the mere bagatelles of a man who was playing it all for laughs, he could insulate himself from the inevitable criticism and ridicule of the *Monthly Review*, *Critical Review*, and other magazines. He hoped to soap and shave the reviewers with his inventions, by showing them they could not tell facts from inventions, or serious from mock-serious, or frivolous from mock-frivolous. Paradoxically, his virtually incessant Shandeism, Scriblerianism, and macaronic wordplay were what most undermined his contemporary public reputation as a published author in the years 1758–1767, before the turning point in his literary career in 1768 when he published his serious journal of a tour to Corsica and his studiously non-whimsical history of that island.

Conclusion

The history of the Soaping Club and its rhetoric of soaping and shaving is a reminder that sociability in eighteenth-century Scotland could be cruel and uncivil as well as polite and genteel. The rowdy social "High Jinks" common in Edinburgh lawyers' culture could damage social trust and cohesion as much as create it.[104] Those who sought a cheerful glass and song in Georgian Edinburgh had to take due care that they chose their merry companions carefully, lest their pride be lathered up and their pretensions shaved away. Boswell's personality was such that while he relished the pranks and plots against others, such as his literary rivals David Mallet or Oliver Goldsmith, his feudal pride resented being made the object of the jest.

Indeed, fairly early in his adult life, Boswell began to question the raucous and satirical nature of low and mixed Scottish sociability. The more months in which he lived in London and experienced a putatively more genteel form of interaction and conversation associated with London clubs, the more he disliked the biting banter, sarcasm, roughness, and high jinks of what he saw as a typical Scottish club. Even worthy but rough civic-minded groups such as the Poker Club could be subjected to his criticism.[105]

Perhaps the culture of raucous Edinburgh sociability, in which he continued to participate in the middle 1760s until the middle 1780s, permanently altered his way of thinking. He observed in an undated observation in his "Boswelliana," that "my head . . . is like a tavern, in which a club of low punch-drinkers have taken up the room that might have been filled with lords who drink Burgundy, but it is not in the landlord's power to dispossess them."[106] His resolutions to leave off soaping and shaving had achieved mixed results. The rhetoric of the Soaping Club resurged in many of the cruel and sarcastic rhymes and news squibs which Boswell published anonymously in the 1780s and 1790s. Old habits of soaping and shaving were especially visible in his pieces of flyting ridicule which mocked the abolitionists and derided Hester Piozzi, his rival in Johnsonian biography.[107] Might it also be fair to say that the method of soaping and shaving appeared covertly in the not infrequent, though subtler, bantering ad hominem attacks on certain personages in *Tour to the Hebrides* (1785) and *The Life of Samuel Johnson* (1791), even though those two works presented themselves as eminently respectable books devoted to the civilized pleasures of polite companionship and clubbability?

NOTES

1. Roger L. Emerson, "The Contexts of the Scottish Enlightenment," in *The Cambridge Companion to the Scottish Enlightenment*, ed. Alexander Broadie (Cambridge: Cambridge University Press, 2003), 9–30; John Robertson, "The Scottish Contribution to the Enlightenment," in *The Scottish Enlightenment: Essays in Reinterpretation*, ed. Paul Wood (Rochester: University of Rochester Press, 2000), 37–62; Mark Towsey, *Reading the Scottish Enlightenment: Books and Their Readers in Provincial Scotland, 1750–1820* (Leiden: Brill, 2010).

2. Jürgen Habermas, *The Structural Transformation of the Public Sphere: An Inquiry into a Category of Bourgeois Society* (1962), trans. Thomas Burger, with the assistance of Frederick Lawrence (Cambridge, MA: MIT Press, 1989), 36–37; Brian Cowan, *The Social Life of Coffee: The Emergence of the British Coffeehouse* (New Haven, CT: Yale University Press, 2005).

3. Lawrence E. Klein, "Politeness and the Interpretation of the British Eighteenth Century," *Historical Journal* 45 (2002): 869.

4. Mark Kingwell, "Politics and the Polite Society in the Scottish Enlightenment," *Historical Reflections / Réflexions Historiques* 19 (1993): 365 and 365n.3.

5. K. Tawny Paul, "A 'Polite and Commercial People'? Masculinity and Economic Violence in Scotland, 1700–60," in *Nine Centuries of Man: Manhood and Masculinities in Scottish History*, ed. Lynn Abrams and Elizabeth L. Ewan (Edinburgh: Edinburgh University Press, 2017), 203–217; alluding to Paul Langford, *A Polite and Commercial People: England, 1727–1783* (London: Oxford University Press, 1989).

6. Barton Swaim, *Scottish Men of Letters and the New Public Sphere, 1802–1834* (Lewisburg, PA: Bucknell University Press, 2009), 72–78.

7. See the prosopographical articles by Richard B. Sher, "Poker Club (*act.* 1762–1784)," in *ODNB*, https://doi:10.1093/ref:odnb/73613; John Dwyer, "Mirror Club (*act.* 1776–1787)," in *ODNB*, https://doi:10.1093/ref:odnb/73612; Roger L. Emerson, "Select Society (*act.* 1754–1764)," in *ODNB*, https://doi:10.1093/ref:odnb/73614; and Paul Wood, "Aberdeen Philosophical Society [Wise Club] (*act.* 1758–1773)," in *ODNB*, https://doi:10.1093/ref:odnb/95092.

8. [James Boswell], "Memoirs of James Boswell, Esq.," *European Magazine* 11 (May 1791): 324.

9. See, e.g., David Stevenson, *The Beggar's Benison: Sex Clubs of Enlightenment Scotland and Their Rituals* (East Linton: Tuckwell Press, 2001).

10. E. P. Thompson, "Patrician Society, Plebeian Culture," *Journal of Social History* 7 (1974): 382–405; [James Townley, possibly with contributions by David Garrick], *High Life Below Stairs. A Farce of Two Acts* (London: J. Newbery et al., 1759); [David Garrick], *Bon Ton; or, High Life Above Stairs. A Comedy. In Two Acts* (London: T. Becket, 1775); Mountstuart E. Grant Duff, *The Club, 1764–1905* (London: printed for private circulation, 1905), 42–43.

11. Corey E. Andrews, "Drinking and Thinking: Club Life and Convivial Sociability in Mid-Eighteenth-Century Edinburgh," *Social History of Alcohol and Drugs* 22 (2007): 65.

12. Ibid., 66.

13. Rosalind Carr, *Gender and Enlightenment Culture in Eighteenth-Century Scotland* (Edinburgh: Edinburgh University Press, 2014), 123–124.

14. Peter Martin, *A Life of James Boswell* (New Haven, CT: Yale University Press, 2000), 81–82.

15. Jason M. Kelly, "Riots, Revelries, and Rumor: Libertinism and Masculine Association in Enlightenment London," *Journal of British Studies* 45 (2006): 777–778.

16. Simon Dickie, *Cruelty and Laughter: Forgotten Comic Literature and the Unsentimental Eighteenth Century* (Chicago: University of Chicago Press, 2011).

17. Boswell to Andrew Erskine, 8 Dec. 1761 (MS version), in *Boswell Gen. Corr. 1757–1763*, 152; Adam Smith, *The Theory of Moral Sentiments*, ed. D. D. Raphael and A. L. Macfie, The Glasgow Edition of the Works and Correspondence of Adam Smith (1976; rev. repr., Indianapolis: Liberty Fund, 1982), 214.

18. 14 Oct. 1762, in *Boswell's London Journal, 1762–1763, Together with Journal of My Jaunt, Harvest 1762*, ed. Frederick A. Pottle (London: Heinemann, 1951), 80.

19. 4 Nov. 1762, in ibid., 104.

20. McElroy, 1952, index.

21. Clark, 131–132, citing Andrew J. Dalgleish, "Voluntary Associations and the Middle Class in Edinburgh, 1780–1820" (PhD diss., University of Edinburgh, 1992).

22. Andrews, "Drinking and Thinking," 65–66, 73.

23. Boswell to Thomas Sheridan, 25 or 26 Nov. 1761, in *Boswell Gen. Corr. 1757–1763*, 142.

24. Dudley Wright, "The Boswells and the Craft," *British Masonic Miscellany* 17 (1927): 118–125.

25. Boswell to Sir William Forbes, 8 May 1787, in *The Correspondence of James Boswell and Sir William Forbes of Pitsligo*, ed. Richard B. Sher (Edinburgh: Edinburgh University Press; New Haven, CT: Yale University Press, 2021), 85; 17 Nov. 1787, in *Boswell: The English Experiment, 1785–1789*, ed. Irma S. Lustig and Frederick A. Pottle (New York: McGraw-Hill, 1986), 154; 4 Jan. 1790, in *Boswell: The Great Biographer, 1789–1795*, ed. Marlies K. Danziger and Frank Brady (New York: McGraw-Hill, 1989), 28.

26. Boswell to Thomas Sheridan, 25 or 26 Nov. 1761, in *Boswell Gen. Corr. 1757–1763*, 141–142.

27. 6 Sept. 1769, in *Boswell in Search of a Wife, 1766–1769*, ed. Frank Brady and Frederick A. Pottle (New York: McGraw-Hill, 1956), 281.

28. Sir David Dalrymple to Boswell, 10 Oct. 1764, Boswell Papers, Yale University (Beinecke Library), Yale MSS, C 1432, published in edited form in *Boswell on the Grand Tour: Germany and Switzerland, 1764*, ed. Frederick A. Pottle (New York: McGraw-Hill, 1953), 242–246; Louis W. Potts, "Lee, Arthur," in *American National Biography* (Oxford: Oxford University Press, 1999), https://doi.org/10.1093/anb/9780198606697.article.0100505.

29. *E-B*; critical edition in *Boswell Gen. Corr. 1757–1763*.

30. [Boswell], "Memoirs of James Boswell, Esq.," 324.

31. *Boswell on the Grand Tour*, 70n3.

32. "Sketch of the Early Life of James Boswell, Written by Himself for Jean Jacques Rousseau, 5 December 1764," in *James Boswell: The Earlier Years, 1740–1769*, by Frederick A. Pottle (New York: McGraw-Hill, 1966), 1–6; Lance Bertelsen, *The Nonsense Club: Literature and Popular Culture, 1749–1764* (Oxford: Clarendon Press; New York: Oxford University Press, 1986).

33. *The Universal Scots Almanack, For the Year of Our Lord, M.DCC.LXIII* (Edinburgh: printed by Walter Ruddiman and John Richardson, 1763), 61.

34. Arthur Lee to Boswell, 10 June 1768, in *The General Correspondence of James Boswell, 1766–1769*, ed. Richard Cargill Cole, Peter S. Baker, and Rachel McClellan, with the assistance of James J. Caudle (New Haven, CT: Yale University Press, 1997), 2:67–69.

35. Dalrymple to Boswell, 10 Oct. 1764, in *Boswell on the Grand Tour*, 242–243; 25 Dec. 1776, in *Boswell in Extremes, 1776–1778*, ed. Charles McC. Weis and Frederick A. Pottle (New York: McGraw-Hill, 1970), 68–69 and 69n6.

36. Dalrymple to Boswell, 10 Oct. 1764, in *Boswell on the Grand Tour*, 242–246.

37. Francis Grose, *A Classical Dictionary of the Vulgar Tongue* (London: S. Hooper, 1785), unpaginated.

38. *OED Online*, s.v. "soaper, n."

39. Boswell to Jean Home, before Nov. 1761, in *Boswell Gen. Corr. 1757–1763*, 118.

40. "B——. A Song," in *A Collection of Original Poems. By Scotch Gentlemen* (Edinburgh: printed by A. Donaldson and J. Reid, 1762), 2:90–91.

41. Andrew Erskine to Boswell, 11 Sept. 1761 (*E-B* version), in *Boswell Gen. Corr. 1757–1763*, 91–92.

42. Boswell's self-image in this period resembles that of Ben Jonson's character Edward Knowell. Boswell's Soapers were not the only clubmen to be inspired by the proverb and Jonson's play. A "Society of Every Man in his Humour" was meeting at the Golden Key in Cock Lane in 1754. F. W. Levander, "The 'Collectanea' of the Rev. Daniel Lysons, F.R.S., F.S.A.," *Ars Quatuor Coronatorum* 29 (1916): 45.

43. William Carew Hazlitt, *English Proverbs and Proverbial Phrases Collected from the Most Authentic Sources* (London: John Russell Smith, 1869), 258; William Harrison, *Mona Miscellany: A Selection of Proverbs, Sayings, Ballads, Customs, Superstitions, and Legends, Peculiar to the Isle of Man*, 2nd ser., Publications of the Manx Society (Douglas, Isle of Man: printed for the Manx Society, 1873), 21:7.

44. 27 Sept. 1762, in *Boswell's London Journal* (1951), 63.

45. Boswell to Andrew Erskine, 9 Jan. 1762 (MS and *E-B* versions), in *Boswell Gen. Corr. 1757–1763*, 180, 182n9.

46. Boswell to Andrew Erskine, 4 May 1762 (*E-B* version), in ibid., 237.

47. Andrew Erskine to Boswell, 13 Dec. 1761 (*E-B* version), in ibid., 164–165.

48. Boswell to Andrew Erskine, 14 Sept. 1761 (*E-B* version), in ibid., 97.

49. Ibid.

50. Boswell to John Johnston, 21 Aug. 1761, in *The Correspondence of James Boswell and John Johnston of Grange*, ed. Ralph S. Walker (New York: McGraw-Hill, 1966), 12.

51. *James Boswell: The Journal of His German and Swiss Travels, 1764*, ed. Marlies K. Danziger (Edinburgh: Edinburgh University Press; New Haven, CT: Yale University Press, 2008), 317.

52. Dalrymple to Boswell, 10 Oct. 1764, in *Boswell on the Grand Tour*, 244.

53. John Locke, *An Essay concerning Human Understanding*, ed. Peter H. Nidditch (Oxford: Clarendon Press, 1975), 253.

54. *OED Online*, s.vv. "soap" ("soap, v.2. a."); "soaper" ("soaper, n.").

55. 12 Aug. 1792, in *Boswell: The Great Biographer*, 151.

56. Boswell to Erskine, 14 Sept. 1761 (*E-B* version), in *Boswell Gen. Corr. 1757–1763*, 97.

57. From the Soaping Club to Boswell, c. 1760–1762, in ibid., 39.

58. *OED Online*, s.vv. "soap," "soaper," (cited above); "shave" ("shave, v. [7.a.]."); "lather" ("lather, n. [1.d.]").

59. Grose, *Classical Dictionary of the Vulgar Tongue*.

60. The earliest example in *DSL* is 1737 from William Meston, *The Poetical Works of the Ingenious and Learned William Meston . . . : To which is Prefixed the Author's Life* (Edinburgh, 1767; 7th ed., Aberdeen: printed by J. Burnett, 1802), 108.

61. 15 Aug. 1773, in *Boswell's Journal of a Tour to the Hebrides with Samuel Johnson, LL.D., 1773*, ed. Frederick A. Pottle and Charles H. Bennett (1936; rev. repr., New York: McGraw-Hill, 1961), 20.

62. William McQuhae to Boswell, 27–30 Dec. 1762, in *Boswell Gen. Corr. 1757–1763*, 351.

63. Boswell to Erskine, 14 Sept. 1761 (*E-B* version), in ibid., 95.

64. Ibid.

65. Erskine to Boswell, 13 Dec. 1761 (*E-B* version), in *Boswell Gen. Corr. 1757–1763*, 163.

66. Grose, *Classical Dictionary of the Vulgar Tongue*.

67. Boswell to John Johnston, 9 July 1763, in *Correspondence of James Boswell and John Johnston*, 86, 86n2.

68. 4 June 1763, in *Boswell's London Journal, 1762–1763*, ed. Frederick A. Pottle (New York: McGraw-Hill, 1950), 272.

69. Matthew Kilburn, "Todd, Sweeney (*supp. fl.* 1784)," in *ODNB*, https://doi:10.1093/ref:odnb/53666; *London Chronicle*, 2 Dec. 1784.

70. Dalrymple to Boswell, 10 Oct. 1764, in *Boswell on the Grand Tour*, 242, 245.

71. *OED Online*, s.vv. "pwn, v."; "punk, v.1 [3.b.]."

72. 13 Oct. 1762, in *Boswell's London Journal* (1951), 79.

73. 5 Nov. 1762, in ibid., 105–106.

74. 11 Nov. 1762, in ibid., 110.

75. 15 Nov. 1762, in *Boswell's London Journal* (1950), 42.

76. Alexander Boswell, Lord Auchinleck to Boswell, 30 May 1763, in ibid., 338, 342.

77. McQuhae to Boswell, 27–30 Dec. 1762, in *Boswell Gen. Corr. 1757–1763*, 351.

78. Boswell to Erskine, 14 Sept. 1761 (*E-B* version), in *Boswell Gen. Corr. 1757–1763*, 97.

79. Anthony W. Lee, "Mentoring and Mimicry in Boswell's *Life of Johnson*," *Eighteenth Century* 51 (2010): 67–85.

80. [James Boswell], *Observations, Good or Bad, Stupid or Clever, Serious or Jocular, on Squire Foote's Dramatic Entertainment, intitled, The Minor. By a Genius* (London: J. Wilkie, 1761), 14–15.

81. Alexander Boswell, Lord Auchinleck to Boswell, 27 Nov. 1762, Boswell Papers, Yale MSS, C 211.

82. Ibid.

83. Alexander Boswell, Lord Auchinleck to Boswell, 30 May 1763, in *Boswell's London Journal* (1950), 338–339.

84. [Boswell], "Memoirs of James Boswell, Esq.," 324.

85. 7 July 1763, *Boswell's London Journal* (1950), 296–297.

86. "B——. A Song," 2:90–91.

87. Ibid. 2:91

88. 17 Feb. 1763, in *Boswell's London Journal* (1950), 192.

89. 16 Feb. 1763, in ibid., 190–191.

90. 20–21, 27 Jan. 1763, in ibid., 162–164, 172–173.

91. 16 Feb. 1763, in ibid., 190–191.

92. Introduction to *Boswell Gen. Corr. 1757–1763*; Terry I. Seymour, *Boswell's Books: Four Generations of Collecting and Collectors* (New Castle, DE: Oak Knoll Press, 2016), catalog items 2278, 4141, 4061, 4075, 4160 and the lists on 424–425.

93. 9 July 1763, in *Boswell's London Journal* (1950), 298; [Boswell], "Memoirs of James Boswell, Esq.," 324.

94. Sir David Dalrymple to Boswell, 30 May 1763, Boswell Papers, Yale MSS, C 1421.

95. John Wagstaff, "Hawkins, Sir John (1719–1789)," in *ODNB*, https://doi:10.1093/ref:odnb/12674; Patrick Cadell, "Dalrymple, Sir David, Third Baronet, Lord Hailes (1726–1792)," in *ODNB*, https://doi:10.1093/ref:odnb/7046; James Fieser, ed., *Early Responses to Hume's History of England* (2002; rev. ed., Bristol: Thoemmes Press, 2005), 8:129.

96. *The Letters of David Hume*, ed. J.Y.T. Greig (Oxford: Clarendon Press, 1932), 1:220.

97. Cadell, "Dalrymple."

98. Dalrymple to Boswell, 30 May 1763.

99. William Creech, *Edinburgh Fugitive Pieces* (Edinburgh: William Creech; London: T. Cadell, 1791), 57–58.

100. *OED Online*, s.v. "pipe, n. 2 [2]."

101. P. G. Wodehouse, *Tales from the Drones Club* (London: Hutchinson, 1982).

102. James Boswell, *An Elegy on the Death of an Amiable Young Lady. With an Epistle from Menalcas to Lycidas. To Which Are Prefixed, Three Critical Recommendatory Letters* (Edinburgh: Alex. Donaldson, 1761), 12–13, 14, 17.

103. *E-B*, "Advertisement" (unpaginated).

104. John Marshall Gest, "The Law and Lawyers of Sir Walter Scott," *American Law Register* 54 (1906): 294.

105. 13 July 1763, in *Boswell's London Journal* (1950), 300.

106. *Boswelliana: The Commonplace Book of James Boswell*, ed. Charles Rogers (London: Grampian Club, 1876), 224.

107. Paul Tankard, ed., *Facts and Inventions: Selections from the Journalism of James Boswell* (New Haven, CT: Yale University Press, 2014), 20.

CHAPTER 6

The "Bohemian Club"

A STUDY OF EDINBURGH'S CAPE CLUB

Rhona Brown

The Cape Club is one of Edinburgh's best known and most enduring convivial societies. This is partly because of its roll call of illustrious members, and partly because it became a "national" club, possessing branches throughout Scotland and, eventually, beyond. But the Cape Club also attracts attention because it has been seen as socially heterogeneous, democratic, and, crucially, "bohemian" in nature. Much of this construction of the Cape finds its foundations in the work of Hans Hecht. Hecht's *Songs from David Herd's Manuscripts* (1904) analyzes the Cape papers of the antiquarian, song collector, and editor David Herd (1732–1810), one of the club's founding members. It situates the Cape Club within a context of Enlightenment Edinburgh sociability, in which

> this familiar fraternity declared and manifested itself in numberless social clubs of every shade and description, which shot up in Edinburgh like mushrooms after rain. It happened one man was a member of fifteen such associations at the same time. The leaders of intellect and society met in the Poker and in the Club of the Crochallan Fencibles, which [William] Smellie had founded, and [Robert] Burns joined as a member. There was a Spendthrift Club, the members of which were not allowed to spend less than fourpence halfpenny a night; a Boar Club the joke of which consisted in the members choosing for themselves, their localities and discourse, expressions referring to the habits of pigs and boars; a Dirty Club, where no member was allowed to appear with clean linen; and so on *ad infinitum*.[1]

Hecht's description is illustrative of the many and sometimes eccentric networks of sociability that existed in Edinburgh in the mid-eighteenth century. However, in common with other traditional accounts from the nineteenth and twentieth centuries, these networks are categorized by Hecht in terms of social class. Indeed, as he later asserts, "unlike the aristocratic and therefore socially homogeneous Poker Club and Crochallan Fencibles, the Knighthood of the Cape was a thoroughly democratic institution."[2] This observation, Hecht argues, is supported by details of the Cape Club members' professions and trades: "The guild of writers sent many members, but tradesmen were in the great majority; shoemakers, tailors, glovemakers, smiths, saddlers, marble-cutters, barbers, brewers were admitted. . . . With them sat a few advocates, writers to the signet, surgeons and doctors, ship owners and naval officers; even a solitary student of divinity appears in the lists."[3] The social diversity of the Cape is such that Hecht "must wonder at the relatively peaceful intercourse of the brethren according to their motto, 'Concordia fratrum decus.'"[4]

Other commentators have followed Hecht's example. According to David Daiches, members of the Cape were "less socially and intellectually pretentious than [those of] the Select Society and the Poker Club," and were "united by a sense of community which drew no social or professional lines at all."[5] For Matthew P. McDiarmid, "It was the composition of its membership that gave the Cape its special character. It was distinctly popular and without pretension to exclusiveness."[6] The club is, in these accounts, set in direct opposition to the Poker Club (1762) and the Select Society (1754): in its diversity, the Cape avoids affectation and elitism. In Robert Chambers's *Traditions of Edinburgh* (1824; rpt. 1868), however, the Cape's social diversity is indicative of a bigger and more serious problem in Scotland's capital in the eighteenth century: "Tavern dissipation, now so rare amongst the respectable classes of the community, formerly prevailed in Edinburgh to an incredible extent, and engrossed the leisure hours of all professional men, scarcely excepting even the most stern and dignified. No rank, class, profession, indeed, formed an exception to this rule. Nothing was so common in the morning as to meet men of high rank and official dignity reeling home from a close in the High Street, where they had spent the night in drinking."[7] Whether positive or negative in inflection, the Cape Club is, for these late nineteenth- and early twentieth-century commentators, evidence of Scotland's supposed egalitarianism and meritocracy during the Enlightenment period. This idea is bolstered in Hecht's account by the very mention of Robert Burns (1759–1796), the "ploughman poet" who nevertheless scaled the heights of Edinburgh's social hierarchy when in 1787 he joined the convivial club known as the Crochallan Fencibles (1778).

Central to this Scottish egalitarian social heterogeneity is what Hecht calls the Cape's "bohemian element."[8] Because the club welcomes tradesmen, artisans, and professionals, it is "democratic." Because it counts many artists, authors, poets, actors, and musicians among its members, it is "bohemian." These descriptions of the Cape Club, many of which find their roots in the critical, cultural, and political assumptions of the early twentieth century, are cross-examined in this chapter through an exploration of the Cape's composition and "bohemian element"; its particular rituals, rules, and regulations; the role of poetry, song, and literary celebrations; and the Cape's engagement with contemporary politics.

The Cape Club as "Bohemian"

Hecht's description of the Cape as "democratic" was challenged in the mid-twentieth century by Davis D. McElroy, who rejects a categorization of Edinburgh clubs based on socio-economic factors, preferring to classify Scottish associations by their aims and objectives. While the Cape Club is designated a "convivial" organization that is "of Literary Interest," it has, following McElroy's methodology, much more in common with the "aristocratic" and "homogeneous" Poker Club than Hecht would allow: "The Cape Club . . . was very similar to the Poker Club. Both were formally constituted about the same time, and both seem to have had at one time a bond of sympathy, in the promotion of adequate defence for the Kingdom of Scotland; the household poker featured largely as a symbol in both their activities, and, like the Poker, accounts of the Cape Club have been a mainstay in many descriptions of Edinburgh's clubs."[9] While the Poker and Cape Clubs utilized, as is shown in greater detail below, the fireside poker as a key component in their rituals and initiations, more significant is their shared quasi-militaristic roots and interest in Scotland's "defence." This collective aim brings into question a construction of the Cape Club based on "bohemian" ideals.

The appropriateness of the term "bohemian" as descriptive of an eighteenth-century society is also challenged by its etymology. According to the *Oxford English Dictionary* (*OED*), the word "bohemian" was "taken from French, in which *bohême* or *bohémien* have been applied to gipsies" but was in modern English transferred to signify a "vagabond, adventurer, person of irregular life or habits." Hecht's conceptualization of the Cape Club is likely to be based on the *OED*'s further definition of the "bohemian" character: "A gipsy of society; who either cuts himself off, or is by his habits cut off, from society for which he is otherwise fitted; especially an artist, literary man, or actor, who leads a free, vagabond, or irregular life, not being particular as to the society he frequents, and despising conventionalities generally."[10] As the *OED* continues, this sense of "bohemian" was introduced only in the mid-nineteenth century by William Makepeace Thackeray, and appeared in English-language periodicals from the 1860s and 1870s. It is, therefore, a thoroughly modern term that had no meaning in eighteenth-century Scotland. Notwithstanding its inappropriateness, Hecht's (and others') use of the term is revealing: it demonstrates not only nostalgia regarding Scotland's apparently democratic Enlightenment past but also a post-Romantic conception of the "artist, literary man, or actor" who, while isolating himself from society, gains "freedom" through his rejection of "conventionalities." This view of the Cape Club is, as I argue below, quite far from the truth, as evidenced in club documents.

The Cape Club's Formation

Although there is some debate about the exact date of its foundation, it appears from club papers that the Cape was formed in Edinburgh in 1764.[11] There are at least three accounts explaining its name. According to Charles Rogers, "Part of the original purpose was to establish branches, whereby provincial and colonial clubs might, with authority derived from the parent society, 'extend the benign influence of their Order to every region under the Grand Cape (or Cope) of Heaven.'"[12] Hecht states that the name derives from "one of its insignia, a curiously shaped head-gear, encircled by a crown, on the Maydays of the club adorned by devoted members with gold and gems."[13] The story, according to Chambers, is rather more unaffected:

> A person who lived in the Calton [a region of Edinburgh outside the Old Town] was in the custom of spending an hour or two every evening with one or two city friends, and being sometimes detained till after the regular period when the Netherbow Port was shut, it occasionally happened that he either had to remain in the city all night, or was under the necessity of bribing the porter who attended the gate. This difficult *pass* . . . the Calton burgher facetiously called *doubling the Cape*; . . . "the Cape" in time became so assimilated with their very existence, that they adopted it as a title; and it was retained as such by the organised club into which, shortly after, they thought proper to form themselves.[14]

Although the truth behind the Cape's title may never be uncovered, we know more about its founding members. According to the manuscript of the first "Sederunt Book of the Knights Companions of the Cape," there were nine "original" members within a total of twenty-four elected in 1764, the first year of the Cape's official existence.[15] These "original" members were James Cockburn, the actor Thomas Lancashire, poets Michael Bruce and Alexander Clapperton, William Fleming, John Ross, Mungo Carrick, William Reid, and James Aitken, all of whom would go on to have long and distinguished associations with the Cape. The twenty-four elected in the Cape's first year were members who, according to the first "Sederunt Book," "preceed [*sic*] all others of the order but have no precedence among themselves."[16] They include David Herd, antiquarian and editor of *Ancient and Modern Scots Songs* (1769); Alexander Runciman, painter; and Gilbert Martin, Herd's printer associate. In 1768, when "Aitken suggested that they adopt fanciful knighthoods,"[17] Cockburn was known as "Sir Tree," Lancashire as "Sir Cape," Herd as "Sir Scrape," Bruce as "Sir Tomas," Clapperton as "Sir Complaints," Fleming as "Sir Fucus," Runciman as "Sir Brimstone," Ross as "Sir Heavypours," Carrick as "Sir Drycape," Donald Smith, Lord Provost, as "Sir Partan," Martin as "Sir Boot," and Aitken as "Sir Poker." This membership grew swiftly across the ensuing century: according to McElroy, "Starting with a nucleus of nine members the Cape multiplied and flourished. In the first ten years it enrolled 200 members, and by 1800 it had bestowed 650 'Knighthoods.'"[18] Members of the Cape were known as "Knights Companions" and were to be addressed only by their pseudonyms when attending the club.

The raison d'être of the Cape was relaxed but at the same time well defined, as the first manuscript "Sederunt Book" outlines: "The purpose and intention of the Society from the beginning was; after the business of the day was over to pass the evening socially with a set of select Companions in an agreeable but at the same time rational and frugal manner; for this purpose Beer or Porter were their liquors fourpence to sixpence each the extent of their usual expence Conversation and song their amusement, Gaming generally prohibited and a freedom for each to come and depart at their pleasure was always considered as essentiall to the Constitution of the Society."[19] This opening description demonstrates that the Cape was at once free and prescriptive, convivial and controlled, welcoming and selective. Although it retained its easy atmosphere, the Cape became more officially managed in 1768, some four years into its existence, when it introduced a defined administration. The chief member was the sovereign, who was assisted by a deputy sovereign, secretary, treasurer, recorder, assistant recorder, chaplain, perpetual councillors, and past sovereigns. At this point, too, insignia and membership diplomas were deemed necessary: "A mace and seal were likewise appointed to be constructed and Diplomas were ordered to be issued. Without being possess'd of one regularly signed by the Sovereign, and sealed with the seal of the order bearing their motto of Concordia Fratrum Decus no person was entitled to the privilege of a member."[20] The Cape Club met every evening from 7:00 P.M. in a tavern (or sometimes the sovereign's home), which was styled "Capehall"; it also held two "Grand Capes," sometimes known as "Turtle Feasts," per year.

Defining Cape Club Rules

As the Cape evolved, it developed its statutes and, particularly, its regulations. In the first "Sederunt Book," beginning in 1764, "gaming" is "prohibited." By 1781, as the manuscript "Analyses of the Cape Club Sederunt Book" outlines, many more activities were deemed unacceptable. Members were now not allowed to "speak or write injuriously of the Cape" or reveal "the secrets or proceedings thereof," and wrongdoers were "liable to the censure of the Cape." "Gaming" and "smoaking tobacco" were forbidden, as was taking another knight's seat. No person who was not a designated knight was allowed entry to Capehall, and members were subject to stringent rules. Bets and wagers were banned, "unless the amount of the wager be instantly tabled, and drank in the same meeting." If a knight removed newspapers from Capehall, "he shall, upon conviction, be fined in a green stoup (i.e. one shilling and fourpence) to the meeting in which he first appears, for each copy so carried off, and shall likewise be obliged to replace the same." Punishment for those who would disturb the Cape's peace is severe: "If any Knight shall disturb the harmony of the Cape, and refuse to submit to such punishment as the Sovereign shall think fit to inflict for the preservation of order, he shall be obliged to leave the company."[21] Despite or perhaps because of these regulations, Hecht states that, in the Cape, "official authority was well maintained."[22] As demonstrated below, rule breaking and punishment were taken seriously in the club, which further destabilizes its twentieth-century reputation as "bohemian" and "vagabond."

Although the Cape grew its quota from 24 original knights in 1764 to 650 in 1800, its membership procedure demonstrates an approach that was simultaneously democratic and highly selective. As the "Analyses of the Cape Club Sederunt Book" outlines,

> Every Candidate for admission to the Cape, shall give in written petition, recommended by two Knights subscribing; which petition shall lie eight days on the table, and he shall then be balloted by the Knights present in Capehall; and, without a majority of two-thirds of the ballots in his favour, he shall not be admitted. The Candidates who are rejected shall have it in their power to present one reclaiming petition *only* to the Ordinary Cape in the same terms; and, if again refuted, no further application can be received; but they shall have it in their power, if they think proper, to enter an appeal for the ensuing Grand Cape, provided it be lodged on the table at least eight days before the same is held.[23]

The prospective knight was therefore to write to the Cape a petition requesting membership. He was then required to be recommended by an existing knight and seconded by at least one other member. At this point, he would be presented at Capehall, and the assembled membership would be balloted on his application. If accepted by at least two-thirds of the vote, he would then be expected to go through an initiation ritual in which he would receive his knightly pseudonym and Cape diploma.

The Cape Club papers in the National Library of Scotland preserve many of these membership petitions and supporting documents,[24] which reveal a great deal about the ways in which the Cape was regarded by outsiders and projected itself as a sociable society. The example of the petition and consideration of one eminent member, the Edinburgh poet Robert Fergusson (1750–1774), provides an understanding of the Cape's membership protocols. "The Petition of Robt. Fergusson Writer in Edinburgh" is addressed "To the Sovereign & Knights Companions of the Cape." In it, Fergusson "humbly prays That he might have the honour of being admitted a Member of their Society." Filed with Fergusson's petition are the minutes of the Cape's consideration of this new member: here we learn that Fergusson was recommended by his friend, the composer and songwriter Cornforth Gilson (Sir Sobersides), and seconded by both David Herd and the heraldic painter, Lyon Clerk and, in time, the first secretary of the Society of Antiquaries, James Cummyng (Sir Nun and Abbess). Fergusson was presented to the Cape on 3 October 1772 and balloted and admitted a member on 10 October, on a vote of thirteen to two. At this point, he would have gone through the Cape's membership initiation. As well as the sovereign's "curious head-gear," the Cape's insignia included, according to Daniel Wilson, "two maces in the form of huge steel pokers, which formed the sword and sceptre of his majesty in Cape Hall."[25] After his petition, recommendation, and ballot, the "novice," as he was known, stood before the sovereign and was required to hold a club poker in his hand while making the Cape pledge:

> I swear devoutly by this light,
> To be a true and faithful Knight,
> With all my might,
> Both day and night,
> So help me Poker!

At the end of the pledge, the novice would kiss the poker, and then be tapped three times on the head by the sovereign using the second poker, as he did so pronouncing the letters "C.F.D.," an abbreviation of the club's motto, "Concordia fratrum decus." The novice would then tell the story of an amusing "scrape" from his past, the details of which would provide his knightly pseudonym.[26] Fergusson's was "Sir Precentor," a sobriquet probably based on an incident that took place while the poet was a student at the University of St. Andrews, where he avoided expulsion only through the intervention of his professors.[27] In common with many other petitions from the Cape's early years, Fergusson's is adorned with an apposite pen drawing, presumably by his artist friend and fellow knight Alexander Runciman, which shows an unkempt Fergusson sitting at a writing desk with book in hand.[28]

The Cape's Social Composition

While Fergusson is generally regarded as a key component of the club's inclusivity and "bohemian element," the Cape's membership list demonstrates that it shared more than an insignia with the socially "elite" Poker Club. Cape members do indeed, as Hecht suggests, come in the main from Edinburgh's trades, but they also include prominent cultural, political, and legal figures. One such member is Andrew Plummer of Middlestead (Sir Care), who served as Cape sovereign from 1771 to 1773 and was eventually elected a "Perpetual Councillor."[29]

Plummer, who would later become sheriff depute for Selkirkshire, and William Robertson of Cardrona (Sir Mirrour), would, according to McDiarmid, "have been at home in the social world that cultivated the Poker Club and the Select Society,"[30] but chose to attend the Cape. Among the watchmakers, coppersmiths, merchants, cutlers, bailies, and many legal clerks (known as writers) who made up the Cape's membership, physicians, surgeons, teachers, captains, solicitors, and advocates were also plentiful in number.

Even if Hecht's branding the Cape as "bohemian" is deemed an inappropriate modern intrusion, many creative individuals were indeed members. Herd and Fergusson were among the Cape's literary membership, alongside Thomas Mercer (Sir Forgetfull), Alexander Clapperton, and Michael Bruce, three unjustly neglected poets. Herd's printers, Gilbert Martin, and John Wotherspoon (Sir Bolt), were also members. The Cape had, moreover, a strong musical constituent. Beside Fergusson's composer and songwriter friend Cornforth Gilson were James Balfour (Sir Tumult) and John Smeaton (Sir Stair), both renowned singers; according to Hecht, Balfour's "skill in rendering Scots songs must have been incomparable."[31] Stephen Clark (Sir Oldwife) was a collaborator of James Johnson and Robert Burns on *The Scots Musical Museum* (1797–1803) song collection, but he was not regarded as a model knight: at the eleventh Grand Cape, held on 9 February 1771, Clark was "expelled and Extruded this Society in all time coming having forfeited all manner of tittle . . . by not complying with the Laws."[32] J.G.C. Schetky (Sir Handle), the German composer working in Edinburgh, was a Cape knight as well as being a member of the Masonic Lodge Canongate Kilwinning No. 2, where he met Burns in 1787.[33] Actors and dramatic men were well represented, with the actor Thomas Lancashire a founding member, as well as his fellow player William Woods and Stephen Kemble, manager of Edinburgh's Theatre Royal. Painters were in plentiful supply, including such celebrated artists as Alexander Runciman, John Brown (Sir Crassus), Jacob More (Sir Byre), Alexander Nasmyth (Sir Thumb), and Henry Raeburn (Sir Discovery) all enjoying membership in the last decades of the eighteenth century.

It is clear that these knights played an important role in club proceedings, with the musical and literary members coming particularly to the fore during special meetings held in memory of deceased knights. One such event took place on 17 June 1773, shortly after the death of a long-standing member, a second knight by the name of James Cockburn (Sir Speak). The first "Sederunt Book" contains this account: "The meeting having been called by the Sovereign That the Knights might have a joint Opportunity of paying a due respect to the memory of the deceased worthy Knight of Speak; A Solemn Dirge Composed for the Occasion by Sir Precentor and sett to Music by Sir Sobersides, was performed by Sir Sobersides and Sir Fender and Sir Precentor—After which the Evening concluded with drinking to the Memory of all the deceast Knights respectively—The Hall being fitted up suitable to the Occasion."[34] This "Dirge" was written and performed by Cornforth Gilson and Robert Fergusson, with the assistance of William Crawford (Sir Fender).

The Cape Club and Literature

In addition to unique events such as private memorials and commemorations, the Cape Club had a special interest in literature that made it, in McElroy's words, "the most poetically inclined club of its day."[35] Among the Cape papers in Edinburgh University Library is "The Capeiad in Three Cantos, Together with Songs of the Cape, being a Complete History in Verse of the Knights Companions of that Illustrious Order, C.F.D."[36] The manuscript is damaged and incomplete, but it is, according to Corey J. Andrews, a good poetic "chronicle of the Cape Club's history and procedures."[37] Although James Aitken is generally considered to be the main author of "The Capeiad," the manuscript contains contributions by others, including "An Excellent New Song to the Tune of Hooly & fairly" by Alexander Clapperton; "An Excellent New Song Entitled the Carter" by Duncan McQueen (Sir Lad); "A Festival Song" by William Woods; "A New Song to the Tune of Push about the Jorum" by Alexander Runciman; the anonymous "Ways and Means" and "Another Capeiad." Robert Fergusson provided many songs for the Cape, including "The Progress of Knighthood," "Cape Song," "A Mournful Ditty from the Knight of Complaints," "Summons," and "On James Cumming," the last of which is dated 1773 and transcribed in the hand of David Herd.[38] Most of these are good-natured drinking songs that make humorous reference to various individual knights' "scrapes" and were presumably intended for community singing, with their recognizable tunes and simple, memorable choruses. Fergusson's songs for the Cape are, as might be expected, in a class of their own. While they do not shy away from celebrating and participating in the club's conviviality, their tone is not straightforward, with Fergusson gleefully (but also seriously and sometimes moralistically) exposing drunken excess.[39]

The Knights of the Cape were also engaged in commemorating their chosen literary heroes: playwright William Shakespeare and James Thomson, author of *The Seasons*. As noted above, the club held two "Grand Capes" per year. The minutes of 2 September 1769 record the resolution that "a Festival in Honour of Shakespeare shall be held in the house where the Knights presently meet on Wednesday next," and the sixth Grand Cape, held at "Austin's" on 6 September 1769, fulfilled this purpose.[40] More fulsome praise and memorialization was given to Thomson. The minutes of 22 September 1769 note details of the knights' Thomson Festival:

> This night being the anniversary of the birth of James Thomson, at an ordinary Cape dedicated to the honour of that Bard a New piece of painting by Sir Kirk exhibiting the Insignia of the Order was hung up and the Hall being

> decorated with laurel, severall songs of Thomson's Composition were performed and the memory of this favourite Poet, the Honour of his Country the Bard of Liberty and Friend of man was drunk round in a Bumper.—It was proposed that on the next return of this anniversary an Ode should be prepared and set to music and a Generall Festivall called for that purpose, as at this meeting there was no other than an ordinary Cape at which there were present the following Members.[41]

This tentative start, which included the dedication of a painting by David Scott (Sir Kirk), toasts, and the singing of Thomson's songs, was followed—as planned—by a more concerted effort in 1770. The tenth Grand Cape of 22 September 1770 was held in honor of Thomson and provides more than a few hints of the ritual that would culminate in the modern Burns Supper:

> In celebrating of this day the hall was Illuminated and Emblematically ornamented with flowers representing the Seasons &c—An Ode wrote for the Occasion by Sir Forgetfull set to music and conducted by Sir Stair was performed by the musical Gentlemen of the Society. After which an Extempore oration pointing out the Capital merits of the Bard was delivered by Sir Crassus.—To this succeeded all the Songs in Thomson's works by way of Garland adapted to Scottish Music by Sir Stair and sung by him and the other respective musical Knights.—And in every demonstration of the art felt Joy Rational Happiness and decent Harmony characteristic of the Bard. The Evening entertainment concluded with a Glass to the particular memorys of Departed Bards, Great Genius's and Good Men.[42]

In this celebration, the musical and literary knights take center stage. While Thomas Mercer (Sir Forgetfull) provided an ode to Thomson's memory, John Smeaton (Sir Stair) gave a musical tribute, and John Brown (Sir Crassus) offered an "oration" on Thomson's achievements in a performance not unlike that of the Burns Supper's "Immortal Memory." This celebration, which was not without controversy in Edinburgh, as various groups vied for ownership of Thomson's memory and the right to commemorate it, was reprised every ten years.[43]

As well as commemoration of deceased authors, the Cape also encouraged new literary developments, particularly through their many links with the theater. As outlined above, alongside Theatre Royal manager Stephen Kemble and actor William Woods was Thomas Lancashire, recently retired from the stage, who, after his death in 1772, was memorialized by Fergusson in his "On the Death of Mr. Thomas Lancashire, Comedian."[44] According to James Grant, "Lancashire the comedian, leaving the stage, seems to have eked out a meagre subsistence by opening in the Canongate a tavern, where he was kindly patronized by the knights of the Cape, and they subsequently paid him visits at 'Comedy Hut, New

Edinburgh,' which he opened somewhere beyond the bank of the North Loch."[45] Grant's account is echoed by Cape Club papers, where it is stated that the ninth Grand Cape of 9 June 1770 was held "in Thomas Lancashire's new house (Comedy Hutt)."[46] The minutes also demonstrate that the knights had a key role in the foundation of Lancashire's establishment. On 29 May 1769 it is recorded that "this night the Sovereign attended by severall Knights laid the first stone of the Comedy Hutt at the end of Princes Street belonging to Sir Cape."[47] Although the club papers offer no further information on the retired actor's new business, they do specify its location and demonstrate the Cape's financial support of its founding member.

This support was also extended to Fergusson during his final illness and incarceration in Edinburgh's asylum for pauper lunatics. The minutes of 2 July 1774 (some two months before Fergusson's death at the age of twenty-four) record details of the club's commitment to its members when in peril: "It was agreed unanimously by the Grand Cape that the remainder of the Fines of the Absentees from this meeting after paying what Extraordinary Charges may attend the same shall be applied for the benefit and assistance of a Young Gentleman a member of the Cape who has been a considerable time past in distress.— And the Gentlemen present in the Grand Cape made a contribution themselves for the same purpose."[48] The Cape was certainly a convivial club and a literary network, but this evidence shows that it was also a support network.

Discipline in the Cape Club

The minutes' mention of "the Fines of the Absentees" illustrates something of the Cape's approach to club discipline. As detailed above, the process of entering the Cape was ritualistic and prolonged, revealing the club's selectivity and prestige. In addition, discipline and order were serious concerns, and, as Hecht outlines, "punishment followed on the heels of trespassers, and the peacebreakers were obliged to apologise."[49] We have already seen how Stephen Clark, the musician and collaborator of Burns and Johnson on *The Scots Musical Museum*, was expelled from the Cape for breaking club rules and regulations. He was certainly not alone. Expulsion came in response to many actions: attending a meeting without one's membership diploma, taking another knight's seat, absenteeism, and breach of the peace would cause a knight to be reprimanded or, depending on the severity of the violation, expelled. There are many examples of such punishments in Cape Club papers. In the minutes for the Grand Cape of 9 February 1771, it is recorded that six knights are to be "extruded and Expelled," while strategies were developed for punishing members' wrongdoings, particularly the unauthorized lifting of Cape newspapers. The thief would "on conviction be fined in a Green Mugg to the meeting in which he first appears after such Conviction for each copy carried off and he shall likewise be obliged to produce the said paper or papers or another copy of them."[50]

At the next Grand Cape, dated 14 May 1771, it is minuted that Sir Speak (James Cockburn) had raised a complaint "against the Knights coming to the Cape when it was late keeping up the people of the house and rendering themselves and others unfitt for attending their lawful business next day."[51] The minutes of 16 March 1772 demonstrate club rules in action when Sir Bile (William Wilson) "abstracted and carried off a book belonging to the Cape containing the Caledonian Mercury for the year 1771" and was "found liable in the sum of £1.8 as the price of said paper and Binding and the further sum of £10 sterling as the Penalty incurred."[52] This hefty fine demonstrates the seriousness with which the Cape administration treated these apparently petty thefts.

Disorder among the knights themselves was not unknown. The minutes of a meeting of council held on 3 March 1775 record details of an altercation between Sir Ship (John Bonnar) and Sir Toe (Thomas Hill), focusing particularly on the vicious behavior of the latter knight: "In being so brutish as to call his friends one after another by the opprobrious name of Lyars without provocation or foundation. In spitting in Sir Ship's face and afterwards stripping to fight him though he Sir Toe was the offending party in raising Riot and Disorder in this peaceful and happy Society and in perpetrating all these Crimes in full & sober Cape and in defiance and high contempt of every member thereof."[53] Although this crime seems infinitely more serious than stealing a book or newspaper, the minutes confirm that Toe was suspended and given an opportunity to apologize. It seems that Toe did not take this chance, for his name appears only once again in Cape minutes, as one of twelve "Knights in Arrears for Diplomas delivered & not yet paid to the Treasurer."[54] Altercations such as this appear to be personal and are rare in the Cape's minute books. Only in the minutes of 16 February 1780 does the worry about indiscipline take a more general turn, as the sovereign, Sir Crassus (John Brown), notes: "This night it was recorded with regret that the ancient virgin slate of the Cape was of late much debauched and it was agreed to restore her maiden state."[55] The 1781 "Analyses of the Cape Club Sederunt Book" therefore details "forfeitures," where the various crimes and misdemeanors of the knights would be recorded for eternity.

The Cape Club and Politics

Although the Cape is not generally seen by commentators as a club with political motivations, it did involve its members in key political decisions and events. This was not, however, an original aim when the Cape Club was officially inaugurated in 1764: despite McElroy's account of the club's apparent interest in the "defence" of Scotland at its beginning, there is no record of direct political engagement until the late 1770s, when Britain was embroiled in conflict with both

America and France. In the minutes of a meeting of 15 January 1778, the following resolution is recorded:

> The Sovereign represented to the Council & other Knights occasionally present that at this time when almost all other Societys [*sic*] of any denomination were emulous for assisting his Majesty by contributing towards the raising of Troops & it would be expected that Knights of the Cape as a Body should likewise give some Testimony of their Loyalty by a voluntary Subscription. It was the opinion of the Meeting that the motion should be adopted; providing upon trial the Contribution should amount to one hundred guineas.—But that if the spirit of the Cape was unequal to that sum it ought to be dropt.[56]

The "spirit of the Cape" was indeed in agreement, as the minutes of the next meeting, dated 9 February, record that they have paid "one hundred Guineas" toward raising "the Royal Edinburgh Volunteers" and have given a transcription of the club's subscription paper.[57]

The Cape's interest in politics appears to have increased after this point, perhaps through a desire to be "emulous" of other societies, and certainly due to the prominence of Britain's troops on the stage of world conflict. The Gordon Riots, sometimes regarded as a turning point in British history and as a domestic disturbance reflecting international quarrels, was another political moment with which the knights engaged. The minutes of 19 June 1780, recorded just over a fortnight after the first riots in London, give a poetic but unequivocal account of the members' political response to this upheaval: "In spite of any man who was educated in France, in spite of any man, who in the end of the eighteenth century, could pretend to be either a John Knox or a Pope man; without deviating from our principles, the honest, unaffected, and unhypocritical constitution of the Cape, wish suspension literal to Lord George Gordon and his accursed London Mob. . . . We have drunk the King, General Clinton, Admiral Arbuthnot, Sir George Bridges Rodney, all the men, who had lived or died in their country's cause."[58] This account, which shows the Cape to be inclusive and "unhypocritical" in its principles, conflates domestic and international politics by at once condemning the anti-Roman Catholic behavior of Lord Gordon and his riotous supporters and drinking toasts to various well-known players in the action of the British army and navy in the American War of Independence.

This patriotic toast is preceded in the minutes of 13 October 1778 with the following poem:

> I come in search of one who now appears,
> Who us'd to laugh at all our foolish fears,
> Surprise, I mean who in's Life will never yield,
> While we've a British Hero for the Field,
> Cornwallis bravely fought and boldly won

> Surprise he knew it ere the Gazette come
> Cornwallis then shall have our loud huzza
> And Britons still shall have America
> And Sir Surprise shall have his huzza.[59]

Sir Surprise is John Wood, one of two knights of the same name: they are recorded in the membership list, one without an occupation and the other as a "Surveyor."[60] Whichever he was, Surprise clearly had an intense interest in Britain's war effort abroad, and was in a position to relay the news of Cornwallis's victory to his fellow knights before the newspapers arrived at Capehall. Sir Surprise later reappears in Cape Club papers when he presents an apparently curious motion, dated 4 April 1791, for a tax on domestic dogs: "That it is the opinion of this respectable and Honourable Society that a Tax upon Dogs at this time would be highly proper beneficial and expedient for this Great Empire and that they hereby resolve to petition Parliament directly for the purpose." While this may seem an odd request from someone so engaged with the American Wars of Independence, it is soon clear that conflict is at the heart of this "domestic" motion:

> It cannot be doubted that on the Event of a War supplies will be wanted and must be granted to defray the extraordinary Expences attending it and what mode of Taxation can be fallen upon more proper or less burdensome to the subject than this one proposed.
>
> When the infinite number of Dogs which swarm in these Realms are considered what Taxation could be so productive and so little felt or what so beneficial for the interest of Society in general, the number of these useless animals are very great and the hurt they occasionally turns [*sic*] to the Public is as great.[61]

The minutes record the promise that this motion will be "fully discussed verbatim," but no other allusion to Surprise's motion has, as yet, been found in Cape papers. What the motion does demonstrate, however, is the Cape Club's increasing awareness of its public and political role as a "respectable and Honourable Society."

Conclusion

If traditional accounts of the Cape Club by commentators such as Hecht and Rogers make much of its "bohemian" and literary nature, they tell only a fraction of the club's story. While there were indeed many literary, musical, dramatic, and artistic knights, the club poetry collected in "The Capeiad" was not the preserve of Fergusson, Mercer, and Clapperton, but rather was the work of all knights who were wont to try their hand at poetry. While the social composition of the club was indeed diverse, it was a selective society in which entry was a ritualistic, protracted affair that required the acquaintance and support of existing knights. While it may have been a convivial society, it nevertheless provided an important literary, social, and support network for young poets such as Fergusson. Most importantly, to label the Cape a "bohemian" club is to do it a disservice; its members were not "cut off from society" or "despising [of] convention." From its convivial beginnings in 1764, the Cape grew increasingly conscious of itself and its role in society, becoming more and more politically active and aware as conflict in Britain and abroad intensified. While the Cape was undoubtedly a genial, supportive, and jocular club, it was also, as its motto "Concordia fratrum decus" emphasizes, greatly concerned with "the preservation of order" within Capehall, Edinburgh, Britain, and the world.[62]

NOTES

1. Hans Hecht, ed., *Songs from David Herd's Manuscripts* (Edinburgh: W. J. Hay, 1904), 34.
2. Ibid., 37–38.
3. Ibid., 38.
4. Ibid., 37. The Cape's motto can be loosely translated as "The agreement of honor among brothers."
5. David Daiches, *Robert Fergusson* (Edinburgh: Scottish Academic Press, 1982), 33–34.
6. *The Poems of Robert Fergusson*, ed. Matthew P. McDiarmid (Edinburgh: William Blackwood and Sons, 1956), 1:53.
7. Robert Chambers, *Traditions of Edinburgh* (1824, rev. 1868; repr., Edinburgh: Chambers, 1996), 138.
8. Hecht, *Herd's Manuscripts*, 38.
9. McElroy, 1952, 2:494.
10. *OED*, s.v. "bohemian."
11. For descriptions of the Cape Club, see Hecht, *Herd's Manuscripts*, 35–50; McElroy, 1969, 145–149; Daniel Wilson, *Memorials of Edinburgh in the Olden Time* (Edinburgh: Hugh Paton, 1848), 2:16–18; Charles Rogers, *Social Life in Scotland from Early to Recent Times* (Edinburgh: William Paterson, 1886), 2:378–382; Chambers, *Traditions of Edinburgh*, 149; Corey E. Andrews, *Literary Nationalism in Eighteenth-Century Scottish Club Poetry* (Lewiston, NY: Edwin Mellen Press, 2004), 115–215; and various articles published in *Book of the Old Edinburgh Club* between 1908 and 1920.
12. Rogers, *Social Life*, 2:378.
13. Hecht, *Herd's Manuscripts*, 36.
14. Chambers, *Traditions of Edinburgh*, 165.
15. Sederunt Book of the Knights Companions of the Cape, NLS, MS 2004:12.
16. Ibid., 9.
17. McElroy, 1969, 145.
18. Ibid.
19. Analyses of the Cape Club Sederunt Book, &c., 1781, NLS, MS 2004:3.
20. Sederunt Book, MS 2004:5.
21. Sederunt Book, MS 2000.
22. Hecht, *Herd's Manuscripts*, 37.
23. Sederunt Book, MS 2000.
24. Cape Club Petitions, vol. 1, NLS, MS 2041.
25. Wilson, *Memorials of Edinburgh*, 2:22.
26. Ibid.; McElroy, 1969, 147.
27. For a fuller account of this "scrape" and an analysis of Fergusson's membership of and poetry for the Cape Club, see Rhona Brown, "'The Cape still flourishes anon': A New Club Poem by Robert Fergusson," *Review of Scottish Culture* 24 (2012): 110–125.

28. For all Cape Club petitions, see NLS, MSS 2041 and 2042.
29. See NLS, MS 2004.
30. *Poems of Robert Fergusson*, 1:53.
31. Hecht, *Herd's Manuscripts*, 38.
32. NLS, MS 2004:59
33. Both Schetky and Burns appear in William Stewart Watson's painting of the imaginary gathering in *The Inauguration of Robert Burns as Poet Laureate of the Lodge* (1846), National Galleries Scotland, PG 946, used for the front cover of this volume. Burns refers to his meeting with Schetky in a letter to Agnes McLehose of 24 January 1788, where he describes socializing with "Mr Schetki, the musician," and the latter's "fine" setting of the song "Clarinda, Mistress of my Soul." *The Letters of Robert Burns*, ed. J. De Lancey Ferguson, 2nd ed., rev. G. Ross Roy (Oxford: Clarendon Press, 1985), 1:218.
34. NLS, MS 2004:95.
35. McElroy, 1969, 148.
36. "The Capeiad in Three Cantos, Together with Songs of the Cape, being a Complete History in Verse of the Knights Companions of that Illustrious Order, C.F.D.," EUL, MS La. 464.
37. Andrews, *Literary Nationalism*, 117. Andrews offers an analysis of "The Capeiad" in the chapter titled "Robert Fergusson, Conviviality, and the Cape Club."
38. See in *Poems of Robert Fergusson*, "The Progress of Knighthood," 2:170; "Cape Song," 2:69; "A Mournful Ditty from the Knight of Complaints," 2:168; Summons," 2:167–168; and "On James Cumming," 2:172–173. "The Progress of Knighthood" is bound in EUL, MS La. 464; "Cape Song" is bound in EUL, MS La.II. 334.
39. A full analysis of Fergusson's songs for the Cape Club can be found in Brown, "'The Cape still flourishes anon'"; it also offers a transcription of, and commentary on, a newly discovered Cape Club poem by Fergusson, which may be consulted at NLS, Acc. 13190.
40. NLS, MS 2004:37, 9.
41. Ibid., 39.
42. Ibid., 51–52.
43. For further analysis of the Cape Club's celebration of James Thomson, see Rhona Brown and Gerard Carruthers, "Commemorating James Thomson, *The Seasons* in Scotland, and Scots Poetry," *Studies in the Literary Imagination* 46 (2013): 71–89.
44. *Poems of Robert Fergusson*, 2:50.
45. James Grant, *Cassell's Old and New Edinburgh: Its History, Its People, and Its Places* (London: Cassell, Petter, Galphin, [1882]), 2:230.
46. NLS, MS 2004:9.
47. Ibid., 34.
48. Ibid., 114–115.
49. Hecht, *Herd's Manuscripts*, 37.
50. NLS, MS 2004:60.
51. Ibid., 76.
52. Ibid.
53. Ibid., 121.
54. Ibid., 126.
55. NLS, MS 2006.
56. NLS, MS 2004:159–160.
57. Ibid., 163–166.
58. NLS, MS 2006, 19 June 1780.
59. Ibid., 13 Oct. 1778.
60. See NLS, MS 2002.
61. NLS, MS 2041, 405–406.
62. Analyses of the Cape Club Sederunt Book, 1781, NLS, MS 2009.

CHAPTER 7

"Caledonia's Bard, Brother Burns"

ROBERT BURNS AND SCOTTISH FREEMASONRY

Corey E. Andrews

Recent scholarship on Freemasonry has underscored the Scottish origins of the association, although, as Mark C. Wallace notes, "the majority of British Masonic histories are written from English perspectives, and as such are largely unrepresentative of eighteenth-century Scottish Freemasonry and its distinctive legacy."[1] David Stevenson has persuasively argued for the distinctively Scottish foundations of modern Freemasonry, documenting the transformation of lodges from artisanal organizations for stonemasons into social associations for "speculative" and "operative" members alike.[2] The continuing presence of operatives was a distinctive feature of Scottish lodges throughout the eighteenth century.[3] In addition, Masonic association not only provided members with an opportunity for fraternal association but also offered mystical justification of Masonry as a superior craft, the ne plus ultra of architecture and manual labor.

In this regard, Scottish Freemasonry continues to be strongly linked with the poet Robert Burns, who was both laborer and mason. Some have seen the unqualified success of Burns's Edinburgh edition of *Poems, Chiefly in the Scottish Dialect* (1787) as the result of direct intervention by fellow masons within Edinburgh's polite society.[4] Many notable masons such as John Clerk (Lord Eldin), Henry Erskine, and Henry Mackenzie literally and figuratively opened their doors to Burns at the time.[5] Of fellow masons, Burns was especially indebted to James Cunningham, fourteenth Earl of Glencairn; J. De Lancey Ferguson notes that Burns often stated that "he owed everything to Glencairn—that the Earl, as he put it, took him by the hand and led him up to fame."[6] Another Masonic connection, Dugald Stewart, introduced the poet to fellow mason Lord Daer, with whom Burns "got on famously."[7]

Contemporary critics have argued for an array of benefits that the poet derived from his association with Freemasonry. Nigel Leask has stated that "egalitarian participation in the 'mystic rites' of Masonry offered Burns a unique opportunity for social mobility . . . as well as a safety net in the eventuality of financial ruin."[8] Robert Crawford has argued that Burns's "career was certainly thoroughly assisted by Masonic networks."[9] However, a closer analysis of Burns's experiences with Freemasonry reveals that the association did not provide him with either lasting sociability or material aid. Although Burns remained a mason throughout his life, the level of his participation changed dramatically over time.[10] In fact, there was a steep decline in Burns's participation after 1792. Burns initially wrote verse for his fellow masons, an activity that he performed for other clubs and groups to which he also belonged, but his enthusiasm for Masonic verse greatly diminished in the early 1790s.

Among other things, one of the reasons for his growing disregard may have been that Freemasonry did not unequivocally promote the ideals of classless brotherhood espoused in so much of Burns's writing. In the Edinburgh lodges, Burns began to socialize with different types of masons than he had previously encountered in the Tarbolton lodges, where he first became a freemason. As Stevenson observes, "By the end of the seventeenth century some lodges were dominated by gentlemen, non-operative members of high social status."[11] These speculative members tried to exert control over the meaning of Freemasonry: "One of the central points of freemasonry is supposed to be that it over-rides differences of social status, yet this definition is based on a snobbish assumption that it is only when the gentry take over the movement that it becomes freemasonry."[12] This chapter looks more closely at the reasons why the poet withdrew from the association during the 1790s, ending with speculation about his motivation and outlook at the time. Although freemasons would claim "brother Burns" to be "Caledonia's Bard," the poet actively withdrew from their support and endorsement.[13]

Burns in the Tarbolton Lodges: St. David and St. James

Burns's involvement with Freemasonry began in 1781, when he was entered as an apprentice in Lodge St. David (Tarbolton) Mauchline No. 174 at the age of twenty-two.[14] Prior to his initiation, there were two Tarbolton lodges (St. David and St. James), and both were in a state of disarray and dysfunction.[15] Little direct evidence of the lodges' reasons for dissension is noted in the minute books from the 1770s, which are largely a record only of meeting dates and member admissions.[16] The first lodge in Tarbolton was Lodge Mother Kilwinning, and dissatisfaction within its ranks had led to the application to the Grand Lodge of Scotland for a new Tarbolton lodge, to be named St. David. According to John Weir, the source of the dissenters' ire lay in the "Scottish passion for schism," which centered on the vying influences of the Grand Lodge of Scotland and Lodge Mother Kilwinning.[17]

The Grand Lodge accepted the group's request to form Lodge St. David, which occurred on 26 February 1773. In a bid for equal recognition, Lodge Mother Kilwinning applied for a charter to the Grand Lodge, which was granted on 24 June 1774. The lodge was then renamed Lodge Tarbolton (Kilwinning) St. James. However, it soon became apparent that Tarbolton was simply not large enough to sustain two Masonic lodges. Lodges relied on dues and assessed fees to members who missed meetings, both of which greatly contributed to the association's overall survival. Robert Lawrence, the historian of Lodge St. David Tarbolton (Mauchline), notes that the Tarbolton masons eventually decided to "form a union of the two Lodges . . . on 25th June 1781, under the name and charter of St. David Tarbolton No.174 since this Lodge held the oldest charter from Grand Lodge."[18]

When Burns was initiated on 4 July 1781, it was only nine days after the lodges had united under the name St. David Tarbolton, and he became a Master Mason (first degree, the most basic) in three months (on 1 October 1781).[19] However, the unified Lodge St. David was dissolved again in June 1782, leading to the restitution of Lodge St. James Tarbolton.[20] St. James became the stronger organization, due (in Weir's account) to the activity of the most prominent seceder, Robert Burns. He notes that "the only person to be initiated and later passed and raised in the united lodge, [Burns] associated himself with the reformed St. James [and] . . . proved himself not only a most enthusiastic freemason but a most competent Depute Master."[21]

Robert Chambers, one of Burns's best-known nineteenth-century editors, attributes the poet's speedy rise from apprentice to Depute Master to his "sociable nature . . . wit and intelligence."[22] The Depute Master was a de facto leadership position, and Burns was re-elected to the post in his lodge from 1786 to 1788.[23] There is little doubt that Burns was a devoted mason at this time of his life. As Depute Master, Burns was the senior administrator below the Worshipful Master, who was, in this case, Sir John Whitefoord.[24] In regard to the Grand Lodge of Scotland, Albert G. Mackey claims that the post of Depute Grand Master was designed "to relieve a nobleman, who was Grand Master, from troublesome details of office."[25] Burns quickly found that there were also many "troublesome details" in the lodge for the Depute Master to relieve.

The first occurred before Burns even assumed the office of Depute Master. In November 1782 (only a year after he had been made a Master Mason), he was enlisted to write a letter appealing for the aid of the Worshipful Master Whitefoord. One of Burns's earliest extant letters, this missive has not survived in manuscript, although it is available in facsimile in Sir Alfred Law's Honresfield Collection.[26] In his letter to the lodge's Worshipful Master, Burns begins with due deference to rank, stating in first-person plural that "as we have the honor of having you for Master of our Lodge, we hope you will excuse this freedom as you are the proper person to whom we ought to apply."[27] Based on the formality of this appeal, it appears that Burns and his fellow masons may have not yet associated with Whitefoord in the lodge.

As the letter continues, however, one can sense Burns's characteristic blend of brio and formal deference as he asserts that "we look on our Mason Lodge to be a serious matter, both with respect to the character of Masonry itself and, likewise, as it is a charitable society."[28] This latter aspect—the lodge's promise of charity and financial aid—was of critical importance to Burns and his brother masons in the Tarbolton lodge. The fact that it was lacking makes the letter to Whitefoord the earliest challenge that Burns made to Freemasonry when its practice did not concur with its theory. In fact, this problem was not isolated to Tarbolton; one of the chief deficiencies of Freemasonry at this time was the frequent absentee status of the lodges' Grand Masters. The Grand Lodge of Scotland states that "in the eighteenth century it was common for a local dignitary to be made the Master of a Lodge and frequently he was a mere figurehead who may or may not have attended the Lodge."[29]

This appears to have been the case for Lodge St. James, for Burns informs the absent Whitefoord that the lodge has fallen on hard times, chiefly financial: "We are sorry to observe that our lodge's affairs with respect to its finances have for a good while been in a wretched situation."[30] To clarify this "wretched situation," Burns goes on to describe "a considerable sum in bills which lye by without being paid or put in execution" and complains that "many of our members never mind their yearly dues or anything else belonging to the lodge."[31] Burns clearly expects that his brother masons (including Whitefoord) must be responsible for upholding the association's ideals, especially those concerning the fiduciary element of membership. The letter exhorts its absent Worshipful Master to return to the lodge and restore accountability among its errant members.

However, even such an overt appeal to the paternalistic hierarchy built into Freemasonry sounds a skeptical note: the lodge is in such a sorry state that "since our separation from St. David's, we are not sure even of our existenc [*sic*] as as [*sic*] a Lodge."[32] Burns concedes to Master Whitefoord that although these issues may "interest you no farther than a benevolent heart is interested in the welfare of its fellow-creatures," he avers that "to us, Sir, who are of *the lower orders of mankind*, to have a fund in view, on which we may, with certainty, depend to be kept from want . . . this is a matter of high importance."[33] Burns ends this rather desperate petition by requesting that Whitefoord "as soon as convenient . . . call a meeting & let us consider some means to retrieve our wretched affairs."[34]

This is a remarkable letter, one in which Burns's ample rhetorical skills are on clear display.[35] Prior to this letter, Burns had written eleven items of correspondence to personal friends (William Niven, Thomas Orr, and Alison Begbie) as well as to his younger brother William. Many of these early letters reveal the considerable extent to which Burns was already obsessing about the purported "benefits" of poverty compared with the vicissitudes of wealth, a theme he would explore in his writing throughout his career. Divisive thinking about wealth and poverty grew from difficult experiences during this period of his life; his family had suffered greatly at the hands of predacious landlords and had only narrowly averted bankruptcy. Burns himself had been unsuccessfully working as a flax-dresser in Irvine, an experiment that ended in a costly fire that left him with less than five shillings to his name.[36]

In this context, the letter to Whitefoord gains a sense of urgency nearly subsumed beneath Burns's mannered syntax. The issue of financial aid was indeed of "high importance" to Burns and his brother Tarbolton masons. Such assistance had been a part of Freemasonry since its beginnings in the seventeenth-century guilds; as Stevenson observes in *The Origins of Freemasonry*, guilds "had 'social welfare' functions, helping members who fell on hard times, providing for the decent burial of members, and giving support to their widows and orphans."[37] However, as the guild transformed into the Masonic lodge, it became "an institution that seemed to reflect the progressive spirit of the age, with ideals of brotherhood, equality, toleration, and reason."[38] It is these ideals, in addition to the association's social welfare functions, that must have resonated so strongly with Burns at this challenging stage in his life.

Keeping this in mind, one can better appreciate the sincerity, directness, and urgency in the letter's request for Whitefoord's intervention. However, it is unclear if Whitefoord took any actions to resolve the problems afflicting the lodge, as there are no extant letters on the subject in Burns's correspondence. When Burns addressed his second (and last) letter to Whitefoord, it was written under very different circumstances. Composed on 1 December 1786 from Edinburgh, the newly famous poet states that a mutual friend has "informed me how you are pleased to interest yourself in my fate as a man, and (what to me is incomparably dearer) my fame as a poet."[39] As in the prior letter, Burns looks for aid and hopes that Whitefoord's reputation for generosity will be realized in direct action. Seeking patronage, he writes that Whitefoord is "the first gentleman in the country whose benevolence and goodness of heart has interested himself for me, *unsolicited and unknown*."[40]

This is one of Burns's many addresses to potential patrons, written in anticipation of the next year's printing of the Edinburgh edition of *Poems, Chiefly in the Scottish Dialect*. While the letter directly appeals for Whitefoord's recognition (and money), it also has the tonal ambiguity of Burns's other letters to men in higher social ranks. For instance, using the metaphor of parasitism, Burns assures Whitefoord that the letter is "not the manœuvre of the needy, sharping author, fastening on those in upper life, who honor him with a little notice of him or his work." Instead, he asserts his difference as a bard "of Nature's making, [with] a certain modest sensibility, mixed with a kind of pride, that will ever keep him out of the way of those windfalls of fortune which frequently light on hardy impudence and foot-licking servility."[41]

Burns's letter speaks to abiding class distinctions that were not (and perhaps could not) be surmounted by the ideals of Freemasonry. Though both were brothers in the lodge, Burns and Whitefoord were strangers in the outside world. Margaret C. Jacob argues that such contradictory experiences within the lodges illuminate a fissure at the heart of Freemasonry, asking, "How did a private society dedicated to equality and fraternity cope with the pressures coming from a deeply hierarchical society?"[42] For masons coming from the laboring classes, the uncertainty of financial support (and burden of dues) may have made the association undesirable. For Burns, maintaining financial independence was a key goal, especially reaching the status where one was recognized as a free and independent individual regardless of class background.

Attaining this status was supposed to be a Masonic ideal put into practice when members commingled in the lodges, irrespective of their social differences. Crawford argues that "eighteenth-century Tarbolton Freemasonry brought together working-men and gentry in an organization at once hierarchical and comparatively classless."[43] Once one has read Burns's letter to Whitefoord, however, it is hard to maintain the view of the "classless" nature of Tarbolton Freemasonry. In Burns's initial experiences in Lodge St. James, Freemasonry failed to live up to its own promises for active leadership and financial aid. Despite this disappointing scenario, Burns continued to participate in the organization. Some of his hopes had been disabused, but perhaps the urban lodges would put theory into practice as the Tarbolton lodges had failed to, providing companionship, equality, and real support.

Burns in the Edinburgh Lodges: The Supposed "Poet Laureate"

Burns arrived in Edinburgh in November 1786, having had a particularly distressing year up to that point. He had planned to leave Scotland in September for Jamaica, largely to avoid the kind of financial collapse that had ruined his father.[44] In addition, he had made Jean Armour pregnant and tendered a written declaration of marriage to her, but her father had destroyed the document and set the law after the poet with a writ. Burns was also at this time involved with "Highland Mary" (Margaret Campbell), who was evidently planning to live with him in Jamaica.[45] Two events occurred that frustrated these designs: Campbell's death and the Kilmarnock printing of *Poems, Chiefly in the Scottish Dialect* in late July. Both forced the poet to change his plans, and the success of the volume encouraged Burns to pursue writing as an occupation.

Burns moved to Edinburgh to seek a printer for a much larger edition of the *Poems*, and he signed over the Mossgiel family farm lease to his brother Gilbert.

He had also been encouraged to come to Edinburgh by the blind poet Thomas Blacklock, who had written Burns a supportive letter about the Kilmarnock volume in early September. Blacklock was a fellow mason who belonged to Lodge Holyroodhouse (St. Luke's) No. 44; he is described by Maurice Lindsay as "a minor poet, but a man of broad culture and keen intellectual power, whose enthusiasm for Burns's work played an important part in the poet's career."[46] He was also the first person to suggest a separate edition of *Poems* to Burns, as well as to introduce him to influential friends in Edinburgh like Dugald Stewart.

Along with Blacklock, Burns had Henry Mackenzie to thank for his warm reception in Edinburgh. Shortly after Burns's arrival, Mackenzie's review of the Kilmarnock volume was published in *The Lounger*; this review not only paved the way for the Edinburgh edition, but it also introduced the idea of Burns as a "heaven-taught ploughman" to the reading public.[47] Burns soon began the process of socializing and networking expected of new literary celebrities, and he quickly learned how the city's population of literati and éminences grises regarded him in these settings. In a letter to Frances Dunlop from 15 January 1787, he described the experience as being "dragged forth to the full glare of learned and polite observation, with all my imperfections of awkward rusticity and crude unpolished ideas on my head."[48]

While he was not entirely satisfied with his "heaven-taught ploughman" persona, Burns recognized that it could help him negotiate this difficult social space, one in which class difference was pronounced and evident to all involved. However, along with his ploughman persona, Burns may have felt that his status as a freemason (shared with many Edinburgh tastemakers) might create common ground for mutual respect and kinship among socially unequal brothers. Initially it might have seemed to Burns that Freemasonry could bridge the social and professional gaps separating masons in the Edinburgh lodges, facilitating potentially valuable connections. This certainly appeared to be the case at the beginning of Burns's visit, but the longer he stayed, the less he learned to expect from his Edinburgh "brothers."

When Burns finally left Edinburgh for Ellisland in 1788, his expectations for aid from his urban brothers had been considerably diminished due to numerous disappointments and a legacy of broken promises. However, the initial response of Burns's brother masons had given him much room for hope. A significant early encounter with Edinburgh masons took place in Lodge Edinburgh St. Andrew No. 48 on 13 January 1787.[49] In a letter to friend John Ballantine written the next day, Burns confides that the masons at the meeting were "most numerous and elegant," coming from "all the different Lodges about town . . . in all their pomp."[50] Francis Charteris, Lord Elcho, who was the Grand Master of Lodge Canongate Kilwinning, presided over the occasion "with great solemnity," and during a round of toasts, Elcho called for one to be made for "Caledonia, & Caledonia's Bard, brother Burns."

Burns informs Ballantine that this toast was met "with multiplied honors and repeated acclamations," causing the bewildered poet to attempt to answer in kind: "As I had no idea such a thing would happen, I was downright thunderstruck and, trembling in every nerve, made the best return in my power." Crawford suggests that this toast signified that Edinburgh had "accepted [Burns] on his own terms," while Catherine Carswell writes that after this official recognition by the masons, "the Edinburgh people were set on doing the thing handsomely, and without pause this unread Laureate of Scotland was bidden to assemblies, concerts, theatres and clubs."[51] Following this social calendar brought increasingly diminishing returns, but when Burns left for Ellisland in June 1788, he had successfully arranged for the publication of the Edinburgh edition of *Poems, Chiefly in the Scottish Dialect* with a lengthy list of subscribers.

Most existing discussion of Burns's experiences in the Edinburgh lodges focuses solely on his supposed "poet laureate" status, with endless dispute over its veracity. For instance, the first book on the topic, James Marshall's *A Winter with Robert Burns, Being Annals of His Patrons and Associates in Edinburgh during the Year 1786–7, and Details of His Inauguration as Poet-Laureate of the Can: Kil:* appeared in 1846, while Wallace Bruce published his book *Robert Burns, Poet-Laureate of Lodge Canongate Kilwinning* in 1893. The next year Hugh C. Peacock wrote his lengthy account titled *Robert Burns, Poet-Laureate of Lodge Canongate Kilwinning: Facts Substantiating His Election and Inauguration on 1st March 1787.*[52] In the twentieth century, Dudley Wright wrote two books on Burns's experiences with Freemasonry, with great attention to the poet's experiences in Edinburgh.[53]

Accounts written in favor of Burns's supposed "inauguration" and "election" are not particularly convincing. The following five reasons have been employed to question the authenticity of Burns's "poet laureate" status:

1. There is no contemporaneous record of the event in the minutes for the meeting.
2. No such office existed before this supposed appointment.
3. No subsequent elections or re-elections to the post are found in the lodge's records from this period.
4. Accounts of the event are not contemporaneous.
5. Burns himself does not mention a Masonic "poet laureate" status in any of his writings.[54]

The only meeting that lists Burns in the minutes occurred on 1 February 1787, during which the poet was raised as a member along with twelve other men. Burns's prowess as a poet is mentioned in the minutes, but he is only admitted as a member of the lodge, not as its "poet laureate."[55]

It is not until the meeting on 1 March 1787 that Burns's purported post as "poet laureate" is mentioned in the lodge's records. Allan Mackenzie's *History* relates that "in course of the evening, the R. W. [Right Worshipful] Master, Alexander Fergusson of Craigdarroch, Advocate, hero of the 'Song of the Whistle,' conferred upon [Burns] the title of Poet-Laureate of the Lodge, and the Minute is signed by the Master,' also by Charles More, D.M., and John Millar, Advocate, J.W."[56] However, Mackenzie has engaged in rather fanciful speculation here, for he does not discuss the actual minute from this meeting; in addition, his account derives from 1883, nearly a hundred years after the supposed inauguration.[57] Concerning the lodge's record keeping, Peacock observes that the "manner of recording business by any one acting as Lodge Secretary was slovenly in the extreme, and shows that the author of the minute was tired of the whole business and wanted to be done with it as speedily as possible."[58]

It was not until 1815 that the masons of Lodge Canongate Kilwinning sought to commemorate their "laureate" by taking a subscription for the erection of a mausoleum in Burns's honor.[59] Because of this event, many masons have assumed that Burns had genuinely been elected the poet laureate of the association.[60] Given the widespread nature of this assumption, it is important to look more closely at the fifth point mentioned in the rebuttal list. Burns never described himself as the masons' poet laureate in his writing or correspondence. Typically he was quite eager to assume any poetic role that would identify him as a national bard. In a letter to Frances Dunlop from 22 March 1787, for example, Burns remarked that "the appelation of, a Scotch Bard, is by far my highest pride; to continue to deserve it is my most exalted ambition."[61]

He may perhaps have privately seen himself as "Caledonia's Bard," the title bestowed upon him by Lord Elcho, but the fact that he never publicly identified himself as the masons' poet laureate should be given much more credence. In fact, it is worth inquiring more thoroughly about the extent to which the post of "poet laureate" of Canongate Kilwinning was of any consequence to the poet himself. In order to answer this question, it is worth reviewing Burns's Masonic poetry to see how his perceptions of Freemasonry changed over time.

Burns's Subversive Experiments in Masonic Verse

Typical specimens of Masonic verse provide exposition of Freemasonry's origins, as well as celebrate its exclusivity. For instance, Alexander Nicol's Masonic poetry includes several examples with these characteristic features. Like Burns, Nicol (bap. 1703) was from the laboring class, his father a packman in Forfarshire. In 1739 he published his first collection of verse, *Nature without Art*. He published only two more collections of verse, *The Rural Muse* (1753) and *Poems on Several Subjects* (1766), and nothing more is known of his life from the 1750s onward.[62] In his collections, Nicol included many explicitly Masonic poems that provide explication of key concepts and beliefs, addressed to fellow masons who would recognize the secret meanings of the works' imagery and symbolism.

For example, "Poem on Masonry" recounts the special role accorded Freemasonry in the world's creation by an unnamed "Master." In the process of creation, Freemasonry is preeminent due to its antiquity among "all arts found by the human race":

> To set aside the Builder of this All,
> Who is the first and great Original;
> Who gives all wisdom, and instructs mankind
> All useful arts and science out to find:
> Yet notwithstanding, and with reverence, we
> May say that he did honour Masonry
> More than all arts found by the human race,
> And long before invention first took place.[63]

Asserting primeval origins establishes not only the antiquity of Freemasonry but also its foundational role in all "civilizing" endeavors. This speaks not only to the artisanal roots of the organization in medieval guilds but also to the emergent voice of Enlightenment ideals in eighteenth-century Freemasonry.

Such triumphalist rhetoric is also found in Masonic verse that praises the exclusivity of the group and seeks to maintain its secrecy at all costs. Nicol affirms this integral aspect of the association in his "Poem, Shewing the Original, Antiquity, Beauty, and Glory of Masonry." He declares that Freemasonry is "a secret kept since first the world began / And still unknown to the most searching man" (1–3, lines 3–4). To "pretenders" to Masonic knowledge who have read only "printed pamphlets" (line 27), Nicol offers, "Let them answer points of entrance, then / I'll call them brothers, and the best of men" (lines 29–30). "Points of entrance" refer to secret signals (handshakes, the Mason Word) that identify brother masons to one another.[64] Nicol ends by asserting the enduring fellowship of all masons who know how to read the poem's "secret" meanings: "All free brothers, known in masonry, / Will in the poem secret beauty see" (lines 37–38).

Nicol's books abound in numerous examples of such orthodox Masonic verse. When Burns tried his hand at the genre, he experienced some difficulty working within its narrow confines; consequently, he wrote only four explicitly Masonic poems. The songs "No Churchman am I" (1783/1784), "The Farewell to the Brethren of St. James's Lodge, Tarbolton " (1786), and "Ye Sons of Old Killie" (1786) directly reference Masonry by name, occasion, or explicit use of Masonic symbolism.[65] Another, "To Dr. John Mackenzie" (1786), indicates its specific purpose in its subtitle, "an invitation to a Masonic Gathering." In addition to these explicitly Masonic poems and songs, Burns also wrote extemporaneous verse, satires, and elegies for his brother masons. It is a limited body of work, but when read in its entirety Burns's Masonic verse complicates his representation as a consummate mason.

The tension between Freemasonry's ideals and practices is explored in Burns's Masonic verse, which ranges in tone and mode from hyperbolic praise to bitter satire. The concept of brotherhood was deeply important to Burns, and on the surface the Masonic ideal of brotherhood appears to coincide with Burns's own. Masonic brotherhood depended in theory upon the denial of existing social differences; as Mary Ann Clawson explains, such differences were symbolically "cleansed" during the Masonic rite of initiation, "in which the candidate enter[ed] the lodge divested of money and jewelry and stripped of all but shirt and pants, thus symbolically detaching [him] from his worldly standing."[66] Indeed, Freemasonry's theory of classless brotherhood may have inspired Burns's anthemic "A Man's a Man for a' That," with its call for universal brotherhood.

However, the concept of classless fraternity did not inspire Burns's Masonic verse in quite the same way. In fact, brotherhood did not spare Burns's fellow masons from his wicked bent for satire, and Burns was notoriously fearless in satirizing anyone whose hypocrisies or pretensions sparked his ire. The most famous Masonic example is the case of John Wilson, recorded for posterity by the poet's brother Gilbert: "Robert was at a mason-meeting in Tarbolton, when the Dominie unfortunately made too ostentatious a display of his medical skill. As [Robert] parted in the evening from this mixture of pedantry and physic, at the place where he describes meeting with Death, one of those floating ideas of apparitions . . . crossed his mind: this set him to work for the rest of the way home."[67] The result of this unhappy evening for Wilson was of course "Death and Dr. Hornbook," one of Burns's best-known satires. Andrew Noble and Patrick Scott Hogg have described the poem as a "hatchet job," commenting that "extraordinarily, either because of innocence, or given the other evidence, gross stupidity, Wilson bore the poet no ill will over this."[68]

Other Masonic victims of Burns's satire were John Manson (subject of the mock-epitaph "On an Innkeeper in Tarbolton"); Thomas Sampson (the report of whose death had been greatly exaggerated by Burns in "Tam Samson's Elegy"); and James Humphrey, whose pretensions to knowledge induced the poet to write the "Epitaph on a Noisy Polemic" (in which Humphrey is described as a "bleth'ran bitch").[69] While this makes for entertaining poetry, it runs counter to the Masonic ideal of brotherhood; in fact, one of the regulations of Lodge St. James stated that "no member of this Lodge shall speak slightingly, detractingly, or calumniously of any of his Brethren behind their backs, so as to damage them in their professions or reputations."[70] Though Burns and Wilson remained friends and corresponded until 1790, "Death and Dr. Hornbook" certainly did not help Wilson's reputation, while Sampson was reported to have protested, "I'm no dead yet."[71]

Burns also praised his fellow masons in elegies and extemporaneous verse. "Elegy on Captain Matthew Henderson" evokes the poet's sincere feeling for his departed friend and brother mason.[72] This is also seen in "Lament for James, Earl of Glencairn," described by Noble and Hogg as a "Bardic lament,"[73] replete with the tone and imagery of Ecclesiastes and Job. The extremity of Burns's emotional relationship to brother masons like the Earl of Glencairn is also found in "Extempore Verses on Dining with Lord Daer," a poem that recounts the poet's first meeting with Daer. The work reveals Burns's rather astonished reaction to dining with "a lord—a peer—an earl's son" who has no obvious

symptoms o' the great,
The gentle pride, the lordly state,
The arrogant assuming.[74]

Burns's meal with Lord Daer appears to certify the Masonic ideal that "One rank as well's another."[75] However, the root of Burns's considerable wonderment in the poem may derive from the fact that a "great and prosperous" mason like Daer actually conformed in behavior to the ideals of Masonic brotherhood.[76]

Burns's explicitly Masonic works reveal a similar ambiguity in their representation of the association's key ideals. His song "No Churchman am I" has generic attributes of eighteenth-century drinking songs and anacreontics, not least in its refrain about the speaker's use of a "big-belly'd bottle" to ease his "cares."[77] However, there is a similar disjuncture between Masonic ideals and practices as that seen in Burns's satires of brother masons. The song's last two lines exhort, "May ev'ry true Brother of th' Compass and Square / Have a big-belly'd bottle when harass'd with care."[78] Such convivial indulgence was not condoned in official Masonic literature, although anti-Masonic tracts "suggested that the Masons had derived their epithet 'free' from their cult of imbibing."[79] In this respect, "No Churchman am I" contravenes orthodox Freemasonry by representing Masonic gatherings as more convivial than secretive and ritualistic in nature, focused primarily on enjoying a "big-belly'd bottle" with brother masons.

In his song "The Farewell to the Brethren of St. James's Lodge, Tarbolton," Burns represents core Masonic ideals quite differently, with rare usage of explicitly Masonic symbolism. For example, the "chearful, festive night" of the masons' meeting is

honor'd with supreme command,
Presided o'er the *Sons of light*:
And by that *Hieroglyphic* bright,
Which none but *Craftsmen* ever saw![80]

By using shorthand symbolism familiar to all masons, Burns concentrates the reader's attention on such rituals of Masonic secrecy as seen in Nicol's verse.[81] The song also directly links Freemasonry with the promise of nationalism in the lines, "Heav'n bless your honor'd, noble Name, / To Masonry and Scotia dear!"[82] However, this early poem is the exception to the rule of Burns's Masonic verse, which tends to record instead the disparity between the association's theory and its practice. Despite being lauded as "Caledonia's Bard" by his brothers, Burns would cease writing Masonic verse after 1790 and dramatically attenuate his participation in Freemasonry for a variety of personal and political reasons.

Conclusion

After leaving Edinburgh in 1788 for Dumfries, Burns continued to attend Masonic meetings and was even admitted as an honorary brother without fee at some lodges.[83] In late 1791 he became a member of Lodge Dumfries St. Andrew and was elected Senior Warden in 1792.[84] His attendance at a meeting of the Dumfries Masonic lodge on 28 January 1796 has been regarded as evidence of his devotion to Freemasonry up until the end of his life.[85] However, his desultory participation during the turbulent 1790s signals Burns's growing dissatisfaction with Freemasonry. At this time in his life, Burns began his project of collecting Scottish songs that would serve as his legacy as a Scottish bard. He also experienced difficulties in reconciling his political beliefs with his occupation as an excise collector in the government's employ. His work began to express openly republican ideals, while at the same time he needed to toe the party line or face severe punishment. Scottish authorities were quite rigorous at this time in transporting radicals who were sentenced for sedition.[86]

Burns's prior dissatisfaction with Freemasonry's practices may have been amplified at this troubled moment. The links connecting Freemasonry with radical politics in the eighteenth century have been examined in depth, with the work of Mark C. Wallace and Margaret C. Jacob contributing much to our understanding of this relationship in Britain and continental Europe.[87] There is still much debate about Freemasonry's relationship to republicanism, but Kenneth Loiselle suggests that "while some aspects of Masonic associational culture may be construed as republican, Freemasonry's reaction to revolutionary events was no different from that of the wider public."[88] Given the fear of sedition that roiled the British government during the 1790s, it seems unlikely that the associational aspirations of Scottish Freemasonry extended far into the public sphere, particularly where politics were concerned. This was an occupational necessity, but it may have been yet another instance of hypocrisy to Burns.

In addition, the realization of core Masonic ideals like brotherhood was counterbalanced in the lodges by internal restrictions placed on political discussion. R. J. Morris explains that "the order insisted on tolerance and the exclusion of contention. . . . The fourth Charge [stated] 'we . . . are resolved against all Politicks, as what never yet conducted to the welfare of the Lodge, nor ever will.'"[89] By avoiding political discussion in the lodges, freemasons could offer plausible deniability when questioned about republicanism. Masonic lodges such as those attended by Burns were content to stay within repressive political structures, as long as Masonic associational practices were not going to be forbidden. The result was that freemasons had no proclivity to practice their own version of democracy in any forum except secret meetings. Such a tangled web of complicities must have gravely disappointed Burns.

British freemasons tended to remain, with few exceptions, politically conservative, and Jacob remarks that many British lodges were in fact "an important vehicle for inculcating loyalism to king and government."[90] In a letter to Henry Erskine about whether to include the political ballad "When Guildford Good" in the 1787 Edinburgh edition of his *Poems*, Burns explained the dilemma he was facing as a mason who held strong political beliefs unwelcome within the confines of the lodge: "I showed the inclosed political ballad to my Lord Glencairn, to have his opinion whether I should publish it; as I suspect my political tenets, such as they are, may be rather heretical in the opinion of some of my best Friends.—I have a few first principles in Religion and Politics which, I believe, I would not easily part with; but . . . I would not have a dissocial word about it with any one of God's creatures; particularly, an honoured Patron, or a respected Friend."[91] Burns was unable to resolve this dilemma to his own satisfaction; he could not assert his political beliefs without offending his Masonic brothers, men who could be useful friends and patrons.

Nonetheless, despite these reservations, Burns followed his political beliefs and included "When Guildford Good" in the expanded Edinburgh edition of his *Poems* (1787). This action reveals that Burns had a much more conflicted attitude toward his fellow masons than it might appear at first glance. Burns withdrew from active participation in Freemasonry after he was elected Senior Warden of Lodge Dumfries St. Andrew, where he attended meetings only sporadically from 1792 to 1796.[92] In addition, he became noticeably less enthusiastic about producing verse for Freemasonry, ceasing to write for the association entirely after 1790. It was precisely his disillusionment with Freemasonry's compromised ideal of brotherhood that led Burns to explore other means of reaching his fellow Scots in his writing. Rather than acting in the guise of "brother Burns," he spent his last years collecting national songs, engaged in a more positive and liberating project that could fulfill his aspirations to be "Caledonia's Bard."

NOTES

1. Mark C. Wallace, *The Great Transformation: Scottish Freemasonry, 1725–1810* (Washington, DC: Westphalia Press, 2018), 2. For more on the Scottish contribution to the development of Freemasonry, see also Lisa Kahler, "Scottish Definitions and Transitions," in *Freemasonry in Context: History, Ritual, Controversy*, ed. Arturo de Hoyos and S. Brent Morris (Lanham, MD: Lexington Books, 2004), 3–18.

2. David Stevenson, *The Origins of Freemasonry: Scotland's Century, 1590–1710* (Cambridge: Cambridge University Press, 1988), 12–25. See also David Stevenson, *The First Freemasons: Scotland's Early Lodges and Their Members* (Aberdeen: Aberdeen University Press, 1988), 1–11. "Operative" freemasons were actual stonemasons, while "speculative" members had no literal ties to the practice of stonemasonry.

3. Stevenson, *Origins of Freemasonry*, 1–12. Stevenson notes that "one of the basic functions of many of the lodges was regulating the working lives of stonemasons. But from the start social and ritual functions lay at the heart of the lodges" (1). In *Great Transformation*, Wallace describes the revival of the Grand Lodge in eighteenth-century Scotland, noting that "Scottish Freemasonry between the year 1740 and 1790 experienced a period of marked growth and development" (56). He also notes that "operatives were still an integral part of many lodges," which led to the movement of masons among various lodges (57).

4. See, e.g., John Campbell Shairp, *Robert Burns*, ed. John Morley (New York: Harper, 1901), 42–59. Burns's *Poems, Chiefly in the Scottish Dialect* was first published in Kilmarnock in 1786.

5. James Marshall, *A Winter with Robert Burns: Being Annals of His Patrons and Associates in Edinburgh during the Year 1786–7, and Details of His Inauguration as Poet-Laureate of the Can: Kil:* (Edinburgh: Peter Brown, 1846), 24–26.

6. J. De Lancey Ferguson, *Pride and Passion: Robert Burns, 1759–1796* (1939; repr., New York: Russell and Russell, 1964), 99. James Mackay has suggested that "Robert regarded Glencairn with adulation bordering on hero-worship and was completely captivated by him" (*RB: A Biography of Robert Burns* [Edinburgh: Mainstream Publishing, 1992], 264). Discussing the nature of this relationship, Robert Crawford states that "Glencairn was able to give Burns the kinds of help required, without clashing with the poet's determined need to preserve inner egalitarian independence" (*The Bard: Robert Burns, a Biography* [Princeton, NJ: Princeton University Press, 2009], 249). It should also be noted that Burns named one of his sons after Glencairn (James Glencairn Burns).

7. Catherine Carswell, *The Life of Robert Burns* (1930; repr., Edinburgh: Canongate, 1990), 174.

8. Nigel Leask, *Robert Burns and Pastoral: Poetry and Improvement in Late Eighteenth-Century Scotland* (Oxford: Oxford University Press, 2010), 12–13.

9. Robert Crawford, "Robert Fergusson's Robert Burns," in *Robert Burns and Cultural Authority*, ed. Robert Crawford (Edinburgh: Edinburgh University Press, 1997), 9.

10. On Burns's experiences with Freemasonry (as well as with a variety of other social clubs), see Corey E. Andrews, *Literary Nationalism in Eighteenth-Century Scottish Club Poetry* (Lewiston, NY: Edwin Mellen Press, 2004), 215–358.

11. Stevenson, *First Freemasons*, 8.

12. Ibid., 9.

13. The Masonic naming of Burns as "Caledonia's Bard" is discussed later in this chapter. "All brothers" refers to the last two lines in "Is There for Honest Poverty," in which the poet claims, "Man to Man, the world o'er / Shall brothers be, for a' that." This well-known song by Burns was published anonymously in the *Morning Chronicle* in 1794. It appears in *Poems and Songs of Robert Burns*, ed. James Kinsley (Oxford: Clarendon Press, 1968), 2:762–763.

14. Marie Roberts, *British Poets and Secret Societies: Freemasons and Clandestine Brotherhoods* (London: Croom Helm, 1986), 52. For other sources concerning Burns's relationship with Freemasonry, see Andrews, *Literary Nationalism*, 349n81.

15. Maurice Lindsay, *The Burns Encyclopedia*, 4th ed., rev. and ed. David Purdie, Kirsteen McCue, and Gerard Carruthers (1959; London: Robert Hale, 2013), 139–140.

16. Ibid.

17. John Weir, "History of Lodge Tarbolton (Mauchline) St. James No. 135," http://www.thefreemasons.org.uk/tarbolton135/history.htm#3 (accessed 17 Nov. 2019).

18. Robert Lawrence, "History of Lodge St David (Tarbolton) Mauchline No. 133," http://www.lodgestdavid133.org/ (accessed 17 Nov. 2019).

19. Ibid. Burns paid twelve shillings for admission.

20. Ibid.

21. Ibid.

22. Robert Chambers, ed., *The Life and Works of Robert Burns*, rev. William Wallace (1851–1852; Edinburgh: W. R. Chambers, 1896), 1:129. Depute Master is a Scottish name for the office of Deputy Master.

23. Albert G. Mackey defines the duties of the "depute master" as the following: "The assistant and, in his absence, the representative of the Grand Master. The office originated in the year 1720, when it was agreed that the Grand Master might appoint both his Grand Wardens and a Deputy Grand Master." Albert G. Mackey, *Encyclopedia of Freemasonry and Its Kindred Sciences* (Philadelphia: McClure, 1917), 239.

24. The "worshipful master" is the senior officer in a Masonic lodge. The adjective "worshipful" was "applied to the symbolic lodge and its master"; see ibid., 1017.

25. Ibid., 239.

26. *The Letters of Robert Burns*, ed. J. De Lancey Ferguson, 2nd ed., rev. G. Ross Roy (Oxford: Clarendon Press, 1985), 1:16. The editors note that "the draft is written on the back of the sheet containing the draft of the first letter to Alison Begbie." The letter is the twelfth item of correspondence in the two-volume collection of correspondence. Further details on Sir Alfred Law's Honresfield edition can be found in Patrick Scott, "A 'Lost' Collection of Robert Burns Manuscripts: Sir Alfred Law, Davidson Cook, and the Honresfield Collection," at https://electricscotland.com/familytree/frank/burns_lives210.htm (accessed 17 Nov. 2019).

27. Ibid., 1:15.

28. Ibid.

29. See "Robert Burns: A Man's a Man, for a' That," Grand Lodge of Scotland, http://www.grandlodgescotland.com/Masonic-subjects/robert-burns/ (accessed 17 Nov. 2019).

30. *Letters of Robert Burns*, 1:16.

31. Ibid.

32. Ibid.

33. Ibid., 1:15–16 (emphasis added).

34. Ibid., 1:16.

35. For analysis of Burns's rhetorical training in club settings, see Andrews, *Literary Nationalism*, 228–251.

36. These events occurred between 1782 and 1784. For a detailed account, see Mackay, *RB*, 91–132.

37. Stevenson, *Origins of Freemasonry*, 13.

38. Ibid.

39. *Letters of Robert Burns*, 1:67.

40. Ibid, 1:67–68 (emphasis added).

41. Ibid., 1:68. The word "servility" is a key marker of derision in Burns's works; its most well-known appearance (in "Robert Bruce's March to Bannockburn") is "your sons in servile chains." *Poems and Songs of Robert Burns*, 2:707–708.

42. Margaret C. Jacob, *The Origins of Freemasonry: Facts and Fictions* (Philadelphia: University of Pennsylvania Press, 2005), 4.

43. Crawford, *Bard*, 94.

44. For more on Burns's decision to immigrate to Jamaica, as well as discussion of the practice of slavery there, see Nigel Leask, "'Their Groves o' Sweet Myrtles': Robert Burns and the Scottish Colonial Experience," in *Robert Burns in Global Culture, 1759–2010*, ed. Murray Pittock (Lanham, MD: Rowman and Littlefield, 2011), 172–188.

45. For more on this period of Burns's life, see Mackay, *RB*, 249–302.

46. Lindsay, *Burns Encyclopedia*, 44–46.

47. For Mackenzie's review, see Donald A. Low, ed., *Burns: The Critical Heritage* (London: Routledge and Kegan Paul, 1974), 67–71. For detailed analysis of Burns's "heaven-taught ploughman" persona, see Corey E. Andrews, *The Genius of Scotland: The Cultural Production of Robert Burns, 1785–1834* (Leiden: Brill Rodopi, 2015), 71–144.

48. *Letters of Robert Burns*, 1:85. The reference to "imperfections" is a nod to *Hamlet.*

49. This lodge is still in existence, and its website provides an interesting account of Burns's relationship to Freemasonry in general (and St. Andrew No. 48 in particular). See the following site: "The Story of Auld Lang Syne," Lodge of Edinburgh St. Andrew No. 48, https://lodge48.webs.com/robertburns.htm (accessed 17 Nov. 2019).

50. *Letters of Robert Burns*, 1:83. All further citations of this letter refer to this page.

51. Crawford, *Bard*, 243; Carswell, *Life of Robert Burns*, 196–197.

52. This is only a small sample of Burns-themed Masonic histories written during the nineteenth century. Given Burns's veneration during this period, it is not unusual to encounter so many accounts that link Scotland's national poet to Freemasonry.

53. See Dudley Wright, *Robert Burns and His Masonic Circle* (London: Cecil Palmer, 1929); and Wright, *Robert Burns and Freemasonry* (Paisley: Alexander Gardner, 1921).

54. This is a paraphrase derived from R. W. Fullarton's introduction to Hugh C. Peacock, *Robert Burns, Poet-Laureate of Lodge Canongate Kilwinning: Facts Substantiating His Election and Inauguration on 1st March 1787*, with the assistance of Allan Mackenzie (Edinburgh: Christie and Son, 1894), xii.

55. The minutes read, "The Right Worshipful Master having observed that Brother Burns was at present in the Lodge, who is well known as a great Poetic Writer, and for a late publication of his works, which have been universally commended, and submitted that he should be assumed a member of this Lodge, which was unanimously agreed to, and he was assumed accordingly" (Allan Mackenzie, *History of the Lodge Canongate Kilwinning No. 2. Compiled from the Records, 1677–1888* [Edinburgh: printed for the Lodge by Brother James Hogg, 1888], 108–109). For analysis of this minute, see Peacock, *Robert Burns*, pt. 2, 6–7.

56. Mackenzie, *History*, 110–111.

57. Mackenzie was the past Master of Lodge Canongate Kilwinning, and he is credited by Peacock with aiding him to prove the "truth" of Burns's poet laureate status. Despite this, Mackenzie's history of the lodge is still a valuable resource, though caveats must be observed regarding his possible bias. For a more recent account of this lodge, see Lisa Kahler, "Canongate Kilwinning Lodge," in *Freemasonry on Both Sides of the Atlantic: Essays concerning the Craft in the British Isles, Europe, the United States, and Mexico*, ed. R. William Weisberger, Wallace McLeod, and S. Brent Morris (Boulder, CO: East European Monographs, 2002), 59–86.

58. Peacock, *Robert Burns*, pt. 2, 8. The records of Lodge Canongate Kilwinning are discussed in detail in part 2 of Peacock's book; he describes the minutes as "very few, imperfect, and brief" and the record keeping itself as "incomplete or hurried," finding that the whole enterprise reveals (in his words) "extraordinary negligence" (pt. 2, 4–5).

59. Mackenzie, *History*, 112–113.

60. The supposed inauguration ceremony is depicted by William Stewart Watson in his painting *The Inauguration of Robert Burns as Poet Laureate of the Lodge* (1846), National Galleries Scotland, PG 946, used for the front cover of this volume. For more on this painting, see National Galleries Scotland, https://www.nationalgalleries.org/art-and-artists/8197/inauguration-robert-burns-poet-laureate-lodge (accessed 17 Nov. 2019).

61. *Letters of Robert Burns*, 1:101.

62. See Richard Ian Hunter, "Nicol, Alexander (*bap.* 1703)," in *ODNB*, https://doi:10.1093/ref:odnb/20161.

63. Alexander Nicol, *The Rural Muse* (Edinburgh: printed for the author, 1753), 6–8, lines 15–22. Further references are to this edition and cited in-text by page and line numbers.

64. For an extended discussion of the Mason Word and other "rituals of identification," see Stevenson, *Origins of Freemasonry*, 125–165.

65. For analysis of these poems, see Andrews, *Literary Nationalism*, 291–297.

66. Mary Ann Clawson, *Constructing Brotherhood: Class, Gender, and Fraternalism* (Princeton, NJ: Princeton University Press, 1989), 76.

67. Quoted in J. G. Lockhart, *Life of Robert Burns*, 4th ed. (London: John Murray, 1838), 72.

68. *The Canongate Burns*, ed. Andrew Noble and Patrick Scott Hogg (Edinburgh: Canongate Classics, 2003), 176.

69. *Poems and Songs of Robert Burns*, 3:47, line 3. Lindsay notes that Humphrey bore the poet no ill will and "was reputed to have been pleased to have been the subject of Burns's muse" (*Burns Encyclopedia*, 166).

70. Quoted in Roberts, *British Poets*, 58.

71. *Canongate Burns*, 198.

72. *Poems and Songs of Robert Burns*, 1:438–442.

73. *Canongate Burns*, 260.

74. *Poems and Songs of Robert Burns*, 1:297–299, lines 14, 37–39.

75. Ibid., 1:299, line 45.

76. Daer was decidedly the exception to the rule; Lindsay notes that he was the first member of the nobility whom Burns met, and he did not disappoint the poet's expectations. Both men were advocates of parliamentary reform and the French Revolution, and Daer was even a member of the radical Friends of the People. For more on Daer, see Bob Harris, *A Tale of Three Cities: The Life and Times of Lord Daer, 1763–1794* (Edinburgh: John Donald, 2015).

77. *Poems and Songs of Robert Burns*, 1:38–39, lines 12, 16, 24, 28. Its tune was known as "Freemasons' March," and the phrase "big-belly'd bottle" derives from a song in Burns's copy of *A Select Collection of English Songs* (1783); see *Poems and Songs of Robert Burns*, 3:1021.

78. *Poems and Songs of Robert Burns*, 1:38–39, lines 27–28. For further links between folk and Masonic songs, see Katherine Campbell, "Masonic Song in Scotland: Folk Tunes and Community," *Oral Tradition* 27 (2012): 85–108; and Stephen W. Brown, "Singing by the Book: Eighteenth-Century Scottish Songbooks, Freemasonry, and Burns," in *From Compositors to Collectors: Essays on Book-Trade History*, ed. John Hinks and Matthew Day (New Castle, DE: Oak Knoll Press; London: British Library, 2012), 249–266.

79. Roberts, *British Poets*, 71.

80. *Poems and Songs of Robert Burns*, 1:270–271, lines 11–14.

81. On the nature of Masonic symbolism, see Stevenson, *Origins of Freemasonry*, 135–152.

82. *Poems and Songs of Robert Burns*, 1:271, lines 27–28.

83. See Wright, *Robert Burns and Freemasonry*, 27–33.

84. Mackay, *RB*, 567. The post of Senior Warden resembles that of the Depute Master; in the event of the Master's absence, the Senior Warden would perform his duties.

85. Ibid., 614. See also Wright, *Robert Burns and Freemasonry*, 101–102. Also confirmed by the Grand Lodge of Scotland, "Robert Burns: A Man's a Man, for a' That," https://www.grandlodgescotland.com/2018/07/23/robert-burns (accessed 17 Nov. 2019).

86. See Liam McIlvanney, *Burns the Radical: Poetry and Politics in Late Eighteenth-Century Scotland* (East Linton: Tuckwell Press, 2003), 15–37.

87. See Wallace, *Great Transformation*; Margaret C. Jacob, *The Radical Enlightenment: Pantheists, Freemasons and Republicans* (London: Allen and Unwin, 1981); and Margaret C. Jacob, *Living the Enlightenment: Freemasonry and Politics in Eighteenth-Century Europe* (New York: Oxford University Press, 1991). For a different perspective on Freemasonry's relationship to radical politics, see Kenneth Loiselle, "Living the Enlightenment in an Age of Revolution: Freemasonry in Bordeaux (1788–1794)," *French History* 24 (2009): 60–81.

88. Loiselle, "Living the Enlightenment," 60.

89. R. J. Morris, "Clubs, Societies, and Associations," in *The Cambridge Social History of Britain, 1750–1950*, vol. 3, *Social Agencies and Institutions*, ed. F.M.L. Thompson (New York: Cambridge University Press, 1990), 401.

90. Jacob, *Living the Enlightenment*, 71.

91. *Letters of Robert Burns*, 1:77.

92. Lindsay, *Burns Encyclopedia*, 140.

CHAPTER 8

Inventing the Public Sphere

FICTIONAL CLUB LIFE IN IRELAND AND SCOTLAND

Martyn J. Powell

The flowering of clubs and societies in both Scotland and Ireland in the course of the eighteenth century can be related in different ways. Some clubs were tied together through fraternal and sociable bonds—Edinburgh's Speculative Society (1764) and the Historical Society of Trinity College Dublin (1770), for example, or the Orange Lodges that spread from Ireland to Scotland from the 1790s. In many Irish societies the nature of club culture—its rituals, the heroes toasted to, the villains toasted against—was linked to a febrile anti-Scottishness that only dimmed with revolution and Union at the end of the century.[1] More positively, in Ulster the club culture had a distinct Scottish impulse thanks to the involvement of Presbyterian Ulster Scots. This dissenting dimension made itself relevant in a particular manner thanks to the way in which the legacy of anti-Stuart Covenanters, protective of their Presbyterian church in Scotland against royal interference, continued to influence naming practices in Irish associational culture. For example, the Irish paramilitary Volunteer regiments established during the American War of Independence frequently used the term "true blue," the Covenanters' adopted color, in the names of their corps.[2]

In both Scotland and Ireland club life fused with print to produce a public sphere that was both "real" and fictional, operating through parody and satire. There has been a relative dearth of focused work on fictive club life.[3] Some of the more famous clubs of this period, such as the Tuesday Club of Annapolis (1745), have received attention, and the playfulness of *The Spectator*, published from 1711 to 1712, with its many fictional clubs, has come under scrutiny in the context of work on politeness.[4] But the broader purpose and implications of the phenomenon require more detailed scrutiny, especially as, unlike the eighteenth-century periodical, newspapers, booming in Ireland in the late eighteenth century, have enjoyed much less attention in this context; and they are addressed in this chapter alongside periodicals. One might argue that the approach to club life by newspapers was just as important as the publications of Joseph Addison and Richard Steele, and an Irish-Scottish newspaper and periodical comparison works particularly well. Irish newspapers like the *Hibernian Journal* and *Dublin Evening Post*, both established in the 1770s, were especially fertile in their imagining of fictional clubs. And in the 1770s and 1780s, as part of the Scottish Enlightenment, Scottish periodicals made a major contribution to intellectual and cultural life in a manner consistent with *The Tatler* (1709–1711) and *The Spectator*; John Dwyer claims that Henry Mackenzie's *The Mirror* (1779–1780) and *The Lounger* (1785–1787) were Addison's "last great literary manifestations," and Mackenzie was even styled the Scottish Addison.[5]

This parodic clubbable world operates on a number of levels: it looks inward and is self-celebrating and self-critiquing; it focuses on the phenomenon of club life itself; and finally it addresses external matters (of state and society)—as we will see, there is a difference between fiction produced by clubs and that produced about clubs. Given the emphasis by some scholars on the very particular nature of the Scottish public sphere in this period, and the critical importance of associational life to it,[6] the comparison between Scottish and Irish commentaries on urban club life at this point in time is worth probing. To what degree were aspects of Irish and Scottish club life becoming disturbing to commentators, and were there national differences? Underpinning my approach to this material is an attempt to move away from cozier Addisonian readings of club culture, and instead to discuss the significance of anti-club language that attacked the very phenomenon of club life.

Biting fictional club satire was present in the early eighteenth century in the writing of Tory polemicist Edward Ward, including his *The History of the London Clubs, or, The Citizens' Pastime* (1709), but it was then displaced by softer approaches, with authors keen to celebrate as well as satirize. Oliver Goldsmith's satirical writings on his imagined clubs, the Choice Spirits, the Muzzy Club, and the Harmonical Society, hint at positive features of club culture, along with its excesses, and the very precise rules of the Harmonical Society were hardly satirical; this was something that Goldsmith would have been aware of as a clubman himself.[7] And yet, the more obvious anti-club language that we see in the German notion of *Vereinsmeirei*—an objectional form of clubbiness—does not entirely disappear. Some of the satirical material produced in Ireland and elsewhere on clubs during the late eighteenth century was directed as much at clubs themselves as at other political and societal targets. But to what extent was this social satire and the targeting of individual clubs transferred to club life in general? At times those who expected most from associational culture—reasoned, polite debate—found it difficult to accept the fact that some clubs merely reinforced the prejudices of their members. Even for those who championed the sociability of the associational world, one does not need to go far to see this sociability transformed into the pursuit of special interests, bringing us a little nearer to some of the implications of the German term.[8]

Despite the outbreak of the American war, during the first few months of 1776, the Irish *Hibernian Journal* opted to devote a substantial number of column inches to the proceedings of the "Board of Bon Ton," a fictional Dublin society whose primary concern was the fashionable world. This chapter will discuss the Board of Bon Ton in some detail, as well as a host of other Irish fictional bodies. And then, in the Scottish context, it will look at Henry Mackenzie's Mirror Club (1776) and the literary club life of a new breed of Scottish periodicals, an Addisonian revival that was very different from the material being produced by Irish newspapers. The Mirror Club was a "real" club, and had morphed out of another Edinburgh club, the Feast of Tabernacles (1770), but there were fictional components, and its usefulness in the pages of its parent printed work was as much about satire as it was about recording the club's goings-on.

As will become clear, fictional club life can be seen to have had a direct relationship with predominant satirical forms, but also with the way in which club culture, and features within it, waxed and waned in different societies. Both Irish and Scottish fictional clubs reveal sharp criticism of female participation in club life, and if Irish fictional clubs were a little more inclusive, then it could be said to reflect the reality of female involvement in the public intellectual scene; Scottish women enjoyed very limited participation in intellectual associational culture before the 1790s.[9] This chapter will also discuss the ways in which class politics intruded into this world and the attendant pushing and shoving that surrounded prevailing notions of politeness in the clubbable context. Comparison of the fictional clubs of Ireland and Scotland would suggest a more relaxed approach in Ireland to a convivial and clubbable public life. In Scotland, on the other hand, the maintenance of a polite culture and codes of behavior was of greater importance. In the first instance, however, it is important to devote some attention to the relationship between clubs and print culture.

Newspapers, Periodicals, and Associational Life

Newspapers like the *Hibernian Journal* (1771–1813), home of the Board of Bon Ton, and periodicals like *The Mirror*, home of the Mirror Club, were key bonding agents in eighteenth-century society, allowing associational life to function. Benedict Anderson has reflected upon the importance of the newspaper both to nation building and to "imagined communities."[10] Peter Clark argues that "the helium of publicity produced by the newspaper press" was vital to the growth of clubs and associations.[11] He might have added that newspapers and periodicals also contributed to a burgeoning public sphere as much by invention as by advertisement—and thus we have the development of the imagined club or society.[12]

Smaller bodies in provincial towns could organize and publicize through face-to-face contact and word of mouth. However, hundreds of societies throughout Ireland and Scotland—some relatively minor—determined that it was worthwhile to place notices of their activities in the press. Indeed, some of these provincial bodies might not have existed without news of metropolitan equivalents. We find the arrangement of meetings, the reporting of proceedings, rules of societies, and the printing of resolutions and toasts. Even if they did not advertise, reports of their activities found their way to the printer, through carefully circulated stories and puffs. Much of this had to do with survival—especially financial survival—and went beyond publicity. Clubs needed subscriptions to function, and the newspaper was the vehicle for reminders, threats, and news of expulsions. Printers also needed the business—and not just advertisements. Thus, printers and bookshops acted as ticket sellers for clubs, or were willing to hold a society's original articles of subscription.[13]

It is also clear that the newspaper-club nexus might be less about the club, its structure, and administration, and more about public opinion and readership. In the case of the Mirror Club, a periodical could arise out of an associational body, and both reflect its activities and act as a publishing outlet for reading materials. Other clubs could be much more political in focus and thrive in periods of adversity—they were groups bonded against external pressures. The Protestant Association (1778) is an obvious example in the Scottish context. In England there were Pitt Clubs, Wilkite Clubs, and Keppel Clubs. The Irish Sea was no boundary for these oppositional clubs, and the reports in the Irish press of the legal travails suffered by John Wilkes and Admiral Augustus Keppel must surely have assisted the formation and longevity of similar societies in Ireland; Dublin had its own Keppel Club (1779), though its most important oppositional club was the Society of Free Citizens of Dublin (1749). Nicholas Rogers stresses the intimate nature of the relationship between the press and the Keppel Clubs in England,[14] and the Dublin Keppel Club was still going, and still very radical politically (with press support), over five years after the admiral's failed court-martial. Although the periodical can be seen as the originator of the intimate club-print link, by the 1780s and 1790s the newspaper was involved in something very similar. Newspapers were being published either by clubs themselves or by individuals attempting to cater for the members of societies. In the Irish context, the first of these was the radical *Volunteer's Journal* (1783–1787), followed by a government alternative, the *Volunteer Evening Post* (1783–1787). The 1790s saw the United Irishmen establish Belfast's *Northern Star* (1792–1797) and Dublin's *The Press* (1797–1798).

Inevitably, the longevity of clubs and their newspaper offspring were connected. The persecution of the United Irishmen was accompanied by the smashing up of their printing presses in 1797. More prosaically, the relationship between clubs and newspapers could also have a commercial basis. A *Lounger* correspondent referenced the importance of the London market, which was a key target for the periodical's printer, William Creech, and apparently provided much-needed encouragement to readers in Edinburgh.[15]

The final point worth discussing as an introduction to the club-print nexus is the way in which it could act as a means of proving active citizenship. Charitable endeavors and political activity were the most obvious means of demonstrating public worth. It was a mode of boosting status—particularly if one was secretary or chairman. Anthony Fox of Dublin's Sons of the Shamrock (1784) (if this was indeed a society) would not have become the focus of the ire of the *Volunteer Evening Post*, had he not appeared as chairman in the *Volunteer's Journal*.[16] Active citizenship could also be demonstrated through a willingness to regulate society and enforce its laws. Dismissals from the associational world meant the stripping of a badge of citizenship and were advertised in the press.[17] Fictional dismissals could also indicate unclubbability—Henry Grattan and Henry Lawes Luttrell both suffered this stain on their characters, the latter from the Knights of Tara (1782), a Dublin fencing society. And yet other clubs might deliberately obscure the names of their membership. The members of Edinburgh's Easy Club (1712) initially took English historical names, eventually switching to more Scottish variants.[18] The Mirror Club also used pseudonyms in printed tales of its proceedings, suggesting that its high-profile members might not want to be identified given the occasionally frivolous and comedic proceedings that were printed. Doubtless there was also homage here to the stock characters familiar in *The Spectator*. In the Scottish case there is no doubt that real clubs like the University of Edinburgh Belles Lettres Society (1759) were heavily influenced by Addison and Steele.[19]

Dublin's Board of Bon Ton and Female Club Life

It is the fictional aspect of club culture that I want to focus upon in this chapter, as perhaps the most intriguing example of the intimate connection between associational life and the press is the establishing of fictional clubs. Along with fictional letters got up by the editorial staff, we find in the press the very fabric of eighteenth-century leisure used as a satirical weapon. There were fictional horseraces, cockfights, and masquerade balls—in the case of the first two the names of the animals were used to score political points, while in the latter it was their chosen character or costume[20]—and as club life was integral to eighteenth-century leisure and the wider public sphere, fictional societies abounded. Marie Mulvey Roberts refers to "the menagerie of the factual, fictional and fantastical clubs that mapped out the pleasures of eighteenth-century London."[21] English newspapers and periodicals were certainly creative, and Moyra Haslett finds no less than thirty-eight clubs in *The Spectator*, almost all imaginary. Among these were Addison's invented Humdrum Club and Sighing Club, and a fictional club was central to the publication: Mr. Spectator's Club featured in the majority of issues.[22] Most fictional clubs appearing in periodicals tended to be less well drawn and more incidental to proceedings. The *Grub-Street Journal* (1730–1737) had a satirical club, and the Blundering Club and the Nonsense Club appeared in the *Gentleman's Magazine* in the 1730s.[23] There was a real Nonsense Club (1750), albeit satirical in its interests, and two of its members—with contributions from others—published the periodical *The Connoisseur,* in which we find the fictional Eating Club (complaining of extravagant diets).[24] The Silent Club (1694) appeared in *The Guardian* (1713), which, again, was produced by Addison, and so unsurprisingly shared *The Spectator*'s approach. This was a club for men whose wives are loud at home.[25]

On the surface, Edward Ward's *A Compleat and Humorous Account of All the Remarkable Clubs and Societies in the Cities of London and Westminster* (1745) is even more fruitful—a selection from which includes the No Noses Club, Surly Club, Tall Club, and Wet Paper Brigade, the last of these for men who liked to read newspapers while the print was still inky.[26] However, unlike in *The Spectator,* where the device of the club is used to encompass a range of characters and opinions, and invite the possibility that amicable fellowship could promote the resolution of disagreements,[27] the satire in Ward's case is closer to later variants, in that the club as institution—possibly as an institution enshrining vice—was being mocked.

In the novel the fictional club has been used as a satirical device by those wishing to prick the pomposity that could be associated with clubbability. In Oliver Goldsmith's *The Citizen of the World* (1760) it is the club of hack writers that comes under scrutiny as Goldsmith lampoons the rage to publish even the most obscure second-rate material—members included Dr. Nonentity and Tim Syllabub.[28] Cabals of writers also appear in Tobias Smollett's *The Expedition of Humphry Clinker* (1771), and in this context it is clear that competitiveness within the clubbable environment could be stultifying.[29] At a society of writers Jery Melford notes that "they seemed afraid and jealous of one another and sat in a state of mutual repulsion." The consequence of the fact that "they are afraid of making free with one another" is that, for Jery, "upon the whole, I never passed a duller evening in my life."[30]

Alternatively, we can see the most ridiculous individuals given pseudo-status through club affiliation, but ultimately brought to heel through the satirical possibilities allowed by the club's structure. The *Hibernian Journal*'s Addisonian-like invention, the Board of Bon Ton, functioned in this manner, focusing in particular on gender and acceptable models of masculinity, though with a liberal dose of (factual) Dublin civic life. It met in the Eagle Tavern in Eustace Street, a popular club venue.[31] Its secretary held audiences in Capel Street between 2:00 P.M. and 4:00 P.M.[32] The unpopular (and real) MP Sir Henry Cavendish was a member, as well as being part of a fictional splinter group, the Insipid Club.

During the Insipid Club's proceedings it discussed the forthcoming mayoral election, with the president toasting to candidate Alderman Nathaniel Warren.[33] The Board of Bon Ton was a Dublin club for the fashionable—its secretary being Sir Thomas Tassell, other members including Timothy Tasteless and Peter Prolix—and for the feckless. In other words, in Ireland some clubs were incompatible with a purely patriotic mindset. The presence of women in the Board of Bon Ton is especially noteworthy. The *Hibernian Journal* opted to use "Coterie," which was more than likely a nod to the formation of the Female Coterie (1769) at Almack's assembly rooms in London, a mixed club run by fashionable women, functioning very much along the lines of a gentleman's club. The term "coterie" became particularly synonymous with female club life, and thus gives the *Hibernian Journal* club a hint of realism. Flirtilla Flaunt attended the board and was also president of the Coterie des Belles. When the breakaway Insipids sought permission for incorporation, it also wanted the "liberty to admit such Females of Character and Discretion as may be found expedient."[34]

One of the ways in which the Habermasian public sphere has been found most wanting is in its approach to gender, and yet women were certainly present—and criticized—in civil society in this period, though the extent of their participation in Scotland and Ireland differed.[35] In 1720 a pamphlet was published purporting to be "an account of the Fair Intellectual-Club in Edinburgh." It was remarkable not only for its depiction of female clubbability regulated in the same manner as male equivalents but also for establishing a positive vision of female associationalism, with improvement at its core. Evidence for the existence of this club is scanty, and this may have been a plea by the author for the formation of such a group. Whether fact or fiction, there was no follow-up. Scottish women would need to wait until the arrival of debating societies in the 1770s before they had access to any kind of club culture.[36] The Dundee Speculative Society was formed by 1772 and Edinburgh's Pantheon Society in 1773, and in this last year women attended Limerick's Juvenile Society, another debating club, though the presence of women in the body did not prevent a resolution that "the Reading of Novels is not of Utility to the fair Sex."[37]

Female participation in the associational public sphere tended to take place in salon-type environments, though there were exceptions—Bath had its female coffeehouse, where women were able to call for the day's newspapers, and some circulating libraries offered similar facilities.[38] Amy Prendergast explores salons in the Irish context, referring to those led by Frances Sheridan, Lady Moira, and Maria Edgeworth, and Scottish equivalents more limited in number. Indeed it is significant that both Prendergast and Rosalind Carr note the paucity of organized intellectual societies that might be willing to accommodate women in eighteenth-century Scotland.[39]

It is clear that commentators took issue with female involvement in public life and clubs and societies in particular, especially through fictional satires.

Jonathan Swift ridiculed Freemasonry by inventing female members in his *A Letter from the Grand Mistress of the Female Free-Masons to Mr Harding the Printer* (1724). Edward Ward referred to a Basket Woman's Club, one of several "Flat-Cap Societies of Female Tatlers."[40] *The Spectator* and *The Tatler* invented a whole series of female clubs, including a Basket Women's Club of Female Tatlers, Kitty Termagent's club of "She-Romps," and the Chit-Chat club.[41] In 1733 the *Grub Street Journal* invented a female society called the Fiddle Faddle Club, which in its obsession with fashion and gossip feels like an early version of the Board of Bon Ton.[42] Salon culture was itself heavily satirized, and Fanny Burney's bluestocking-esque club run by Lady Smatter in *The Witlings* (1779) is an obvious example.[43] Many of the satires on female fictional clubs tend to be directed at such informal gatherings, often in private houses, without a surfeit of rules and regulations. In 1792 the *Northern Star*, and by extension the United Irishmen, was dismissive of the English bluestockings: terming them as "an association of illiterate Literati" and "stale old Maids."[44]

In the Scottish context, the *Edinburgh Courant*, with perhaps a greater degree of hostility than the *Hibernian Journal* showed, invented a similar society, the Jezebel Club, with Lydia Harridan in the chair.[45] Two Mirror Club members, Lord Kames, and Henry Mackenzie himself, were both critical of a certain female literary type.[46] And though women were a major part of the intended audience of *The Mirror* and *The Lounger*, it appears that club culture, however important to the language of these periodicals, was not something to which the female readership could aspire. Female appearance at the assembly and theater was criticized by Colonel Caustic in pieces written by Mackenzie.[47] William Creech, printer of *The Mirror* and *The Lounger*, and ex officio Mirror Club member, even disapproved of the sociability of the circulating library. Rather, a woman's place was the educative—though not too educative—domestic sphere. The fact that Mrs. Careful and Lady Benevolus, referenced in the fictional Mirror Club, educated their daughters at home rather than let them loose at an early stage into the public sphere was a matter of praise. Significantly, Creech selected the Jezebel Club satire for inclusion in his compilation, *Edinburgh Fugitive Pieces* (1791). Creech's influence on *The Mirror* and *The Lounger*, which he saw, particularly in their collected editions, as money-makers in both Edinburgh and London, should not be underestimated.[48]

It is important to recognize that the Board of Bon Ton and other societies like it were as much about the feminization of society as the admission of women into clubs.[49] The 1770s saw both excessive macaroni fashions—elaborate female wigs, tight male breeches, and waistcoats—and the formation of several high-profile clubs and salons that allowed women to participate, most notably the Female Coterie, and it was only to be expected that the press would combine the two developments.[50] Thus the Board of Bon Ton made resolutions relating to the wearing of certain hairpieces, and resolved that its membership should ape the vicereine's new hat at public assemblies. The Coterie des Belles advocated a fund to make fashionable life possible without recourse to skinflint husbands, reflecting broader concerns about unregulated female expenditure.[51] MPs were criticized for slovenly dress, depriving woolen drapers, hosiers, and hairdressers of work, though praised for their economy, as more could be given to the poor.[52] In contrast the female members of the Jezebel Club were rather less public-spirited. They passed motions approving of dancing masters, hairdressers, theaters, and lending libraries, but with the obvious motivation of self-interest. Further bite is added through criticism of blatantly impolite behavior—drinking and swearing. These were some of the dangers of club life for either gender, and the participation of women made the criticism particularly pointed.[53]

Edinburgh's Mirror Club: Improving Satire

The notion of a Scottish Enlightenment that was improving in character has perhaps led to an underestimation of some of its more playful characteristics. The Beggar's Benison (1732) of Anstruther is a notable exception, and Edinburgh's Oyster Club (c. 1778), founded by Adam Smith, Joseph Black, and James Hutton, and including Henry Mackenzie in the membership, combined the improving with the playful; Edinburgh's Poker Club (1762) was less fun than it sounded, even if David Hume missed its "plain roughness" when in Paris.[54] It is clear that the historiography of Enlightenment Scotland has, for the most part, been more interested in documenting the clubs that made direct commercial or scientific contributions to Scotland's university-connected policies of improvement.[55] In some ways this reflected the trajectory of clubs moving away from the literary or philosophical concerns of bodies like the Easy Club and the Rankenian Club (1716/17), active in the early eighteenth century. Social, political, and economic questions dominated the discussions of the Select Society (1754).[56] The Philosophical Society of Edinburgh (1737) had as one of its objects the promotion of literature, but it gradually became much more scientific in its focus. Nevertheless, in each case it should be recognized that the promotion of politeness was always a constant.[57] Yet through engagement with an earlier English periodical culture, and the novel post–Samuel Richardson and Henry Fielding, it is clear that Scottish clubs—even those with a serious intent like the Edinburgh University Belles Lettres Society or the Speculative Society, the latter established "for improvement in Literary Composition and Public Speaking"—began to immerse themselves in narrative techniques.[58] Nowhere was this more obvious than in Henry Mackenzie's publications, *The Mirror* and *The Lounger*, and the later Edinburgh periodical, *The Bee* (1790–1794), which imagined itself as a virtual coffeehouse, and saw polite conversation as key to the civilizing process.[59] In these periodicals there were signs of a more frivolous approach, and this could include the fabricated and the fictional.

James Arbuckle's Tribune Club in his Dublin periodical of the same name of 1729 was indebted to the great Addisonian publications for its use of fictional spectators as part of the landscape of club life—Thomas Verger, Will Truman, Sir Humphry Thorowgood—and the same can be said for these Scottish exemplars.[60] Addison's use of fictional stock characters to describe members of a real club was certainly apparent in references to the Mirror Club in the periodical, *The Mirror.* Not only was there a Mr. Spectator, a Mr. Lounger, and a Mr. Mirror, but there was a Colonel Caustic and a Lord and Lady Benevolus. Not all of these characters were, of course, club members, though they did interact with the club; Colonel Caustic and Mr. Wilfull engaged with Mr. Lounger, and a member of the Mirror Club invited Mr. Lounger to attend the society.[61] The blurring of fact and fiction was made all the more pronounced through the publication of tales involving members of the real Mirror Club in both *The Mirror* and *The Lounger.* A lady known to one correspondent, and member of that Mirror Club, told him that "I know every person described here as well as if they had given us their names at full length." The Mirror Club member was not of her mind, as when she recounted some of her acquaintance, "these persons and characters were equally unknown to me, and even whose names I never heard mentioned before."[62] The same could be said, however, for the real Mirror Club itself, which was, it seems, exercised by the character of Sir Bobby Button: "Of our forty-five members it may, without offence, be said, that some of them are *manu quam lingua promptiores*, readier at a blow than a word; and we were told, that they seriously intended to make the author of the Mirror speak out, and say, whether, in the modern language of Parliament, *he meant any thing personal.*" There was then a dislocation (at least in print) between club members and the characters populating the print output, with the printer being at the heart of any deception.[63] Such interventions in print could be part of a protective carapace—using frivolity as a means of self-protection—or a means of professing innocence to the public and, perhaps more importantly, the state.[64] A piece in *The Lounger* written by Alexander Abercromby that combined (obvious) mendacity with puffery denied that the periodical was a group effort by the men of letters of Scotland; a club member stated that "there was not one of our Club who ever published a single sentence, or in likelihood ever would have done it, had it not been for the accidental publication of the *Mirror.*" The same article also suggested that *The Mirror* was a club production and *The Lounger* was not.[65]

The Mirror Club which went on to feature in *The Lounger* was very different in nature from the club of the same name that was at the heart of *The Mirror.* The former seemed much more fictive in character. Indeed, if the descriptions in *The Lounger* were accurate, it was hardly a club at all, given that it only met once a year on the day that the first issue was published. On these occasions they would "talk over the little anecdotes which gave us so much pleasure in the *Mirror.*"[66] The descriptions of this later Mirror Club indicated that there were forty-five members, a very potent number in both Whig and Scottish politics in this period, as an allusion to the Jacobite rising, and also to John Wilkes, that contrasted with the apolitical nature of much of the content. The fictional readership of *The Lounger* delighted in a languid disengagement, the publication satirizing the studied boredom of the fashionable world in the same manner as Frances Burney's novel *Camilla* (1796). The fictional lounger's world was the public sphere offered by so many urban centers, including Edinburgh: "In the morning, the political lounger betakes himself to his coffee-house, the literary lounger to his bookseller's shop, the saunterer to the public walks, the dreamer to his usual occupation of counting the sign-posts. In the evening, clubs, card parties, and public places, furnish a rendezvous for loungers of all denominations."[67]

This playfulness with the indolence fostered by the public sphere was characteristic of the Board of Bon Ton and a society celebrated in print in Edinburgh's *The Bee* in 1792 called the Nonsensical Club. The latter certainly feels like an Edward Ward club:

> 'Tis nonsense we sing, and we deal in,
> And gen'rously deal it about;
> And if common sense chance should steal in,
> We kick the precise rascal out.[68]

As with the Board of Bon Ton, the Nonsensical Club showed concern for the fashionable and the foolish. If they should be deprived of conversation, "The beau pick his teeth must for ever, / The chatt'ring coquette be undone." There was also more barbed criticism aimed at writers, lawyers, and nonconformist preachers:

> The bards would have little to write on,
> The lawyers have little to say;
> The critics would nought have to bite on,
> The Non Cons not know how to pray.[69]

Class and Politics in Fictional Club Life

In the Board of Bon Ton Alderman Warren was sniped at by another member for his background in the brewing trade. The class issue is noteworthy, as it was one of the other targets of fictional clubs. The creation of ludicrous clubs placed a barrier between the clubbable wealthy and the unclubbable hoi polloi. For the Mirror Club the associational ideal was a grouping of the wealthy and landed. In Ireland, which arguably saw a much earlier entry of the lower orders into the reality of club life, the satire was particularly scabrous. To give one example, Dublin's "ancient and numerous society" of cripples, the blind, and the aged was said to have met in a pub by the Liffey in 1754.[70] As Toby Barnard notes, this may have been "a satire on the vogue for clubs or a cover for indulgence."[71] A similar society appears in the *Hibernian Journal* in 1776, based in Channel Row, notorious for gin shops and low life. In both cases material is styled in the manner of a political club addressing either a senior figure in the society or a member of Parliament. In 1754 it was Hackball, a famed beggar who worked on the Old Bridge, known as king of the mendicants. By 1776 he had been replaced by "Benjamin the First, King of Beggars," though Hackball is still referred to in one of this club's songs.[72] The concerns of the latter body of beggarly clubmen—the promotion of local manufactures, in this case the decidedly unfashionable fabrics moreen, a tough woolen cloth used in upholstery, and hemp—were pertinent to the patriotic climate in Dublin in 1776. There was also reference to a society ritual, during which beggars visited Benjamin and were invited to kiss his arse.[73] Ritualistic behavior was evident in the fictional chimney sweepers' and shoe boys' club, which met to plan an elaborate parade to Gallows-green with the hated Richard Twiss's *A Tour in Ireland* (1775), an event that would climax with the burning of the book.[74]

In these cases, however, though an invasion of club life by the masses is a concern, their treatment is comical, even generous. Indeed they are viewed as allies in the patriotic cause, though the humor was broad-brush—this particular club met at the King of Morocco's Head in Sooty Lane. Its president, "who can read," was Jack Ketch, doubtless named after Charles II's infamous executioner.[75] There is a difference in the way that these clubs are portrayed in the press, compared with those that followed the agitation for parliamentary reform in the early 1780s. The unclubbable membership of the semi-fictional "Fishmongers" Volunteers, the Bog of Allen Light Infantry, the Ruffian Levellers, and the Drunken Club of Carlow were treated in a much more hostile fashion in 1784. The new leaders were Colonel Stitch-bone (the stay maker) and Lieutenant Trowel.[76] The Dublin underworld was back, this time as the, also fictional, Channel Row Volunteer corps. Though based on real artisan regiments and clubs, these societies became fiction in the newspapers—complete with a plan to assassinate John Foster and replace him with French finance minister Jacques Necker.[77] In these cases the satire is darker—there is real disdain, and it is much more spiteful, which, of course, could be because the chimney sweeps and beggars appeared in the patriotic *Hibernian Journal*, and the artisan clubs and Volunteers in the government-supporting *Volunteer Evening Post*. The threat of radicalism in the 1790s ensured that such practices continued. In 1794 Robert Jephson, sometime government hack-writer, published his *The Confessions of James Baptiste Couteau, Citizen of France*. In this he gave Ireland's urban houghers—those with a penchant for taking a cleaver to the hamstrings of Ireland's soldiery—club status. Couteau had a letter of introduction to both the United Irishmen and the houghers, and he described the latter as a "nursery of Reformers." Jephson's satire degraded both the United Irishmen and the very notion of reform clubs through his vision of clubbable houghers.[78] Of course, it was also possible to take the opposite tack.

Sydney, Lady Morgan, wrote tar and feathering bands, the Strugglers Club, and the United Irishmen into a romantic mélange in her *The O'Briens and the O'Flahertys* (1827).[79]

In Smollett's *Humphry Clinker*, Jery Melford introduces the reader to a society of cawdies, or errand boys, who organize an entertainment for the gentlemen attending the races at Leith. The cawdies were known, according to Jery, for being able to provide gentlemen with prostitutes. At the dinner, Jery finds himself in a hall with "fourscore, lords and lairds and other gentlemen, courtesans and cawdies, mingled together, as the slaves and their masters were in the time of the Saturnalia in Ancient Rome." As with Morgan's novel, however, the treatment of lower-class involvement in club life is not particularly negative. Jery Melford has his own predilections—and veers toward the rakish—but he is reasonably dispassionate. He is wryly amused by the cawdies: "The toastmaster who sat at the upper end, was one cawdy Fraser, a veteran pimp, distinguished by his humor and sagacity, well known and much respected in his profession by all the guests, male and female, that were here assembled." Fraser, as toastmaster, not only made toasts in imitation of his wealthier guests, but he aped their dress as well: "He himself wore a periwig with three tails."[80]

Similarly, in 1793 *The Bee* detailed the activities of the Ram's Head Club, which may have been fictional. Edinburgh did have a Sheep Heid Inn, but the Ram's Head was said to have met in the house of a "jolly widow." At the Ram's Head Club, "each member pays fourpence; for which he gets value in ham, porter, beer, a pipe of tobacco, and exhilarating glass. The president entertains his guests with a song and asks all the company in their turn to do the like, and so the night passes away."[81] The commentary here was not particularly judgmental. *The Bee* was aimed at Edinburgh business and commercial types; indeed Jon Mee notes its willingness to tolerate "a more outgoing form of sociability" than Mackenzie's publications.[82] Its final lines hinted at commonplace but uninspiring club culture: "It would fill five hundred Bees to give the names of all the clubs of this sort that subsist in Britain;—but who would read them?"[83] In *Humphry Clinker* the Society for the Encouragement of the Arts (1754) is cited in positive tones, and both Jery and Matthew Bramble join, but the need for exclusivity for clubs to survive is indicated through Jery's concerns that the benefits accrued to society would only be possible "if, from its democratical form, it does not degenerate into cabal and corruption."[84]

Issues of class, fashion, and politics are all found in Irish newspaper fictional club satires. What is not seen, however, is a general willingness to ridicule the Dublin club scene, as was apparent in England and, to an extent, Scotland. In the English/Scottish context there were satirical attacks upon clubs of connoisseurs and virtuosos, such as in Smollett's *Peregrine Pickle* (1751) and *Ferdinand Count Fathom* (1753). Robert J. Allen notes that here the device "is turned not only against a social type, but also against the club as an institution."[85] As mentioned above, in Germany the word *Vereinsmeir* defines a "club fanatic," and a potential target for those frustrated by the rules, debates, votes, and procedures of club life.[86] The correspondence between Andrew Erskine and James Boswell hints at similar frustrations, as they criticized the constraints placed on club life by the rules and rigmarole of toasting.[87] As discussed in this volume by James J. Caudle, the Edinburgh Soaping Club's motto of "Every man soap his own Beard" was indicative of this longed-for greater freedom in club conduct, and was praised in the *Public Advertiser.*[88] Scotland's fictional Nonsensical Club seemed of a similar view: "Thus free from restraint, in we rattle / Inslav'd by no precepts or rules."[89] In many ways the Nonsensical Club was an anti-club—to have no rules was the very point of its existence.

The nature of Scottish periodical culture—harking back to the Addisonian tradition—allowed for a criticism of excessive clubbability that would have been unfamiliar to the readers of Irish newspapers. In February 1779 the printer of *The Mirror* claimed to have received a letter criticizing the conduct of a "certain club," which "continues, in defiance of decency and good manners, to insult the public in Large Characters, in the front of every newspaper in town." The correspondent added that this "moves my indignation the more, when I consider that several of its principal members are arrived at a period of life, which should teach decorum, at least, if it does not extinguish vice."[90] This may have been incestuous and playful satire, but 1779 was also a tricky year in Scottish club life, as it witnessed the rapid growth of Lord George Gordon's Protestant Association, a development that was criticized by a range of Irish newspapers.

If we turn to Dublin's Board of Bon Ton we find that it interacted with other clubs in a proper and respectful manner; and there is an obvious contrast here with the debauched activities of Ward's Bawds Initiating Club and even his Basket Woman's Club, whose members "as soon as their Business is over, Liquor their weather-beaten Hides at the Tavern adjacent to the Markets they use."[91] The Board of Bon Ton bought tickets for a production of Judas Maccabeus for the benefit of imprisoned debtors, as prize for the best idea to chase away ennui.[92] It also discussed a masquerade to be given at the Rotunda by the anti-dueling club, the Knights of Tara—with no real antipathy toward the event. The concerns of the board—theatrical gossip, masquerade costumes of the famous, conditions of the streets, crime—were exactly the same as those featuring in the *Hibernian Journal*'s news columns, which arguably undermines the satirical intentions.

Fictional clubs could also be used to damage a political career, or score political points, the most notorious example of this in eighteenth-century Britain being the attempts to mire Sir Francis Dashwood in the salacious activities of the Medmenham Monks (c. 1750).[93] In the Irish context there is an early example in 1729 in James Arbuckle's Tribune Club, which was an Addisonian vehicle for his Whiggish commonwealthman politics, and in Swift's Legion Club, which in 1736 satirized the Irish Parliament. The Bon Ton Board's discussion of masquerade costumes for the Knights of Tara ball left one in little doubt as to their thoughts on the earl of Bective-Lovegold the Miser, and the Lord Chancellor–Moses the Jew.[94] In Edinburgh both the Cape Club (1764) and the Poker Club had connections with campaigns to form a national militia. And although these were real societies with distinguished membership lists, some of the predictable club rituals hinted at satire. Fifteen members of the Poker Club were determined by nomination, the remainder by ballot or "fisticuffs." The chairman was chosen at the beginning of each meeting by means of a staring contest. William Pitt's minister in Scotland, Henry Dundas, whose nickname Grand Manager of Scotland was itself a pun on the chief Masonic office, was a member of the Poker Club. But in Dublin at a time when the Free Citizens of Dublin and the Monks of the Screw (1779) (who opted for monkish garb as compared with the Cape Club's knightly costumes) dominated Irish club life, the notion of a homosocial government equivalent appeared both threatening and perhaps a little ridiculous. In February 1784 the *Dublin Evening Post* claimed that Dublin Castle loyalists were forming a new club, "to celebrate the memory of the Northington Administration, similar to that formed at the departure of [the ex-viceroy] Lord Townshend." Rather than styling themselves the Northington Club, it was claimed that they preferred "the Anti-Reformist Society." It continued: "This society will not be merely convivial, it being intended as a standing committee, for the purpose of managing an opposition, in and out of Parliament, to any Reform or innovation whatever in the Representation of the kingdom."[95]

There was a degree of overlap here with another fictional group: the Sons of Freedom, who in 1784 are described as meeting at Liberty Tavern. They had resolved to call for a more equal representation of the people in Ireland, but the signatories revealed the club to be bogus. Its membership included leading lights from the government benches such as John Beresford, John Fitzgibbon, and John Scott, as well as turncoat patriots like Denis Daly, George Ogle, and Charles Francis Sheridan. The notion of print war through clubs is given further credence here by the inclusion of John Giffard, printer of *Faulkner's Dublin Journal*, and John Exshaw, printer of *Exshaw's Gentleman's and London Magazine*, as members.[96] Marie Mulvey Roberts notes that fictional clubs were often used as a way of attacking enemies in the world of print and journalism, two of the most famous examples being Daniel Defoe's Scandalous Club (1704) and Henry Fielding's Skull Club (1740). Here again, in these Irish government fictional clubs we have the blurring of fact and fiction. This kind of political lobbying society had a precedent in Dublin's Monks of the Screw, a society that was formed to provide some focus to the activities of Ireland's parliamentary opposition. Also, the membership was similar to the group that met to celebrate Lord Townshend's birthday. Indeed, there is evidence to suggest that a government grouping dined as a body on other occasions, such as on Queen Charlotte's birthday. Although the report of this also had a fictional dimension, as unlikely toasts included "Annihilation to the Volunteers" and "the British Interest."[97]

The Mirror and *The Lounger* were largely apolitical in clubbable content, but *The Bee* published letters from the Society of the Friends of the People (1792), and its engagement with radical politics eventually saw its editor James Anderson taken up for sedition in December 1792.[98] By 1793 it had retreated from this position, and in July *The Bee* invented the Magnum Bonum Sunday's Club, a society formed in hell by Satan and his followers. In a poem describing their conversation, one demon said: "Our viceregents on earth leave us little to do." This may, of course have been referencing the bloody events in revolutionary France, themselves club-connected, or the political upheaval in Britain. *The Bee* was also notable for its antipathy to the slave trade: "These flesh and blood demons have learned so well / The art of our calling, they laugh at our hell."[99]

Politeness and Fictional Clubs

Other than an obsession with rule making and ritual, the other preoccupation shown by some Scottish periodicals in their approach to club life was the issue of politeness. In the early eighteenth century the Rankenian Club had a number of members who were influenced by the writings of Lord Shaftesbury.[100] The Easy Club, according to its journal, met "in order that by a Mutual improvement in Conversation that they may become more adapted for fellowship with the politer part of mankind," and the name was said to be a "check to all unruly and disturbing behaviour" among the membership.[101] Indeed the initial practice of using pseudonyms in the Easy Club—"Sir Isaac Newton," "Sir Roger L'Estrange," "Rochester"—was less about comedy and more to ensure that for the name holder it "makes it impossible he should forget to copy what is laudable in him and what is not so to reject."[102] Concerns with politeness continued to occupy the memberships of some later eighteenth-century clubs. Henry Mackenzie was writing about self-control as well as sentimentality, and he was critical of luxury in a late edition of *The Lounger*. His publisher, William Creech, was unimpressed by the influence of ballad sellers in the 1780s, and he was generally disapproving of "modern manners."[103] The Speculative Society, of which Creech was a co-founder, had in its establishing articles the stipulation that any member who interrupted another by laughing should be reprimanded by the president. A member guilty of swearing would be fined sixpence and then one shilling; for a third offense the penalty was expulsion.[104] A major difficulty for clubs in Scotland and Ireland looking to enforce politeness was the structure and ritual that, by the late eighteenth century, had become a key component of club culture, although in some ways a culture of gourmandizing could disguise other more potent forms of activity.

More pertinent in Scotland and Ireland was the association of the club with the public house—there were plenty of drinking clubs in eighteenth-century Edinburgh. A letter to *The Mirror* in 1779 suggested that Mr. Mirror had been courted by the tavern keepers of Edinburgh in order that they could secure the position of the meetinghouse of the Mirror Club. The author went on to list a number of Edinburgh clubs that did meet in public houses, including the Capillaire, Whin-bush, Knights of the Cap and Feather, Tabernacle, Stoic, Poker, Humdrum, and Antemanum.[105] The critical role of the public house—as host, facilitator, and observer of impolite antics—was reflected by the fact that Mr. Mirror asked the landlords of the taverns (rather than the chairmen of the clubs) that hosted these institutions "to transmit me a short account of the origin and nature of these societies."[106] In this sense not only did tavern and club become one and the same—a natural confusion given that some clubs were born out of taverns—but the landlord became observer, and possibly even guardian, of decorum; clubs could bring disorder to taverns rather than the other way around. Some landlords had an even closer relationship with club life. An innkeeper was among the new recruits joining the Edinburgh Philosophical Society between 1768 and 1783.[107]

As suggested above, criticism of toasting featured in a number of newspapers, periodicals, and novels. Toasting itself had an early connection with a semi-fictional club. According to *The Tatler*, it was the primary activity of the satirical chivalric order called the Knights of the Toast.[108] Edward Ward's fictional Calves-Head Club of 1701, based on societies that allegedly gathered at the end of the seventeenth century to celebrate the execution of Charles I, and later used by Swift, toasted in a "Calve's-Scull fill'd with Wine" to "the Pious Memory of those worthy Patriots that had kill'd the Tyrant, and deliver'd their Country from his Arbitrary Sway."[109] The head of the calf, and its use in the ritual of toasting was therefore central to its identity, and the club's anniversary anthems had references to toasting as a central motif: "Let every smiling Glass with Mirth be Crown'd, / While Healths to England's Native Rights go round." More threatening was:

> Then fill the Calves Cranium to a Health so Divine,
> The Cause, the Old Cause shall ennoble our Wine;
> Charge briskly around, fill it up, fill it full,
> 'Tis the Last and Best Service of a Tyrannick Scull.[110]

Though Oliver Cromwell was toasted in some radical Irish clubs, the reference to the "Old Cause"—the parliamentary struggle against the monarchy, as badged by the Cromwellian army—would have been rather more scandalous, and made the act of toasting a threatening practice in itself. Another verse seemed to suggest that the sacred nature of drinking in club life rendered seditious toasts an innocent pastime:

Advance the Emblem of the Action!
Fill the Calve's Scull full of Wine,
Drinking ne'er was Counted Faction,
Men and Gods adore the wine.

The footnote to this stanza comments, ironically: "Admirable Doctrine in the Mouths of Hypocrites, that pretend to so much sanctity."[111] This was presumably a jibe at nonconformist republicans, and it is clear that the head of the calf had a link to sectarianism dating back at least to the 1640s.[112]

The rituals and the toasts of Ward's Calves-Head Club, which, as Michelle Orihel has shown, came with its own complex literary/fictive history, have clear echoes in the practices of the Aldermen of Skinner's Alley (1690), a Dublin-based proto-Orange society.[113] And while there can be no proof that the club—which itself had an early fictional-sounding life in the prose of Jonah Barrington and a later one via Joseph Sheridan Le Fanu—was influenced by the Calves-Head, it should be noted that Ward's fictional work *The Secret History of the Calves-Head Club* (1701) was reprinted in Dublin in 1705. Perhaps more importantly, there is a sense that clubs like the Calves-Head and the Aldermen of Skinner's Alley morphed in and out of reality thanks to their very close relationship with print. The target of the Calves-Head's ire, Charles I, complete with severed head buttons, found expression in Dublin's Block and Axe Club (c. 1783), which may also have had a fictional dimension.[114] The blurring between fact and fiction that we see in the Block and Axe Club—with a real civic membership but a perhaps too playful edge—is reversed in the case of Ward's original in that the fiction is given a hint of realism through the believable club anthems and toasts, and indeed the political language utilized. Brutus, a favorite of Irish and English Whiggism, is referenced twice in the Calves-Head anthems.[115] Throughout the various iterations of the Calves-Head there is also a clear attempt to link fictional Calves-Head members with prominent republicans like John Toland and John Milton.[116]

Smollett satirized toasting rituals in the fictional Scottish club visited by Jery Melford in *Humphry Clinker*. Jery's visit to the cawdies' entertainment in Leith would not have been so drunken without the toasts given by the cawdy toastmaster. The toasts themselves were mostly unexceptional, though they did include "The beggar's benison," a reference to the Anstruther libertine club (1732) of the same name, with a branch in Edinburgh; there was also one in Ireland, though this was a hunting society and did not seem to have a direct connection.[117] The toasting glasses used by the Anstruther original were highly sexualized, and the "beggar's benison" toast, based on stories of James V's sexual proclivities, was a literal health to the male genitals.[118] The Edinburgh Beggar's Benison (1752) clearly had more sober moments, as during the American war the club advertised in the press that it would give each new recruit to the Edinburgh regiment one guinea "and the Beggar's Benison over and above all other bounties and rewards."[119]

The practice of toasting was subject to a good deal of criticism in *The Mirror* and *The Lounger*, though authors and club members appearing in print did raise a glass from time to time.[120] The notion of toasting "sentiments" was referred to in a number of issues, echoing criticisms made in the London press in the 1760s.[121] This particular brand of toasting—which was also satirized in the poems produced by Jonathan Swift's circle on Dan Jackson's nose[122]—caused offense due to the often ribald tone of the healths given. A lengthy piece in the *Public Advertiser* in 1763 criticized a variety of toasting practices, including the role of the toastmaster, the types of toasts given to ladies, and the toasting of sentiments, as well as more political toasts likely to divide the company.[123] It is perhaps dangerous to assume that toasting was more acceptable in Irish circles, but it does seem that there was very little public debate on its merits. In Scotland an ode recited in a radical club in December 1791 did not see a contradiction between revolutionary politics and excessive sociability:

> Hither drawer! Bring us claret,
> Quickly fill us flowing bowls!
> Mouldy cash!—Why should we spare it?
> Banish dull unsocial souls.

Later in the poem: "In this bumper blooms a treasure, Chears the care-corroded breast!"[124]

The excesses encouraged by toasting rituals contributed to the pressures exerted upon some clubs and their members to find ways of moderating their proceedings. Both Irish and Scottish clubs of a certain kind placed restrictions on the amount of alcohol that could be consumed in a given evening, though in many cases this was attributable to clubs wishing to restrict expenditure rather than binge drinking.[125] One correspondent of *The Lounger* observed in 1786: "I was a member too of a weekly club, which met on the Saturday evenings, most of them people of talents, and some of them not unknown in the world of letters. Here the entertainment was truly *Attic*. A single bottle was the modicum, which no man was allowed to exceed. Wit and humour flowed without reserve, where all were united by the bonds of intimacy; and learning lost her gravity over the enlivening glass."[126] The sociable rules of Edinburgh's Poker Club were deliberately staid. Dinner was set at 2:00 P.M. and the alcohol available was restricted to wine, sherry, and claret. The bill had to be called for by 6:00 P.M.

The Mirror Club itself preferred claret to port wine,[127] and for many of the writers of the Mirror Club, even though enmeshed in club life themselves, there was an unease about excessive sociability and a championing of the sober responsibilities of domesticity. This championing of the domestic over the urban is a thread that runs counter to both Spectatorial satire and Irish newspapers' clubbable fictions. The Mirror Club's Colonel Caustic was critical of female participation in assemblies and theatrical entertainments in Edinburgh.[128] The fictional club in Mackenzie's poem "The Old Batchelor" reveals common practices in club life that ran counter to his ideal of domestic sociability. These included the discussion of politics—"And oft on politics the preachments ran"; lurid comedy—"And oft they chuckl'd loud at jest or jeer / Or bawdy tale the most, thilk much they lov'd to hear"; the failure to appreciate the attractions of domestic happiness—"No honest love they knew, no melting smile"; and, of course, toasting and the excessive consumption of alcohol—"Then pledg'd their hands, and toss'd their bumpers o'er / And lo! Bacchus! sung, and own'd no other pow'r."[129] Mackenzie's anti-political sentiments were later reflected in his dissatisfaction with the politics of the *Edinburgh Review* after 1802, though they did not stop him attacking Thomas Paine in print in 1791.[130]

It is clear, then, that for a sentimental—and indeed at times sententious—part of the Scottish Enlightenment there was a strand of anti-club rhetoric that can be seen to have fed in to nineteenth- and twentieth-century anti-club sentiment. This is why these periodicals also ran fictional tales about real clubs, which could be as powerful a mode of satire on clubbable excess as the invention of wholly fictional clubs (with, in some cases, real people as members). A piece published in Edinburgh's *The Bee* in 1791, on idleness, criticized the habits of those who attended London's Brooks's club (1764). An idler "drew upon my father, with his approbation, for three thousand pounds, the price I paid to a broker for a Cornish borough, got into Brookes's club, and the other fashionable societies in town, kept a girl, shook my elbow with the best company." He "sung a catch with the best in the club."[131] Later in the tale he lost five hundred at Brooks's at the age of twenty-five.[132] British and Irish newspapers delighted in tales, many doubtless fictional, about Irish dueling (though the only two clubs in Ireland connected to dueling, the Friendly Brothers of St. Patrick [c. 1750] and the Knights of Tara, were, in fact, formed in opposition to the practice). In *The Mirror* there was gentle mockery of two members of the Jockey Club (1750), who had been involved in a duel. One of them "had systematized the art of duelling to a wonderful degree." He could, it seems, aim with some success at any part of an opponent's body. The editor disapproved: "These arts . . . resemble, methinks, a loaded die, or a packed deal, and I am inclined to be of opinion, that a gentleman is no more obliged to fight against the first, than to play against the latter."[133]

Conclusion

Moyra Haslett suggests that fictional clubs had a very practical purpose—they could be responsible for notions an author would like to anonymize and they were convenient modes of shorthand—particularly in terms of social classes or types. Irish fortune hunters were included in Erasmus Jones's *A Trip Through London* (1728), and there was a fictional Irish club called the Welters in Anthony Pasquin's response to Christopher Anstey's *New Bath Guide* (1766).[134] Fictional clubs also chimed with a recognizable associational world and immediately lent credibility to a piece of satire. However, this was an associational world that was changing. By the end of the eighteenth century, groups like those celebrating Lord Townshend's birthday in Dublin had moved out of the tavern and into the private members' club, in that case from the King's Arms to Daly's Club House. Indeed, the original Daly's gaming club had shifted from public chocolate house to private premises.[135] And while the titled, the gentry, and the respectable middle classes were meeting in private, the radicals now had to meet in secret.

There is a temptation to see the French Revolution as a line of demarcation between different kinds of club life, as some contemporaries certainly did.[136] This of course does not mean a decline in club life, or indeed the removal of clubs from the world of print. Charitable bodies, if anything, expanded after the Union, and newspapers remained key to their activities. But the fictional club, at least in its mushroom phase, was a casualty (though the nineteenth century did see Charles Dickens's Pickwick Club). Haslett notes that while English fictional clubs became a rhetorical fashion during the early eighteenth century, it was a fashion that was dying out after mid-century. This might have been due to trends in club life, but it was equally down to fashions in satire: the end of Augustan irony and playfulness. There is less evidence of this in the Irish context, perhaps because fictional club life was driven more by a patriotic newspaper press that was booming during the 1770s and 1780s than by periodicals. In the Scottish context the fictive dimension of club life was linked to the arrival from the late 1770s of a new breed of Edinburgh periodicals that owed much to *The Tatler* and *The Spectator*; though, like other periodical titles, *The Lounger* was also reprinted in full issue form—in the *Caledonian Mercury* newspaper—as a mode of advertisement.[137] In these periodicals we are treated again to the Spectatorial approach to club life that envisages the readership as a logical extension of the club itself, with the downsides being the implications for polite culture of some clubbable activities, and the threat to society from those who were not clubbable. In Scotland one of the most significant examples of the genre, the Edinburgh-based "Noctes Ambrosianae" appearing in *Blackwood's Edinburgh Magazine*, comes as late as 1822.

Much of what newspapers and periodicals did, and the point of them being in the public arena, was to determine who exactly was clubbable. In the sharper Irish satires, women were perhaps not, though they led clubbable lives, in charitable clubs, debating clubs, catch and glee clubs, and a variety of other coteries and salons. Their inclusion was debated by the Spectator Club (1711), but they were never admitted, except, in the same periodical, to their own breed of fictional bodies; and even these suggested that a female "clubman" was ridiculous rather than club life itself.[138] The lower orders were also problematic clubmen, as were the effeminate and, at times, the fashionable. In the case of Irish fictional societies, all were given club status for the purpose of ridicule. This public versus private dichotomy is one of the most interesting aspects of the club-newspaper nexus. Newspapers ensured that the privacy and exclusivity of club life was, in an oxymoronic fashion, publicized. And this feels somewhat different from the cozier, more intimate approach of the periodical. But whatever the organ, the details that we get in the press are the public face, the open activities of societies rather than the precise details of their meetings. And here again, the use of fictive clubs and fictive proceedings could be protective as well as aggressive, ensuring that privacy and secrecy were maintained.

The final point worth making here is that in terms of press coverage—of fictional and nonfictional clubs—notions of clubbability went largely unchallenged in the Irish context. Any attack of this nature in Ireland, at least prior to the 1790s, tended to focus on unclubbable people and individual clubs. Clubs could be dangerous, but club life itself was still a prized component of the public sphere. Hunting clubs were criticized "for trampling the green corn of poor industrious tenants in pursuit of a harmless hare,"[139] the Block and Axe Club for its radical tendencies, the Irish Whig Club (1789), by John Fitzgibbon, lord chancellor and Dublin castle loyalist, for gluttony. In Scotland, whether in the new breed of periodicals or in the fiction of Smollett, there is a focus upon polite culture, and satirical writing was directed against the dangers inherent in raucous clubbable activities. Neither in Scotland nor in Ireland was there anything like the all-out assaults on club life undertaken earlier by Edward Ward. If we are looking for the *Vereinsmeirei* sniping of modern Germany, then in the late eighteenth century the nearest we see is the ridicule of certain clubbable practices that are increasingly regarded as impolite: excessive drinking and gluttony, swearing, and other forms of obscenity found in lurid toasts. These were far more of a concern for the Scottish periodicals, as politeness was a more pressing matter for Mackenzie and his fellows. The writers of the Mirror Club, according to Barbara M. Benedict, "promulgated conservative social attitudes sympathetic to the landed gentry."[140] Irish club life in fiction and reality remained a little more fun-filled, blurred, and incestuous. The Monks of the Screw were real, as was the Mirth and Good Humour Club (actually a Roscommon hunt).[141] Our understanding of club culture must by necessity be informed by the views of its critics, else historians fall prey to a tendency to see the development of civil society groups as an unalloyed good, and proto-democratic. Fictional club life offers insight into contemporary criticisms and enables comparative discussion, while giving a sense of how deeply embedded associational culture can be in national life. It also had its own impact on the development of that culture, encouraging clubbable proliferation and democratization in some cases and stultifying these impulses in others.

NOTES

1. Martyn J. Powell, "Scottophobia versus Jacobitism : Political Radicalism and the Press in Late Eighteenth-Century Ireland," in *Cultures of Radicalism in Britain and Ireland*, ed. John Kirk, Michael Brown, and Andrew Noble (London: Pickering and Chatto, 2013), 49–62.

2. Martyn J. Powell, "'Associate for the Purposes of Deliverance and Glory': The Club-Life of the Irish Volunteers," in *Associational Culture in Ireland and Abroad*, ed. R. V. Comerford and Jennifer Kelly (Dublin: Irish Academic Press, 2010), 27–46.

3. For print and the public sphere, see David S. Shields, *Civil Tongues and Polite Letters in British America* (Chapel Hill: University of North Carolina Press, 1997); Moyra Haslett, *Pope to Burney, 1714–1779: Scriblerians to Bluestockings* (Basingstoke: Palgrave Macmillan, 2003); Richard B. Sher, *The Enlightenment and the Book: Scottish Authors and Their Publishers in Eighteenth-Century Britain, Ireland, and America* (Chicago: University of Chicago Press, 2006); Jon Mee, *Conversable Worlds: Literature, Contention, and Community, 1762–1830* (Oxford: Oxford University Press, 2011); Alex Benchimol, "Periodicals and Public Culture," in *The Edinburgh Companion to Scottish Romanticism*, ed. Murray Pittock (Edinburgh: Edinburgh University Press, 2011), 84–99.

4. Alexander Hamilton, *The History of the Ancient and Honourable Tuesday Club*, ed. Robert Micklus (Chapel Hill: University of North Carolina Press, 1990); Marie Mulvey Roberts, "Pleasures Engendered by Gender: Homosociality and the Club," in *Pleasure in the Eighteenth Century*, ed. Roy Porter and Marie Mulvey Roberts (Basingstoke: Macmillan, 1996), 48–76.

5. John Dwyer, "Enlightened Spectators and Classical Moralists: Sympathetic Relations in Eighteenth-Century Scotland," in "Sociability and Society," 97; John Dwyer, "Mirror Club (*act.* 1776–1787)," in *ODNB*, https://doi:10.1093/ref:odnb/73612.

6. See Benchimol, "Periodicals and Public Culture," 87, 91.

7. Oliver Goldsmith, *Essays and Criticisms* (London: J. Johnson, 1798), 1:20–33.

8. Haslett, *Pope to Burney*, 2, 27.

9. See Rosalind Carr, *Gender and Enlightenment Culture in Eighteenth-Century Scotland* (Edinburgh: Edinburgh University Press, 2014), 73–101.

10. Benedict Anderson, *Imagined Communities: Reflections on the Origin and Spread of Nationalism* (London: Verso, 1991).

11. Clark, 172.

12. Haslett refers to readers forming "an imagined community, made present only in the consciousness of belonging to a print culture" (*Pope to Burney*, 53).

13. Martyn J. Powell, "'Beef, Claret, and Communication': Convivial Clubs in the Public Sphere, 1750–1800," in *Clubs and Societies in Eighteenth-Century Ireland*, ed. James Kelly and Martyn J. Powell (Dublin: Four Courts, 2010), 353–372.

14. Nicholas Rogers, "The Dynamic of News in Britain during the American War: The Case of Admiral Keppel," *Parliamentary History* 25 (2006): 49–67.

15. *The Lounger*, 27 Aug. 1785.

16. *Volunteer's Journal*, 17 May 1784, 28 May 1784.

17. *Volunteer's Journal*, 21 May 1784, 21 June 1784.

18. Murray Pittock, *Enlightenment in a Smart City: Edinburgh's Civic Development, 1660–1750* (Edinburgh: Edinburgh University Press, 2018), 201–202.

19. Paul Bator, "The University of Edinburgh Belles Lettres Society (1759–64) and the Rhetoric of the Novel," *Rhetoric Review* 14 (1996): 281.

20. See Martyn J. Powell, *The Politics of Consumption in Eighteenth-Century Ireland* (Basingstoke: Palgrave Macmillan, 2005), chap. 4.

21. Mulvey Roberts, "Pleasures Engendered by Gender," 49.

22. Haslett, *Pope to Burney*, 42.

23. Mulvey Roberts, "Pleasures Engendered by Gender," 57; *Gentleman's Magazine*, Mar. 1732, 647; Sept. 1735, 554.

24. Haslett, *Pope to Burney*, 11, 42.

25. *The Guardian*, 30 July 1713.

26. Edward Ward, *A Compleat and Humorous Account of All the Remarkable Clubs and Societies in the Cities of London and Westminster* (London: printed for the author, 1745).

27. Haslett, *Pope to Burney*, 122–123.

28. Ibid., 41.

29. *Humphry Clinker*, 105–106.

30. Ibid., 128–129.

31. *HJ*, 2–5 Jan. 1784.

32. *HJ*, 24–26 Mar. 1784.

33. *HJ*, 9–12 Jan. 1784.

34. *HJ*, 2–5 Jan. 1784.

35. Jürgen Habermas, *The Structural Transformation of the Public Sphere: An Inquiry into a Category of Bourgeois Society* (1962), trans. Thomas Burger, with the assistance of Frederick Lawrence (Cambridge, MA: MIT Press, 1989). For criticisms, see Joanna Meehan, ed., *Feminists Read Habermas: Gendering the Subject of Discourse* (New York: Routledge, 1995); Carr, *Gender and Enlightenment Culture*, 39–41.

36. *An Account of the Fair Intellectual-Club in Edinburgh: In a Letter to a Honourable Member of the Athenian Society there. By a young Lady, the Secretary of the Club* (Edinburgh: printed by J. McEuen, 1720). Also see Carr, *Gender and Enlightenment Culture*, 78–79.

37. Carr, *Gender and Enlightenment Culture*, 82–92; *Limerick Chronicle*, 29 Mar. 1773.

38. See Rose McCormack, "Leisured Women and the English Spa Town in the Long Eighteenth Century: A Case Study of Bath and Tunbridge Wells" (PhD diss, University of Aberystwyth, 2015), chap. 3.

39. Amy Prendergast, *Literary Salons across Britain and Ireland in the Long Eighteenth Century* (Basingstoke: Palgrave Macmillan, 2015), 106–133; Carr, *Gender and Enlightenment Culture*, 73–101.

40. Edward Ward, *The History of the London Clubs, or, The Citizens' Pastime* (1709; repr., London: J. Dutten, [1896]), 20.

41. *The Spectator*, 8 Nov. 1711, 28 June 1714.

42. *Grub Street Journal*, 10 May 1733; also see Haslett, *Pope to Burney*, 42, 145.

43. See Mee, *Conversable Worlds*, 111–115.

44. *Northern Star*, 4–7 Apr. 1792.

45. Barbara M. Benedict, "'Service to the Public': William Creech and Sentiment for Sale," in "Sociability and Society," 119, 135.

46. Ibid., 124.

47. *The Lounger*, 26 Feb. 1785, 12 Mar. 1785.

48. Benedict, "'Service to the Public,'" 133–134, 136.

49. Mulvey Roberts, "Pleasures Engendered by Gender," 69.

50. For the positioning of these associations within the gendered London club landscape, see Valérie Capdeville, "Gender at Stake: The Role of Eighteenth-Century London Clubs in Shaping a New Model of English Masculinity," *Culture, Society and Masculinities* 4 (2012): 18–19.

51. *HJ*, 23 Jan. 1784.

52. *HJ*, 29 Feb. 1784, 1–3 Mar. 1784.

53. Benedict, "'Service to the Public,'" 135.

54. Mee, *Conversable Worlds*, 63.

55. Roger L. Emerson, "The Philosophical Society of Edinburgh, 1768–1783," *Br J Hist of Sci* 18 (1985): 275. The "Sociability and Society" special issue of *Eighteenth-Century Life* goes some way toward redressing the balance.

56. Emerson, "Philosophical Society of Edinburgh, 1768–1783," 295.

57. For the Rankenian Club, see M. A. Stewart, "Berkeley and the Rankenian Club," *Hermathena* 89 (1985): 25–45; Emerson, "Philosophical Society of Edinburgh, 1768–1783," 264.

58. Bator, "Edinburgh Belles Lettres Society," 290; *The History of the Speculative Society, 1764–1904* (Edinburgh: printed for the Society, 1905), 2.

59. Haslett, *Pope to Burney*, 122; John Dwyer, "Introduction—A 'Peculiar Blessing': Social Converse in Scotland from Hutcheson to Burns," in "Sociability and Society," 9.

60. *James Arbuckle: Selected Works*, ed. Richard Holmes (Lewisburg, PA: Bucknell University Press, 2014), xxxii. I am grateful to Michael Brown for this reference.

61. *The Lounger*, 27 Aug. 1785.

62. Ibid.

63. Ibid.

64. Shields, *Civil Tongues*, 177.

65. *The Lounger*, 27 Aug. 1785.

66. Ibid.

67. *The Mirror*, 17 Aug. 1779.

68. *The Bee*, 3 Oct. 1792.

69. Ibid.

70. *The Beggars (of St Mary's Parish) Address, to Their Worthy Representative, Hackball* ([Dublin?], 1754), in Toby Barnard, *Making the Grand Figure: Lives and Possessions in Ireland, 1641–1770* (New Haven, CT: Yale University Press, 2004), 370.

71. Ibid., 370.

72. *HJ*, 1–3 Jan. 1776.

73. *HJ*, 12–15 Jan. 1776.

74. *Finn's Leinster Journal*, 28–31 Aug. 1776.

75. Ibid.

76. *Volunteer Evening Post*, 27–29 May 1784.

77. *Volunteer Evening Post*, 5–8 June 1784.

78. Robert Jephson, *The Confessions of James Baptiste Couteau, Citizen of France* (London: J. Debrett, 1794), 2:172.

79. Sydney, Lady Morgan, *The O'Briens and the O'Flahertys: A National Tale* (London: H. Colburn, 1828), 1:242–243, 270–282.

80. *Humphry Clinker*, 226–228.

81. *The Bee*, 10 July 1793.

82. Jon Mee, "The Buzz about the *Bee*: Policing the Conversation of Culture in the 1790s," in *Before Blackwood's: Scottish Journalism in the Age of Enlightenment*, ed. Alex Benchimol, Rhona Brown, and David Shuttleton (London: Routledge, 2015), 71.

83. *The Bee*, 10 July 1793.

84. *Humphry Clinker*, 115.

85. Robert J. Allen, *The Clubs of Augustan London* (Cambridge, MA: Harvard University Press, 1933), 166.

86. Roger Chickering, "Political Mobilization and Associational Life," in *Elections, Mass Politics, and Social Change in Modern Germany*, ed. Larry Eugene Jones and James Retallack (Cambridge: Cambridge University Press, 2002), 309.

87. *E-B*.

88. *Public Advertiser*, 16 Apr. 1763.

89. *The Bee*, 3 Oct. 1792.

90. *The Mirror*, 26 Feb. 1779.

91. Ward, *Compleat and Humorous Account*, 269–274; Ward, *History of the London Clubs*, 20.

92. *HJ*, 23–26 Jan. 1784.

93. James Sambrook, "Franciscans [Monks of Medmenham] (*act. c.* 1750–*c.* 1776)," in *ODNB*, https://doi:10.1093/ref:odnb/71306.

94. *HJ*, 23–26 Jan. 1784.

95. *Dublin Evening Post*, 12 Feb. 1784.

96. *Volunteer's Journal*, 12 Jan. 1784.

97. James Kelly, "Monks of the Screw [Monks of the Order of St. Patrick] (*act.* 1779–1789)," in *ODNB*, https://doi:10.1093/ref:odnb/96301; *Dublin Evening Post*, 9 Mar. 1784; *HJ*, 16–19 Jan. 1784.

98. Mee, "Buzz about the *Bee*," 72–73.

99. *The Bee*, 10 July 1793, 37–40. Fielding presented fashionable society as a fictional club with the devil rumored to be the president. See Haslett, *Pope to Burney*, 47.

100. Stewart, "Berkeley and the Rankenian Club," 29.

101. Allan Ramsay, "Journal of the Easy Club," in *The Works of Allan Ramsay*, vol. 5, ed. Alexander M. Kinghorn and Alexander Law (Edinburgh: William Blackwood and Sons, 1972), 5.

102. Ibid.

103. Dwyer, "Introduction—A 'Peculiar Blessing,'" in "Sociability and Society," 7; Dwyer, "Enlightened Spectators," 114; John Scally, "Cheap Print on Scottish Streets," in *The Edinburgh History of the Book in Scotland*, vol. 2, *Enlightenment and Expansion, 1707–1800*, ed. Stephen W. Brown and Warren McDougall (Edinburgh: Edinburgh University Press, 2012), 379; Barbara M. Benedict, "Creech, William [*pseud.* Theophrastus] (1745–1815)," in *ODNB*, https://doi:10.1093/ref:odnb/6662.

104. *History of the Speculative Society, 1764–1904*, 3.

105. *The Mirror*, 3 July 1779.

106. Ibid.

107. Emerson, "Philosophical Society of Edinburgh, 1768–1783," 271.

108. *The Tatler* 24 (24 Jan. 1709).

109. Edward Ward, *The Secret History of the Calves-Head Club, or, The Republican Unmasqu'd* (Dublin, 1705), 8; Jonathan Swift, *T—l—nd's Invitation to Dismal: To Dine With the Calve's-Head Club, Imitated from Horace Epist. 5 Lib. 1* ([Dublin?], 1712).

110. Ward, *Secret History*, 9–11.

111. Ibid., 14.

112. Michelle Orihel, "'Treacherous Memories' of Regicide: The Calves-Head Club in the Age of Anne," *The Historian* 73 (2011): 446.

113. See ibid.; Martyn J. Powell, "The Aldermen of Skinner's Alley: Ultra-Protestantism before the Orange Order," in Kelly and Powell, *Clubs and Societies*, 203–224.

114. Powell, "Aldermen of Skinner's Alley," 203–223.

115. Ward, *Secret History*, 9–10.

116. Orihel, "'Treacherous Memories,'" 462.

117. David Stevenson, *The Beggar's Benison: Sex Clubs of Enlightenment Scotland and Their Rituals* (East Linton: Tuckwell Press, 2001); Martyn J. Powell, "Hunting Clubs and Societies," in Kelly and Powell, *Clubs and Societies*, 392–408.

118. David Stevenson, "'The Gudeman of Ballangeich': Rambles in the Afterlife of James V," *Folklore* 15 (2004): 194.

119. *London Evening Post*, 7 Feb. 1778.

120. *The Lounger*, 27 Aug. 1785.

121. One particular toast or sentiment was described in *The Lounger* as given "in terms shockingly gross and indecent." *The Lounger*, 7 May 1785.

122. See Moyra Haslett, "Swift and Conversational Culture," *Eighteenth-Century Ireland*, 29 (2014): 11–30.

123. *Public Advertiser*, 16 Apr. 1763.

124. *The Bee*, 8 Feb. 1792.

125. Powell, "'Beef, Claret, and Communication,'" 370.

126. *The Lounger*, 15 Apr. 1786.

127. *The Lounger*, 27 Aug. 1785.

128. John Dwyer, *Virtuous Discourse: Sensibility and Community in Late Eighteenth-Century Scotland* (Edinburgh: John Donald, 1987), 123–124.

129. Henry Mackenzie, "The Old Batchelor. After the Manner of Spenser," *Town and Country Magazine* 3 (Mar. 1771): 158–160.

130. Dwyer, *Virtuous Discourse*, 191–192; "Brutus to the Opposition," *SM*, May 1791. I am grateful to Michael Brown for this latter reference.

131. *The Bee*, 25 May 1791.

132. Ibid.

133. *The Mirror*, 2 Mar. 1779.

134. Anthony Pasquin, *A Postscript to the New Bath Guide: A Poem* (London: J. Strahan, 1790), 94–97.

135. *Dublin Evening Post*, 9 Mar. 1784; *Saunders's News-Letter*, 8 Mar. 1793.

136. Mee, *Conversable Worlds*, 90.

137. Dwyer, *Virtuous Discourse*, 14.

138. Haslett, *Pope to Burney*, 123.

139. *Finn's Leinster Journal*, 22–25 Feb. 1775.

140. Benedict, "'Service to the Public,'" 119.

141. *Faulkner's Dublin Journal*, 12–14 Dec. 1776.

PART IV

Gender and Associational Culture

CHAPTER 9

Achieving Manhood in Associational Culture

STUDENT SOCIETIES AND MASCULINITY IN ENLIGHTENMENT EDINBURGH

Rosalind Carr

Student-led debating societies were more than another subdivision of associational culture in eighteenth-century Scotland. They were a significant educational space, facilitating the transmission of Enlightenment ideas and entrance into a culture of polite manhood. Located in universities, these societies were a voluntary part of higher education. The debates and discussions within them combined the conversational education begun in childhood with the development of the art of rhetoric, necessary for a career in the church, the law, and other professions.

Mimicking more mature intellectual societies—such as Edinburgh's preeminent Select Society (1754)—in form and topics debated, student societies provide insight into the experience of youth in urban Scotland.[1] While in some respects distinct, the youth culture enacted in these societies was not dissimilar to the homosocial culture of intellectual societies primarily composed of adult men who had achieved professional or landholding status or both, and participation in them provided a path to socially recognized manhood.[2] The exact form this manhood would take was not, however, predetermined; student-led debating societies offered the polish and self-command necessary for professional and married life, but also provided an avenue for a tavern-based libertine masculinity. Within the male culture of the university, these conflicting masculinities, both conferring elite male privilege, could be complementary and thus, as Alexandra Shepard argues in a study of early modern Cambridge, remained "unthreatening to social and political order."[3] Focusing on Edinburgh University, and utilizing alumni life writing, college archives, and records from the

Belles Lettres Society (1759) and the Speculative Society (1764), this chapter explores the role of student societies in the formation of manliness in Enlightenment Scotland.

Associations, Youth, and Character Formation

As Susan Manning and Thomas Ahnert have discussed, the Scottish Enlightenment "science of man" emphasized sociability as a crucial influence in the formation of character. The "close development between the moral self and the social life" meant that formal education was not enough to form one's character. Rather, it was formed and judged through social exchange in domestic and public arenas.[4] While character formation was a lifelong endeavor, the transitional phase of youth was particularly important, and student societies are an example of Enlightenment character formation in action. In early modern Europe, youth denoted an important stage in an individual's life cycle, marking a transitional period from childhood to adulthood, and indicated by events such as entering work outside the family unit or attending university. Embracing the period before adulthood was achieved via marriage and heading a household or establishing a business, the life stage of youth and adolescence in early modern England has been summarized by Ilana Krausman Ben-Amos as "a long and dynamic phase in the life cycle—a phase which consisted of a series of mental, social and economic processes through which the young were transformed into adults."[5] Ben-Amos's study examines the lower and middling sorts for whom work, such as entering service, was crucial in the transition to adulthood.

For many elite men, the experience of education away from home at school and university was a distinguishing characteristic of the transition from youth to manhood. For Thomas Somerville, born in Hawick, Roxburghshire, in 1741, removal "from intercourse with my beloved father"—when placed in a school in Duns—"contributed to my advantage in later life" because "indulgence at home . . . might have unfitted me for the exertions I had to make."[6] This development of independence was combined with a need to develop a foundational knowledge. In school, Matthew D. Eddy explains in his study of the later Enlightenment period, children developed a "spatial knowledge that laid the foundation for the forms of systematic classification that undergirded the Enlightenment vision of an ordered mind."[7]

Examining youth and school education in England, Anthony Fletcher has noted parents' recognition that the teenage years were those "when a child was old enough to imbibe patterns of behavior and learn the polite accomplishments that would stand them in good stead in adult life."[8] For boys, the initial separation from family instigated by schooling was often followed by university study, and Henry French and Mark Rothery have explored English gentry families' understanding of university as "a valuable staging post in the development of masculine independence."[9] In *My Own Life and Times, 1741–1814* (1861), written when he was in his early seventies, Somerville reflected on his studies at Edinburgh University, which began in November 1756 at age fifteen. Somerville drew particular attention to the influence of the Belles Lettres Society and the Theological Society (1759) on the formation of his character and establishment of his professional identity.[10] Eventually becoming minister at Minto in 1767, and later Jedburgh, and serving as a tutor to the family of Sir Gilbert Elliot of Minto, Somerville considered his initial education in these student societies to have had a significant and positive long-term impact: "To my attendance on these societies, more than to any branch of reading or study, I impute any progress I have made in literature, in composition, and in solid intellectual improvement. I thus acquired, especially, some facility and correctness of expression, and, what I deem of still greater importance, an estimation and love of truth."[11] This statement speaks to the importance of student societies in the formation of men's moral character during the transitional phase from youth to manhood, and Somerville's use of the term "improvement" and emphasis on "truth" places this process in the context of both Presbyterian and Enlightenment discourse.

The Scottish Enlightenment was not a secular project, and Somerville, a peripheral participant who published pamphlets on the American and French Revolutions and the slave trade, as well as *The History of Great Britain during the Reign of Queen Anne* (1798), exemplifies the connection between religion and Enlightenment in Scotland.[12] In a similar fashion, William Lothian's participation in the Belle Lettres Society while a student at Edinburgh is emphasized by Jeng-Guo S. Chen as crucial to his development of oratory skills and a Moderate philosophy that promoted "both polite culture and moral sense."[13] As Chen argues, the society exemplified the fact that "divinity students of the day were expected to mix not in scholastic culture but in polite society."[14]

Participation in polite society, including sociable debate, was considered to have a reforming and polishing influence, but conviviality could pose a threat to polite Presbyterian manhood. Somerville's Presbyterian perspective influenced his reflections on youthful conviviality, presenting an uncertain but largely condemnatory opinion of it. Somerville describes the Theological Society as "not only a school of mental improvement, but a nursery of brotherly love and kind affections."[15] Yet it was this very brotherly love, coupled with the freedom from the constraints that professional life and domesticity imposed, that most threatened Somerville's moral character: "If the time of my liberty had been prolonged, it is more than probable that the love of pleasure might have relaxed my application to study; for I was, perhaps to a culpable degree, fond of convivial meetings, and my company began to be courted by many young men of a similar disposition, who were not under the restraints which my principles, pecuniary circumstances, and professional views imposed upon me."[16] Somerville's unease about the effects of conviviality were shared by moral philosopher (and Select Society founding member) Adam Smith. Describing the ideal prudent man, Smith writes that "he is always very capable of friendship," but "he rarely frequents, and more rarely figures in those convivial societies which are distinguished for the jollity and gaiety of their conversation. Their way of life might too often interfere with the regularity of his temperance, might interrupt the steadiness of his industry, or break in upon the strictness of his frugality."[17]

Across Britain, the influence of education on the character of middling and elite men—from infancy to the grand tour and university—was a subject of debate, and part of a growing concern with character during this period.[18] In Scotland, for example, Aberdeen professors debated whether university students should be housed on campus or allowed to live in town, indicating a concern for the susceptibility of youth to moral corruption, in particular the allures of the town.[19] These practical considerations were part of a broader philosophical discourse on education: in February 1755 the Select Society questioned "Whether a University in a metropolis, or in a remote town be most proper for the place of the education of youth," while Aberdeen's Philosophical Society (1758) asked "How far the ancient method of Education in Public Seminaries from earliest Infancy was preferable or Inferior to Modern Practice."[20] Considering similar issues in 1763, the student-led Belles Lettres Society heard a discourse on "Whether a publick or private Education is best," and in 1766 and 1768 the Speculative Society discussed "Whether the Spartan or present method of Education be most preferable" and "Whether virtue is the product of Nature or of Education."[21] As the similarity in questions debated suggest, student-led intellectual societies, such as the Belles Lettres and Speculative societies at Edinburgh, were part of a shared urbane culture that encompassed other voluntary associations, convivial societies, and emerging social realms such as the music concert and theater. In this context they represent an ideal of youth culture, as spaces for the formation of rhetorical skill and self-command via controlled intellectual exchange.

As I have explored elsewhere in relation to adult male intellectual associations, adherence to these behavioral codes was crucial to the performativity of a masculine politeness deemed to be symbolic of civility and commercial civilization.[22] Involving teenagers typically from landed or professional backgrounds, student societies were an important part of the education of men on the cusp of adulthood, functioning alongside university lectures and other sites of education such as dancing and language instruction. This complementary role can be gleaned, for instance, in the establishment of libraries by student societies, supplementing the texts available in university libraries and recommended by professors. As Roger L. Emerson suggests, these libraries served "the needs of men in classes, and in their leisure hours."[23] Occurring in the predominantly male space of the university and continuing in the exclusively male professions, men's learning often occurred in a different context from women's, but it is important not to overstate this difference regarding the complementarity of education within and outside the domestic home.

In her study of elite Scotswomen, Katharine Glover explores the importance to the formation of female politeness of education at home and in private schools. As with boys, the removal of elite girls from the home and their placement in schools in Edinburgh or London was considered a key stage in their life cycle, and was normally accompanied by their first public engagements in polite society.[24] Great emphasis was placed on women's role in conversation in eighteenth-century Britain, and their education was primarily intended to enable them to fulfill this role. Conversation was not only important to women, however. As Michèle Cohen explains, the informal education of children through conversation and exposure to polite company was—for "families of leisure and education"—considered essential to the development of critical thinking (a skill not necessarily encouraged by rote learning in schools). Through conversation, children learned the social arts of politeness while expanding their intellectual knowledge.[25]

In an era when, following the philosophy of John Locke, the self was increasingly understood to be formed by education, the questions debated in societies indicate a concern with appropriate masculine character formation. This construction of a specific, polite, manhood can also be gleaned from other topics discussed in the Speculative Society, such as Mr. Hepburn's "discourse on friendship" on 3 May 1764, and another discourse on the same subject in December 1770. A similar debate, engaging with philosophical discussions of friendship and sociability, was held on 20 December 1765, when the society's members discussed "Whether we should pay greater regard to the Interests of our Country or our friends," and on 21 January 1767, "Whether is Friendship or Love the noblest passion."[26] The society was also concerned with virtue. For instance, on 22 November 1765 they debated "whether Tragedy or Comedy tend most to the Encouragement of Virtue," and in November the following year considered "the importance of Virtue to the Happiness of Society."[27] Reflecting concerns present in the moral philosophy of Henry Home, Lord Kames, Hugh Blair, and James Fordyce, among others, regarding the corrupting influence of luxury on men's character, the debate in November 1768, "Is Luxury advantageous to any state?," can be read as an indirect engagement with appropriate forms of masculinity.[28] Indeed, all these debates and discourses, and others, such as that on 24 November 1772, "Have the modern laws of Honour tended to the improvement of morals?," represent an intellectual engagement with the formation of masculine character.[29] Yet they went further than this. In the context of debates and discourses, these societies provided a space for men to enact, and through reiterative practice to learn and make natural, a virtuous polite masculinity.[30]

Gender Performativity in the Belles Lettres and Speculative Societies

Learning through conversation remained important during the youth life stage, and motivated the formation of mixed-sex social spaces in the public sphere—from gatherings centered on tea drinking to assemblies and the theater. As David Hume insisted: "What better school for manners, than the company of virtuous women; where the mutual endeavour to please must insensibly polish the mind, where the example of the female softness and modesty must communicate itself to their admirers, and where the delicacy of that sex puts every one on his guard, lest he give offence by any breach of decency?"[31]

The importance of femininity to the formation of polite male identities encouraged mixed-sex sociability, but conversation was also crucial in homosocial spaces, from the tavern to the intellectual club.[32] The specific character of this conversation, for example, bawdy or polite, was dependent on its cultural, geographic, and spatial location.[33] As in other associational spaces, in student societies conversation was controlled and directed by rules and set topics of discussion. These codes made the ideals of polite manhood behavioral, writing them on the body. Rule 7 of the Speculative Society asserted, "That every Person who shall interrupt another while speaking, Debating or Reading by laughing or by any other improper Behaviour, shall be solemnly reprimanded by the President."[34] It was a similar situation in the Belles Lettres Society, where in 1759 Mr. Andrew Smith was expelled for behavior "deemed inconsistent with the Decency and Decorum hitherto observed in this Society," and Mr. Govane was banned from taking the role of president for six months after he acted in an "ungenteel and uncivil manner" toward Mr. Grant.[35] In the Speculative Society, it was a combination of behavior during meetings and moral credit in society that determined whether a young man could become a member, with rule 10 stating: "That no person of immoral Character can be admitted, whatever his abilities in other respects may be; and that every member who is heard swear, or use unbecoming Language in the Society, shall for the first fault be fined in Six pence, for the second in a Shilling, and the third time shall be excluded."[36]

The polite debates in student societies continued the skills learned in the domestic realm in a homosocial environment, combining manly rhetoric with feminine-tinged polite conversation. This conversation could also occur informally between professors and students; as a student of professor of medicine William Cullen remarked in 1764: "We convene at his own house once or twice a week, where after lecturing for one hour, we spend another in an easy conversation upon the subject of the last evening's lecture, & every one is encouraged to make his remarks or objections with the greatest freedom & ease."[37]

This shared conversation with professors suggests a common culture of genteel learning, which was also reflected in student societies, existing at Edinburgh since at least the early eighteenth century.[38] Also, societies' role within the institution was not necessarily an inferior one; as Emerson explains, the establishment of mid-century societies such as the Belles Lettres occurred at the same time as significant changes to the curriculum at Scottish universities. These changes included the establishment of a chair of rhetoric and belles lettres at Edinburgh in 1761, an emphasis on empiricism by new professors such as Adam Smith at Glasgow, and an increasing use of English- and French-language books alongside traditional Latin texts.[39] Formed in 1759 and meeting on the grounds of Edinburgh University, the Belles Lettres Society has been credited by Paul Bator with providing a unique example of the contribution of students to the cultural and intellectual output of the Scottish Enlightenment, especially in relation to interpretations of romance and the idea of the novel as an improving rather than corrupting genre.[40] The society was also conscious of its role in the formation of manhood, stating that members' speeches on the liberal arts were "now looked upon as necessary to compleat the Scholar and the Gentleman."[41] This notion illustrates the influence of broader Enlightenment culture on the society, with many members being students of Hugh Blair, professor of rhetoric and belles lettres. Reinforcing the society's relations with the university, Blair and other professors such as Adam Ferguson were honorary members.

In student societies, young men established and reinforced links with a professional world dominated by the law and the church, with success in both requiring good networks and a talent for public speaking.[42] Somerville cited his involvement in student societies as a significant factor in his later professional success: "My exertions in both these societies also contributed in various respects to my advantage, by procuring me the esteem of several of my fellow-students."[43] Men to whom Somerville had access through the Belles Lettres Society included Henry Dundas, later Viscount Melville. He also honed his skills in public speaking and developed his self-command, recording that at the Belles Lettres Society, he spoke "only on such subjects as I believed to be within the compass of my understanding, and to embrace and defend that side of the question which accorded with my genuine sentiments, and appeared to be supported by the most solid arguments."[44]

The conversation of intellectual associations—including student societies—was, in theory, not the same as the mixed-sex conversation of the drawing room or assembly hall. Cultural rules of politeness ensured that it was non-combative, but the importance of argument undermined the gallantry and acquiescence that were considered important behavioral traits in ideal manifestations of mixed-sex conversation.[45] Instead, the art of rhetoric was essential. In the early years of the Speculative Society, its weekly meetings included a debate, a paper, and a member of the society reading "in prose and in verse."[46] This society was self-aware of its place in the professional world, asking in April 1768 "which of the three great Professions has the most extensive sphere of usefulness—Physic—

or Law—or Divinity." Over time its membership came to include men from the professions as well as students.[47]

As well as membership, the institutional and geographical location of the Speculative and Belles Lettres Societies place them as part of Enlightenment culture. Together with the universities of Aberdeen and Glasgow, the University of Edinburgh was a center for the formulation and dissemination of Enlightenment thought, particularly under the leadership of the historian Rev. William Robertson, principal from 1762 to 1793. In addition to Blair, other significant Enlightenment thinkers held professorships at the university, including Adam Ferguson, William Cullen, Dugald Stewart, and Joseph Black. Besides this, the location of the university in Scotland's capital was significant, giving the young male students access to the center of a publishing revolution and an urbane public sphere that was growing in size and cultural dominance.[48] Alongside theaters and assemblies, this public sphere included other intellectual societies, such as the Edinburgh Philosophical Society (1737) (later the Royal Society of Edinburgh [1783]), and professional associations, including the Faculty of Advocates. It was to this public world that students in the Speculative Society most readily sought to associate themselves, in the process demonstrating the integration of town and gown in mid-eighteenth-century Edinburgh.[49]

The importance of Edinburgh in forming polite, enlightened men was emphasized by Rev. Dr. Alexander Carlyle, who, comparing his experiences studying at Edinburgh and Glasgow universities, wrote that while Glasgow placed great importance on formal learning, only in Edinburgh could men attain "knowledge of the world, and a certain manner and address that can only be attained in the capital."[50] He complained that although there were dancing assemblies every fortnight, "There never was but one concert the two winters I was at Glasgow."[51] Illustrating this culture, the club Carlyle attended at Mr. Dugald's tavern "admitted a mixture of young gentlemen" and "conversation was almost entirely literary."[52] These Glasgow clubs are explored by Ralph McLean in his chapter in this volume. As he indicates, Carlyle was also a student member of Glasgow's Anderston Club (c. 1745), established by Robert Simson, professor of mathematics. While Glasgow may have been lacking in urbane culture, this youthful associational culture helped to forge the adult professional man. As Carlyle mused, "These societies tended much to our improvement; and as moderation and early hours were inviolable rules of both institutions, they served to open and enlarge our minds."[53]

In Edinburgh, the desire to forge a space in polite, professional society was particularly marked in the Speculative Society. Referred to by Nicholas Phillipson as "the grandest of student societies" and by Davis D. McElroy as "the most successful debating society of the century," the Speculative Society demonstrated its powerful position by obtaining rooms in the new college (now called Old College) when the building was completed in 1819. This was as Robertson intended when, in the 1780s, the new college was first planned with leading neoclassical architect Robert Adam.[54]

Alternative Student Masculinities

The place of the Belles Lettres and Speculative societies in the polite, urbane culture of Enlightenment Scotland provides a different image of student life to the riotous students of the late seventeenth century, when according to Phillipson, "student unrest was endemic," resulting in the 1694 Act against Tumults and Disorders in Colleges and Universities by the Scottish Privy Council and a 1701 ban by Edinburgh's town council on students playing games, throwing stones, carrying weapons, and visiting taverns.[55] Yet the change in student culture during the eighteenth century should not be overstated: while Enlightenment values of self-command and refinement were reflected in student life, the disorderly, challenging aspects of student life did not disappear.

In 1755 two medical students were initially denied the opportunity to sit their exams by the University Senate after they failed to make proper apology for a riot at the playhouse and then behaved in an "indecent and scandalous manner" at a public entertainment given by the magistrates who had fined them for their initial riot. The penalty imposed by the university prompted an apology to the magistrates, after which the two students were allowed to take their exams and "if found qualified" obtain the degree of MD.[56] This case provides unique evidence of student disorder dealt with by the university's governing body during this period, and it possibly came before the Senate Academicus because it was reported in the papers. However, the apparent lack of other evidence of student drunkenness in the Senate minutes does not necessarily mean that these teenagers always behaved in a sober, upstanding manner.[57]

While the primary function of student societies was to polish boys by encouraging polite but rigorous debate, they did not place them on a single, linear path to manhood. In his autobiography, Somerville admits to the "darkest side of the history of this Society, which diminished, perhaps counterbalanced the advantages derived from it. . . . Our tavern adjournments, which succeeded our weekly meetings in the College, were the cause of expense, and sometimes of excess and irregularity, unsuitable to our circumstances and professional views."[58] Although these sociable interactions gave Somerville pleasure and encouraged affection toward his peer group, he also noted the "baneful habits by which some of the worthiest of my earliest contemporaries have been enthralled, and which I have too much reason to think germinated in the fascinating indulgences I have described." By Somerville's reckoning, as well as being immoral by the standards of Presbyterianism, drinking undermined oeconomy and respectability, and it was by "a narrow escape my own health and character have been maintained."[59] This participation in "immoral" activities in youth was also part of Carlyle's experience of student life; for instance, while studying at Edinburgh, during his spare time he began to spend his money "at a billiard-table, which unluckily was within fifty yards of the College." However, being "sensible of the folly of this," he had abandoned this practice by the next year.[60]

The different impact that university study could have on a man's adult character is indicative of its importance as a transitional life stage. For men like Somerville, drinking to excess in taverns was part of youth culture and not something to be carried into adult professional or domestic manhood. Studies of early modern England have shown that drunkenness, violence, and sexual libertinism during youth—whether as an apprentice or student—provided a means to establish a masculine identity distinct from the sober manhood of the married and financially independent adult man.[61] Men such as the diarist and biographer James Boswell demonstrate that for some, excessive alcohol consumption and sexual libertinism remained connected to polite and professional culture in Edinburgh, while contemporaries such as Somerville placed it as a distinct youth stage. Both men regretted their behavior, and Boswell is known for his regular self-condemnation after getting drunk and purchasing sex from women. Unlike Somerville, he continued this behavior into adulthood, including during his marriage (when violence was also part of his drunken behavior).[62] And there is nothing to suggest that the youthful libertinism of Somerville, unlike that of Boswell, extended to paying women for sex.[63] While they led different lives, the involvement of both of these men in associational and tavern-based convivial culture attests to the connections between these spaces in Edinburgh, and their significance to elite and professional men's lived experience, particularly in youth. As James J. Caudle's chapter in this volume explores, Boswell was active in the Soaping Club (c. 1760). This Edinburgh convivial club was primarily composed of men in their twenties and offered a space for the performance of a less genteel masculinity than intellectual societies such as the Select Society, of which he was also a member.

Boswell's mixed experiences at university support French and Rothery's contention that this life stage "placed men in an ambiguous position between degrees of childish dependence and aspirations to genteel manhood."[64] In a short sketch of his early life written for Jean Jacques Rousseau, Boswell writes positively about his first experience at Edinburgh University, where from the age of thirteen he studied arts, attesting: "There I had more freedom [compared to studying under his governor]. The place rather pleased me, and during the three years that I was studying languages, I gained high distinction and my professors said I would be a very great man."[65] This is in stark contrast to his experiences several years later, studying civil law at the behest of his father. Returning from London, he records that his mind, "once put in ferment, could never apply itself again to solid learning. I had no inclination whatever for the Civil Law. I learned it very superficially. My principles became more and more confused.

I ended a complete sceptic. I held all things in contempt, and I had no idea except to get through the passing day agreeably. I had intrigues with married actresses. My fine feelings were absolutely effaced."[66]

These contrasting formative experiences occurred in the same city, only a few years apart. They were influenced less by the character of the place and more by the subjects studied and Boswell's state of mind (specifically, the resentment of a maturing man at being forced into an unwanted profession by his father, a Court of Session judge). The adoption of masculine identities distinct to patriarchal manhood should, French and Rothery argue, be recognized as "a sub-set of legitimate values, rather than a replacement for them."[67] Just as financial probity and marriage indicated manly independence, in certain homosocial contexts drinking and whoring established a man's maturity and autonomy, though if it resulted in a loss of self-control it could destroy a man's social credit.[68] Also, this alternative tavern-based masculinity did not wholly define male youth culture. As Somerville suggests—although there was a close interrelationship between them—there was a clear distinction between society meetings and tavern conviviality, and the formation of student societies committed to polite debate reveals a youth culture attuned to the dominant elite culture of politeness. In this culture, the performance of a manly sensibility formed by self-command and displayed in non-combative intellectual and other social interaction was an indicator of enlightened manhood.

Conclusion: Routes to Manhood

Connected to male work patterns, such as the completion of apprenticeships and achievement of financial autonomy, marriage was the typical route to manhood in the early modern period, with governance over a wife and children (and often servants) indicating men's self-command and social credit.[69] During the eighteenth century, Joanne Bailey argues, sensibility encouraged "a benign form of fatherly government," but this government continued to be a crucial marker of manhood.[70] As Katie Barclay reminds us, marriage should not be understood as a single life-cycle phase, as this "simplifies the complex and evolving experience of a marital relationship that could last a significant part of a person's life."[71] While not a single stage, nor unchanging in its core characteristics, marriage and fatherhood were a common means to achieve and display manhood. Yet marrying was not the only route to socially recognized manhood.

Considering the fact that leading literati such as Adam Smith and David Hume did not marry, integration into associational culture via participation in societies and professional bodies can be understood as a means of achieving and asserting manhood. That they were bachelors did not negate their manhood. In Karen Harvey's study of men, domesticity, and economy, she provides examples of men who remained unmarried yet demonstrated a financial probity that enabled them to claim manhood.[72] In addition to financial independence, in Scotland at least, intellectual men of wealth and status could display manliness by performing polite sensibility and establishing their reputation via participation in learned societies, professional achievement, and the publication of influential texts. Indeed, Hume, who had been a member of the Physiological Library (1724) when at Edinburgh University in the 1720s and a founding member of the Select Society as an adult, focuses on his intellectual, professional, and social achievements in his short autobiography "My Own Life," written shortly before his death, in April 1776.

Hume concludes his brief autobiography with an assessment of his character, declaring himself "a man of mild dispositions, of command of temper, of an open, social, and cheerful humour, capable of attachment, but little susceptible of enmity, and of great moderation in all my passions."[73] This summary of his manly status is indicative of the focus on the inner self rather than outward behavior or status in determining character in Enlightenment thought. In Hume's work, as well as that of Smith, Blair, and others, the formation of this inner self was not separate from society.

This alternative route to manhood was not confined to leading literati, who established a scholarly reputation among contemporaries. A recent study of Gilbert Innes by Barclay has demonstrated that an upper-middling man could achieve manhood outside of marriage through leadership of cultural institutions such as Edinburgh's Assembly, of which Innes was a director in the early decades of the nineteenth century. Innes was involved in some aspects of fatherhood by ensuring the maintenance of his illegitimate children, but in a Presbyterian culture (however moderate) it was not this that proved his manhood in society. Rather, it was his public engagement and overall financial probity.[74]

Across the eighteenth century, student societies were an important part of men's education, providing a sociable and educational adjunct to the formal learning of the university lecture. Encouraging polite debate and enabling men to network, they were particularly important to the formation of an urbane manliness, and thus played a significant role in young men's transition to adulthood. However, as the comparison of Boswell and Somerville shows, the convivial aspects of student associational culture could lead men down different paths, and the character of Enlightenment men was not homogenous.

NOTES

1. Davis D. McElroy refers to student societies as miniatures of Enlightenment clubs and societies. See McElroy, 1969, 104. See also Roger L. Emerson, *Essays on David Hume, Medical Men and the Scottish Enlightenment: Industry, Knowledge and Humanity* (Farnham: Ashgate, 2009), 66–67.

2. For the social status of men in Enlightenment societies, see Emerson, *Essays on David Hume*, 291–329.

3. Alexandra Shepard, "Student Masculinity in Early Modern Cambridge," in *Frühneuzeitliche Universitätskulturen: Kulturhistorische Perspektiven auf die Hochschulen in Europa*, ed. Barbara Krug-Richter and Ruth-E. Mohrmann (Cologne: Böhlau, 2009), 56.

4. Thomas Ahnert and Susan Manning, "Introduction: Character, Self, and Sociability in the Scottish Enlightenment," in *Character, Self, and Sociability in the Scottish Enlightenment*, ed. Thomas Ahnert and Susan Manning (New York: Palgrave Macmillan, 2011), 6–11.

5. Ilana Krausman Ben-Amos, *Adolescence and Youth in Early Modern England* (New Haven, CT: Yale University Press, 1994), 8.

6. Thomas Somerville, *My Own Life and Times, 1741–1814*, ed. Richard B. Sher (1861; repr., Bristol: Thoemmes Press, 1996), 8.

7. Matthew D. Eddy, "The Shape of Knowledge: Children and the Visual Culture of Literacy and Numeracy," *Science in Context* 26 (2013): 221.

8. Anthony Fletcher, "Courses in Politeness: The Upbringing and Experiences of Five Teenage Diarists, 1671–1860," *Transactions of the Royal Historical Society* 12 (2002): 417.

9. Henry French and Mark Rothery, *Man's Estate: Landed Gentry Masculinities, 1660–1900* (Oxford: Oxford University Press, 2012), 91.

10. Somerville, *My Own Life*, 10–45.

11. Ibid., 39–40.

12. Sher, introduction to Somerville, *My Own Life*, ix–xi. For the entanglement of church and Enlightenment in Scotland, see Richard B. Sher, *Church and University in the Scottish Enlightenment: The Moderate Literati of Edinburgh* (Edinburgh: Edinburgh University Press; Princeton, NJ: Princeton University Press, 1985).

13. Jeng-Guo S. Chen, "William Lothian and the Belles Lettres Society of Edinburgh: Learning to Be a Luminary in Scotland," *J for 18th Cent Stud* 27 (2004): 183.

14. Ibid., 175.

15. Somerville, *My Own Life*, 42.

16. Ibid., 51.

17. Adam Smith, *The Theory of Moral Sentiments*, ed. D. D. Raphael and A. L. Macfie, The Glasgow Edition of the Works and Correspondence of Adam Smith (1976; rev. repr., Indianapolis: Liberty Fund, 1982), 214.

18. See French and Rothery, *Man's Estate*; see also Mary Hilton and Jill Shefrin, eds., *Educating the Child in Enlightenment Britain: Beliefs, Cultures, Practices* (Farnham: Ashgate, 2009); Anthony Fletcher, *Gender, Sex, and Subordination in England, 1500–1800* (New Haven, CT: Yale University Press, 1995), 297–322.

19. Paul Wood, *The Aberdeen Enlightenment: The Arts Curriculum in the Eighteenth Century* (Aberdeen: Aberdeen University Press, 1993), 68–69. See also Rosalind Carr, *Gender and Enlightenment Culture in Eighteenth-Century Scotland* (Edinburgh: Edinburgh University Press, 2014), 64.

20. "Minutes of the Select Society," NLS, Adv. MS 23.1.1, 45; H. Lewis Ulman, ed., *The Minutes of the Aberdeen Philosophical Society, 1758–1773* (Aberdeen: Aberdeen University Press, 1990), 191.

21. "Belles Lettres Society of Edinburgh, 1761–1764," NLS, Adv. MS 5.1.6; Speculative Society Minute Book, vol. 1 (1764–1775), EUL, Mic M 1076.

22. Carr, *Gender and Enlightenment Culture*, 36–72.

23. Emerson, *Essays on David Hume*, 68, 73.

24. Katharine Glover, *Elite Women and Polite Society in Eighteenth-Century Scotland* (Woodbridge, UK: Boydell and Brewer, 2011), 24–49.

25. Michèle Cohen, "'A Proper Exercise for the Mind': Conversation and Education in the Long Eighteenth Century," in *The Concept and Practice of Conversation in the Long Eighteenth Century, 1688–1848*, ed. Katie Halsey and Jane Slinn (Newcastle: Cambridge Scholars Publishing, 2008), 104–110.

26. Speculative Society Minute Book, vol. 1; Lisa Hill and Peter McCarthy, "Hume, Smith and Ferguson: Friendship in Commercial Society," *Critical Review of International Social and Political Philosophy* 2 (1999): 33–49.

27. Speculative Society Minute Book, vol. 1.

28. John Dwyer, *Virtuous Discourse: Sensibility and Community in Late Eighteenth-Century Scotland* (Edinburgh: John Donald, 1987); Speculative Society Minute Book, vol. 1.

29. Speculative Society Minute Book, vol. 1.

30. For a discussion of gender performativity, including reiterative practice, see Judith Butler, *Gender Trouble: Feminism and the Subversion of Identity* (New York: Routledge, 1990); and Butler, *Bodies That Matter* (New York: Routledge, 1993).

31. David Hume, "Of the Rise and Progress of the Arts and Sciences" (1742), in *Essays Moral, Political, and Literary*, ed. Eugene F. Miller (Indianapolis: Liberty Classics, 1987), 134.

32. Carr, *Gender and Enlightenment Culture*, see esp. chaps. 2–3.

33. For instance, in the London context, see Vic Gatrell, *The First Bohemians: Life and Art in London's Golden Age* (London: Allen Lane, 2013). Gatrell illustrates the importance of the spaces of Covent Garden in fostering a bohemian culture opposed to dominant religious and polite values. See also Helen Berry, "Rethinking Politeness in Eighteenth-Century England: Moll King's Coffee House and the Significance of 'Flash Talk,'" *Transactions of the Royal Historical Society* 11 (2001): 65–81; and Kate Davison, "Occasional Politeness and Gentlemen's Laughter in Eighteenth-Century England," *Historical Journal* 57 (2014): 921–945.

34. Speculative Society Minute Book, vol. 1; Rules of the Speculative Society, EUL, Mic M 1076.

35. "Belles Lettres Society," 1759, NLS, Adv. MS 22.3.8, 25 Mar. 1759 and 30 Nov. 1759.

36. Speculative Society Minute Book; Rules of the Speculative Society.

37. Quoted in Nicholas Phillipson, "The Making of an Enlightened University," in *The University of Edinburgh: An Illustrated History*, ed. Robert D. Anderson, Michael Lynch, and Nicholas Phillipson (Edinburgh: Edinburgh University Press, 2003), 84.

38. Early eighteenth-century student societies included the Physiological Library and the Royal Medical Society (1737); the latter is discussed in Jacqueline Jenkinson's chapter in this volume.

39. Emerson, *Essays on David Hume*, 67–72.

40. Paul Bator, "The University of Edinburgh Belles Lettres Society (1759–64) and the Rhetoric of the Novel," *Rhetoric Review* 14 (1996): 280–298.

41. Ibid., quoted on 282.

42. McElroy, 1969, 104.

43. Somerville, *My Own Life*, 40.

44. Ibid.

45. See, e.g., Hume, "Rise and Progress," 131–134.

46. Speculative Society Minute Book; Rules of the Speculative Society.

47. Speculative Society Minute Book, 5 Apr. 1768.

48. Roger L. Emerson, "The Contexts of the Scottish Enlightenment," in *The Cambridge Companion to the Scottish Enlightenment*, ed. Alexander Broadie (Cambridge: Cambridge University Press, 2003), 9–30.

49. Phillipson, "Enlightened University," 72–73.

50. Carlyle, 82.

51. Ibid., 83.

52. Ibid., 85.

53. Ibid., 86–87.

54. Phillipson, "Enlightened University," 89–93; McElroy, 1969, 111.

55. Phillipson, "Enlightened University," 56–58.

56. *Minutes of Senatus Academicus*, 2 vols. (1733–1855), vol. 1, 15 June 1755, EUL.

57. Other cases of eighteenth-century student discipline in the Minutes of the Senate are two cases of a pistol being brandished in class (with one being fired in Feb. 1755) and ball playing within university grounds, causing broken windows.

58. Somerville, *My Own Life*, 43–44.

59. Ibid., 44–45.

60. Carlyle, 54.

61. Alexandra Shepard, *Meanings of Manhood in Early Modern England* (Oxford: Oxford University Press, 2003), 93–126; Tim Reinke-Williams, "Misogyny, Jest-Books and Male Youth Culture in Seventeenth-Century England," *Gender and History* 21 (2009): 324–339.

62. *Boswell's Edinburgh Journals, 1767–1786*, ed. Hugh M. Milne (Edinburgh: Birlinn, 2013); Philip Carter, "James Boswell's Manliness," in *English Masculinities, 1660–1800*, ed. Tim Hitchcock and Michèle Cohen (London: Routledge, 1999), 111–130.

63. James Boswell, *London Journal, 1762–1763*, ed. Gordon Turnbull (London: Penguin, 2010); *Boswell's Edinburgh Journals*; Carr, *Gender and Enlightenment Culture*, 122–124.

64. French and Rothery, *Man's Estate*, 123.

65. "Sketch of the Early Life of James Boswell, Written by Himself for Jean Jacques Rousseau, 5 December 1764," in *James Boswell: The Earlier Years, 1740–1769*, by Frederick A. Pottle (New York: McGraw-Hill, 1966), 4.

66. Ibid., 5.

67. French and Rothery, *Man's Estate*, 131–132.

68. K. Tawny Paul, "Credit, Reputation, and Masculinity in British Urban Commerce: Edinburgh, c. 1710–70," *Economic History Review* 66 (2013): 242–243; Elizabeth Foyster, *Manhood in Early Modern England: Honour, Sex, and Marriage* (London: Routledge, 1999), 40–41; Shepard, *Meanings of Manhood*, 103–111.

69. Shepard, *Meanings of Manhood*; Foyster, *Manhood*.

70. Joanne Bailey, "'A Very Sensible Man': Imagining Fatherhood in England, c. 1750–1830," *History* 95 (2010): 283.

71. Katie Barclay, "Intimacy and the Life Cycle in the Marital Relationships of the Scottish Elite during the Long Eighteenth Century," *Women's History Review* 20 (2011): 203.

72. Karen Harvey, *The Little Republic: Masculinity and Domestic Authority in Eighteenth-Century Britain* (Oxford: Oxford University Press, 2012).

73. David Hume, "My Own Life," in *Essays Moral, Political, and Literary*, xl.

74. Katie Barclay, "Illicit Intimacies: The Imagined 'Homes' of Gilbert Innes of Stow and His Mistress (1751–1832)," *Gender and History* 27 (2015): 576–579.

CHAPTER 10

Women's Associations in Scotland, 1790–1830

Jane Rendall

Speaking at a meeting of the Edinburgh Bible Society in May 1813, the Baptist physician and former Church of Scotland minister Dr. Charles Stuart felt that he had to pay tribute to "the present age on the existence of societies unknown to the days of my youth; but of highest utility, not only to the objects to which they attend, but to the females who compose them. Female societies for the relief of aged and indigent women—female subscriptions for supporting native missionaries in India—female associations for supporting schools for girls—females engaged in gratuitous teaching—female Bible societies, are a pledge to me, while conducted with delicacy and privacy, of better times to come." To Stuart, these institutions brought into employment "the moral, intellectual and social powers of some of the most amiable part of our species, too generally dormant, or in danger of being wasted in vain frivolity."[1] Yet there is a note of qualification and ambiguity in Stuart's call for "delicacy and privacy." Women had played virtually no role in the convivial and sociable clubs of eighteenth-century Scotland; though they entered into the world of voluntary associations in the late 1790s, there remained hostility to their participation, and many tensions within female and mixed associations. This response and the accompanying tensions became apparent as women's place in the changing fabric of Scottish civil society began to shift.

The explosion of philanthropic activity among women of the upper and middle classes in England in the years after 1795 was clearly identified in 1974 by F. K. Prochaska in a pioneering article, which traced both female contributions to male-led societies and the expanding number of female societies.[2] Since then many historians have contributed to our understanding of this development from both national and local perspectives, although there is still no overall study of the movement in England.[3] Some historians have emphasized the circumscribed nature of women's power in these societies.[4] Others have argued that in spite of undoubted limitations, through these voluntary associations women came to play a distinctive role as part of a modernizing elite, sharing a commitment to the moral and social improvement of their society.[5] For Scotland, this movement remains largely untraced, though it clearly followed a similar if not identical chronology.[6] Stana Nenadic has, for Glasgow, suggested that women were reluctant to focus on the practical business, the organized meetings, and the formal committees of voluntary associations; but this suggestion is not borne out by a wider view of the growth of female associations across Scotland.[7]

Charles Stuart was right to identify the range and diversity of female associations in 1813. Two hundred and fifty-five women's associations founded between 1789 and 1830 have been identified for this chapter, though this is a provisional and incomplete list; further local research would find many more.[8] Four overlapping types of association are considered here: friendly societies, political reform societies, philanthropic and educational societies, and Bible and missionary societies. The majority were founded by middle-class and elite women, though working women also set up and were strongly represented in friendly societies, reform societies, and Bible associations. They are distributed across southern, central, and eastern Scotland, with only two found in the western Highlands, and the most northerly in Stromness.

Edinburgh Beginnings

The earliest formal associations identified, with one exception, were found in Edinburgh from 1797; they clearly drew their inspiration in part from a group of Edinburgh ministers sympathetic both to philanthropic enterprises and to the new, evangelical, missionary movement marked by the foundation of the London Missionary Society in 1795. The leaders of this group came not only from the Church of Scotland but also from the seceding and dissenting churches, with support from evangelically minded Episcopalian ministers. In February 1796 Rev. James Peddie, a minister in the New Light Burgher Church, founded, with others, the Edinburgh (later Scottish) Missionary Society; in the same year Rev. Greville Ewing, then a minister in the Church of Scotland, which he left for the Congregational Church in 1798, became the co-founder and editor of the Edinburgh-based *Missionary Magazine*.[9] However, this chapter suggests that the expansion of female associations cannot be entirely attributed to the impetus of evangelicalism, though that was undoubtedly the predominant impulse. Women in Scotland as elsewhere might alternatively draw upon a rational Christianity, a commitment to benevolence, the language of civic virtue, and the assumptions of a liberal political economy.[10] Kathryn Gleadle emphasizes that women's philanthropic activities can be interpreted not only in religious terms but as "an informed response to contemporary economic issues," whether in the language of traditional moral economy or that of political economy.[11] Rosemary Sweet has suggested a more flexible definition of urban citizenship, resting on women's participation in some if not all aspects of public life, allowing them to display civic feeling in the pursuit of improvement.[12] Female philanthropists in Scotland were also, like their male counterparts, inspired by the prospects of a regulated program of social and moral improvement and, in Bob Harris's words, "stimulated by enlightenment confidence in the capacity of well-designed institutions (bridewells, schools, savings banks, dispensaries, and infirmaries) to restore balance in society."[13]

The case for female association was made within the pages of the *Missionary Magazine*. In July 1797 "A Female Reader"—who can be identified as a Miss Jamieson—contributed a letter, "On Female Associations," in which she asked why women alone were to be excluded from a share in philanthropic labors. Though she proclaimed, "I am no advocate for the fancied equality of the sexes," she also argued that "the united efforts of godly women" might achieve much in ministering to the needs of their own sex and in superintending the education of poor children. She suggested that the accounting and minute-keeping needed was well within the capabilities of middle-class women. Ewing, as editor, added an approving note to this article.[14] Another contributor, "Melissa," surveyed the societies and charity schools run by women in England, as well as the existing male benevolent societies in Scotland, whose purposes, she argued, could be as easily achieved by Scottish women.[15]

In the same year, 1797, the first female philanthropic societies in Edinburgh, the Edinburgh Senior and Junior Female Societies for the Relief of Aged and Indigent Women, were founded.[16] This development may have been influenced by the first visit to Edinburgh of the Anglican evangelical Rev. Charles Simeon, who associated himself with the group described above; in the following year a similar society was established in Leith as a direct result of his second visit.[17] In August 1798 James Peddie and Rev. David Black of Lady Yester's Church set up the Edinburgh Philanthropic Society on the model of the London Philanthropic Society and determined to found a refuge for women to be reclaimed from the Edinburgh Bridewell and the streets of Edinburgh.[18] In November of that year, in response to an invitation from the society, a committee of twelve ladies met in the newly founded Edinburgh Philanthropic Society House, later known as the Magdalene Asylum, in the West Bow, charged with taking particular care of the women admitted, especially their work, dress, and conduct. One of these ladies was Eliza Fletcher, later Enlightenment hostess and autobiographer.[19] Her presence signals that the impetus to benevolence and improvement was not confined to those identified with the city's evangelical movement; it could extend to those inspired by a reforming commitment to improve the situation of the city's poor.

Fletcher had already demonstrated that commitment in April 1798, when in company with other ladies she founded the Edinburgh New Town Female

Friendly Society. In the preliminary to the regulations of this society it was noted that "these societies . . . have hitherto, in this part of the kingdom, been confined solely to men, whilst it is obvious that they may and ought to be extended to women . . . to prevent or alleviate many of those distresses to which females in the lower industrious class of society are exposed."[20] The female friendly society is often excluded from discussions of voluntary associations, yet it appeared in Scotland simultaneously with other female societies, even if Fletcher was not entirely accurate in claiming priority.

The Growth of Female Friendly Societies in Scotland

One example of the female friendly society prior to 1798 has been identified, the Dumfries Female Society, founded in 1789 and registered with the Justices of the Peace of Dumfriesshire on 5 August 1794, about which nothing else is known.[21] Male friendly societies are known to have existed from the early seventeenth century.[22] However, in 1793 an Act of Parliament, introduced by George Rose, secretary to the Treasury, for the first time prescribed a form for friendly societies and encouraged them to register with local justices of the peace to give them legal status; such societies were seen as a means of encouraging independence among the poor and of limiting the increasingly high cost of the English Poor Law.[23] Although the specific provisions relating to the Poor Law were irrelevant to Scotland, the general intentions underlying the act appeared by no means irrelevant to those observing the Scottish system of voluntary poor relief. The act encouraged the growth of male and female friendly societies, which, though they might be set up by working-class initiatives, also came to be seen as part of a range of philanthropic measures for addressing local poverty and encouraging independence and self-help.

Sixty-six female friendly societies and nine mixed friendly societies have been identified in Scotland across the period from 1798 to 1830.[24] This is certainly an underestimate. Many societies did not trouble to register their rules, and many of the minute books of the justices of the peace have not survived for this period; except for Orkney and Shetland, all those that do survive have been consulted. The rules exist for twenty-three out of these seventy-five societies, mostly in the later form in which they were submitted to an Edinburgh-based barrister as required by the Act of 1829;[25] others have been identified through brief references in directories, urban histories, and *The New Statistical Account of Scotland* (1845). This last source is patchy and unreliable; the minister of Maybole in Ayrshire gives a very full account of the history of the seven friendly societies—including two female ones—in his parish, but the incumbent of Irvine in the same county does not mention the four female friendly societies that we know existed there.[26]

In comparison, 458 female friendly societies were recorded for England in 1803 alone by parish overseers, itself a significant underestimate.[27] It would seem that even given the difference in population, the female friendly society was much less prevalent in Scotland than in England in these years.[28] The geographical distribution of the Scottish societies is striking: thirty-two of the sixty-six female societies are found in Ayrshire, including eight in Kilmarnock, six in Ayr, and four in Irvine. Nicola Sian Reader's analysis of English female friendly societies has also found a clustering in areas of proto-industrial employment for women, notably in Lancashire, though not such a remarkable dominance; these were areas where male societies were strong, as was also the case in Ayrshire.[29] The rules of nine of the sixty-six societies indicate that they included both honorary and ordinary members, as did the Edinburgh New Town society; these received financial support from the honorary members, who were sometimes powerful patrons, and were viewed by them as philanthropic enterprises. But many more such societies would have had such female patrons. The ministers writing in *The New Statistical Account* mention a number, including the Countess of Crawford in Ayr, Lady Lilias Oswald in St. Quivox, and Mrs. Crawfurd of Ardmillan in Girvan.[30]

The resistance expressed in some places toward female friendly societies is illustrated in the attempts made by the Edinburgh New Town society to register its rules with the justices of the peace for Midlothian. In 1798 the autobiographer Eliza Fletcher recalled that the act of founding a female friendly society aroused hostility and suspicion from magistrates, who regarded her and her associates as "ladies suspected of democratic principles"; that suspicion, she said, marked "the spirit of the time at that period in Edinburgh, both as regards politics, and with regard to the condition of women."[31] The minute books of the Midlothian justices for that year have not survived. But from later evidence it is apparent that they refused to register the society on the grounds that neither female societies nor societies with honorary members came within the intention of the statutes.[32] They subsequently refused all applications from female and mixed societies until, in 1825, Fletcher enlisted the help of no less an advocate than Francis Jeffrey, who pointed out in the *Memorial for the Edinburgh New-Town Female Friendly Society* that such societies were perfectly conformable to the Act of 1793, and had been universally approved and registered across the rest of Britain since that date.[33] The Midlothian justices finally agreed to registration in May 1825.[34] But the absence of other female friendly societies in the major urban centers of Scotland is striking.

Of the twenty-three sets of rules that have been identified, only nine are contemporary with the foundation of the society; the rules of the first society set up in Ayr, and that of Elgin, both dating from 1804, are the earliest.[35] The remaining fourteen survive in the form in which they were submitted and amended, as prescribed by the Act of 1829. Nevertheless, the constitutions that they outline are broadly similar. The great majority appear to be clearly organized and headed by women, who held the offices of president, or preses, and treasurer, with a female committee of between eight and twelve members, from whom visitors to the sick were normally drawn; the elections were made either by the annual general meeting of the society or through the rotation of members. Most societies provided for the appointment of a paid male clerk to take minutes and arrange the general meeting. But there were many variants.

The Kilmarnock Dutiful Female Society (1811) and the Paisley Female Union Friendly Society (1820) provided for a committee of up to five men to assist with the society's investments.[36] Only the Kilmarnock Good Intent Female Society (1819) specifically mentioned that the clerk could be female.[37] The Edinburgh New Town society required all officers, including committee members, to be unmarried, and specified that the committee was to be made up of seven honorary and four general members.[38] The Edinburgh Institution for the Benefit of Female Teachers and Governesses (before 1809) was managed by its members but had five male trustees, including ex officio the lord advocate and the solicitor general for Scotland.[39] The Edinburgh-based Scottish Friendly Society of Governesses and Female Teachers (1830) allowed an equal role to honorary and ordinary members.[40] Men might also be honorary members. Three so-called female societies, those of Elgin (1804), Brechin (before 1812), and Montrose (1808), had male officers. The rules of the Female Friendly Society of Elgin state that the management of the society was the responsibility of the male honorary members, together with the husbands of ordinary members, who alone were to attend the general meeting; however, four "women of good character" could be appointed as visitors. In 1805 two of these were midwives.[41] Although the Montrose Female Friendly Society was established by a leading female philanthropist—Susan Carnegie, founder of the Montrose Lunatic Asylum in 1781—its officers were all male, with the exception of two women who kept the keys of the society's box.[42] In all the mixed societies, the officers were entirely male, though the rules of the Kildrummy Male and Female Friendly Society (1826) allowed women to attend general meetings and vote.[43]

All societies imposed admission requirements, using some such phrase as this, from the rules of the Galston Female Society (1811): "They shall be of a healthy constitution, good moral character, and able to manage their affairs."[44] Health and age were important if the society was to survive financially. The upper age limit of the Galston society was fifty; in 1815, with fifty-five members, it was described as "in a very thriving state."[45] The Irvine and Halfway Young Female Provident Society (1820) accepted only those aged between sixteen and twenty-five.[46] The Edinburgh New Town society was intended particularly, though not exclusively, for domestic servants, though it also allowed honorary members to become ordinary ones should their circumstances change. It admitted married women only with the consent of their husbands.[47] The occupational base of the two Edinburgh societies for governesses and female teachers was unique. Societies charged an entrance fee as well as regular contributions. For all, the maintenance of respectability and good behavior was a constant concern, with expulsion a common penalty for "a vicious and disorderly life," as in the Beith rules (1818).[48] The Maxwelltown society (1817) expelled a member for the birth of an illegitimate child, though for others the denial of benefit was a sufficient penalty.[49] The Paisley society was exceptional in permitting women to remain in the society after the birth of a second illegitimate child, though it barred them from receiving benefits for six months.[50]

The primary aim of all these societies was to provide financial benefits for women unable to work through sickness, as long as such sickness was not self-imposed through "vicious or intemperate living";[51] most did not make provision for childbirth, unless a woman was still incapable of work fourteen days after a birth. Most made a grant toward funeral expenses; only the Paisley society promised an annuity of four pounds a year to women reaching the age of seventy.[52] The Society of Governesses kept an annuity fund separate from the sickness fund.[53] All faced financial problems in the absence of any reliable calculations on female sickness and mortality rates. The most prestigious attempt at such calculations, by the Highland Society of Scotland at Edinburgh (1784), deliberately chose to focus only on male sickness and mortality rates, though its work was still used by the female societies.[54]

It is hard from the rules that survive to recover a picture of the levels of sociability of such societies, some of which were clearly based on one area of a town, as in Kilmarnock and Irvine. The most frequent meeting places for the annual general meeting were venues such as a local schoolroom or chapel, though the rules may have been amended at a later date to stress the respectability of such meetings. It is occasionally mentioned that committee meetings, held sometimes quarterly, sometimes more frequently, might take place in the home of the president. The Ruthwell Female Friendly Society, founded in 1801 by the minister of Ruthwell, accompanied the male society in a procession to church, with music and flags flying before their annual meeting. Once a year the female society also drank tea together.[55] Women's participation in the procession at Maybole, in February 1811, has already been referred to in this volume.[56] A similarly stage-managed procession took place in Montrose in August 1814, when the Montrose Female Friendly Society took advantage of the annual procession of St. John's Lodge of Free Gardeners, to accompany them through the town: "They . . . walked, in mutual procession, through the principal streets of the town. The steady and uniform conduct of both Females and Gardeners—the former dressed in white, and the latter adorned with the choicest flowers of the season, together with the fineness of the day, made the whole appear truly great. The novelty of the scene drew forth a great concourse of spectators." The women were preceded by their patroness, Susan Carnegie, supported by the two lady key-keepers. This account, in the Montrose newspaper, was followed by hostile comments: "It is the first time we ever heard of females marching, in martial order, to the sound of a drum, since the Amazons of ancient times."[57] Carnegie replied as "A Friend to the Montrose Female Society" in a letter taking up two full columns, defending both the principle and the decorum of the march, which generated much further angry correspondence.[58] These public associational displays are also relevant to the few political societies formed by women.

Political Radicalism and Female Reform Societies

Only two female societies for political reform have been identified, both found in 1819–1820 in the heart of the radical politics of western Scotland, where women were actively participating in the mass actions of radical reformers, in demonstrations, and in theatrical and ritualized meetings. They were fully aware of the existence of female reform societies in England, in Manchester, Stockport, and Blackburn. The Galston Female Reform Society (c. 1819) marched to the gathering of radical reformers at Galston on 23 October 1819, accompanied by a band: "When they came within 20 yards of the hustings, a vocal band sung '*Scots who ha'e wi' Wallace bled*,' and moving on 'solemn and slow,' to the music, a deputation of female Reformers mounted the hustings, and one of them placed a splendid cap of liberty on the head of the Chairman, and another presented a flag, inscribed 'Annual Parliaments, Universal Suffrage, Election by Ballot'; reverse 'Rise, Britons and assert your rights'; and a third presented an address from the Galston Female Reform Society, consisting of 279 members."[59] In April 1820 Jean Reid, a grocer's daughter from Johnstone, gave evidence at the trial of a local schoolmaster, John Frazer, that she had attended a meeting of the Female Reform Society there, with about twelve present. She had contributed sixpence toward the cost of a cap of liberty of "blue satin or sarsnet," and had asked Frazer to write an address to be delivered on presenting the cap to the president of a meeting of Renfrewshire radicals.[60] Newspaper accounts of this and other radical meetings in Glasgow, Ayr, and Kilmarnock all describe deputations of female reformers and the presentation of caps of liberty. At Ayr on 30 October 1819, women wore striking black gowns with white scarves, and headdresses in white studded with black knots, in memory of those killed in Manchester at St. Peter's Field on 16 August 1819.[61] Only two societies can be firmly identified, and these were probably short-lived; but the activism of so many women in Ayrshire and Renfrewshire must have owed something to existing patterns of organization through female friendly societies in those areas.

"Philanthropic Labours": The Work of Female Philanthropic and Educational Societies

The philanthropic and educational societies that were growing rapidly across Scotland in these years have left few records. Sixty-four have been identified from published charity sermons, directories, newspaper references, *The New Statistical Account*, and a few rule books and reports. The first societies in Edinburgh, Leith, and Glasgow were clearly founded as part of the evangelical movement of the late 1790s, as suggested above, but soon cut across theological boundaries. There may, however, have been tensions. In Edinburgh in 1806 the Senior and Junior Female Societies split, and the newly founded Charitable Female Society, with a distinguished list of patrons, absorbed the Junior Society. The reasons for this are not clear, but it may be significant that the first sermon for the Charitable Female Society, in the Cowgate Episcopal Chapel, was given by the Episcopalian minister for Haddington, Miles Jackson.[62] The numbers of these societies grew rapidly, mainly in the larger urban centers and provincial towns of Scotland. Of the sixty-four, twenty-six were in Edinburgh, Glasgow, Aberdeen, and Perth. Among the early societies there was a particular concern for the aged and indigent female poor, with sixteen of the sixty-four announcing this commitment in their titles.

Following the Edinburgh initiatives, the Glasgow Female Society, for the relief of "poor and indigent women," was founded in 1799.[63] The Female Society of Aberdeen for the Relief of Aged and Indigent Women (1804) made it clear in its regulations that it was inspired by the first Edinburgh societies. These regulations established a committee of six managers and six visitors, with a clerk and treasurer and a membership qualified by the payment of a minimum of one shilling and sixpence each quarter. All officers appear to have been female, though a subscription list of 181 names in 1816 included 11 male names. The funds were to be applied for the benefit of the elderly female poor, preferably "those of a religious character and such as do not receive aid from any public institution."[64] The society maintained an effective public presence. The four extant published sermons appealing for funds, by leading local ministers of the Church of Scotland, all reflected on the disproportionate need for the relief of elderly women, brought about by demographic imbalance, by economic changes affecting women's employment in the city, and by war; they referred to the pitiable state of those "who have reached the extreme verge of human life"; and they called for more women to participate in "an inexhaustible field of improvement" and "philanthropic labours, from which the timidity of the loveliest natures might be apt to retire."[65] Regular appeals for funds throughout this period appear in the *Aberdeen Journal*, where in 1816 the society even attracted a poetic tribute, "Address to the Female Society."[66]

The much smaller Beith Female Benevolent Society (1817) was founded after "several ladies in the parish" became aware of a legacy of twenty pounds to the poor of the town. The main objects of this Ayrshire society were to relieve the "necessitous Poor" with food, blankets, and fuel, but also "to embrace other useful and benevolent purposes, such as paying for the instruction of poor female children, in Reading, Writing, Sewing &c &c." The management of the society would "chiefly devolve upon Females," but men were admitted as members and their donations and subscriptions were always acceptable; the female committee of twelve was to be assisted by a committee of five gentlemen. Though the preses, vice-preses, and committee were women, the secretary and treasurer were men.[67]

Such initiatives were accompanied by clothing societies, houses of industry, and the provision of small-scale education for girls. These were normally run by a female committee; the first rule of the Arbroath Female Benevolent Society (1818) was that "this Society shall consist entirely of Females."[68] Clothing societies were a natural extension of concern for the poor and elderly. The Glasgow Benevolent Society for Clothing the Poor was established in 1812 as an auxiliary to the Glasgow Female Society, and its committee of sixteen met weekly to make clothes and coordinate the collection of those made at home by members.[69] The first society directed specifically toward the needs of mothers in childbirth appears to have been the Edinburgh Society for Relief of Poor Married Women of Respectable Character when in Child-Bed (1822), which gave boxes of lying-in clothes, coals according to season, and food for the mother, and sometimes helped husbands find employment.[70]

Philanthropy also involved education, in reading and writing and in skills useful for employment and for domestic work. In 1802 "Alpha," a contributor to the *Missionary Magazine*, had suggested "the erection of Female Societies, for completing the education of poor female children," and many emerged in the following years.[71] The Glasgow Charity Sewing School (1812) was founded "for the purpose of teaching Girls, who are employed at the public works, to Sew, Knit and Spin," and was superintended by a committee of ladies.[72] The Arbroath Female Benevolent Society saw its purpose as educating orphans and children of poor parents, and "rendering such other assistance to necessitous young persons, as our funds will admit," to counter "the vice and depravity which disgrace the present age."[73] The same concerns are evident in *Address to the Ladies of Leith Walk, Greenside and Broughton* (1819), which describes the establishment of a school for girls at the head of Leith Walk in Edinburgh, to be managed by a committee of ladies and a general meeting of subscribers.[74] Such schools also benefited from the patronage of aristocratic and well-to-do ladies; the Perth Female School was established in 1817 with Lady Gray as patroness and a committee of ladies.[75] The number of such schools was growing rapidly by the 1820s.

The practice of all these societies, and the sermons preached in their support, emphasized extensive visiting; all applicants were to be personally approved either by committee members or by designated visitors. Members of the Glasgow Female Society visited every month all those to whom they gave relief, and this served several purposes: observation of the state of the family, encouragement to "cleanliness, industry and economy," and the recommendation of Bible-reading, church attendance, and the education—especially the religious education—of children.[76] There was a continuing anxiety that charity should not be directed to the unworthy; these societies were committed to a policy of social improvement and religious inspiration that looked both to the relief of extreme poverty and to the encouragement of personal independence among the "industrious poor."

The income of societies rested first on that from subscribers and donors. This frequently needed to be supplemented by collections in churches, especially following sermons in aid of the cause, and by public appeals. And the place that these societies occupied in the life of Scotland was influenced by the practice of the Old Poor Law, administered largely through kirk sessions and rooted in the principle of charitable giving.[77] In the larger cities, where town councils had by the late eighteenth century mostly taken over the responsibilities of the kirk, female societies rapidly became part of a charitable establishment, one of a number of institutions and societies through which town councils distributed funds from major events, court fines, and legacies to the poor. So, in 1815 the Town Council of Edinburgh distributed £1,500, the profits of the Edinburgh Musical Festival, to seventeen institutions and societies; the Royal Infirmary received £400, the Senior Female Society £50, and the Leith Female Society £30.[78] In smaller towns like Beith, the foundation of a philanthropic society appears to have formalized the informal assistance often given to the poor by the wives of local landowners and heritors. In March 1836 the minister of Cupar in Fife wrote of the Female Society there as one of a number of sources of support for the poor which meant that no assessment for a poor rate was necessary.[79]

At the same time as female societies were emerging, in some organizations—especially those whose aims were directed toward poor women and girls—ladies' committees were established and took on substantial though not necessarily executive responsibilities. Two early examples were the Edinburgh Magdalene Asylum, mentioned above, and the Edinburgh House of Industry, founded in 1801. The surviving minutes of the ladies' committee of the Magdalene Asylum show the detailed care they gave to its internal administration.[80] The House of Industry from its beginning included an industrial school for girls; in November 1806 the male committee appealed to "a number of ladies every way qualified for so important a trust" to take charge of what were described as "the internal arrangements of the house . . . as this is entirely a female institution." The committee of ladies then set up included the novelist Elizabeth Hamilton. Other ladies were invited to join and attend the next general meeting.[81] By 1815 the ladies are described in the annual report as having the sole management of the institution.[82]

Other societies followed this practice. The Edinburgh Society for the Suppression of Beggars, established in January 1813 and modeled on similar societies elsewhere, aimed not only to suppress begging on Edinburgh streets but to relieve "the Industrious and Destitute Poor" of whom the female poor were "by far the most numerous class we have." The committee of the society looked to "a Committee of Ladies" to help set up a repository for work to be taken on for the poor to execute and to teach poor children useful skills.[83] The repository was opened in March 1813, and it is clear that the female committee played a major part in superintending its organization and in the society more generally.[84] The Edinburgh Lancastrian School Society was set up in 1810, along with others in Glasgow and Aberdeen, to develop the monitorial methods of teaching that Joseph Lancaster had developed in his Southwark school. When a new schoolhouse was found for the Edinburgh school in 1813, with space for separate boys' and girls' schools, the directors reported in May 1813 that "as the detail of female education properly falls within the province of the ladies," the superintendence of the girls' school would be given to "a number of respectable ladies residing in Edinburgh."[85] The female visitors rapidly became a ladies' committee.[86] On a smaller scale, the Newhaven Education Society, which took over a local schoolhouse in 1822, in 1823 established a female branch that set up a girls' school and later an infant school; in May 1827 the male and female branches reunited, which apparently considerably helped the funds of the parent society.[87] The extent of this gendered division of philanthropic labor remains to be traced more generally and was certainly not confined to Edinburgh.[88] The Dundee Orphan Institution, founded in 1815, was governed by a large and mixed committee of ordinary directors including, in 1815, twenty-five women and twenty-eight men, together with a further mixed committee of extraordinary directors, or patrons and patronesses.[89]

The advantages of this extension of female philanthropy were clearly apparent to male societies. Middle-class women had both time and energy to devote to such work, much of it work to which they seemed best suited given the extent of female poverty. They were also, clearly, enthusiastic fund-raisers. In December 1826 a ladies' committee raised £1,500 from a bazaar in the Assembly Rooms, Glasgow; the day after, they distributed the receipts, including £1,000 to the "industrious poor" of Glasgow and £300 to those of Paisley, and £50 each to the Clothing Society, the Female Society, the Aged Women's Society (1811), and the Old Man's Friend Society (1814).[90]

Three societies had aims which went beyond the relief of poverty in Scotland. On her visit to Glasgow in September 1818, Elizabeth Fry helped to establish a Ladies' Society for Visiting the Prison, to provide moral and religious instruction for the prisoners. This society lasted only until 1826, when the jail was closed, and the prisoners transferred to solitary confinement in the Bridewell; the ladies' committee, however, wrote of the benefits of their instruction and the "permanent reformation" of at least ten of the prisoners.[91] The Scottish Ladies' Society for Promoting the Education of Greek Females was founded at an exceptionally well-attended meeting in Edinburgh in April 1825, at which no woman spoke. Rev. Thomas McCrie and Rev. Henry Grey gave supportive accounts of how "some of the ladies in this place" had originated the idea of encouraging female education in Greece and had corresponded with the Greek Committee and the British and Foreign School Society (1808) in London. The society clearly encountered problems, but in early 1830 was able to send out its first female agent, a Miss Robertson, to Corfu, by then part of the British Protectorate of the Ionian Islands.[92] And in November 1830 the first female anti-slavery society in Scotland—the Edinburgh Female Anti-Slavery Association—met, its formation encouraged by the evangelical campaigner for immediate abolition, Rev. Andrew Thomson.[93] Its rules established a secretary, treasurer, and committee, and declared the aims of the association to include the circulation of anti-slavery books and tracts, the improvement of the welfare of Africans, and the encouragement of the use of free-grown sugar.[94] These last two societies suggest a campaigning force extended beyond the local and domestic concerns of philanthropy to imperial issues, which drew upon and overlapped with the dynamism of the Bible and missionary movements discussed below.

Spreading the Word: Women's Religious Associations

The largest group of women's associations discussed here are the Bible and missionary societies, of which 124 have been identified in Scotland, dating from 1809. The sources for these are mainly the donation lists of the Edinburgh Bible Society (1809), the Glasgow Bible Society (1812), and the Society for the Support of Gaelic Schools (1810), and the pages of the *Edinburgh Christian Instructor* and *Scottish Missionary and Philanthropic Register*. The impetus for their growth came from the establishment in London of the immensely successful British and Foreign Bible Society (BFBS) in 1804. Its primary aim was the unsectarian distribution of the text of the Bible, at home and overseas, and to do so it constructed a network of auxiliary and branch associations, of which by far the most successful were the Ladies' Bible Associations.[95]

The Edinburgh Bible Society was established in 1809 to begin the task of constructing a similar network in Scotland and was followed by the Glasgow Bible Society in 1812. The first women's societies emerged simultaneously, probably encouraged by local ministers. In 1811 the Edinburgh society received a donation of twenty pounds from the already established Aberdeen Female Servants' Society for Promoting the Diffusion of the Scriptures (1809).[96] Charles Stokes Dudley, a Quaker minister who became the main organizer of ladies' associations within the BFBS, acknowledged its claim to be the first in Britain.[97] The published account of its foundation has a deprecating quality, describing how "a few female servants in Aberdeen," desiring to "support . . . these excellent institutions formed of late in the country, for sending the Scriptures, and, by them, the knowledge of salvation, to such as are yet destitute of that inestimable privilege," resolved to meet together; with local ministers presiding, they formed themselves into a society. Its rules allowed it to decide where to send donations;

another twenty pounds was sent to aid the Bible translations undertaken by missionaries at Serampore, near Calcutta.[98] The Paisley Female Bible Association was formed in 1811, with a structure not unlike that advocated by the BFBS. It had a treasurer and secretary, seven directors, and thirty-two collectors, two for each of the town's sixteen wards. Dudley noted, however, that like the Aberdeen society the committee chose independently to distribute its funds between various causes and, disapprovingly, that "this mode of proceeding is peculiar to Scotland."[99]

The preferred structure of Dudley and the BFBS followed the hierarchy of male societies, in which an auxiliary society—with accepted geographical boundaries—was subdivided into districts roughly approximating to parishes, each with its own Bible association through which the poor might subscribe, at the rate of a penny a week, for a cheap Bible. Auxiliary societies might establish their own ladies' branches, with parallel district ladies' associations. All funds collected were to go to the men's auxiliary society for transmission to London. The BFBS found that within districts the bulk of the work was done by women, acting as collectors of subscriptions from the poor, undertaking the day-to-day work of the society, and keeping all necessary accounts. Leslie Howsam has written of ladies' associations as "enormously more successful and widespread than those of gentlemen"; nevertheless, they were excluded from any part in the direction of auxiliaries and relied on ministers to preside in public at annual meetings.[100]

It is difficult to know how the practice of the Scottish Bible society movement compared to Dudley's ideal structure; the term "auxiliary" seems to be used quite loosely. By 1814 the Edinburgh Bible Society was welcoming the appearance of a number of all-female societies including those from Dairsie, Dunbar, and Stevenston, all dating from the previous year, and calling for the establishment of a Ladies' Auxiliary Bible Society in Edinburgh.[101] But this did not happen until 1818, when, prompted by the parent society, a meeting for Edinburgh ladies was rapidly organized by the secretaries of the society.[102] However, its form met with some disapproval from within the Church of Scotland. The *Edinburgh Christian Instructor* wrote critically of "public and advertised meetings of the ladies of a great city and its vicinity, where they are to hold up their hands in token of their approbation, and go through various other manoeuvres, to show that they are very zealous, and would be very masculine if they could."[103]

On its clearly successful foundation, the Edinburgh Ladies' Auxiliary Bible Society had fifteen aristocratic patronesses and a committee of sixty-eight; it emphasized that such auxiliary societies "call for no sacrifice of delicacy, or *valuable* seclusion" and that they would collect funds not only from the well-to-do but from "the smaller contributions of their fellow creatures in the lower and domestic walks of life."[104] In 1819 this auxiliary collected £347 10s. 6d., more than any of the other fifteen auxiliaries, and over a third of the total income of the Edinburgh Bible Society.[105]

The Paisley society founded in 1811 did not survive in its older form; by 1820 it had been reorganized into four, later five, separate parish-based societies, each divided into districts for the purpose of collecting subscriptions, all of which were transmitted to the Paisley and East Renfrewshire Bible Society (before 1814) in accordance with Dudley's system.[106] At the second annual meeting of the Glasgow Auxiliary Bible Society in 1814 a Mr. Wigham asked, in relation to local penny-a-week societies: "May we not look with the best founded expectations to the female part of the community for their formation? They stand conspicuous for their benevolence in the establishment of societies for relieving the wants and increasing the comforts of the poor; and surely the objects of this Society are not less worthy their attention."[107] This suggestion was clearly frequently repeated. However, the committee of the Glasgow society chose to wait for some years for a visit from Dudley, so that it was not until his visit could be arranged in 1824 that the Glasgow ladies' branch and eighteen local ladies' associations were formed along approved lines. The existing local male associations then immediately dissolved, resigning the "field of benevolent labour" to the ladies, who were to prove extremely successful. Only one local association was not included in this reorganization, the Lanark Ladies' Auxiliary Bible Society (1821), "under the immediate patronage of Lady Honyman and Lady Mary Ross."[108] Many associations did maintain a degree of independence from the officially approved model, choosing to make their own distribution of the funds collected, especially if they had powerful female patrons.

And there were increasing demands upon their funds. The Edinburgh Society for the Support of Gaelic Schools was founded in 1810; by 1818 it was attracting significant support from existing female associations. Like many other societies, the Saltcoats Female Bible Society (before 1814), which had made a donation to it in 1814, transformed itself by 1818 into the Saltcoats Female Bible and Gaelic School Society.[109] The ladies' auxiliary of the Edinburgh-based parent society was founded in 1817, and by 1825 was the most successful of its fund-raising auxiliaries across Scotland.[110]

The Edinburgh (later Scottish) Missionary Society and the Glasgow Society for Foreign Missions had both been founded in 1796 by ministers from the seceding churches and the Church of Scotland, although the General Assembly of the Church of Scotland rejected engagement in missionary activity until 1824. Long before then the missionary field had attracted a wide-ranging network of support, including significant numbers of female associations. From 1820 the *Scottish Missionary and Philanthropic Register* recorded the existence of Bible and missionary societies across the country; again, by then the ladies' committee of the Scottish Missionary Society was the largest single contributor to the funds of its parent society.[111] Two examples of the way in which local societies balanced the competing claims on their funds may be given. The Fenwick Female Association for Religious Purposes (1821) was founded from the congregations of the local parish church and the Relief Church, another Scottish Presbyterian denomination. The annual fund-raising sermon alternated between the two; this association elected all female officeholders and a committee of ten. In 1823 it divided the funds collected between the Scottish Missionary Society, the Glasgow Gaelic School Society (1812), the London-based Society for Promoting Christianity among the Jews (1809), the Glasgow Missionary Society (1797), and the Dublin Tract Society (before 1811).[112] Similarly the Easter Ross, Cromarty, and Sutherlandshires Ladies' Bible and Missionary Society (1818) chose to divide its funds in 1822 mainly between the Scottish Missionary Society and the London-based Hibernian Society (1806), with a small donation to the education of poor children in Tain.[113] Female associations were linked to a wide range of religious purposes including, besides those mentioned, the Kirriemuir Female Society for the Education of Females in India (1823), and the Ladies' Committee of the Glasgow Continental Society for the Promotion of Protestantism in Catholic Europe (1826).[114]

Conclusion

Many of the societies discussed here were ephemeral. Many female friendly societies failed because of their financial vulnerability, as recorded in the pages of *The New Statistical Account*, though some survived into the later nineteenth century. Yet though the two political reform societies mentioned here were probably very short-lived, their concerns were to re-emerge in the growth of female Chartism across Scotland in the 1830s.[115] Middle-class and elite women's philanthropic associations in Scotland, especially in urban areas, were to become increasingly more significant throughout the nineteenth century. The dynamic growth of female Bible associations came to an end with the bitter schism in the late 1820s between the Scottish societies and the parent society over the inclusion of the books of the Apocrypha in Bibles circulated in Europe.[116] But growing interest in the missionary movement and its endorsement by the Church of Scotland in 1824 meant continuity in such women's societies from this period onward, though they were increasingly reorganized along denominational lines.[117]

In Scotland as in the rest of Great Britain this period saw the entry of a small minority of women into the world of formally structured voluntary associations, though the timetable and the concerns of Scottish women's involvement were distinctive. That entry was both welcomed and contested. It was welcomed because the energy, time, and ability that women brought to religious and philanthropic enterprises were invaluable to elite men in the shared aim of shaping the moral and social regulation of their society. Howsam's comment that within Bible societies women demonstrated themselves to be "active organizers, persuasive collectors and powerful contributors" could be extended more widely.[118] Yet women's roles in voluntary organizations were also contested, because they were at odds with dominant ideological requirements for women to exercise the "delicacy and privacy" of which Charles Stuart spoke. This anxiety was shared by women themselves. Male assistance was often requested. Women presiding over a mixed meeting or speaking in public to mixed audiences remained rare, though not unknown, and the autonomy of their associations within wider movements was limited. Nevertheless, all these boundaries were tested in this period. The tensions and the debates stimulated around women's role in voluntary associations and civil society more generally remained unresolved, but their presence, by 1830, was well established.

NOTES

1. *Proceedings of the Fourth Annual Meeting of the Edinburgh Bible Society, Held on Monday 31st May 1813* (Edinburgh: printed by A. and J. Aikman, 1813), 11–12.

2. F. K. Prochaska, "Women in English Philanthropy, 1790–1830," *International Review of Social History* 9 (1974): 426–445.

3. See, for instance, Leonore Davidoff and Catherine Hall, *Family Fortunes: Men and Women of the English Middle Class, 1780–1850*, rev. ed. (1987; London: Routledge, 2002), 429–436; Donna T. Andrew, *Philanthropy and Police: London Charity in the Eighteenth Century* (Princeton, NJ: Princeton University Press, 1989); Amanda Vickery, introduction to *Women, Privilege, and Power: British Politics, 1750 to the Present*, ed. Amanda Vickery (Stanford, CA: Stanford University Press, 2001), 24–25; Rosemary Sweet, "Women and Civic Life in Eighteenth-Century England," in *Women and Urban Life in Eighteenth-Century England: On the Town*, ed. Rosemary Sweet and Penelope Lane (Aldershot: Ashgate, 2003), 39–41.

4. Martin Gorsky, *Patterns of Philanthropy: Charity and Society in Nineteenth-Century Bristol* (Woodbridge, UK: Boydell and Brewer, 2011), 164–172.

5. Vickery, introduction to *Women, Privilege, and Power*, 25; Sweet, "Women and Civic Life," 39–41.

6. However, see Olive Checkland, *Philanthropy in Victorian Scotland: Social Welfare and the Voluntary Principle* (Edinburgh: John Donald, 1980), chaps. 1–2; Andrew J. Dalgleish, "Voluntary Associations and the Middle Class in Edinburgh, 1780–1820" (PhD diss., University of Edinburgh, 1992); Bob Harris, "Cultural Change in Provincial Scottish Towns, c. 1700–1820," *Historical Journal* 54 (2011): 139–140.

7. Stana Nenadic, "The Middle Ranks and Modernisation," in *Glasgow*, vol. 1, *Beginnings to 1830*, ed. T. M. Devine and Gordon Jackson (Manchester: Manchester University Press, 1995), 295.

8. This list has been compiled through consulting the catalogs of the NRS, the Scottish Archive Network, the National Records of Archives for Scotland, and the Consortium of Online Public Access Catalogues (COPAC), now Library Hub Discover. I have also used Ian MacDougall, ed., *A Catalogue of Some Labour Records in Scotland and Some Scots Records outside Scotland* (Edinburgh: Scottish Labour History Society, 1978); *NSA*; *AJ*; *CM*; *ECI*; *GH*; *Inverness Courier*; *SMPR*; and the annual reports of the Edinburgh and Glasgow Bible Societies and the Edinburgh Society for the Support of Gaelic Schools. These sources have been supplemented by selected urban histories and directories. The list is available upon request.

9. See, for this group, William Law Mathieson, *Church and Reform in Scotland: A History from 1797 to 1843* (Glasgow: James MacLehose and Sons, 1916), chaps. 1–2; for James Peddie, see Kenneth B. E. Roxburgh, "Peddie, James (1759–1845)," in *ODNB*, https://doi:10

.1093/ref:odnb/21753; and for Greville Ewing, see W. G. Blaikie, "Ewing, Greville (1767–1841)," rev. David Huddleston, in *ODNB*, https://doi:10.1093/ref:odnb/9018.

10. Donna T. Andrew has with reference to London charities argued for a shift by the late eighteenth century away from earlier goals of increasing both population and wealth. The foundation of the Philanthropic Society (1788) and Sir Thomas Bernard's London-based Society for Bettering the Condition and Increasing the Comforts of the Poor (1795) were both signs that charity was being united with the principles of liberal political economy. Andrew, *Philanthropy and Police*, 184; see also Sarah Lloyd, *Charity and Poverty in England, 1680–1820: Wild and Visionary Schemes* (Manchester: Manchester University Press, 2009); and Karen Sonnelitter, *Charity Movements in Eighteenth-Century Ireland: Philanthropy and Improvement* (Woodbridge, UK: Boydell Press, 2016).

11. Kathryn Gleadle, "Gentry, Gender, and the Moral Economy during the Revolutionary and Napoleonic Wars in Provincial England," in *Economic Women: Essays on Desire and Dispossession in Nineteenth-Century British Culture*, ed. Lana L. Dalley and Jill Rappoport (Columbus: Ohio State University Press, 2013), 25–40.

12. Sweet, "Women and Civic Life," 39–41.

13. Bob Harris, "The Enlightenment, Towns and Urban Society in Scotland, c. 1760–1820," *English Historical Review* 126 (2011): 1135; see also Hugh Cunningham, introduction to *Charity, Philanthropy and Reform: From the 1690s to 1850*, ed. Hugh Cunningham and Joanna Innes (Basingstoke: Macmillan, 1998), 11.

14. A Female Reader, "On Female Associations," *MM* 2 (1797): 360–362; J. J. Matheson, *Memoir of Greville Ewing* (London: W. Tegg, 1847), 88–90.

15. Melissa, "On Female Associations," *MM* 2 (1797): 551–554.

16. For the later history of these societies, see Viviene Cree, *A Family Concern: A History of the Indigent Old Women's Society, 1797–2002* (Edinburgh: University of Edinburgh, 2005) at https://www.pure.ed.ac.uk/ws/files/15242135/A_Family_Concern.pdf (accessed 20 June 2020). The Senior and Junior Female Societies amalgamated in 1907, under the title of the Indigent Old Women's Society, which survived until January 2002.

17. William Carus, ed., *Memoirs of the Life of the Rev. Charles Simeon, with a Selection from His Writings and Correspondence*, 3rd ed. (London: J. Hatchard and Son, 1848), 98, 119–120.

18. For the London Philanthropic Society, see Andrew, *Philanthropy and Police*, 182–186; David Black, *Christian Benevolence Recommended and Enforced by the Example of Christ. A Sermon Preached before the Edinburgh Philanthropic Society* (Edinburgh: printed by John Brown, 1798), 26–47.

19. Ladies' Committee Minute Book, Magdalene Asylum, 23 Nov. 1798, ECA, SL 237/2/1.

20. *Regulations for the Edinburgh New Town Female Friendly Society, Instituted 19th April 1798*, NRS, FS1/17/58 (Edinburgh, 1832).

21. Sederunt Book of the Justices of the Peace for the County of Dumfriesshire, 1779–1815, Ewart Library, Dumfries, EGD 046/2, fols. 67v–68, 5 Aug. 1794.

22. W. Hamish Fraser, *Conflict and Class: Scottish Workers, 1700–1838* (Edinburgh: John Donald, 1988), 41, 54–55, 76; MacDougall, *Catalogue of Some Labour Records*, 2–30.

23. George Rose, *Observations on the Act for the Relief and Encouragement of Friendly Societies* (London: S. Brookes, 1794); Simon Cordery, *British Friendly Societies, 1750–1914* (Basingstoke: Palgrave Macmillan, 2003), 5, 45–47.

24. For a more detailed discussion of female friendly societies in Scotland, see Jane Rendall, "'The Principle of Mutual Support': Female Friendly Societies in Scotland, c. 1789–1830," *Journal of Scottish Historical Studies* 40 (2020): 17–39.

25. Cordery, *British Friendly Societies*, 85–87.

26. *NSA*, 5:377, 619–636.

27. Nicola Sian Reader, "Female Friendly Societies in Industrialising England, 1780–1850" (PhD diss., University of Leeds, 2005), 66.

28. The population of Scotland in 1801 was 1.6 million, that of England and Wales 9.2 million. Jeremy Gregory and John Stevenson, *The Longman Companion to Britain in the Eighteenth Century* (London: Longman, 2000), 289.

29. Reader, "Female Friendly Societies," 65–66, 80; in Galston, Ayrshire, in 1815, the majority of men over the age of sixteen were said to belong to one or more of the friendly societies. "Benefit Societies Galston," *The Irvine and County of Ayr Miscellany, from September, 1814 to July, 1815* (Irvine: J. Mennons and Sons, 1815), Feb. 1815, 268–269.

30. *NSA*, 5:80, 125, 405.

31. *Autobiography of Mrs. Fletcher with Letters and Other Family Memorials*, ed. Mary Richardson (Edinburgh, Edmonston and Douglas, 1875), 76.

32. Francis Jeffrey and Robert Hunter, *Memorial for the Edinburgh New-Town Female Friendly Society: Submitted to the Honourable the Justices of the Peace for the County of Edinburgh* ([Edinburgh], 1825), 3.

33. E.g., see Minute-Book of the Justices of the Peace for Midlothian, 1810–1826, 30 Sept. 1818, NRS, JP4/2/2, fols. 144–145; and Jeffrey and Hunter, *Memorial*, 4–6.

34. Minute-Book of the Justices of the Peace for Midlothian, 17 May 1825, fol. 408.

35. "Rules and Regulations of the Female Friendly Society for the Town and Parish of Ayr, instituted Decr 1st, 1804, sanctioned 29th Octr 1805," Ayrshire Archives, Ayr, B6/39/71.

36. "Rules and Regulations of the Kilmarnock Dutiful Female Society. Instituted 8th February 1811. Revised and Sanctioned May 1835," chap. 2, art. 4, NRS, FS1/2/42; "Paisley Female Union Friendly Society, Instituted Dec. 1820, Remodelled June 1837," art. 7, NRS, FS1/21/29. Where the rules of a friendly society are unpaginated, references are given to articles.

37. "Regulations of the Kilmarnock Good Intent Female Society, instituted 6th March 1819," art. 13, NRS, FS1/2/44.

38. *Regulations for the Edinburgh New Town Female Friendly Society*, 4.

39. Maxwell Garthshore, "Account of the Edinburgh Institution, for the Benefit of Female Teachers and Governesses," in *The Reports of the Society for Bettering the Condition and Increasing the Comforts of the Poor* (London: printed for the Society, 1814), 6:29–40.

40. *Rules of the Scottish Friendly Society of Governesses and Female Teachers* ([Edinburgh]: Caledonian Mercury Press, 1830), art. 2, NRS, FS1/17/122.

41. *Rules and Regulations of the Female Friendly Society of Elgin* (Inverness: printed by J. Young, 1804), 2, 4–6.

42. Alexander A. Cormack, *Susan Carnegie, 1744–1821: Her Life of Service* (Aberdeen: Aberdeen University Press for the author, 1966), 307–309; *Angus and Mearns Register for 1812, containing Accurate Lists of the Nobility, Clergy, [&c]* (Montrose: John Smith, 1812), 38.

43. "Rules and Regulations of the Kildrummy Male and Female Friendly Society," art. 11, NRS, FS1/1/28.

44. *Regulations for the Galston Female Society* (Kilmarnock: H. Crawford, 1811), 3.

45. Ibid.; "Benefit Societies Galston."

46. "Articles and Regulations of the Irvine & Halfway Young Female Provident Society," art. 2, NRS, FS1/2/32.

47. *Regulations for the Edinburgh New Town Female Friendly Society*, 6, 8.

48. *Regulations of the Beith Female Friendly Society* (Beith: printed by A. Gibson, 1826), 4.

49. Maxwelltown Female Friendly Society, *Proposed Regulations of a Female Friendly Society . . . in Maxwelltown* (Dumfries: printed by C. Munro, 1817), 10.

50. "Paisley Female Union Friendly Society," art. 12.

51. "Regulations of the Ayr Relief Juvenile Female Society 1838," art. 5, NRS, FS1/2/8. This society was founded in 1827.

52. "Paisley Female Union Friendly Society," art. 16.

53. *Rules of the Scottish Friendly Society of Governesses and Female Teachers*, arts. 1 and 3.

54. Committee of the Highland Society of Scotland, *Report on Friendly or Benefit Societies, Exhibiting the Law of Sickness, as Deduced from Returns by Friendly Societies in Different Parts of Scotland* (Edinburgh: A. Constable, 1824), 24, 113.

55. George John C. Duncan, *Memoir of the Rev. Henry Duncan, Minister of Ruthwell* (Edinburgh: William Oliphant and Sons, 1848), 66.

56. See the introduction to this volume, 1.

57. *Montrose, Arbroath, and Brechin Review*, 5 Aug. 1814; see also previous correspondence in this newspaper in relation to the Female Friendly Society in procession on 29 Apr. and 15 July 1814, and in *CM*, 8 Aug. 1814.

58. *CM*, 19 and 26 Aug.; 2, 9, and 16 Sept. 1814.

59. *GH*, 28 Oct. 1819, quoted in Elaine Chalus and Fiona Montgomery, "Women and Politics," in *Women's History: Britain, 1700–1850; An Introduction*, ed. Hannah Barker and Elaine Chalus (London: Routledge, 2005), 242.

60. Precognition v. John Frazer, schoolmaster in Johnstone, 12 Apr. 1820, NRS, SC58/55/24, cited in Christopher A. Whatley, *Scottish Society, 1707–1830: Beyond Jacobitism, towards Industrialisation* (Manchester: Manchester University Press, 2000), 312.

61. *Glasgow Courier*, 2, 4, and 23 Nov. 1819; Whatley, *Scottish Society*, 312; Anna Clark, *The Struggle for the Breeches: Gender and the Making of the British Working Class* (Berkeley: University of California Press, 1995), 160–161.

62. Miles Jackson, *The Constraining Power of the Love of Christ. A Sermon, Preached on Tuesday, Oct. 28, 1806, in the Episcopal Chapel, Cowgate, for the Benefit of the Charitable Female Society, Edinburgh* (Edinburgh: Ogle and Aikin, 1806), 33–35, app.

63. James Cleland, *Annals of Glasgow, Comprising an Account of the Public Buildings, Charities, and the Rise and Progress of the City* (Glasgow: printed by James Hedderwick, 1816), 1:249.

64. "Rules of the Aberdeen Female Society for the Relief of Aged and Indigent Women, Aberdeen 19 December 1804," appended to William Laurence Brown, *On the True Excellence of the Female Character: A Sermon . . . for the Benefit of the Female Society* (Aberdeen: J. Chalmers, 1807).

65. John Lee, *A Sermon, Preached in the West Church of Aberdeen, . . . for the Aberdeen Female Society* (Cupar: printed by R. Tullis, 1821), 21, 28–29; see also Brown, *True Excellence of the Female Character*; George Skene Keith, *The Union of Benevolence and Purity of Heart: A Sermon . . . , for the Benefit of the Female Society of Aberdeen, for the Relief of Aged and Indigent Women* (Aberdeen: printed by D. Chalmers, 1812); Duncan Grant, *The Claims of the Afflicted on the Compassion of Friends: A Sermon, . . . for the Benefit of the Female Society of Aberdeen, for the Relief of Aged and Indigent Women* (Aberdeen: printed by D. Chalmers, 1816).

66. *AJ*, 28 Feb. 1816.

67. *Regulations of the Beith Female Benevolent Society, Instituted 22nd Nov. 1817* (Paisley: printed by J. Neilson, 1817), 3–8.

68. *Amended Rules and Regulations of the Arbroath Female Benevolent Society: Under the Patronage of Miss A. Gardyne: Instituted 24th July, 1818* (Arbroath: printed by P. Cochran, 1823), 2.

69. Cleland, *Annals of Glasgow*, 1:264–265.

70. *First Annual Report of the Edinburgh Society for Relief of Poor Married Women, of Respectable Character when in Child-Bed* (Edinburgh: printed by Anderson and Bryce, 1822).

71. Alpha, "Plan for Female Schools," *MM* 7 (1802): 291–292.

72. Cleland, *Annals of Glasgow*, 1:267.

73. *Amended Rules and Regulations of the Arbroath Female Benevolent Society*, 1–2.

74. *Address to the Ladies of Leith Walk, Greenside and Broughton* (Edinburgh, 1819), EUL, C.R.15.3.16/16–17.

75. Harriet Howell, *Record of Religious Persecution in Scotland* (London: A. J. Valpy, 1836), 60.

76. Cleland, *Annals of Glasgow*, 1:249.

77. See Rosalind Mitchison, *The Old Poor Law in Scotland: The Experience of Poverty, 1574–1845* (Edinburgh: Edinburgh University Press, 2000); and, for the problems faced by Scottish towns in this period, see Harris and McKean, 460–463.

78. *CM*, 1 Dec. 1815.

79. *NSA*, 9:17.

80. Ladies' Committee Minute Book 1798–1834, for the Magdalene Asylum, ECA, SL 237/2/1.

81. *CM*, Nov. 27, 1806; "Account of the Edinburgh House of Industry," *SM* 71 (Jan. 1809): 20–22.

82. *CM*, 9 Jan. 1815.

83. *Society for the Suppression of Beggars, for the Relief of Occasional Distress, and the Encouragement of Industry among the Poor, within the City and Environs of Edinburgh* (Edinburgh: Alex. Lawrie, 1813), 11–17.

84. See [Edinburgh] Society for the Suppression of Beggars, *First Report of the Society, Instituted in Edinburgh on 25th January 1813, for the Suppression of Beggars* (Edinburgh: Alex. Smellie, 1814), 9–16, 25–28; and subsequent reports of this society, 1815–1824.

85. *Reports of the Ordinary Directors of the Edinburgh Lancastrian School Society to the General Meetings of the Society, Held in the Assembly Rooms, George's Street, on July 2 and November 15, 1813* (Edinburgh: printed by Alex. Lawrie, 1813), 7.

86. Ibid., 24.

87. Howell, *Record of Religious Persecution in Scotland*, 18–19.

88. For Edinburgh, see Jane Rendall, "Gender, Philanthropy and Civic Identities in Edinburgh, 1795–1830," in *The Routledge History Handbook of Gender and the Urban Experience*, ed. Deborah Simonton (London: Routledge, 2017), 209–220.

89. Alexander Abbot, *Dundee Directory for 1818* (Dundee: printed by A. Colville, [1818]), 178–180.

90. *CM*, 25 Dec. 1826.

91. *CM*, 14 Sept. 1818; *GH*, 10 Apr. 1826.

92. *CM*, 2 Apr. 1825; *SMPR* 11 (1830): 294–295.

93. Iain Whyte, *Scotland and the Abolition of Black Slavery, 1756–1838* (Edinburgh: Edinburgh University Press, 2006), 197.

94. *Resolutions and Rules of the Edinburgh Female Anti-Slavery Association* (Edinburgh: printed by Ballantine, 1830).

95. See the excellent account in Leslie Howsam, *Cheap Bibles: Nineteenth-Century Publishing and the British and Foreign Bible Society* (Cambridge: Cambridge University Press, 1991), 52–61.

96. *Second Report of the Edinburgh Bible Society, . . . 1811* (Edinburgh: printed for the Society, 1811), 43–44.

97. Charles Stokes Dudley, *An Analysis of the System of the Bible Society* (London: printed by R. Watts, 1821), 356.

98. *Second Report of the Edinburgh Bible Society*, 43–44.

99. Dudley, *Analysis of the System*, 358–359.

100. Howsam, *Cheap Bibles*, 42–44, 53.

101. *Fourth Report of the Edinburgh Bible Society, . . . 1813*, 7–9.

102. *ECI* 16 (Feb. 1818): 128.

103. *ECI* 16 (Apr. 1818): 267–268.

104. *Ninth Report of the Edinburgh Bible Society, . . . 1818*, 23–25.

105. *Tenth Report of the Edinburgh Bible Society, . . . 1819*, 13–14.

106. *ECI* 9 (Nov. 1814): 339; 20 (Oct. 1821): 701–703.

107. *Proceedings at the Second Annual Meeting of the Glasgow Auxiliary Bible Society . . . 24th February 1814* (Glasgow: printed by Andrew Duncan, 1814), 15.

108. *SMPR* 5 (1824): 487–491.

109. [Edinburgh] Society for the Support of Gaelic Schools, *Third Annual Report of the Society for the Support of Gaelic Schools* (Edinburgh: printed for the Society, 1814), 20; *Seventh Annual Report of the Society for the Support of Gaelic Schools* (Edinburgh: printed for the Society, 1818), 26.

110. [Edinburgh] Society for the Support of Gaelic Schools, *Seventh Annual Report*, 29, 39–40; *Fourteenth Annual Report of the Society for the Support of Gaelic Schools* (Edinburgh: printed for the Society, 1825), 15.

111. *SMPR* 1 (1820): 160.

112. "Minute Book of the Fenwick Female Association for Religious Purposes formed 1821," Ayrshire Archives, Ayr, Acc. 978.

113. "Minutes of a Meeting of the Easter Ross, Cromarty and Sutherlandshires Ladies Society held at Tain on 14 August 1822," NRS, GD305/1/161/126.

114. *SMPR* 6 (1825): 95; 7 (1826): 530.

115. Sue Innes and Jane Rendall, "Women, Gender and Politics," in *Gender in Scottish History since 1700*, ed. Lynn Abrams et al. (Edinburgh: Edinburgh University Press, 2006), 56–57; Clark, *Struggle for the Breeches*, 228–229.

116. Howsam, *Cheap Bibles*, 13–15.

117. Esther Breitenbach, *Empire and Scottish Society: The Impact of Foreign Missions at Home, c. 1790 to c. 1914* (Edinburgh: Edinburgh University Press, 2009), 54–56.

118. Howsam, *Cheap Bibles*, 59.

Acknowledgments

The idea for this work originated with Mark Wallace, in Edinburgh over dinner at Vittoria on the Bridge and a conspiratorial pint (or two) at the Jolly Judge with his good friend David Allan. Mark Wallace would, with great pleasure, like to thank David Allan publicly for his contributions, not just in terms of encouragement and creativity, but for his willingness to contribute to this book and read and comment on drafts of the introduction. Additionally, he is sincerely appreciative of the enthusiasm and willingness shown by Roger Emerson, Susan Sommers, Judith Robey, and Christopher Whatley, all of whom read and edited portions of the work. Many of the resources that he needed for research and consultation were not immediately available, and he is indebted to Rob Austin, Camille Beary, Robert Kraphol, and Kathy Whittenton for tolerating many loan requests and tracking down obscure titles in relatively short periods of time. Jane Rendall would like to thank Mark Towsey for reading and commenting with such insight on a late draft of the introduction, and Jon Mee, with whom she has enjoyed many profitable conversations on improving clubs and societies. We would both like to thank the anonymous readers for Bucknell University Press for their careful readings and suggestions for improvement of this volume, and Cheryl Hirsch and Jane M. Lichty for all their assistance in the final preparation of the text. Finally, we would like to acknowledge with gratitude the generous grant made by the Strathmartine Trust toward publication costs.

A tremendous thanks is due to all the contributors to *Association and Enlightenment* for their efforts and patience. The editors greatly appreciated Christopher Whatley's kindness in reading the introduction and writing the foreword. We are grateful to the Eighteenth-Century Scottish Studies Society for publishing the book series in which this volume appears—Studies in Eighteenth-Century Scotland—and especially to Rick Sher, who has generously guided us through the entire process, offering invaluable advice, timely evaluation, extensive commentary, and frequent editorial support on many versions of the book. Finally, Mark Wallace would like to thank his wife, Melinda, for her support and reassurance, which were essential to the completion of this book, and Jane Rendall would like to thank Adam Middleton for his continuing encouragement and toleration of editorial activities.

Bibliography

PRIMARY SOURCES

Abbot, Alexander. *Dundee Directory for 1818*. Dundee: printed by A. Colville, [1818].

An Account of the Fair Intellectual-Club in Edinburgh: In a Letter to a Honourable Member of the Athenian Society there. By a young Lady, the Secretary of the Club. Edinburgh: printed by J. McEuen, 1720.

Angus and Mearns Register for 1812, containing Accurate Lists of the Nobility, Clergy, [&c]. Montrose: John Smith, 1812.

Arbroath Female Benevolent Society. *Amended Rules and Regulations of the Arbroath Female Benevolent Society: Under the Patronage of Miss A. Gardyne: Instituted 24th July, 1818*. Arbroath: printed by P. Cochran, 1823.

Arbuckle, James. *James Arbuckle: Selected Works*. Edited by Richard Holmes. Lewisburg, PA: Bucknell University Press, 2014.

Arnot, Hugo, ed. *A Collection and Abridgement of Celebrated Criminal Trials in Scotland. From A.D. 1536 to 1784. With Historical and Critical Remarks*. Glasgow: printed by A. Napier, 1812.

"B——. A Song." In *A Collection of Original Poems. By Scotch Gentlemen*, 2:90–91. Edinburgh: A. Donaldson, 1762.

Beith Female Benevolent Society. *Regulations of the Beith Female Benevolent Society, Instituted 22nd Nov. 1817*. Paisley: printed by J. Neilson, 1817.

Beith Female Friendly Society. *Regulations of the Beith Female Friendly Society*. Beith: printed by A. Gibson, 1826.

Beith Humane Society. *Articles of the Beith Humane Society, Constituted 27th March 1800*. Dalry: printed by J. Gemmill, 1801.

Black, David. *Christian Benevolence Recommended and Enforced by the Example of Christ. A Sermon Preached before the Edinburgh Philanthropic Society*. Edinburgh: printed by John Brown, 1798.

Blair, Hugh. *Lectures on Rhetoric and Belles Lettres*. 2 vols. London: W. Strahan and T. Cadell; Edinburgh: W. Creech, 1783.

Boswell, James. *Boswelliana: The Commonplace Book of James Boswell*. Edited by Charles Rogers. London: Grampian Club, 1876.

———. *Boswell in Extremes, 1776–1778.* Edited by Charles McC. Weis and Frederick A. Pottle. New York: McGraw-Hill, 1970.

———. *Boswell in Search of a Wife, 1766–1769.* Edited by Frank Brady and Frederick A. Pottle. New York: McGraw-Hill, 1956.

———. *Boswell on the Grand Tour: Germany and Switzerland, 1764.* Edited by Frederick A. Pottle. New York: McGraw-Hill, 1953.

———. *Boswell's Edinburgh Journals, 1767–1786.* Edited by Hugh M. Milne. Edinburgh: Birlinn, 2013.

———. *Boswell's Journal of a Tour to the Hebrides with Samuel Johnson, LL.D., 1773.* Edited by Frederick A. Pottle and Charles H. Bennett. London, 1936. Rev. reprint, New York: McGraw-Hill, 1961.

———. *Boswell's London Journal, 1762–1763.* Edited by Frederick A. Pottle. New York: McGraw-Hill, 1950.

———. *Boswell's London Journal, 1762–1763, Together with Journal of My Jaunt, Harvest 1762.* Edited by Frederick A. Pottle. London: Heinemann, 1951.

———. *Boswell: The English Experiment, 1785–1789.* Edited by Irma S. Lustig and Frederick A. Pottle. New York: McGraw-Hill, 1986.

———. *Boswell: The Great Biographer, 1789–1795.* Edited by Marlies K. Danziger and Frank Brady. New York: McGraw-Hill, 1989.

———. *The Correspondence of James Boswell and John Johnston of Grange.* Edited by Ralph S. Walker. New York: McGraw-Hill, 1966.

———. *The Correspondence of James Boswell and Sir William Forbes of Pitsligo.* Edited by Richard B. Sher. Edinburgh: Edinburgh University Press; New Haven, CT: Yale University Press, 2021.

———. *An Elegy on the Death of an Amiable Young Lady. With an Epistle from Menalcas to Lycidas. To Which Are Prefixed, Three Critical Recommendatory Letters.* Edinburgh: Alex. Donaldson, 1761.

———. *The General Correspondence of James Boswell, 1757–1763.* Edited by David Hankins and James J. Caudle. Edinburgh: Edinburgh University Press; New Haven, CT: Yale University Press, 2006.

———. *The General Correspondence of James Boswell, 1766–1769.* Edited by Richard Cargill Cole, Peter S. Baker, and Rachel McClellan, with the assistance of James J. Caudle. 2 vols. New Haven, CT: Yale University Press, 1993–1997.

———. *James Boswell: The Journal of His German and Swiss Travels, 1764.* Edited by Marlies K. Danziger. Edinburgh: Edinburgh University Press; New Haven, CT: Yale University Press, 2008.

———. *Letters between the Honourable Andrew Erskine, and James Boswell, Esq.* London: W. Flexney, 1763.

———. *Letters of James Boswell.* Edited by Chauncey Brewster Tinker. 2 vols. Oxford: Clarendon Press, 1924.

———. *London Journal, 1762–1763.* Edited by Gordon Turnbull. London: Penguin, 2010.

———. "Sketch of the Early Life of James Boswell, Written by Himself for Jean Jacques Rousseau, 5 December 1764." In *James Boswell: The Earlier Years, 1740–1769*, by Frederick A. Pottle, 1–6. New York: McGraw-Hill, 1966.

[Boswell, James]. "Memoirs of James Boswell, Esq." *European Magazine* 11 (May 1791): 322–326; (June 1791): 404–407.

———. *Observations, Good or Bad, Stupid or Clever, Serious or Jocular, on Squire Foote's Dramatic Entertainment, intitled, The Minor.* London: J. Wilkie, 1761.

[Boswell, James, Andrew Erskine, and George Dempster]. *Critical Strictures on the New Tragedy of Elvira: Written by Mr. David Malloch.* London: W. Flexney, 1763.

Brewster, David, ed. *The Edinburgh Encyclopaedia.* 18 vols. Edinburgh: William Blackwood, 1808–1830.

Broadie, Alexander, ed. *The Cambridge Companion to the Scottish Enlightenment.* Cambridge: Cambridge University Press, 2003.

Brown, William Laurence. *On the True Excellence of the Female Character: A Sermon . . . for the Benefit of the Female Society.* Aberdeen: J. Chalmers, 1807.

Burke, Edmund. *Revolutionary Writings.* Edited by Iain Hampsher-Monk. Cambridge: Cambridge University Press, 2014.

———. *The Writings and Speeches of Edmund Burke.* Vol. 8, *The French Revolution, 1790–1794*, edited by L. G. Mitchell. Oxford: Clarendon Press, 1989.

Burns, Robert. *The Canongate Burns.* Edited by Andrew Noble and Patrick Scott Hogg. Edinburgh: Canongate Classics, 2003.

———. *Commonplace Books, Tour Journals, and Miscellaneous Prose.* Edited by Nigel Leask. Vol. 1 of The Oxford Edition of the Works of Robert Burns. Oxford: Oxford University Press, 2014.

———. *The Letters of Robert Burns.* Edited by J. De Lancey Ferguson. 2nd ed. Revised by G. Ross Roy. 2 vols. Oxford: Clarendon Press, 1985.

———. *The Poems and Songs of Robert Burns.* Edited by James Kinsley. 3 vols. Oxford: Clarendon Press, 1968.

———. *Poems, Chiefly in the Scottish Dialect* (Kilmarnock: John Wilson, 1786).

Carlyle, Alexander. *Autobiography of the Rev. Dr. Alexander Carlyle, Minister of Inveresk.* 3rd ed. Edinburgh: William Blackwood and Sons, 1861.

Carus, William, ed. *Memoirs of the Life of the Rev. Charles Simeon, with a Selection from His Writings and Correspondence.* 3rd ed. London: J. Hatchard and Son, 1848.

Cleland, James. *Annals of Glasgow, Comprising an Account of the Public Buildings, Charities, and the Rise and Progress of the City.* 2 vols. Glasgow: printed by James Hedderwick, 1816.

Cochrane, Andrew. *The Cochrane Correspondence regarding the Affairs of Glasgow, 1745–46.* Edited by James Dennistoun. Glasgow: Maitland Club, 1836.

Committee of the Highland Society of Scotland. *Report on Friendly or Benefit Societies, Exhibiting the Law of Sickness, as Deduced from Returns by Friendly Societies in Different Parts of Scotland.* Edinburgh: A. Constable, 1824.

Cooper, Anthony Ashley, third Earl of Shaftesbury. *Characteristicks of Men, Manners, Opinions, Times.* Edited by Lawrence E. Klein. Cambridge: Cambridge University Press, 1999.

Crawfurd, George, and William Semple. *The History of the Shire of Renfrew.* Paisley: printed by Alex. Weir, 1782.

Creech, William. *Edinburgh Fugitive Pieces.* Edinburgh: William Creech; London: T. Cadell, 1791.

Dudley, Charles Stokes. *An Analysis of the System of the Bible Society.* London: printed by R. Watts, 1821.

The Dundee Register of Merchants and Trades, With All the Public Offices, &c for M,DD, LXXXIII. Dundee, 1782. Reprint. Edited by A. C. Lamb. Dundee: A. C. Lamb, 1879.

Edinburgh Bible Society. *Proceedings of the Fourth Annual Meeting of the Edinburgh Bible Society, Held on Monday 31st May 1813*. Edinburgh: printed by A. and J. Aikman, 1813.

———. *Reports of the Edinburgh Bible Society.* 50 vols. Edinburgh: printed for the Society, 1810–[1860].

Edinburgh Education Society. *Report of the Committee of Directors of the Edinburgh Education Society, to the General Meeting of the Society . . . on November 28, 1814*. Edinburgh: Alex. Lawrie, 1814.

Edinburgh Female Anti-Slavery Association. *Resolutions and Rules of the Edinburgh Female Anti-Slavery Association*. Edinburgh: printed by Ballantine, 1830.

Edinburgh Lancastrian School Society. *Reports of the Ordinary Directors of the Edinburgh Lancastrian School Society to the General Meetings of the Society, Held in the Assembly Rooms, George's Street, on July 2 and November 15, 1813*. Edinburgh: printed by Alex. Lawrie, 1813.

Edinburgh Society for Relief of Poor Married Women of Respectable Character when in Child-Bed. *First Annual Report of the Edinburgh Society for Relief of Poor Married Women, of Respectable Character When in Child-Bed*. Edinburgh: printed by Anderson and Bryce, 1822.

[Edinburgh] Society for the Support of Gaelic Schools. *Annual Reports of the Society for the Support of Gaelic Schools*. 38 vols. Edinburgh: printed for the Society, 1811–1849.

[Edinburgh] Society for the Suppression of Beggars. *First Report of the Society, Instituted in Edinburgh on 25th January 1813, for the Suppression of Beggars*. Edinburgh: Alex. Smellie, 1814.

———. *Society for the Suppression of Beggars, for the Relief of Occasional Distress, and the Encouragement of Industry among the Poor, within the City and Environs of Edinburgh*. Edinburgh: Alex. Lawrie, 1813.

The Emmet; A Selection of Original Essays, Tales, Anecdotes, Bon Mots, Choice Sayings, &c. 2 vols. Glasgow: Purvis and Aitken, 1824.

Female Friendly Society of Elgin. *Rules and Regulations of the Female Friendly Society of Elgin*. Inverness: printed by J. Young, 1804.

Ferguson, Adam. *An Essay on the History of Civil Society.* Edited by Fania Oz-Salzberger. Cambridge: Cambridge University Press, 1995.

———. *The History of the Progress and Termination of the Roman Republic.* 3 vols. London: W. Strahan and T. Cadell; Edinburgh: W. Creech, 1783.

———. *Institutes of Moral Philosophy.* Edinburgh: A. Kincaid and J. Bell, 1769.

Fergusson, Robert. *The Poems of Robert Fergusson*. Edited by Matthew P. McDiarmid. 2 vols. Edinburgh: William Blackwood and Sons, 1954–1956.

Fieser, James, ed. *Early Responses to Hume's History of England*. 10 vols. Bristol, 2002. Rev. ed. Bristol: Thoemmes Press, 2005.

Galston Female Society. *Regulations for the Galston Female Society.* Kilmarnock: H. Crawford, 1811.

Galt, John. *The Entail, or The Lairds of Grippy.* Edinburgh, 1823. New ed. Edited by Ian A. Gordon. London: Oxford University Press, 1970.

[Garrick, David]. *Bon Ton; or, High Life Above Stairs. A Comedy. In Two Acts.* London: T. Becket, 1775.

Garthshore, Maxwell. "Account of the Edinburgh Institution, for the Benefit of Female Teachers and Governesses." In *The Reports of the Society for Bettering the Condition and Increasing the Comforts of the Poor*, 6:29–40. London: printed for the Society, 1814.

A General History of Stirling. Stirling: printed by C. Randall, 1794.

Glasgow Auxiliary Bible Society. *Proceedings at the Second Annual Meeting of the Glasgow Auxiliary Bible Society . . . 24th February 1814.* Glasgow: printed by Andrew Duncan, 1814.

Goldsmith, Oliver. *Essays and Criticisms.* 3 vols. London: J. Johnson, 1798.

Grant, Duncan. *The Claims of the Afflicted on the Compassion of Friends: A Sermon, . . . for the Benefit of the Female Society of Aberdeen, for the Relief of Aged and Indigent Women.* Aberdeen: printed by D. Chalmers, 1816.

Gray, Nathan, ed. "Sir David Hume, Lord Crossrig, 'A Narrative of the Rise, Progress and Success of the Societies of Edinburgh for Reformation of Manners,' 1701." *Miscellany of the Scottish History Society*, 6th ser., vol. 4, miscellany XIV (2013): 111–138.

Gregory, John. *Lectures on the Duties and Qualifications of a Physician.* London: W. Strahan and T. Cadell, 1772.

Grierson, William. *Apostle to Burns: The Diaries of William Grierson.* Edited by John Davies. Edinburgh: William Blackwood, 1981.

Grose, Francis. *A Classical Dictionary of the Vulgar Tongue.* London: S. Hooper, 1785.

Hamilton, Alexander. *The History of the Ancient and Honourable Tuesday Club.* Edited by Robert Micklus. 3 vols. Chapel Hill: University of North Carolina Press, 1990.

Hazlitt, William Carew. *English Proverbs and Proverbial Phrases Collected from the Most Authentic Sources.* London: John Russell Smith, 1869.

Heron, Robert. *Observations Made in a Journey through the Western Counties of Scotland in the Autumn of 1792.* 2nd ed. 2 vols. Perth: R. Morison and Son; Edinburgh: Bell and Bradfute; London: Vernor and Hood, 1799.

Home, Henry. Lord Kames. *Sketches of the History of Man.* 2 vols. Edinburgh: W. Creech; London: W. Strahan and T. Cadell, 1774.

Howell, Harriet, *Record of Religious Persecution in Scotland.* London: A. J. Valpy, 1836.

Hume, David. *Enquiries concerning Human Understanding and concerning the Principles of Morals.* Edited by L. A. Selby-Bigge. 3rd ed. Revised by Peter H. Nidditch. Oxford: Oxford University Press, 1975.

———. *An Enquiry concerning the Principles of Morals.* London: A. Millar, 1751.

———. *Essays, Moral and Political.* 3rd ed. London: A. Millar; Edinburgh: A. Kincaid, 1748.

———. *The Letters of David Hume.* Edited by J.Y.T. Greig. 2 vols. Oxford: Clarendon Press, 1932.

———. "My Own Life." In *Essays Moral, Political, and Literary*, edited by Eugene F. Miller, xxxi–xli. Indianapolis: Liberty Classics, 1987.

———. "Of National Characters." In *Essays Moral, Political, and Literary*, edited by Eugene F. Miller, 202–220. Indianapolis: Liberty Classics, 1987.

———. "Of Refinement in the Arts." In *Essays Moral, Political, and Literary*, edited by Eugene F. Miller, 268–280. Indianapolis: Liberty Classics, 1987.

———. "Of the Rise and Progress of the Arts and Sciences." In *Essays Moral, Political, and Literary*, edited by Eugene F. Miller, 111–137. Indianapolis: Liberty Classics, 1987.

Hutcheson, Francis. *An Essay on the Nature and Conduct of the Passions and Affections, with Illustrations on the Moral Sense.* Edited by Aaron Garrett. Indianapolis: Liberty Fund, 2002.

———. *An Inquiry into the Original of Our Ideas of Beauty and Virtue.* Edited by Wolfgang Leidhold. Indianapolis: Liberty Fund, 2004.

Jackson, Miles. *The Constraining Power of the Love of Christ. A Sermon, Preached on Tuesday, Oct. 28, 1806, in the Episcopal Chapel, Cowgate, for the Benefit of the Charitable Female Society, Edinburgh*. Edinburgh: Ogle and Aikin, 1806.

Jeffrey, Francis, and Robert Hunter. *Memorial for the Edinburgh New-Town Female Friendly Society: Submitted to the Honourable the Justices of the Peace for the County of Edinburgh*. [Edinburgh], 1825.

Jephson, Robert. *The Confessions of James Baptiste Couteau, Citizen of France*. 2 vols. London: J. Debrett, 1794.

Johnstone, Christian Isobel. *The Cook and Housewife's Manual; . . . by Mrs Margaret Dods*. Edinburgh: printed for the author, 1826. 2nd ed. Edinburgh: Oliver and Boyd, 1827.

Keith, George Skene. *The Union of Benevolence and Purity of Heart: A Sermon . . . , for the Benefit of the Female Society of Aberdeen, for the Relief of Aged and Indigent Women*. Aberdeen: printed by D. Chalmers, 1812.

Kelso Records. Kelso, 1789.

Kennedy, William. *Annals of Aberdeen*. 2 vols. London: A. Brown, 1818.

Lee, John. *A Sermon, Preached in the West Church of Aberdeen, . . . for the Aberdeen Female Society*. Cupar: printed by R. Tullis, 1821.

Lettice, John. *Letters on a Tour through Various Parts of Scotland, in the Year 1792*. London: T. Cadell, 1794.

Locke, John. *An Essay concerning Human Understanding*. Edited by Peter H. Nidditch. Oxford: Clarendon Press, 1975.

Maitland, William. *The History of Edinburgh, from its Foundation to the Present Time*. Edinburgh: printed by Hamilton, Balfour and Neill, for the author, 1753.

Marshall, James. *A Winter with Robert Burns, Being Annals of His Patrons and Associates in Edinburgh during the Year 1786–7, and Details of His Inauguration as Poet-Laureate of the Can: Kil:*. Edinburgh: Peter Brown, 1846.

Maxwelltown Female Friendly Society. *Proposed Regulations of a Female Friendly Society . . . in Maxwelltown*. Dumfries: printed by C. Munro, 1817.

Medical Society [of Edinburgh]. *Medical Essays and Observations*. 4th ed. 5 vols. Edinburgh: Hamilton, Balfour and Neill, 1752.

Mercer, A. *The History of Dunfermline, from the Earliest Period Down to the Present Time*. Dunfermline: John Miller, 1828.

Meston, William. *The Poetical Works of the Ingenious and Learned William Meston . . . : To which is Prefixed the Author's Life*. Edinburgh, 1767. 7th ed. Aberdeen: printed by J. Burnett, 1802.

Millar, John. *An Historical View of the English Government*. London: A. Strahan and T. Cadell, and J. Murray, 1787.

———. *Observations Concerning the Distinctions of Ranks in Society*. London: J. Murray, 1771.

———. *The Origin of the Distinction of Ranks*. 4th ed., 1806. Reprint. Edited by Aaron Garrett. Indianapolis: Liberty Fund, 2006.

Miller, James. *The History of Dunbar: From the Earliest Records to the Present Period*. Dunbar: W. Miller, 1830.

Moore, John. "The Life of T. Smollett." In *The Works of Tobias Smollett, M.D.*, 1:lxxxixvii–ccx. London: B. Law et al., 1797.

Morgan, Sydney, Lady. *The O'Briens and the O'Flahertys: A National Tale.* 4 vols. London: H. Colburn, 1828.

Natural History Society of Edinburgh. *Laws of the Society Constituted at Edinburgh MDCCLXXXII for the Investigation of Natural History.* Edinburgh: C. Stewart, 1803.

Neville, Sylas. *The Diary of Sylas Neville, 1767–1788.* Edited by Basil Cozens-Hardy. London: Oxford University Press, 1950.

Nicol, Alexander. *The Rural Muse.* Edinburgh: printed for the author, 1753.

Observations upon the Propriety of Establishing a Lancastrian School in Edinburgh. Edinburgh, 1811.

Pasquin, Anthony. *A Postscript to the New Bath Guide: A Poem.* London: J. Strahan, 1790.

Philosophical Society of Edinburgh. *Essays and Observations: Physical and Literary.* 3 vols. Edinburgh: G. Hamilton and J. Balfour, 1754–1771.

Pigot, J. *Pigot & Co.'s New Commercial Directory of Scotland, for 1825–6.* London: J. Pigot, 1825.

Ramsay, Allan. "Journal of the Easy Club." In *The Works of Allan Ramsay,* vol. 5, edited by Alexander M. Kinghorn and Alexander Law, 1–58. Edinburgh: William Blackwood and Sons, 1972.

———. *The Works of Allan Ramsay.* Edited by Burns Martin, John W. Oliver, Alexander M. Kinghorn, and Alexander Law. 6 vols. Edinburgh: William Blackwood and Sons, 1945–1974.

Robertson, George. *Topographical Description of Ayrshire; More Particularly of Cunninghame.* Irvine: Cunninghame Press, 1820.

Rose, George. *Observations on the Act for the Relief and Encouragement of Friendly Societies.* London: S. Brookes, 1794.

Scott, Sir Walter. *The Antiquary.* Edited by David Hewitt. Vol. 3 of The Edinburgh Edition of the Waverley Novels. Edinburgh: Edinburgh University Press, 1995.

———. *Saint Ronan's Well.* Edited by Mark Weinstein. Vol. 16 of The Edinburgh Edition of the Waverley Novels. Edinburgh: Edinburgh University Press, 1995.

Short Account of the Town of Dumfries. Dumfries, 1828.

Sinclair, Sir John, ed. *The Statistical Account of Scotland.* 21 vols. Edinburgh: W. Creech, 1791–1799.

Smith, Adam. *Correspondence of Adam Smith.* Edited by Ernest Campbell Mossner and Ian Simpson Ross. Rev. ed. The Glasgow Edition of the Works and Correspondence of Adam Smith. Oxford, 1987. Reprint, Indianapolis: Liberty Fund, 1987.

———. *Essays on Philosophical Subjects.* Edited by W.P.D. Wightman and J. C. Bryce. The Glasgow Edition of the Works and Correspondence of Adam Smith. Oxford, 1980. Reprint, Indianapolis: Liberty Fund, 1982.

———. *Lectures on Rhetoric and Belles Lettres.* Edited by J. C. Bryce. The Glasgow Edition of the Works and Correspondence of Adam Smith. Oxford, 1983. Reprint, Indianapolis: Liberty Fund, 1985.

———. *The Theory of Moral Sentiments.* Edited by D. D. Raphael and A. L. Macfie. The Glasgow Edition of the Works and Correspondence of Adam Smith. Oxford, 1976. Rev. reprint, Indianapolis: Liberty Fund, 1982.

Smollett, Tobias. *The Expedition of Humphry Clinker.* Edited by Louis M. Knapp. Revised by Paul-Gabriel Boucé. Oxford: Oxford University Press, 1998.

Society for the Encouragement of Arts and Sciences, Greenock. *Observations on the Best Mode of Promoting the Society Instituted for the Encouragement of Arts and Sciences, in Greenock*. Glasgow: Mennons, 1814.

Somerville, Thomas. *My Own Life and Times, 1741–1814*. Edinburgh, 1861. Reprint. Edited by Richard B. Sher. Bristol: Thoemmes Press, 1996.

Stewart, Dugald. "Account of the Life and Writings of Adam Smith, LL.D." In *Essays on Philosophical Subjects*, edited by W.P.D. Wightman and J. C. Bryce, 269–351. The Glasgow Edition of the Works and Correspondence of Adam Smith. Oxford, 1980. Reprint, Indianapolis: Liberty Fund, 1982.

Swift, Jonathan. *T—l—nd's Invitation to Dismal: To Dine With the Calve's-Head Club, Imitated from Horace Epist. 5 Lib. 1*. [Dublin?, 1712].

[Thom, William]. *The Defects of an University Education, and Its Unsuitableness to a Commercial People*. London: E. Dilly, 1762.

[Townley, James, possibly with contributions by David Garrick]. *High Life Below Stairs. A Farce of Two Acts*. London: J. Newbery et al., 1759.

The Universal Scots Almanack, For the Year of Our Lord, M.DCC.LXIII. Edinburgh: printed by Walter Ruddiman and John Richardson, 1763.

Ward, Edward. *A Compleat and Humorous Account of All the Remarkable Clubs and Societies in the Cities of London and Westminster*. London: printed for the author, 1745.

———. *The History of the London Clubs, or, The Citizens' Pastime*. 1709. Reprint, London: J. Dutten, [1896].

———. *The Secret History of the Calves-Head Club, or, The Republican Unmasqu'd*. Dublin, 1705.

Weir, Daniel. *History of the Town of Greenock*. Greenock: Daniel Weir; Glasgow: Robertson and Atkinson; Edinburgh: John Boyd; London: Whittaker, 1829.

Wight, William. *Heads of a Course of Lectures on Civil History*. Glasgow: printed by Robert and Andrew Foulis, 1767.

———. *Heads of a Course of Lectures on Civil History*. Glasgow: printed by Robert and Andrew Foulis, 1772.

SECONDARY SOURCES

Abrams, Lynn, and Elizabeth L. Ewan, eds. *Nine Centuries of Man: Manhood and Masculinities in Scottish History*. Edinburgh: Edinburgh University Press, 2017.

Abrams, Lynn, Eleanor Gordon, Deborah Simonton, and Eileen Janes Yeo, eds. *Gender in Scottish History since 1700*. Edinburgh: Edinburgh University Press, 2006.

Ahnert, Thomas, and Susan Manning, eds. *Character, Self, and Sociability in the Scottish Enlightenment*. New York: Palgrave Macmillan, 2011.

———. "Introduction: Character, Self, and Sociability in the Scottish Enlightenment." In *Character, Self, and Sociability in the Scottish Enlightenment*, edited by Thomas Ahnert and Susan Manning, 1–30. New York: Palgrave Macmillan, 2011.

Allan, David. *Scotland in the Eighteenth Century: Union and Enlightenment*. Harlow: Longman, 2002.

———. "The Scottish Enlightenment and the Politics of Provincial Culture: The Perth Literary and Antiquarian Society, ca. 1784–1790." *Eighteenth-Century Life* 27 (2003): 1–30.

Allen, Robert J. *The Clubs of Augustan London*. Cambridge, MA: Harvard University Press, 1933.

Anderson, Benedict. *Imagined Communities: Reflections on the Origin and Spread of Nationalism*. London: Verso, 1991.

Anderson, Robert D., Michael Lynch, and Nicholas Phillipson, eds. *The University of Edinburgh: An Illustrated History*. Edinburgh: Edinburgh University Press, 2003.

Andrew, Donna T. *Philanthropy and Police: London Charity in the Eighteenth Century*. Princeton, NJ: Princeton University Press, 1989.

Andrews, Corey E. "Drinking and Thinking: Club Life and Convivial Sociability in Mid-Eighteenth-Century Edinburgh." *Social History of Alcohol and Drugs* 22 (2007): 65–82.

———. *The Genius of Scotland: The Cultural Production of Robert Burns, 1785–1834*. Leiden: Brill Rodopi, 2015.

———. *Literary Nationalism in Eighteenth-Century Scottish Club Poetry*. Lewiston, NY: Edwin Mellen Press, 2004.

———. "The Mirror Club: Periodicals as Tastemakers in Eighteenth-Century Scotland." In *The Scottish Enlightenment and Literary Culture*, edited by Ralph McLean, Ronnie Young, and Kenneth Simpson, 171–184. Lewisburg, PA: Bucknell University Press, 2016.

Bailey, Joanne. "'A Very Sensible Man': Imagining Fatherhood in England, c. 1750–1830." *History* 95 (2010): 267–292.

Barclay, Katie. "Illicit Intimacies: The Imagined 'Homes' of Gilbert Innes of Stow and his Mistress (1751–1832)." *Gender and History* 27 (2015): 576–590.

———. "Intimacy and the Life Cycle in the Marital Relationships of the Scottish Elite during the Long Eighteenth Century." *Women's History Review* 20 (2011): 189–206.

Barker, Hannah, and Elaine Chalus, eds. *Women's History: Britain, 1700–1850; An Introduction*. London: Routledge, 2005.

Barnard, Toby. *Making the Grand Figure: Lives and Possessions in Ireland, 1641–1770*. New Haven, CT: Yale University Press, 2004.

Bartlett, T., D. Dickson, and D. Keogh, eds. *The Irish Rebellion of 1798: A Bicentennial Perspective*. Dublin: Four Courts, 2003.

Bator, Paul. "The University of Edinburgh Belles Lettres Society (1759–64) and the Rhetoric of the Novel." *Rhetoric Review* 14 (1996): 280–298.

Bell, J. F. "Adam Smith, Clubman." In *Adam Smith: Critical Assessments*, edited by John Cunningham Wood, 1:94–101. London: Routledge, 1983.

Ben-Amos, Ilana Krausman. *Adolescence and Youth in Early Modern England*. New Haven, CT: Yale University Press, 1994.

Benchimol, Alex. "Periodicals and Public Culture." In *The Edinburgh Companion to Scottish Romanticism*, edited by Murray Pittock, 84–99. Edinburgh: Edinburgh University Press, 2011.

Benchimol, Alex, Rhona Brown, and David Shuttleton, eds. *Before Blackwood's: Scottish Journalism in the Age of Enlightenment*. London: Routledge, 2015.

Benedict, Barbara M. "Creech, William [*pseud.* Theophrastus] (1745–1815)." In *Oxford Dictionary of National Biography*. Oxford University Press, 2004; online ed. https://doi:10.1093/ref:odnb/6662.

———. "'Service to the Public': William Creech and Sentiment for Sale." In "Sociability and Society in Eighteenth-Century Scotland," edited by John Dwyer and Richard B. Sher. Special issue, *Eighteenth-Century Life* 15, nos. 1–2 (1991): 96–146.

Berry, Helen. "Rethinking Politeness in Eighteenth-Century England: Moll King's Coffee House and the Significance of 'Flash Talk.'" *Transactions of the Royal Historical Society* 11 (2001): 65–81.

Bertelsen, Lance. *The Nonsense Club: Literature and Popular Culture, 1749–1764.* Oxford: Clarendon Press; New York: Oxford University Press, 1986.

Bettany, George Thomas. "Duncan, Andrew, the Elder (1744–1828)." Revised by Lisa Rosner. In *Oxford Dictionary of National Biography.* Oxford University Press, 2004; online ed. https://doi:10.1093/ref:odnb/8212.

Blaikie, W. G. "Ewing, Greville (1767–1841)." Revised by David Huddleston." In *Oxford Dictionary of National Biography.* Oxford University Press, 2004; online ed. https://doi:10.1093/ref:odnb/9018.

Booker, R. Michael. "Orange Alba: The Civil Religion of Loyalism in the Southwestern Lowlands of Scotland since 1798." PhD diss., University of Tennessee, Knoxville, 2010.

Breitenbach, Esther. *Empire and Scottish Society: The Impact of Foreign Missions at Home, c. 1790 to c. 1914.* Edinburgh: Edinburgh University Press, 2009.

Brims, J. D. "From Reformers to 'Jacobins': The Scottish Association of the Friends of the People." In *Conflict and Stability in Scottish Society, 1700–1850,* edited by T. M. Devine, 31–50. Edinburgh: John Donald, 1990.

———. "The Scottish Democratic Movement in the Age of the French Revolution." PhD diss., University of Edinburgh, 1983.

Brown, Michael. "The Meal at the Saracen's Head: Edmund Burke and the Scottish Literati." *Studies in Burke and His Time* 22 (2011): 13–44.

Brown, Rhona. "'The Cape still flourishes anon': A New Club Poem by Robert Fergusson." *Review of Scottish Culture* 24 (2012): 110–125.

Brown, Rhona, and Gerard Carruthers. "Commemorating James Thomson, *The Seasons* in Scotland, and Scots Poetry." *Studies in the Literary Imagination* 46 (2013): 71–89.

Brown, S. C., ed. *Philosophers of the Enlightenment.* Brighton: Harvester Press, 1979.

Brown, Stephen W. "Singing by the Book: Eighteenth-Century Scottish Songbooks, Freemasonry, and Burns." In *From Compositors to Collectors: Essays on Book-Trade History,* edited by John Hinks and Matthew Day, 249–266. New Castle, DE: Oak Knoll Press; London: British Library, 2012.

———. "Smellie, William (1740–1795)." In *Oxford Dictionary of National Biography.* Oxford University Press, 2004; online ed. https://doi:10.1093/ref:odnb/25753.

———. "William Smellie and Natural History: Dissent and Dissemination." In *Science and Medicine in the Scottish Enlightenment,* edited by Charles W. J. Withers and Paul Wood, 191–214. East Linton: Tuckwell Press, 2002.

Brown, Stephen W., and Warren McDougall, eds. *The Edinburgh History of the Book in Scotland.* Vol. 2, *Enlightenment and Expansion, 1707–1800.* Edinburgh: Edinburgh University Press, 2012.

Bryson, Gladys. *Man and Society: The Scottish Inquiry of the Eighteenth Century.* Princeton, NJ: Princeton University Press, 1945.

Butler, Judith. *Bodies That Matter.* New York: Routledge, 1993.

———. *Gender Trouble: Feminism and the Subversion of Identity.* New York: Routledge, 1990.

Bynum, W. F., and Roy Porter, eds. *William Hunter and the Eighteenth-Century Medical World.* Cambridge: Cambridge University Press, 1985.

Cadell, Patrick. "Dalrymple, Sir David, Third Baronet, Lord Hailes (1726–1792)." In *Oxford Dictionary of National Biography.* Oxford University Press, 2004; online ed. https://doi:10.1093/ref:odnb/7046.

Campbell, Katherine. "Masonic Song in Scotland: Folk Tunes and Community." *Oral Tradition* 27 (2012): 85–108.

Campbell, Roy Hutcheson, and Andrew S. Skinner, eds. *The Origins and Nature of the Scottish Enlightenment*. Edinburgh: John Donald, 1982.

Capdeville, Valérie. "Gender at Stake: The Role of Eighteenth-Century London Clubs in Shaping a New Model of English Masculinity." *Culture, Society and Masculinities* 4 (2012): 13–32.

Carr, Rosalind. *Gender and Enlightenment Culture in Eighteenth-Century Scotland*. Edinburgh: Edinburgh University Press, 2014.

Carr-Saunders, A. M., and P. A. Wilson. *The Professions*. Oxford: Clarendon Press, 1933.

Carswell, Catherine. *The Life of Robert Burns*. London, 1930. Reprint, Edinburgh: Canongate, 1990.

Carter, Philip. "James Boswell's Manliness." In *English Masculinities, 1660–1800*, edited by Tim Hitchcock and Michèle Cohen, 111–130. London: Routledge, 1999.

Chalkin, C. W. "Capital Expenditure on Building for Cultural Purposes in Provincial England, 1730–1830." *Business History* 22 (1980): 51–70.

Chalmers, John, ed. *Andrew Duncan Senior: Physician of the Enlightenment*. Edinburgh: National Museums Scotland, 2010.

———. "Medical Clubs and Societies Founded by Andrew Duncan." In *Andrew Duncan Senior: Physician of the Enlightenment*, edited by John Chalmers, 114–133. Edinburgh: National Museums Scotland, 2010.

Chalus, Elaine, and Fiona Montgomery. "Women and Politics." In *Women's History: Britain, 1700–1850; An Introduction*, edited by Hannah Barker and Elaine Chalus, 217–259. London: Routledge, 2005.

Chambers, Robert, ed. *The Life and Works of Robert Burns*. 4 vols. Edinburgh, 1851–1852. Revised by William Wallace. Edinburgh: W. R. Chambers, 1896.

———. *Traditions of Edinburgh*. Edinburgh, 1824. Revised 1868. Reprint, Edinburgh: Chambers, 1996.

Checkland, Olive. *Philanthropy in Victorian Scotland: Social Welfare and the Voluntary Principle*. Edinburgh: John Donald, 1980.

Chen, Jeng-Guo S. "William Lothian and the Belles Lettres Society of Edinburgh: Learning to Be a Luminary in Scotland." *Journal for Eighteenth-Century Studies* 27 (2004): 173–187.

Chickering, Roger. "Political Mobilization and Associational Life." In *Elections, Mass Politics, and Social Change in Modern Germany*, edited by Larry Eugene Jones and James Retallack, 307–328. Cambridge: Cambridge University Press, 2002.

Chitnis, Anand C. "Provost Drummond and the Origins of Edinburgh Medicine." In *The Origins and Nature of the Scottish Enlightenment*, edited by Roy Hutcheson Campbell and Andrew S. Skinner, 86–97. Edinburgh: John Donald, 1982.

———. *The Scottish Enlightenment: A Social History*. London: Croom Helm, 1976.

Clark, Anna. *The Struggle for the Breeches: Gender and the Making of the British Working Class*. Berkeley: University of California Press, 1995.

Clark, Arthur Melville. "The Background." In *History of the Speculative Society*, 9–53. Bicentenary ed. Edinburgh: printed for the Society by T. and A. Constable, 1968.

Clark, Peter. *British Clubs and Societies, 1580–1800: The Origins of an Associational World*. Oxford: Oxford University Press, 2000.

———. *The English Alehouse: A Social History, 1200–1830*. London: Longman, 1983.

Clawson, Mary Ann. *Constructing Brotherhood: Class, Gender, and Fraternalism*. Princeton, NJ: Princeton University Press, 1989.

Clerk, Sir John. *Memoirs of the Life of Sir John Clerk of Penicuik*. Edited by John M. Gray. Edinburgh: Scottish History Society, 1892.

Clive, John, and Bernard Bailyn "England's Cultural Provinces: Scotland and America." *William and Mary Quarterly*, 3rd ser., 11 (1954): 163–179.

Cockburn, Harry A. "An Account of the Friday Club." *Book of the Old Edinburgh Club* 3 (1910): 105–178.

———. *History of the New Club, Edinburgh, 1787–1937*. Edinburgh: W. and R. Chambers, 1938.

Cockburn, Henry. *Memorials of His Time*. Edinburgh, 1856. New ed. Edited by Harry A. Cockburn. Edinburgh: T. N. Foulis, 1909.

Cohen, Michèle. "'A Proper Exercise for the Mind': Conversation and Education in the Long Eighteenth Century." In *The Concept and Practice of Conversation in the Long Eighteenth Century, 1688–1848*, edited by Katie Halsey and Jane Slinn, 103–127. Newcastle: Cambridge Scholars Publishing, 2008.

Comerford, R. V., and Jennifer Kelly, eds. *Associational Culture in Ireland and Abroad*. Dublin: Irish Academic Press, 2010.

Comrie, John D. *History of Scottish Medicine to 1860*. London: Wellcome Historical Medical Museum, 1927.

Conrad, Stephen A. *Citizenship and Common Sense: The Problem of Authority in the Social Background and Social Philosophy of the Wise Club of Aberdeen*. New York: Garland, 1987.

Cordery, Simon. *British Friendly Societies, 1750–1914*. Basingstoke: Palgrave Macmillan, 2003.

Cormack, Alexander A. *Susan Carnegie, 1744–1821: Her Life of Service*. Aberdeen: Aberdeen University Press for the author, 1966.

Couper, W. J. *The Millers of Haddington, Dunbar and Dunfermline: A Record of Scottish Bookselling*. London: T. F. Unwin, 1914.

Coutts, James. *A History of the University of Glasgow, from Its Foundation in 1451 to 1909*. Glasgow: James MacLehose and Sons, 1909.

Cowan, Brian. *The Social Life of Coffee: The Emergence of the British Coffeehouse*. New Haven, CT: Yale University Press, 2005.

Craig, John. "The Aberdeen Medico-Chirurgical Society." *Medical Press and Circular* 195 (1968): 302–330.

Cramond, William. *Annals of Banff*. 2 vols. Aberdeen: New Spalding Club, 1891.

Crawford, Robert. *The Bard: Robert Burns, a Biography*. Princeton, NJ: Princeton University Press, 2009.

———, ed. *Robert Burns and Cultural Authority*. Edinburgh: Edinburgh University Press, 1997.

———. "Robert Fergusson's Robert Burns." In *Robert Burns and Cultural Authority*, edited by Robert Crawford, 1–22. Edinburgh: Edinburgh University Press, 1997.

Cree, Viviene. *A Family Concern: A History of the Indigent Old Women's Society, 1797–2002*. Edinburgh: University of Edinburgh, 2005. https://www.pure.ed.ac.uk/ws/files/15242135/A_Family_Concern.pdf (accessed 20 June 2020).

Cunningham, Hugh. Introduction to *Charity, Philanthropy and Reform: From the 1690s to 1850*, edited by Hugh Cunningham and Joanna Innes, 1–14. Basingstoke: Macmillan, 1998.

Cunningham, Hugh, and Joanna Innes, eds. *Charity, Philanthropy and Reform: From the 1690s to 1850*. Basingstoke: Macmillan, 1998.

Daiches, David. *The Paradox of Scottish Culture: The Eighteenth-Century Experience*. London: Oxford University Press, 1964.

———. *Robert Fergusson*. Edinburgh: Scottish Academic Press, 1982.

Dalgleish, Andrew J. "Voluntary Associations and the Middle Class in Edinburgh, 1780–1820." PhD diss., University of Edinburgh, 1992.

Dalley, Lana L., and Jill Rappoport, eds. *Economic Women: Essays on Desire and Dispossession in Nineteenth-Century British Culture*. Columbus: Ohio State University Press, 2013.

Davidoff, Leonore, and Catherine Hall. *Family Fortunes: Men and Women of the English Middle Class, 1780–1850*. London, 1987. Rev. ed. London, Routledge, 2002.

Davis, Michael T. "United Scotsmen (*act.* 1797–1802)." In *Oxford Dictionary of National Biography*. Oxford University Press, 2004; online ed. https://doi:10.1093/ref:odnb/95551.

Davison, Kate. "Occasional Politeness and Gentlemen's Laughter in Eighteenth-Century England." *Historical Journal* 57 (2014): 921–945.

Dennis, Victoria Solt. *Discovering Friendly and Fraternal Societies: Their Badges and Regalia*. Princes Risborough: Shire, 2005.

Devine, T. M., ed. *Conflict and Stability in Scottish Society, 1700–1850*. Edinburgh: John Donald, 1990.

———. *The Tobacco Lords: A Study of the Tobacco Merchants of Glasgow and Their Trading Activities, c. 1740–90*. Edinburgh: Edinburgh University Press, 1975.

Devine, T. M., and Gordon Jackson, eds. *Glasgow*. Vol. 1, *Beginnings to 1830*. Manchester: Manchester University Press, 1995.

[Dialectic Society of Edinburgh]. *History of the Dialectic Society*. Edinburgh: printed for the Society 1887.

Dick, Alexander. "'A good deal of trash': Reading Societies, Religious Controversy and Networks of Improvement in Eighteenth-Century Scotland." *Journal for Eighteenth-Century Studies* 38 (2015): 585–598.

Dickie, Simon. *Cruelty and Laughter: Forgotten Comic Literature and the Unsentimental Eighteenth Century*. Chicago: University of Chicago Press, 2011.

Donald, T. F. *The Hodge Podge Club, 1752–1900*. Glasgow: James MacLehose and Sons, 1900.

Duff, Mountstuart E. Grant. *The Club, 1764–1905*. London: printed for private circulation, 1905.

Dunan-Page, Anne, and Clotilde Prunier, eds. *Debating the Faith: Religion and Letter Writing in Great Britain, 1550–1800*. Dordrecht: Springer, 2013.

Duncan, George John C. *Memoir of the Rev. Henry Duncan, Minister of Ruthwell*. Edinburgh: William Oliphant and Sons, 1848.

Duncan, Ian. *Scott's Shadow: The Novel in Romantic Edinburgh*. Princeton, NJ: Princeton University Press, 2007.

Duncan, William James, ed. *Notices and Documents Illustrative of the Literary History of Glasgow*. Glasgow: Maitland Club, 1831.

Durkacz, Victor Edward. *The Decline of the Celtic Languages*. Edinburgh: John Donald, 1983.

Dwyer, John. "Enlightened Spectators and Classical Moralists: Sympathetic Relations in Eighteenth-Century Scotland." In "Sociability and Society in Eighteenth-Century

Scotland," edited by John Dwyer and Richard B. Sher. Special issue, *Eighteenth-Century Life* 15, nos. 1–2 (1991): 96–118.

———. "Introduction—A 'Peculiar Blessing': Social Converse in Scotland from Hutcheson to Burns." In "Sociability and Society in Eighteenth-Century Scotland," edited by John Dwyer and Richard B. Sher. Special issue, *Eighteenth-Century Life* 15, nos. 1–2 (1991): 1–22.

———. "Mirror Club (*act.* 1776–1787)." In *Oxford Dictionary of National Biography.* Oxford University Press, 2004; online ed. https://doi:10.1093/ref:odnb/73612.

———. *Virtuous Discourse: Sensibility and Community in Late Eighteenth-Century Scotland.* Edinburgh: John Donald, 1987.

Dwyer, John, and Richard B. Sher, eds. "Sociability and Society in Eighteenth-Century Scotland." Special issue, *Eighteenth-Century Life* 15, nos. 1–2 (1991).

Eddy, Matthew D. "The Shape of Knowledge: Children and the Visual Culture of Literacy and Numeracy." *Science in Context* 26 (2013): 215–245.

Elliott, Paul. "The Origins of the 'Creative Class': Provincial Urban Society, Scientific Culture and Socio-political Marginality in Britain in the Eighteenth and Nineteenth Centuries." *Social History* 28 (2003): 361–387.

Emerson, Roger L. *Academic Patronage in the Scottish Enlightenment: Glasgow, Edinburgh and St Andrews Universities.* Oxford: Oxford University Press, 2008.

———. "The Contexts of the Scottish Enlightenment." In *The Cambridge Companion to the Scottish Enlightenment*, edited by Alexander Broadie, 9–30. Cambridge: Cambridge University Press, 2003.

———. "The Edinburgh Society for the Importation of Foreign Seeds and Plants, 1764–1773." *Eighteenth-Century Life* 7 (1982): 73–95.

———. "The Enlightenment and Social Structures." In *City and Society in the Eighteenth Century*, edited by Paul Fritz and David Williams, 99–124. Toronto: Hakkert, 1973.

———. *Essays on David Hume, Medical Men and the Scottish Enlightenment: Industry, Knowledge and Humanity.* Farnham: Ashgate, 2009.

———. *Neglected Scots: Eighteenth Century Glaswegians and Women.* Edinburgh: Humming Earth, 2015.

———. "The Philosophical Society of Edinburgh, 1737–1747." *British Journal for the History of Science* 12 (1979): 154–191.

———. "The Philosophical Society of Edinburgh, 1747–1768." *British Journal for the History of Science* 14 (1981): 133–176.

———. "The Philosophical Society of Edinburgh, 1768–1783." *British Journal for the History of Science* 18 (1985): 255–303.

———. "Science and the Origins and Concerns of the Scottish Enlightenment." *History of Science* 26 (1988): 333–366.

———. "The Scottish Enlightenment and the End of the Philosophical Society of Edinburgh." *British Journal for the History of Science* 21 (1988): 33–66.

———. "Select Society (*act.* 1754–1764)." In *Oxford Dictionary of National Biography.* Oxford University Press, 2004; online ed. https://doi:10.1093/ref:odnb/73614.

———. "Sir Robert Sibbald, Kt, the Royal Society of Scotland and the Origins of the Scottish Enlightenment." *Annals of Science* 45 (1988): 41–72.

———. "The Social Composition of Enlightened Scotland: The Select Society of Edinburgh, 1754–1764." *Studies on Voltaire and the Eighteenth Century* 114 (1973): 291–329.

Emerson, Roger L., and Jennifer Macleod, "The Musick Club and the Edinburgh Musical Society." *Book of the Old Edinburgh Club* 10 (2014): 45–62.

Emerson, Roger L., and Paul Wood. "Science and Enlightenment in Glasgow, 1690–1802." In *Science and Medicine in the Scottish Enlightenment*, edited by Charles W. J. Withers and Paul Wood, 79–142. East Linton: Tuckwell Press, 2002.

Ferguson, J. De Lancey. *Pride and Passion: Robert Burns, 1759–1796*. New York, 1939. Reprint, New York: Russell and Russell, 1964.

Finkelstein, David, ed. *Print Culture and the Blackwood Tradition, 1805–1930*. Toronto: Toronto University Press, 2006.

Fletcher, Anthony. "Courses in Politeness: The Upbringing and Experiences of Five Teenage Diarists, 1671–1860." *Transactions of the Royal Historical Society* 12 (2002): 417–430.

———. *Gender, Sex, and Subordination in England, 1500–1800*. New Haven, CT: Yale University Press, 1995.

Fletcher, Eliza. *Autobiography of Mrs. Fletcher with Letters and Other Family Memorials*. Edited by Mary Richardson. Edinburgh: Edmonston and Douglas, 1875.

Forbes, Duncan. "'Scientific Whiggism': Adam Smith and John Millar." *Cambridge Journal* 9 (1953–1954): 643–670.

Foyster, Elizabeth. *Manhood in Early Modern England: Honour, Sex, and Marriage*. London: Routledge, 1999.

Fraser, W. Hamish. *Conflict and Class: Scottish Workers, 1700–1838*. Edinburgh: John Donald, 1988.

French, Henry, and Mark Rothery. *Man's Estate: Landed Gentry Masculinities, 1660–1900*. Oxford: Oxford University Press, 2012.

Fritz, Paul, and David Williams, eds. *City and Society in the Eighteenth Century*. Toronto: Hakkert, 1973.

Fulton, Henry L. *Dr. John Moore, 1729–1802: A Life in Medicine, Travel, and Revolution*. London: Rowman and Littlefield, 2015.

Gatrell, Vic. *The First Bohemians: Life and Art in London's Golden Age*. London: Allen Lane, 2013.

Gest, John Marshall. "The Law and Lawyers of Sir Walter Scott." *American Law Register* 54 (1906): 289–309, 352–372.

Gleadle, Kathryn. "Gentry, Gender, and the Moral Economy during the Revolutionary and Napoleonic Wars in Provincial England." In *Economic Women: Essays on Desire and Dispossession in Nineteenth-Century British Culture*, edited by Lana L. Dalley and Jill Rappoport, 25–40. Columbus: Ohio State University Press, 2013.

Glover, Katharine. *Elite Women and Polite Society in Eighteenth-Century Scotland*. Woodbridge, UK: Boydell and Brewer, 2011.

Gorsky, Martin. *Patterns of Philanthropy: Charity and Society in Nineteenth-Century Bristol*. Woodbridge, UK: Boydell and Brewer, 2011.

Grant, James. *Cassell's Old and New Edinburgh: Its History, Its People, and Its Places*. 3 vols. London: Cassell, Petter, Galphin, [1882].

Gray, James. *History of the Royal Medical Society of Edinburgh, 1737–1937*. Edinburgh: Edinburgh University Press, 1952.

Gregory, Jeremy, and John Stevenson. *The Longman Companion to Britain in the Eighteenth Century*. London: Longman, 2000.

Guerrini, Anita. "Monro, Alexander, Primus (1697–1767)." In *Oxford Dictionary of National Biography*. Oxford University Press, 2004; online ed. https://doi:10.1093/ref:odnb/18964.

Guthrie, Douglas. "The Aesculapian Club of Edinburgh." *Edinburgh University Journal* 23 (1968): 245–250.

Habermas, Jürgen. *The Structural Transformation of the Public Sphere: An Inquiry into a Category of Bourgeois Society*. 1962. Translated by Thomas Burger, with the assistance of Frederick Lawrence. Cambridge, MA: MIT Press, 1989.

Halsey, Katie, and Jane Slinn, eds. *The Concept and Practice of Conversation in the Long Eighteenth Century, 1688–1848*. Newcastle: Cambridge Scholars Publishing, 2008.

Hamilton, Douglas J. *Scotland, the Caribbean and the Atlantic World, 1750–1820*. Manchester: Manchester University Press, 2005.

Harris, Bob. "Cultural Change in Provincial Scottish Towns, c. 1700–1820." *Historical Journal* 54 (2011): 105–141.

———. "The Enlightenment, Towns and Urban Society in Scotland, c. 1760–1820." *English Historical Review* 126 (2011): 1097–1136.

———. *The Scottish People and the French Revolution*. London: Routledge, 2008.

———. *A Tale of Three Cities: The Life and Times of Lord Daer, 1763–1794*. Edinburgh: John Donald, 2015.

Harris, Bob, and Charles McKean. *The Scottish Town in the Age of the Enlightenment, 1740–1820*. Edinburgh: Edinburgh University Press, 2014.

Harrison, William. *Mona Miscellany: A Selection of Proverbs, Sayings, Ballads, Customs, Superstitions, and Legends, Peculiar to the Isle of Man*. 2nd ser. Publications of the Manx Society, vol. 21. Douglas, Isle of Man: printed for the Manx Society, 1873.

Harvey, Karen. *The Little Republic: Masculinity and Domestic Authority in Eighteenth-Century Britain*. Oxford: Oxford University Press, 2012.

Haslett, Moyra. *Pope to Burney, 1714–1779: Scriblerians to Bluestockings*. Basingstoke: Palgrave Macmillan, 2003.

———. "Swift and Conversational Culture." *Eighteenth-Century Ireland* 29 (2014): 11–30.

Hecht, Hans, ed. *Songs from David Herd's Manuscripts*. Edinburgh: W. J. Hay, 1904.

Henderson, Ebenezer. *The Annals of Dunfermline and Vicinity from the Earliest Authentic Period to the Present Time, A.D. 1069–1878*. Glasgow: J. Tweed, 1879.

Herman, Arthur. *The Scottish Enlightenment: The Scots' Invention of the Modern World*. London: Fourth Estate, 2001.

Hill, Lisa, and Peter McCarthy. "Hume, Smith and Ferguson: Friendship in Commercial Society." *Critical Review of International Social and Political Philosophy* 2 (1999): 33–49.

Hilton, Mary, and Jill Shefrin, eds. *Educating the Child in Enlightenment Britain: Beliefs, Cultures, Practices*. Farnham: Ashgate, 2009.

Hinks, John, and Matthew Day, eds. *From Compositors to Collectors: Essays on Book-Trade History*. New Castle, DE: Oak Knoll Press; London: British Library, 2012.

Hitchcock, Tim, and Michèle Cohen. *English Masculinities, 1660–1800*. London: Routledge, 1999

Holcomb, Kathleen. "A Dance in the Mind: The Provincial Scottish Philosophical Societies." *Studies in Eighteenth-Century Culture* 21 (1991): 89–100.

———. "Thomas Reid in the Glasgow Literary Society." In *The Glasgow Enlightenment*, edited by Andrew Hook and Richard B. Sher, 95–110. East Linton: Tuckwell Press, 1997.

Hook, Andrew, and Richard B. Sher, eds. *The Glasgow Enlightenment.* East Linton: Tuckwell Press, 1997.

Howsam, Leslie. *Cheap Bibles: Nineteenth-Century Publishing and the British and Foreign Bible Society.* Cambridge: Cambridge University Press, 1991.

Hoyos, Arturo de, and S. Brent Morris, eds. *Freemasonry in Context: History, Ritual, Controversy.* Lanham, MD: Lexington Books, 2004.

Hunter, Richard Ian, "Nicol, Alexander (*bap.* 1703)." In *Oxford Dictionary of National Biography.* Oxford University Press, 2004; online ed. https://doi:10.1093/ref:odnb/20161.

Innes, James. "The Harveians of Edinburgh: Their First Two Hundred Years." *Scottish Medical Journal* 28 (1983): 285–289.

Innes, Sue, and Jane Rendall, "Women, Gender and Politics." In *Gender in Scottish History Since 1700*, edited by Lynn Abrams, Eleanor Gordon, Deborah Simonton, and Eileen Janes Yeo, 43–83. Edinburgh: Edinburgh University Press, 2006.

Jacob, Margaret C. *Living the Enlightenment: Freemasonry and Politics in Eighteenth-Century Europe.* New York: Oxford University Press, 1991.

———. *The Origins of Freemasonry: Facts and Fictions.* Philadelphia: University of Pennsylvania Press, 2005.

———. *The Radical Enlightenment: Pantheists, Freemasons and Republicans.* London: Allen and Unwin, 1981.

James, R. I. "Bristol Society in the Eighteenth Century." In *Bristol and Its Adjoining Counties*, edited by C. M. MacInnes and W. F. Whittard, 231–241. Bristol: British Association for the Advancement of Science, 1955.

Jenkinson, Jacqueline. *Scottish Medical Societies, 1731–1939: Their History and Records.* Edinburgh: Edinburgh University Press, 1993.

Jones, Larry Eugene, and James Retallack, eds. *Elections, Mass Politics, and Social Change in Modern Germany.* Cambridge: Cambridge University Press, 2002.

Kahler, Lisa. "Canongate Kilwinning Lodge." In *Freemasonry on Both Sides of the Atlantic: Essays concerning the Craft in the British Isles, Europe, the United States, and Mexico*, edited by R. William Weisberger, Wallace McLeod, and S. Brent Morris, 59–86. Boulder, CO: East European Monographs, 2002.

———. "Freemasonry in Edinburgh, 1721–1746: Institutions and Context." PhD diss., University of St. Andrews, 1998.

———. "Scottish Definitions and Transitions." In *Freemasonry in Context: History, Ritual, Controversy*, edited by Arturo de Hoyos and S. Brent Morris, 3–18. Lanham, MD: Lexington Books, 2004.

Kelly, James. "Monks of the Screw [Monks of the Order of St. Patrick] (*act.* 1779–1789)." In *Oxford Dictionary of National Biography.* Oxford University Press, 2004; online ed. https://doi:10.1093/ref:odnb/96301.

Kelly, James, and Martyn J. Powell, eds. *Clubs and Societies in Eighteenth-Century Ireland.* Dublin: Four Courts, 2010.

Kelly, Jason M. "Riots, Revelries, and Rumor: Libertinism and Masculine Association in Enlightenment London." *Journal of British Studies* 45 (2006): 759–795.

Kidd, Colin. "The Phillipsonian Enlightenment." *Modern Intellectual History* 11 (2014): 175–190.

Kilburn, Matthew. "Todd, Sweeney (*supp. fl.* 1784)." In *Oxford Dictionary of National Biography.* Oxford University Press, 2004; online ed. https://doi:10.1093/ref:odnb/53666.

Kingwell, Mark. "Politics and the Polite Society in the Scottish Enlightenment." *Historical Reflections / Réflexions Historiques* 19 (1993): 363–387.

Kirk, John, Michael Brown, and Andrew Noble, eds. *Cultures of Radicalism in Britain and Ireland*. London: Pickering and Chatto, 2013.

Klein, Lawrence E. "Politeness and the Interpretation of the British Eighteenth Century." *Historical Journal* 45 (2002): 860–898.

———. *Shaftesbury and the Culture of Politeness: Moral Discourse and Cultural Politics in Early Eighteenth-Century England*. Cambridge: Cambridge University Press, 1994.

Krug-Richter, Barbara, and Ruth-E. Mohrmann, eds. *Frühneuzeitliche Universitätskulturen: Kulturhistorische Perspektiven auf die Hochschulen in Europa*. Cologne: Böhlau, 2009.

Langford, Paul. *A Polite and Commercial People: England, 1727–1783*. London: Oxford University Press, 1989.

Lawrence, Christopher J. "Medicine as Culture: Edinburgh and the Scottish Enlightenment." PhD diss., University of London, 1984.

Leask, Nigel. *Robert Burns and Pastoral: Poetry and Improvement in Late Eighteenth-Century Scotland*. Oxford: Oxford University Press, 2010.

———. "'Their Groves o' Sweet Myrtles': Robert Burns and the Scottish Colonial Experience." In *Robert Burns in Global Culture, 1759–2010*, edited by Murray Pittock, 172–188. Lanham, MD: Rowman and Littlefield, 2011.

Lee, Anthony W. "Mentoring and Mimicry in Boswell's *Life of Johnson*." *Eighteenth Century* 51 (2010): 67–85.

Levander, F. W. "The 'Collectanea' of the Rev. Daniel Lysons, F.R.S., F.S.A." *Ars Quatuor Coronatorum* 29 (1916): 7–100.

Lindsay, Maurice. *The Burns Encyclopedia*. London, 1959. 4th ed. Revised and edited by David Purdie, Kirsteen McCue, and Gerard Carruthers. London: Robert Hale, 2013.

"Literary and Philosophical Societies of Edinburgh during the Eighteenth Century." *Hogg's Instructor* 8 (1852): 44–46.

Lloyd, Sarah. *Charity and Poverty in England, 1680–1820: Wild and Visionary Schemes*. Manchester: Manchester University Press, 2009.

Lockhart, J. G. *Life of Robert Burns*. 4th ed. London: John Murray, 1838.

Loiselle, Kenneth. "Living the Enlightenment in an Age of Revolution: Freemasonry in Bordeaux (1788–1794)." *French History* 24 (2009): 60–81.

Low, Donald A., ed. *Burns: The Critical Heritage*. London: Routledge and Kegan Paul, 1974.

Macdonald, Fiona. "Medicine." In *The Edinburgh History of the Book in Scotland*, vol. 2, *Enlightenment and Expansion, 1707–1800*, edited by Stephen W. Brown and Warren McDougall, 494–502. Edinburgh: Edinburgh University Press, 2012.

MacDougall, Ian, ed. *A Catalogue of Some Labour Records in Scotland and Some Scots Records outside Scotland*. Edinburgh: Scottish Labour History Society, 1978.

MacInnes, C. M., and W. F. Whittard, eds. *Bristol and Its Adjoining Counties*. Bristol: British Association for the Advancement of Science, 1955.

Mackay, James. *RB: A Biography of Robert Burns*. Edinburgh: Mainstream Publishing, 1992.

Mackenzie, Allan. *History of the Lodge Canongate Kilwinning No. 2. Compiled from the Records, 1677–1888*. Edinburgh: printed for the Lodge by Brother James Hogg, 1888.

Mackey, Albert G. *Encyclopedia of Freemasonry and Its Kindred Sciences*. Philadelphia: McClure, 1917.

Mackintosh, James. *Memoirs of the Life of the Right Honourable Sir James Mackintosh*. Edited by Robert James Mackintosh. 2nd ed. 2 vols. London: Edward Moxon, 1836.

Manley, K. A. *Books, Borrowers, and Shareholders: Scottish Circulating and Subscription Libraries before 1825; A Survey and Listing*. Edinburgh: Edinburgh Bibliographical Society in association with the National Library of Scotland, 2012.

Martin, Peter. *A Life of James Boswell*. New Haven, CT: Yale University Press, 2000.

Marwick, Sandra. *Sons of Crispin: The St Crispin Lodges of Edinburgh and Scotland*. Newcastle upon Tyne: Cambridge Scholars Publishing, 2014.

Matheson, Ann. "Religion." In *The Edinburgh History of the Book in Scotland*, vol. 2, *Enlightenment and Expansion, 1707–1800*, edited by Stephen W. Brown and Warren McDougall, 459–470. Edinburgh: Edinburgh University Press, 2012.

Matheson, J. J. *Memoir of Greville Ewing*. London: W. Tegg, 1847.

Mathew, W. M. "The Origins and Occupations of Glasgow Students, 1740–1839." *Past and Present* 33 (1966): 74–94.

Mathieson, William Law. *Church and Reform in Scotland: A History from 1797 to 1843*. Glasgow: James MacLehose and Sons, 1916.

McCormack, Rose. "Leisured Women and the English Spa Town in the Long Eighteenth Century: A Case Study of Bath and Tunbridge Wells." PhD diss., University of Aberystwyth, 2015.

McElroy, Davis D. "Literary Clubs and Societies of Eighteenth-Century Scotland." PhD diss., 2 vols., University of Edinburgh, 1952. Index, with Lucille McElroy, University of Edinburgh, 1955.

———. *Scotland's Age of Improvement: A Survey of Eighteenth-Century Literary Clubs and Societies*. Pullman: Washington State University Press, 1969.

McFarland, Elaine. *Ireland and Scotland in the Age of Revolution: Planting the Green Bough*. Edinburgh: Edinburgh University Press, 1994.

McIlvanney, Liam. *Burns the Radical: Poetry and Politics in Late Eighteenth-Century Scotland*. East Linton: Tuckwell Press, 2003.

McKean, Charles. "Was There a British Georgian Town? A Comparison between Selected Scottish Burghs and English Towns." *Historical Research* 86 (2013): 253–291.

McLean, Ralph. "Rhetoric and Literary Criticism in the Early Scottish Enlightenment." PhD diss., University of Glasgow, 2009.

McLean, Ralph, Ronnie Young, and Kenneth Simpson. Introduction to *The Scottish Enlightenment and Literary Culture*, edited by Ralph McLean, Ronnie Young, and Kenneth Simpson, 1–18. Lewisburg, PA: Bucknell University Press, 2016.

———, eds. *The Scottish Enlightenment and Literary Culture*. Lewisburg, PA: Bucknell University Press, 2016.

Mee, Jon. "The Buzz about the *Bee*: Policing the Conversation of Culture in the 1790s." In *Before Blackwood's: Scottish Journalism in the Age of Enlightenment*, edited by Alex Benchimol, Rhona Brown, and David Shuttleton, 63–74. London: Routledge, 2015.

———. *Conversable Worlds: Literature, Contention, and Community, 1762–1830*. Oxford: Oxford University Press, 2011.

Meehan, Joanna, ed. *Feminists Read Habermas: Gendering the Subject of Discourse*. New York: Routledge, 1995.

Memorabilia of Inverness. Inverness, 1912.

Miller, James. *The Lamp of Lothian; or, The History of Haddington*. Haddington: Allan, 1844.

Mitchison, Rosalind. *The Old Poor Law in Scotland: The Experience of Poverty, 1574–1845*. Edinburgh: Edinburgh University Press, 2000.

Moore, James. "Evangelical Calvinists versus the Hutcheson Circle: Debating the Faith in Scotland, 1738–1739." In *Debating the Faith: Religion and Letter Writing in Great Britain, 1550–1800*, edited by Anne Dunan-Page and Clotilde Prunier, 177–193. Dordrecht: Springer, 2013.

Morrell, J. B. "Reflections on the History of Scottish Science." *History of Science* 12 (1974): 81–94.

———. "The University of Edinburgh in the Late Eighteenth Century: Its Scientific Eminence and Academic Structure." *Isis* 62 (1971): 158–171.

Morris, R. J. "Civil Society and the Nature of Urbanism: Britain, 1750–1850." *Urban History* 25 (1998): 289–301.

———. "Clubs, Societies, and Associations." In *The Cambridge Social History of Britain, 1750–1950*, vol. 3, *Social Agencies and Institutions*, edited by F.M.L. Thompson, 395–444. New York: Cambridge University Press, 1990.

———. "Voluntary Societies and British Urban Elites, 1780–1850: An Analysis." *Historical Journal* 26 (1983): 95–118.

Mulvey Roberts, Marie. "Pleasures Engendered by Gender: Homosociality and the Club." In *Pleasure in the Eighteenth Century*, edited by Roy Porter and Marie Mulvey Roberts, 48–76. Basingstoke: Macmillan, 1996.

———. *See also* Roberts, Marie.

Murray, David. *Early Burgh Organisation in Scotland*. 2 vols. Glasgow: MacLehose, Jackson, 1924–1932.

———. *Memories of the Old College of Glasgow*. Glasgow: Jackson and Wylie, 1927.

———. *Robert and Andrew Foulis and the Glasgow Press*. Glasgow: James MacLehose and Sons, 1913.

Nenadic, Stana. "The Middle Ranks and Modernisation." In *Glasgow*, vol. 1, *Beginnings to 1830*, edited by T. M. Devine and Gordon Jackson, 278–311. Manchester: Manchester University Press, 1995.

The New Statistical Account of Scotland. 15 vols. Edinburgh: William Blackwood and Sons, 1845.

Notes of a Tour through the Shires of Fife, Forfar, Perth, and Stirling in 1800. Dundee: printed for private circulation, 1898.

Orihel, Michelle. "'Treacherous Memories' of Regicide: The Calves-Head Club in the Age of Anne." *The Historian* 73 (2011): 435–462.

Paul, James Balfour. *The History of the Royal Company of Archers, the Queen's Bodyguard for Scotland*. Edinburgh: William Blackwood and Sons, 1875.

Paul, K. Tawny. "Credit, Reputation, and Masculinity in British Urban Commerce: Edinburgh, c. 1710–70." *Economic History Review* 66 (2013): 226–248.

———. "A 'Polite and Commercial People'? Masculinity and Economic Violence in Scotland, 1700–60." In *Nine Centuries of Man: Manhood and Masculinities in Scottish History*, edited by Lynn Abrams and Elizabeth L. Ewan, 203–222. Edinburgh: Edinburgh University Press, 2017.

Peacock, Hugh C. *Robert Burns, Poet-Laureate of Lodge Canongate Kilwinning: Facts Substantiating His Election and Inauguration on 1st March 1787*. With the assistance of Allan Mackenzie. Edinburgh: Christie and Son, 1894.

Penny, George. *Traditions of Perth, containing Sketches of the Manners and Customs of the Inhabitants, and Notices of Public Occurrences, during the Last Century.* Perth: Dewar, Sidey, Morison, Peat, and Drummond, 1836.

Pentland, Gordon. *The Spirit of the Union: Popular Politics in Scotland, 1815–1820.* London: Pickering and Chatto, 2011.

Perkins, Pam. "A Taste for Scottish Fiction: Christian Johnstone's *Cook and Housewife's Manual.*" *European Romantic Review* 11 (2000): 248–258.

Phillipson, Nicholas. *Adam Smith: An Enlightened Life.* London: Allen Lane, 2010.

———. "Culture and Society in the Eighteenth-Century Province: The Case of Edinburgh and the Scottish Enlightenment." In *The University in Society,* edited by Lawrence Stone, 2:407–448. Princeton, NJ: Princeton University Press, 1975.

———. "Hume as Moralist: A Social Historian's Perspective." In *Philosophers of the Enlightenment,* edited by S. C. Brown, 140–161. Brighton: Harvester Press, 1979.

———. "The Making of an Enlightened University." In *The University of Edinburgh: An Illustrated History,* edited by Robert D. Anderson, Michael Lynch, and Nicholas Phillipson, 51–102. Edinburgh: Edinburgh University Press, 2003.

———. "Towards a Definition of the Scottish Enlightenment." In *City and Society in the Eighteenth Century,* edited by Paul Fritz and David Williams, 125–147. Toronto: Hakkert, 1973.

Phillipson, Nicholas, and Rosalind Mitchison, eds. *Scotland in the Age of Improvement: Essays in Scottish History in the Eighteenth Century.* Edinburgh: Edinburgh University Press, 1970.

Pittock, Murray, ed. *The Edinburgh Companion to Scottish Romanticism.* Edinburgh: Edinburgh University Press, 2011.

———. *Enlightenment in a Smart City: Edinburgh's Civic Development, 1660–1750.* Edinburgh: Edinburgh University Press, 2018.

———, ed. *Robert Burns in Global Culture, 1759–2010.* Lanham, MD: Rowman and Littlefield, 2011.

Porter, Roy, and Marie Mulvey Roberts, eds. *Pleasure in the Eighteenth Century.* Basingstoke: Macmillan, 1996.

Potts, Louis W. "Lee, Arthur." In *American National Biography.* 24 vols. Oxford: Oxford University Press, 1999; online ed. https://doi.org/10.1093/anb/9780198606697.article.0100505.

Powell, Martyn J. "The Aldermen of Skinner's Alley: Ultra-Protestantism before the Orange Order." In *Clubs and Societies in Eighteenth-Century Ireland,* edited by James Kelly and Martyn J. Powell, 203–224. Dublin: Four Courts, 2010.

———. "'Associate for the Purposes of Deliverance and Glory': The Club-Life of the Irish Volunteers." In *Associational Culture in Ireland and Abroad,* edited by R. V. Comerford and Jennifer Kelly, 27–46. Dublin: Irish Academic Press, 2010.

———. "'Beef, Claret, and Communication': Convivial Clubs in the Public Sphere, 1750–1800." In *Clubs and Societies in Eighteenth-Century Ireland,* edited by James Kelly and Martyn J. Powell, 353–372. Dublin: Four Courts, 2010.

———. "Hunting Clubs and Societies." In *Clubs and Societies in Eighteenth-Century Ireland,* edited by James Kelly and Martyn J. Powell, 392–408. Dublin: Four Courts, 2010.

———. *The Politics of Consumption in Eighteenth-Century Ireland.* Basingstoke: Palgrave Macmillan, 2005.

———. "Scottophobia versus Jacobitism: Political Radicalism and the Press in Late Eighteenth-Century Ireland." In *Cultures of Radicalism in Britain and Ireland*, edited by John Kirk, Michael Brown, and Andrew Noble, 49–62. London: Pickering and Chatto, 2013.

Prendergast, Amy. *Literary Salons across Britain and Ireland in the Long Eighteenth Century*. Basingstoke: Palgrave Macmillan, 2015.

Prochaska, F. K. "Women in English Philanthropy, 1790–1830." *International Review of Social History* 9 (1974): 426–445.

Purviance, Susan M. "Intersubjectivity and Sociable Relations in the Philosophy of Francis Hutcheson." In "Sociability and Society in Eighteenth-Century Scotland," edited by John Dwyer and Richard B. Sher. Special issue, *Eighteenth-Century Life* 15, nos. 1–2 (1991): 23–80.

Rae, John. *The Life of Adam Smith*. London, 1895. Reprint, New York: Cosimo, 2006.

Ramsay, Alexander. *History of the Highland and Agricultural Society of Scotland*. Edinburgh: William Blackwood and Sons, 1879.

Ramsay, John. *Scotland and Scotsmen in the Eighteenth Century*. Edited by Alexander Allardyce. 2 vols. Edinburgh: William Blackwood and Sons, 1888.

Reader, Nicola Sian. "Female Friendly Societies in Industrialising England, 1780–1850." PhD diss., University of Leeds, 2005.

[Reid, William]. *History of the Juridical Society of Edinburgh*. Edinburgh: printed for the Society, 1875.

Reinke-Williams, Tim. "Misogyny, Jest-Books and Male Youth Culture in Seventeenth-Century England." *Gender and History* 21 (2009): 324–339.

Rendall, Jane. "Gender, Philanthropy and Civic Identities in Edinburgh, 1795–1830." In *The Routledge History Handbook of Gender and the Urban Experience*, edited by Deborah Simonton, 209–220. London: Routledge, 2017.

———. "'The Principle of Mutual Support': Female Friendly Societies in Scotland, c. 1789–1830." *Journal of Scottish Historical Studies* 40 (2020): 17–39.

Risse, Guenter B. *Hospital Life in Enlightenment Scotland: Care and Teaching at the Royal Infirmary of Edinburgh*. Cambridge: Cambridge University Press, 1986.

Roberts, Marie. *British Poets and Secret Societies: Freemasons and Clandestine Brotherhoods*. London: Croom Helm, 1986.

———. *See also* Mulvey Roberts, Marie.

Robertson, John. "The Scottish Contribution to the Enlightenment." In *The Scottish Enlightenment: Essays in Reinterpretation*, edited by Paul Wood, 37–62. Rochester: University of Rochester Press, 2000.

Rogers, Charles. *Social Life in Scotland from Early to Recent Times*. 2 vols. Edinburgh: William Paterson, 1884–1886.

Rogers, Nicholas. "The Dynamic of News in Britain during the American War: The Case of Admiral Keppel." *Parliamentary History* 25 (2006): 49–67.

Rosner, Lisa. *Medical Education in the Age of Improvement: Edinburgh Students and Apprentices, 1760–1826*. Edinburgh: Edinburgh University Press, 1991.

———. "Monro, Alexander, Secundus (1733–1817), Anatomist." In *Oxford Dictionary of National Biography*. Oxford University Press, 2004; online ed. https://doi:10.1093/ref:odnb/18965.

Ross, Alasdair. "The Bannatyne Club and the Publication of Scottish Ecclesiastical Cartularies." *Scottish Historical Review* 85 (2006): 202–233.

Roxburgh, Kenneth B. E. "Peddie, James (1759–1845), Minister of the Secession Church." In *Oxford Dictionary of National Biography*. Oxford University Press, 2004; online ed. https://doi:10.1093/ref:odnb/21753.

Sambrook, James. "Franciscans [Monks of Medmenham] (*act. c.* 1750–*c.* 1776)." In *Oxford Dictionary of National Biography*. Oxford University Press, 2004; online ed. https://doi:10.1093/ref:odnb/71306.

Scally, John. "Cheap Print on Scottish Streets." In *The Edinburgh History of the Book in Scotland*, vol. 2, *Enlightenment and Expansion, 1707–1800*, edited by Stephen W. Brown and Warren McDougall, 372–381. Edinburgh: Edinburgh University Press, 2012.

Schofield, Robert E. *The Lunar Society of Birmingham*. London: University of London Press, 1963.

Scott, Hew. *Fasti Ecclesiae Scoticanae: The Succession of Ministers in the Church of Scotland from the Reformation*. Vol. 3, *Synod of Glasgow and Ayr*. Edinburgh: Oliver and Boyd, 1920.

Scott, Patrick. "A 'Lost' Collection of Robert Burns Manuscripts: Sir Alfred Law, Davidson Cook, and the Honresfield Collection." https://electricscotland.com/familytree/frank/burns_lives210.htm (accessed 17 Nov. 2019).

Scott, W. R. *Adam Smith as Student and Professor*. Glasgow: Jackson and Son, 1937.

Semple, David. *Paisley Town's House, Public Inn, or Saracen's Head Inn: Its History*. Paisley, 1870.

Seymour, Terry I. *Boswell's Books: Four Generations of Collecting and Collectors*. New Castle, DE: Oak Knoll Press, 2016.

Shairp, John Campbell. *Robert Burns*. Edited by John Morley. New York: Harper, 1901.

Shapin, Steven. "The Audience for Science in Eighteenth-Century Edinburgh." *History of Science* 12 (1974): 95–121.

———. "Property, Patronage, and the Politics of Science: The Founding of the Royal Society of Edinburgh." *British Journal for the History of Science* 7 (1974): 1–41.

Shepard, Alexandra. *Meanings of Manhood in Early Modern England*. Oxford: Oxford University Press, 2003.

———. "Student Masculinity in Early Modern Cambridge." In *Frühneuzeitliche Universitätskulturen: Kulturhistorische Perspektiven auf die Hochschulen in Europa*, edited by Barbara Krug-Richter and Ruth-E. Mohrmann, 53–74. Cologne: Böhlau, 2009.

Sher, Richard B. *Church and University in the Scottish Enlightenment: The Moderate Literati of Edinburgh*. Edinburgh: Edinburgh University Press; Princeton, NJ: Princeton University Press, 1985.

———. "Commerce, Religion and the Enlightenment in Eighteenth-Century Glasgow." In *Glasgow*, vol. 1, *Beginnings to 1830*, edited by T. M. Devine and Gordon Jackson, 312–359. Manchester: Manchester University Press, 1995.

———. "Corporatism and Consensus in the Late Eighteenth-Century Book Trade: The Edinburgh Booksellers' Society in Comparative Perspective." *Book History* 1 (1998): 32–90.

———. *The Enlightenment and the Book: Scottish Authors and Their Publishers in Eighteenth-Century Britain, Ireland, and America*. Chicago: University of Chicago Press, 2006.

———. "Poker Club (*act.* 1762–1784)." In *Oxford Dictionary of National Biography*. Oxford University Press, 2004; online ed. https://doi:10.1093/ref:odnb/73613.

Sher, Richard B., and Andrew Hook. "Introduction: Glasgow and the Enlightenment." In *The Glasgow Enlightenment*, edited by Andrew Hook and Richard B. Sher, 1–17. East Linton: Tuckwell Press, 1997.

Shields, David S. *Civil Tongues and Polite Letters in British America*. Chapel Hill: University of North Carolina Press, 1997.

Simonton, Deborah, ed. *The Routledge History Handbook of Gender and the Urban Experience*. London: Routledge, 2017.

Smout, T. C. *A History of the Scottish People, 1560–1830*. London: Fontana, 1998.

Snodgrass, Charles. "*Blackwood's* Subversive Scottishness." In *Print Culture and the Blackwood Tradition, 1805–1930*, edited by David Finkelstein, 90–116. Toronto: Toronto University Press, 2006.

Sonnelitter, Karen. *Charity Movements in Eighteenth-Century Ireland: Philanthropy and Improvement*. Woodbridge, UK: Boydell Press, 2016.

Speculative Society of Edinburgh. *History of the Speculative Society of Edinburgh, from Its Institution in 1764*. Edinburgh: printed for the Society, 1845.

———. *The History of the Speculative Society, 1764–1904*. Edinburgh: printed for the Society, 1905.

Stevenson, David. *The Beggar's Benison: Sex Clubs of Enlightenment Scotland and Their Rituals*. East Linton: Tuckwell Press, 2001.

———. *The First Freemasons: Scotland's Early Lodges and Their Members*. Aberdeen: Aberdeen University Press, 1988.

———. "'The Gudeman of Ballangeich': Rambles in the Afterlife of James V." *Folklore* 15 (2004): 187–200.

———. *The Origins of Freemasonry: Scotland's Century, 1590–1710*. Cambridge: Cambridge University Press, 1988.

Stewart, George. *Curiosities of Glasgow Citizenship*. Glasgow: James MacLehose, 1881.

Stewart, M. A. "Berkeley and the Rankenian Club." *Hermathena* 89 (1985): 25–45.

Stone, Lawrence, ed. *The University in Society*. 2 vols. Princeton, NJ: Princeton University Press, 1975.

Strang, John. *Glasgow and Its Clubs: Or Glimpses of the Condition, Manners, Characters, and Oddities of the City, during the Past and Present Centuries*. 3rd ed. Glasgow: John Smith, 1864.

Swaim, Barton. *Scottish Men of Letters and the New Public Sphere, 1802–1834*. Lewisburg, PA: Bucknell University Press, 2009.

Sweet, Rosemary. "Women and Civic Life in Eighteenth-Century England." In *Women and Urban Life in Eighteenth-Century England: On the Town*, edited by Rosemary Sweet and Penelope Lane, 21–42. Aldershot: Ashgate, 2003.

Sweet, Rosemary, and Penelope Lane, eds. *Women and Urban Life in Eighteenth-Century England: On the Town*. Aldershot: Ashgate, 2003.

Tankard, Paul, ed. *Facts and Inventions: Selections from the Journalism of James Boswell*. New Haven, CT: Yale University Press, 2014.

Tarbuck, Derya Gurses. "Exercises in Women's Intellectual Sociability in the Eighteenth Century: The Fair Intellectual Club." *History of European Ideas* 41 (2015): 375–386.

Terry, Charles Sanford. *A Catalogue of the Publications of Scottish Historical and Kindred Clubs and Societies . . . 1780–1908*. Glasgow: James MacLehose and Sons, 1909.

Thale, Mary. "Women in London Debating Societies in the 1780s." *Gender and History* 7 (1995): 5–24.

Thompson, E. P. "Patrician Society, Plebeian Culture." *Journal of Social History* 7 (1974): 382–405.

Tocqueville, Alexis de. *The Old Regime and the Revolution*. Translated by John Bonner. New York: Harper and Brothers, 1856. http://oll.libertyfund.org/titles/tocqueville-the-old-regime-and-the-revolution-1856 (accessed 10 May 2018).

Towsey, Mark. "First Steps in Associational Reading: Book Use and Sociability at the Wigtown Subscription Library, 1795–9." *Papers of the Bibliographical Society of America* 103 (2009): 455–495.

———. *Reading the Scottish Enlightenment: Books and Their Readers in Provincial Scotland, 1750–1820*. Leiden: Brill, 2010.

———. "'Store their Minds with Much Valuable Knowledge': Agricultural Improvement at the Selkirk Subscription Library, 1799–1814." *Journal for Eighteenth-Century Studies* 38 (2015): 569–584.

Trevor-Roper, H. R. "The Scottish Enlightenment." *Studies on Voltaire and the Eighteenth Century* 58 (1967): 1635–1658.

Ulman, H. Lewis, ed. *The Minutes of the Aberdeen Philosophical Society, 1758–1773*. Aberdeen: Aberdeen University Press, 1990.

Valentine, James. "A Society of Aberdeen Philosophers One Hundred Years Ago." *Macmillan's Magazine* 8 (1863): 436–444.

Vickery, Amanda. Introduction to *Women, Privilege, and Power: British Politics, 1750 to the Present*, edited by Amanda Vickery, 1–55. Stanford, CA: Stanford University Press, 2001.

———, ed. *Women, Privilege, and Power: British Politics, 1750 to the Present*. Stanford, CA: Stanford University Press, 2001.

Wagstaff, John. "Hawkins, Sir John (1719–1789)." In *Oxford Dictionary of National Biography*. Oxford University Press, 2004; online ed. https://doi:10.1093/ref:odnb/12674.

Wallace, Mark C. *The Great Transformation: Scottish Freemasonry, 1725–1810*. Washington, DC: Westphalia Press, 2018.

Weinbren, Daniel. *The Oddfellows, 1810–2010: 200 Years of Making Friends and Helping People*. Lancaster: Carnegie Publishing, 2010.

Weisberger, R. William, Wallace McLeod, and S. Brent Morris, eds. *Freemasonry on Both Sides of the Atlantic: Essays concerning the Craft in the British Isles, Europe, the United States, and Mexico*. Boulder, CO: East European Monographs, 2002.

Whatley, Christopher A. *Scottish Society, 1707–1830: Beyond Jacobitism, towards Industrialisation*. Manchester: Manchester University Press, 2000.

Whyte, Iain. *Scotland and the Abolition of Black Slavery, 1756–1838*. Edinburgh: Edinburgh University Press, 2006.

Wilson, Daniel. *Memorials of Edinburgh in the Olden Time*. 2 vols. Edinburgh: Hugh Paton, 1848.

Wilson, Robert. *History of Hawick*. 2nd ed. Hawick: printed by R. Armstrong, 1841.

Wilson, Walter. *The History and Antiquities of Dissenting Churches and Meeting Houses in London, Westminster, and Southwark*. 4 vols. London, 1808.

Withers, Charles W. J. "Kirk, Club and Culture Change: Gaelic Chapels, Highland Societies and the Urban Gaelic Subculture in Eighteenth-Century Scotland." *Social History* 10 (1985): 171–192.

Withers, Charles W. J., and Paul Wood, eds. *Science and Medicine in the Scottish Enlightenment*. East Linton: Tuckwell Press, 2002.

Wodehouse, P. G. *Tales from the Drones Club*. London: Hutchinson, 1982.

Wold, Atle L. *Scotland and the French Revolutionary War, 1792–1802*. Edinburgh: Edinburgh University Press, 2015.

Wood, John Cunningham, ed. *Adam Smith: Critical Assessments*. 4 vols. London: Routledge, 1983.

Wood, Paul. *The Aberdeen Enlightenment: The Arts Curriculum in the Eighteenth Century*. Aberdeen: Aberdeen University Press, 1993.

———. "Aberdeen Philosophical Society [Wise Club] (*act.* 1758 1773)." In *Oxford Dictionary of National Biography*. Oxford University Press, 2004; online ed. https://doi:10.1093/ref:odnb/95092.

———, ed. *The Scottish Enlightenment: Essays in Reinterpretation*. Rochester: University of Rochester Press, 2000.

Wright, Dudley. "The Boswells and the Craft." *British Masonic Miscellany* 17 (1927): 118–125.

———. *Robert Burns and Freemasonry*. Paisley: Alexander Gardner, 1921.

———. *Robert Burns and His Masonic Circle*. London: Cecil Palmer, 1929.

Wright–St. Clair, Rex E. *Doctors Monro: A Medical Saga*. London: Wellcome Historical Medical Library, 1964.

Zachs, William. *The First John Murray and the Late Eighteenth-Century Book Trade*. Oxford: Oxford University Press, 1998.

Ziolkowski, Theodore. *Lure of the Arcane: The Literature of Cult and Conspiracy*. Baltimore: Johns Hopkins University Press, 2013.

Notes on Contributors

DAVID ALLAN was a reader in Scottish history at the University of St. Andrews until his retirement in 2019. He taught previously at Lancaster University and also held visiting fellowships at Yale, Harvard, and Brown. He has published widely on Scottish and British intellectual history, particularly in the eighteenth century, and his most recent publications include *Commonplace Books and Reading in Georgian England* (2010) and *Scottish History: A Complete Introduction* (2015).

COREY E. ANDREWS is a professor of English at Youngstown State University. He is the author of *The Genius of Scotland: The Cultural Production of Robert Burns, 1785–1834* (2015) and has published articles and reviews in the *International Journal of Scottish Literature*, *Scottish Literary Review*, *Burns Chronicle*, and *Eighteenth-Century Scotland.*

RHONA BROWN is a senior lecturer in Scottish literature at the University of Glasgow. She specializes in the work of eighteenth-century Scottish poets and, in particular, their relationship with the periodical press and sociable networks. She is the author of *Robert Fergusson and the Scottish Periodical Press* (2012) and co-editor of *Before Blackwood's: Scottish Journalism in the Age of Enlightenment* (2015). She has recently published a digital edition of a radical 1790s newspaper, the *Edinburgh Gazetteer*, and is an editor on the forthcoming editions of Robert Burns's correspondence and Allan Ramsay's poetry and prose.

ROSALIND CARR is an honorary senior research fellow at Queen Mary, University of London, and was previously a senior lecturer in history at the University of East London. She completed her PhD at the University of Glasgow and held a postdoctoral fellowship with the Institute for Advanced Studies in the Humanities, University of Edinburgh. She has published articles and book chapters on women and early modern Scottish political history and Scottish masculinities and is the author of *Gender and Enlightenment Culture in Eighteenth-Century*

Scotland (2014). She is currently working on a study of Enlightenment, politeness, and violence in Warrane/Sydney, 1788–1815.

James J. Caudle is a research associate at the Centre for Robert Burns Studies at the University of Glasgow, currently working with the team creating the first-ever edition of Burns's complete correspondence for *The Oxford Edition of the Works of Robert Burns*. He has published numerous essays on James Boswell, most recently, "Affleck Generations: The Libraries of the Boswells of Auchinleck, 1695–1825," in *Before the Public Library: Reading, Community, and Identity in the Atlantic World, 1650–1850* (2018), and "The Case of the Missing Hottentot: John Dun's Conversation with Samuel Johnson in James Boswell's *Tour to the Hebrides* as Reported by Boswell and Dun," in *Community and Solitude: New Essays on Johnson's Circle*, ed. Anthony W. Lee (2019). As the associate editor of the Yale Boswell Editions from 2000 to 2017, he was co-editor of a volume of Boswell's earliest correspondence and, as a member of the editorial group, contributed documentary transcriptions and annotations to other volumes in the series. He also writes on the history of the book, political thought in early modern mass media such as sermons, and the role of social verse in Georgian culture.

Bob Harris is a professor of British history and Harry Pitt Fellow and tutor in history at Worcester College, Oxford. He is joint author, with Charles McKean, of *The Scottish Town in the Age of the Enlightenment, 1740–1820* (2014), which won the Saltire Society Scottish Book of the Year Award for 2014. He is currently completing a book on gambling and speculation in Britain, circa 1689–1830.

Jacqueline Jenkinson is a senior lecturer in modern British history at the University of Stirling. She has published widely on British and Scottish social and political history of the nineteenth and twentieth centuries. Her monographs in the history of medicine are *Scotland's Health, 1919–1948* (2002) and *Scottish Medical Societies, 1731–1939: Their History and Records* (1993). She also co-authored, with Michael Moss and Iain Russell, *The Royal: The History of the Glasgow Royal Infirmary, 1794–1994* (1994). Her most recent articles in this field include "More 'Marginal Men': A Prosopography of Scottish Shop-Keeping Doctors in the Late Nineteenth and Early Twentieth Centuries," *Social History of Medicine* 29 (2016): 89–111 (reprinted by the American Institute of the History of Pharmacy in *Pharmacy in History* 57 [2016]: 67–84), and "A 'Crutch to Assist in Gaining an Honest Living': Dispensary Shopkeeping by Scottish General Practitioners and the Responses of the British Medical Elite, ca. 1852–1911," *Bulletin for the History of Medicine* 86 (2012): 1–36.

Ralph McLean is curator of manuscripts for the Long 18th Century Collections at the National Library of Scotland. He previously worked as a research associate at the University of Glasgow on the project Editing Robert Burns for the 21st Century, funded by the Arts and Humanities Research Council. He has published a number of articles on Robert Burns and the Scottish Enlightenment, and along with Ronnie Young and Kenneth Simpson recently edited a collection of essays titled *The Scottish Enlightenment and Literary Culture* (2016).

MARTYN J. POWELL is a professor and head of the School of Humanities at the University of Bristol. He is a specialist in Irish political, cultural, and social history, and his publications include *Britain and Ireland in the Eighteenth-Century Crisis of Empire* (2003), *The Politics of Consumption in Eighteenth-Century Ireland* (2005), *Piss-Pots, Printers and Public Opinion in Eighteenth-Century Dublin* (2009), *Clubs and Societies in Eighteenth-Century Ireland* (2010) (edited with James Kelly), and many articles and essays. He is currently working on a study of violence in Irish society, titled "Houghers and Chalkers: The Knife in Revolutionary Ireland, 1760–1815," and an edition of the political works of Richard Brinsley Sheridan, part of a Leverhulme-funded research project.

JANE RENDALL is an honorary fellow of the History Department and the Centre for Eighteenth Century Studies at the University of York. She has published many articles on the history of the Enlightenment and on women's and feminist history, especially in Scotland, in the eighteenth and nineteenth centuries. Most recently, she is one of the editors of *The New Biographical Dictionary of Scottish Women* (2018).

MARK C. WALLACE is a former associate professor of history at Lyon College, and a fellow of the Royal Historical Society. He has lectured on a wide range of subjects including British imperialism; Scottish cultural, social, and intellectual history from the fifteenth century to the present; and the Scottish Enlightenment. A former visiting research fellow at the Institute for Advanced Studies in the Humanities at the University of Edinburgh, he has written extensively on Scottish Freemasonry and Scottish clubs and societies, particularly in the eighteenth century. He is the author of *The Great Transformation: Scottish Freemasonry, 1725–1810* (2018) and is researching the influence of Scottish historical and literary clubs on the preservation and publication of Scottish texts

CHRISTOPHER A. WHATLEY is a professor of Scottish history at the University of Dundee, where until 2013 he was vice principal. He has published extensively in the fields of Scottish economic, social, and political history. His best-known books are *Scottish Society, 1707–1830: Beyond Jacobitism, towards Industrialisation* (2000) and the award-winning *The Scots and the Union* (2006, 2007, 2014). More recently, he has combined aspects of cultural history with a social history of the legacy of Robert Burns: *Immortal Memory: Burns and the Scottish People* (2016). He recently published a history of a small Scottish island, Pabay, where members of his family lived and worked. He is a fellow of the Royal Society of Edinburgh; in 2015 his services to Scottish history education were recognized with an Order of the British Empire.

Index

Abercorn, Earl of. *See* Hamilton, James
Aberdeen, 3, 8, 13, 23, 86; clubs of, 7, 10, 12, 73, 80, 81, 214, 217, 218–219; Marischal College, 10, 80; medical developments in, 70, 73, 80; ministers of, 214, 218; professors of, 10, 37, 194; University of, 10, 37, 70, 80, 194, 198
Aberdeen Philosophical Society, or Wise Club (1758), 2, 10–11, 19, 73, 93, 194
Adam, Robert, 12, 20, 52, 199
Addison, Joseph, 7, 8, 34–38, 39, 46, 162, 163, 165–166, 170, 174
admission procedures to clubs, 18–19, 76, 132–133, 145, 153, 157n19, 211; satires on, 175. *See also* rituals
Ahnert, Thomas, 192
Aldermen of Skinner's Alley (1690), 178
Allan, David, 7, 8–9, 22
American War of Independence, 92, 138–140, 161, 163, 178, 193
Anderson, Benedict, 163
Anderson, James, 176
Anderston Club (c. 1744), 10, 22, 86, 89–91, 198
Andrews, Corey E., 18, 23, 104, 106, 135
Arbroath, 52, 53, 54, 57, 60, 215
Arbuckle, James, 170, 174
Arouet, François-Marie. *See* Voltaire
associations, 1–2, 9, 13–15, 39, 59, 61, 73, 129, 163, 197; female, 206–222; and fraternal ideals, 143–144, 146–148, 149, 152–156; political, 2, 5, 16–17; professional, 11, 41, 69–71, 74, 75–77, 80–81, 198; voluntary, 2, 20, 42, 45, 194, 206–207, 209, 221. *See also* women
Auchinleck, Lord. *See* Boswell, Alexander
Ayr, 8, 12, 18, 52, 53, 56, 59, 210, 213

Bailey, Joanne, 201
Banff, 54, 62n2, 64n36
Bannatyne Club (1812), 15
Baptist Church, 206. *See also* evangelicals
Barclay, Katie, 201, 202
Barnard, Toby, 171
Bee, The, 169, 171, 173, 176, 180
Beggar's Benison (1732), 12, 169, 178–179
Beith, 16, 212, 214–215, 216
Belfast, 164
Belles Lettres Society (1759), 9, 104, 107, 165, 169, 192, 193, 194, 196–199; rules of, 19–20, 93
Ben-Amos, Ilana Krausman, 192
Black, David, 208
Black, Joseph, 9, 93, 169, 198
Blacklock, Thomas, 149
Blackwood's Edinburgh Magazine, 22, 181
Blair, Hugh, 9, 40–41, 195, 197–198, 202
Block and Axe Club (c.1783), 178, 182
Board of Bon Ton (1776), 163, 166–167, 168–169, 171, 174, 175
bohemianism, 127, 128–130, 132, 133–134, 140–141, 204n33
Boswell, Alexander: Lord Auchinleck, 108, 111, 114–116, 200–201
Boswell, James, 12, 21, 23, 104–122, 174, 200–201, 202; clubs of, 107; *The Life of Samuel Johnson*, 122; poems of, 116, 120; *Tour to the Hebrides*, 122. *See also* Soaping Club (c.1760)
Bradfute, John, 91

Braemar, 16
Brechin, 17, 211
British and Foreign Bible Society (1804), 218
British and Foreign School Society (1814), formerly the Royal Lancastrian Society (1808), 218
British empire, 5, 54, 72, 87, 117, 130, 140, 218. *See also* West Indies
Buchan, Earl of. *See* Erskine, David Steuart
burghs, 6–7, 49–62
Burke, Edmund, 22, 34, 43, 45, 46
Burn, William, 52
Burnett, James, Lord Monboddo, 11, 12
Burney, Frances, 168, 171
Burns, Robert, 12, 15, 20, 21, 92, 127, 128, 134, 137, 158n44; and Freemasonry, 11, 18, 23, 143–156; Masonic verse of, 144, 151, 152–155, 156; *Poems, Chiefly in the Scottish Dialect*, 11, 143, 147, 148–149, 150, 156; as "poet laureate," 142n33, 144, 149–151, 155, 156; and radical politics, 155–156; satires on masons, 152–153, 154
Burns clubs, 60
Burns suppers, 136

Calves-Head Club (1701), 177–178
Calvinism, 15. *See also* Church of Scotland; Presbyterianism
Cameronians, 39
Campbell, George, 10
Cape Club (1764), 12, 19, 23, 127–141, 175; rules and regulations of, 131–133, 137–138
Carlyle, Alexander, 86, 87, 89, 90–91, 96, 198, 199–200
Carnegie, Susan, 211, 212–213
Carr, Rosalind, 5, 9, 11, 23, 79, 105, 167
Carswell, Catherine, 150
Catholicism, 51; anti-Catholicism, 7, 13, 139. *See also* sectarianism
Cavendish, Sir Henry, 166
Chambers, Robert, 128, 130, 145
character, formation of, 35–37, 38, 86, 192–195, 199–200, 202. *See also* improvement
Charteris, Francis, Lord Elcho, 149, 151
Chen, Jeng-Guo S., 193
Church of England, 107, 108, 109, 207. *See also* Episcopalians
Church of Scotland, 14, 87, 90, 119, 206, 207, 214, 219, 220, 221. *See also* Presbyterianism
Clark, Peter, 4–5, 6, 13, 33, 70, 74, 76, 85, 106, 163
Cleikum Club (1826), 22
Clerk, John, Lord Eldin, 143
Clerk of Penicuik, Sir James, 91
club and society types: agricultural, 3, 8, 59, 118; antiquarian, 15, 22; anti-slavery, 6, 13, 218; bawdy, 1, 12; bible, 13, 14, 206, 207, 218–221, 222n8; book and reading, 12, 14 15, 16; Burns, 60; economic, 1, 86, 169; educational, 14, 16, 18–19, 34, 41, 206–207, 214–215, 217–218, 221; farmers', 1, 59; fictitious, 18, 20–22, 23, 75, 106, 119–120, 161–183; horticultural, 1; hunting, 55, 58, 59, 178, 182; loyalist, 6, 13, 16–17, 22, 60, 107, 172, 175; medical, 6, 10, 23, 69–81, 84n54; missionary, 1, 14, 206, 207, 218, 220–221; mixed, 14–15, 18, 20, 167–168, 170, 206, 209–211, 214–215, 217, 222; musical, 1, 11–12; philanthropic, 1, 4, 13, 14, 15–16, 18–19, 23, 206–210, 213–218, 221; philosophical, 1, 2, 3, 10, 89, 104, 169; political, 9, 60–61, 107, 109, 164, 172, 175–176, 179; reforming and radical, 6, 16, 22, 60, 109, 164, 175–179, 207, 213, 221; regional, 1, 19; religious, 1, 10, 18, 19, 23, 109, 218–221; scientific, 1, 3, 4, 9–10, 55, 71, 73, 84n54, 86, 94, 169; sporting, 1, 13, 59, 60, 165; student, 1, 3, 9, 11, 18–20, 33–34, 78–80, 90, 106, 191–202; women's, 17–18, 23–24, 167–169, 206–222. *See also* convivial and drinking clubs; debating clubs; friendly societies; libraries; literary societies; medical corporations; politics; women
Cochrane, Andrew, 87–88, 94
Cockburn, Henry, Lord Cockburn, 33–34, 40, 76
coffeehouses, 56–57, 58, 103, 169, 171; and women, 167
Cohen, Michèle, 195
Colquitt, Edward "Ned", 107–108, 116
Congregational Church, 207
conversation, 20, 22, 36, 37, 41, 116, 120, 121, 131, 171, 194; and education, 89, 191, 195, 196, 198; and Enlightenment philosophy, 4; and improvement, 1, 40, 176; mixed-sex, 86, 196, 197; and polite culture, 4, 7, 169
convivial and drinking clubs, 1–4, 6, 12, 14, 19–20, 35, 92, 105–109, 119–120, 173–174; and women, 18. *See also* Cape Club (1764); conviviality
conviviality, 9, 10, 13, 21–22, 104–109, 111, 121, 163, 175–180, 182; and Freemasonry,

154; in medical clubs, 69, 76–77, 78, 81; and youth culture, 193–194, 199–200, 202. *See also* convivial and drinking clubs; inns; taverns
Cooper, Antony Ashley, third Lord Shaftesbury, 8, 37, 39, 46, 176
Covenanters, 39, 161. *See also* Presbyterianism
Craig, William, 93, 95–96
Crawford, Robert, 144, 148, 150, 157n6
Creech, William, 11, 165, 168, 176
Critical Review, 121
criticisms of clubs, 23, 34, 40–41, 118–120, 162–163, 166–169, 173–174, 179, 180–183
Crochallan Fencibles (1778), 12, 21, 127–128
Cullen, William, 80, 89, 93, 196, 198
Cummyng, James, 133
Cunningham, James, fourteenth Earl of Glencairn, 11, 143, 153–154, 156
Cupar, 8, 53, 59, 216

Daer, Lord. *See* Douglas, Basil
Daiches, David, 128
Dairsie, 219
Dalgleish, Andrew J., 13, 20
Dalrymple, Sir David, Lord Hailes, 11, 109, 111, 113–114, 115, 116, 118–119
Dalrymple, Sir John, 93, 94
Dashwood, Sir Francis, 174
debating, 4, 55, 74, 81; and civil society, 40–41, 86, 87, 103, 162; in club proceedings, 8, 10, 19, 73, 89, 92–95; and youth culture, 193–197, 199, 201–202. *See also* debating clubs
debating clubs, 1, 3, 12, 61, 106; criticisms of, 41, 49; for students, 33, 79, 191, 198; and women, 18, 167, 181. *See also* debating
Dempster, George, 34, 53, 108, 114, 116, 117–118, 120
Devine, T. M., 96
Dickie, Simon, 105
discipline in clubs and societies, 19–20, 93, 131–132, 137–138, 164, 165, 176, 196, 211–212
dissenters, 161, 207. *See* Baptist Church; Congregational Church; seceding churches
Donaldson, Alexander, 109
Douglas, Basil, Lord Daer, 143, 154, 160n76
Dublin, 8, 172, 173, 175, 178, 181, 182; clubs of, 161, 163, 164–167, 170, 171–172, 174, 175, 178, 221
Dublin Evening Post, 162, 175
Dudley, Charles Stokes, 218–220
dueling, 5; and clubs, 174, 180
Dumfries, 51–52, 55, 57, 60, 63n13, 64n37, 66n75, 155, 156, 209
Dunbar, 50, 51, 52, 55, 219
Duncan, Andrew, senior, 21, 75, 76–77, 80, 81
Duncan, Ian, 22
Dundas, Henry, 10, 175, 197
Dundee, 18, 52, 53, 55, 56–57, 59, 60, 61, 64n38, 66n75; clubs of, 12, 13–14, 16, 34, 47n6, 50, 60, 62n3
Dundee Orphan Institution (1815), 14, 217
Dundee Speculative Society (fl. 1772), 12, 49, 167
Dunfermline, 51, 53, 57
Dunlop, Frances, 149, 151
Duns, 12, 59, 192
Dwyer, John, 4, 9, 162

Easy Club (1712), 1, 7, 26n36, 36–37, 165, 169, 176
Eddy, Matthew D., 192
Edinburgh: hospitals of, 70; Magdalene Asylum, 216; Masonic lodges of, 23, 144, 149–151; medical developments in, 69–81; ministers of, 4, 107–108, 207, 208, 214, 218, 220; as provincial capital, 3, 34, 81, 128, 198; Royal College of Physicians of (1681), 3, 6, 69, 83n33; Royal Infirmary of, 70, 71, 78, 79, 81, 216; town council of, 6, 14, 72–73, 81, 199, 216. *See also* Edinburgh, University of
Edinburgh, University of, 3, 20, 33–34, 107, 165, 169, 191, 193–194, 196–202; Library, 135; and medical education, 69–70, 71, 72–73, 78–80, 81, 83n33; principals of, 8, 198; professors of, 40, 71, 73, 78, 79–80, 83n33, 89, 196–197, 198, 200
Edinburgh Christian Instructor, 218, 219
[Edinburgh] Fair Intellectual Club (1720), 17–18, 21, 167
Edinburgh Female Anti-Slavery Association (1830), 218
Edinburgh Junior Female Society for the Relief of Aged and Indigent Women (1797), later the Charitable Female Society (1806), 208, 214, 223n16
Edinburgh Lancastrian School Society (1810), later Edinburgh Education Society (1814), 13, 14, 20, 217
Edinburgh Medical Journal, 75
Edinburgh Philanthropic Society (1798), later the Society for Support of the Magdalene Asylum (1799), 208, 216. *See also* Edinburgh, Magdalene Asylum

Edinburgh Review, 22, 180
Edinburgh Senior Female Society for the Relief of Aged and Indigent Women (1797), 208, 214, 216, 223n16
Edinburgh Society for the Support of Gaelic Schools (1810), 13, 14, 20, 218, 220, 222n8
Edinburgh Society for the Suppression of Beggars (1813), 14, 216–217
Eglinton, Earl of. *See* Montgomerie, Alexander
Elcho, Lord. *See* Charteris, Francis
Eldin, Lord. *See* Clerk, John
Elgin, 210, 211
Elliot, Charles, 75
Elliot of Minto, Sir Gilbert, 193
Elliott, Paul, 86
Emerson, Roger L., 3, 10, 70–71, 72, 73, 93, 194, 197
English Society for the Propagation of the Gospel in Foreign Parts (1701), 7
Episcopalians, 51, 109, 207, 214. *See also* Church of England
Erskine, Andrew, 106, 108–110, 112, 113, 114, 116–118, 120, 174
Erskine, David Steuart, eleventh Earl of Buchan, 15, 95
Erskine, Henry, 143, 156
evangelicals, 5, 14, 15, 90, 93, 208, 214, 218. *See also* religion; *and individual denominations*
Ewing, Greville, 207, 208

factionalism, 22, 36, 38–41, 46, 144–145, 221. *See also* sectarianism
Female Coterie (1769), 167, 168
Fenwick, 220–221
Ferguson, Adam, 9, 46, 48n33, 48n35, 86, 197, 198
Ferguson, J. DeLancey, 143
Fergusson, Robert, 19, 23, 132–135, 136–137, 140–141
Ferrier, Susan, 22
Fielding, Henry, 169, 175, 186n99
Fletcher, Anthony, 192
Fletcher, Eliza, 208–209, 210
Forfar, 53–54, 58, 59, 61, 65n52
Forres, 55
Foulis, Andrew, 89, 93, 94, 95
Foulis, Robert, 89, 93, 94, 95
Foulis Press, 88, 94
Free Gardeners, Independent Order of, 7, 17, 19, 53, 212
Freemasonry, 1, 4, 6, 11, 12–13, 107, 134, 143–156, 175; class distinctions in, 7, 144, 145–146, 147, 149, 153, 154; Grand Lodge of Scotland, 12, 17, 144–145, 146, 157n3; growth of, 7, 12, 17, 143, 147, 152, 157n3; lodge buildings, 49, 51, 52–53; and politics, 17, 23, 155–156; rituals of, 7, 13, 17, 19, 144, 152, 153, 154, 157n3; and satire, 21, 152–153, 154, 168; Scottish foundations of, 5, 7, 143; "speculative" and "operative" members, 7, 19, 109, 143, 144. *See also* Burns, Robert
French, Henry, 192–193, 200, 201
French Revolution, 16, 34, 46, 60, 155, 160n76, 176, 181, 193
Friday Club (1803), 2, 13–14, 21–22
friendly societies, 1–2, 4, 6–7, 13, 15–16, 19, 50, 61; female, 1, 16, 18, 66n77, 207, 208–213, 221; male, 1, 15–16, 209, 210; mixed, 209, 210, 211
Fry, Elizabeth, 217
Fulton, Henry L., 91

Gaelic Club of Glasgow (1780), 19
Gaelic language, 7, 13, 14, 16, 19. *See also* Highlands; schools
Galston, 211, 213
Galt, John, 21–22
Garrick, David, 104
gender, 5, 17–18, 23, 24, 167; and femininity, 5, 105, 168–169, 196; and masculinity, 5, 22, 23, 105, 166, 168–169, 182, 191–202. *See also* women
Gilson, Cornforth, 133, 134–135
Glasgow: medical developments in, 69, 70, 73, 76; merchants of, 10, 20, 23, 73, 85–89, 91, 93, 95–97; ministers of, 10, 23, 85–86, 87, 90–91, 93, 95–96, 97, 218; reading room of, 56; Royal Infirmary of, 73, 76. *See also* Glasgow, University of
Glasgow, University of, 23, 46, 80, 85, 89–91, 96–97, 198; medical education in, 70, 73, 76; principal of, 11; professors of, 9–11, 38, 44, 73, 76, 80, 85–90, 93–97, 197–198
Glasgow Highland Society (1727), 19
Glasgow Literary Society (1752), 10–11, 73, 86, 87, 92–96
Glassford, John, 87, 88–89
Gleadle, Kathryn, 207–208
Glencairn, Earl of. *See* Cunningham, James
Glover, Katharine, 195
Goldsmith, Oliver, 121, 162, 166
Gordon Mill's Farming Club (1758), 10

Gordon Riots, 139. *See also* Protestant Association (1778)
Govan, 85
Grattan, Henry, 165
Greenock, 51, 52–53, 54, 55, 58, 59
Gregory, John, 9, 10, 78, 79
Grey, Henry, 217–218
Grose, Francis, 112, 113
Grub Street Journal, 166, 168

Habermas, Jürgen, 103, 105, 167
Hailes, Lord. *See* Dalrymple, Sir David
Hamilton, Douglas J., 92
Hamilton, Elizabeth (novelist), 216
Hamilton, Elizabeth, eighth Duchess of Hamilton, 58
Hamilton, James, eighth Earl of Abercorn, 58
Hamilton, John, third Earl of Selkirk, 6
Hamilton, Thomas (architect), 52,
Hamilton, Thomas (professor of anatomy and botany), 89, 93
Harris, Bob, 6, 13–14, 16–17, 20, 22–23, 208
Harvey, Karen, 201–202
Haslett, Moyra, 165, 180–181
Hawick, 12, 52, 55, 58, 192
Hazlitt, William Carew, 110
Hecht, Hans, 127–130, 132, 133–134, 137, 140
Herd, David, 127, 130, 133, 134, 135
Hibernian Journal, 162, 163, 166–167, 168, 172, 174
Highlands, 7, 13, 14, 15, 16, 19, 52, 58, 60, 207. *See also* Gaelic language
Highland Society of Edinburgh (1784), 2, 18, 29n112, 212
historiography, of clubs and societies, 2–6, 33, 103–105, 169, 206–207
Hodge Podge Club (1750), 10, 86, 91–92
Hogg, James, 22
Home, Henry, Lord Kames, 42–44, 46, 105–106, 107, 168, 195
Honourable the Society for Improvement in the Knowledge of Agriculture (1723), 3, 8
Howsam, Leslie, 219, 221
Hume, David, 3, 9, 10, 46, 94, 117, 119, 169, 201–202; and Glasgow Literary Society (1752), 93, 94–95; ideas about sociability, 9, 22, 38, 41–42, 86, 104, 196
Hutcheson, Francis, 4, 9, 22, 38, 39–40, 46, 85, 90, 91, 95–96

improvement, 1, 5, 18, 46, 103–104, 106, 167, 169, 197, 214; agricultural, 3, 8, 10, 15, 59, 95, 118; in burghs, 23, 50, 51, 54–56, 58–59, 61–62; cultural, 7, 8; and education, 9, 11, 16, 42, 91, 108, 119, 169, 193; and Freemasonry, 12–13; landowners and, 3, 9, 10; and medicine, 71, 76, 81; moral, 195, 208; national, 2–3, 8, 9, 15, 20, 21; self-, 1, 9, 16, 33, 36–37, 40, 42, 108, 117, 176, 198; social, 207, 208, 216. *See also* character, formation of
inns, 22, 23, 50, 51, 52–53, 56, 57–61, 65n52, 110, 177. *See also* taverns
Inverness, 13, 14, 15, 52, 63n29
Ireland, 2, 5, 11, 17, 39; anti-Scottishness in, 161; clubs of, 23, 161–183; legacy of Scottish Presbyterianism in, 161; and Union of 1800, 161, 181
Irish Whig Club (1789), 182
Irvine, 60, 147, 209, 210, 211, 212

Jacob, Margaret, 148, 155, 156
Jacobitism, 7, 13, 39, 87, 171; and clubs, 6, 26n36, 109; and rebellion of 1715, 33
Jamaica, 148, 158n44
Jedburgh, 59, 115, 193
Jeffrey, Francis, 210
Jephson, Robert, 172
Jezebel Club (1791), 168–169
Johnson, Samuel, 104, 107, 111, 112, 116, 121–122
Johnston, John (professor of medicine), 73, 98n38
Johnston, John, of Grange, 111, 113, 116, 118
Johnstone, 213
Johnstone, Christian Isobel, 22

Kames, Lord. *See* Home, Henry
Kelly, Jason M., 105
Kelso, 12, 58, 59
Kemble, Stephen, 134, 136
Keppel Clubs (after 1779), 164
Kildrummy, 211
Kilmarnock, 49, 56, 60, 91, 148–149, 210, 211, 212, 213
Kingwell, Mark, 103
Kirkcaldy, 51, 52
Kirkcudbright, 53
Kirriemuir, 66n75, 221
Klein, Lawrence, 103

Lancastrian school movement, 13, 14, 20, 217. *See also* British and Foreign School Society (1814), formerly the Royal Lancastrian Society (1808); Edinburgh Lancastrian School Society (1810), later Edinburgh Education Society (1814)

Langford, Paul, 103
Lauder, 59
Lawrence, Christopher J., 69
Leask, Nigel, 144
Lee, Arthur, 108
Leechman, William, 90, 93, 96
libraries, 18, 51, 52, 53, 54–55, 169, 194; circulating, 51, 167; subscription, 12, 13, 14–15, 18, 49, 53. *See also* reading rooms
Lindsay, Hercules, 89, 93
Linlithgow, 55, 59
literary societies, 1, 2–3, 4, 9, 33, 35, 50, 106, 135–137, 169, 197–198; and antiquarianism, 15; of Glasgow, 89–96; of London, 107, 108
Locke, John, 35, 38, 111, 195
Loiselle, Kenneth, 155
London, 18, 36, 39, 58, 80, 139, 165, 184n50, 204n33, 219; clubs of, 12, 16, 107–108, 116, 166–167, 180, 207–8, 218, 221, 223n10; education in, 195; influence in Scotland of, 3, 5, 7, 8; James Boswell in, 105–108, 109, 110, 114, 115–116, 117, 118, 121, 200; print culture of, 7, 56, 75, 108, 109, 165, 168, 179; Royal Society of, 9
London Corresponding Society (1792), 16
London Missionary Society (1795), 207
Lothian, William, 9, 193
Lounger, The, 10, 104, 149, 162, 164–165, 168, 169–171, 176, 179, 181
loyalism. *See* politics
Luttrell, Henry Lawes, 165

Macdonald, Fiona, 72
Mackenzie, Allan, 150, 151, 159n57
Mackenzie, Henry, 149, 162, 168, 173, 176, 180, 182; and Freemasonry, 11, 12, 143; membership of clubs, 21, 22, 169; and the Mirror Club (1776), 4, 9, 163, 168
Mackey, Albert, 145
Mackintosh, James, 79
MacLaurin, Colin, 8, 9, 37
MacLaurin, John, 90, 96
Mallet, David, 117–118, 121
Manning, Susan, 192
Martin, Peter, 105
Marwick, Sandra, 6
Mathew, W. M., 87, 96
Maxwelltown, 212
Maybole, 1, 17, 209, 212
McCrie, Thomas, 217–218
McDiarmid, Matthew P., 128, 134
McElroy, Davis D., 2–3, 21, 33, 70, 88, 92–93, 198; on the Cape Club (1764), 131, 135, 138; taxonomy of clubs, 106, 129
McLehose, Agnes, 92, 142n33
medical corporations, 23, 69–70, 77–78. *See also* club and society types
Medical Society (1731), 10, 71–72, 74, 75, 76, 77–78, 80, 81; *Medical Essays and Observations*, 71–72, 73, 74, 77, 80, 81
medicine, 9, 69–81
Mee, Jon, 173
meeting places of clubs and societies, 9, 17, 20, 22–23, 61, 131, 135, 177, 181, 212; and new urban buildings, 52–53, 58–60. *See also* burghs; inns; taverns
Millar, John, 22, 44–46
Miller, George, 50, 51
Mirror, The, 10, 104, 162, 163, 168–170, 174, 176, 177, 179, 180
Mirror Club (1776), 4, 10, 104, 108, 163–165, 168, 170–171, 177, 179–180, 182; and the Feast of Tabernacles (1770), 9, 96, 104, 163
Missionary Magazine, 207, 208, 215
Moderates, 4, 15, 90, 96, 119, 193, 202. *See also* Church of Scotland; Presbyterianism
Moffat, 52
Monboddo, Lord. *See* Burnett, James
Monkland Friendly Society (1789), 15
Monro, Alexander, primus, 71, 72, 74, 77, 80, 81
Monro, Alexander, secundus, 11, 74, 80
Montgomerie, Alexander, tenth Earl of Eglinton, 118
Monthly Review, 121
Montrose, 14, 52, 53, 211, 212–213
Moor, James, 89, 93
Moore, John, 85, 91–92
More, Jacob, 134
Morgan, Sydney, Lady Morgan, 173
Morrell, J. B., 70, 73
Morris, R. J., 155
Mossner, Ernest Campbell, 89
Murray, John, 75

Nasmyth, Alexander, 11, 134
Nenadic, Stana, 207
Neville, Sylas, 79
New Light Burgher Church, 207. *See also* seceding churches
newspapers, 2, 20, 49, 56, 64nn37–38, 199, 214; club copies of, 132, 137–138, 140; representations of clubs in, 21, 23, 161–162, 163–165, 166–169, 171–175, 177, 179–182, 212–213. *See also* periodicals; print culture
New Statistical Account of Scotland, The (1845), 209, 210, 214, 221

Nicol, Alexander, 151–152, 154
nonconformists, 171, 178
Northern Star (Belfast), 164, 168

Oddfellows, Independent Order of, 17, 29n107
Orange Order, 17, 161, 178
Oyster Club (1778), 12, 169

Paisley, 51, 53, 56–57, 58, 64n40, 91, 217; clubs of, 60, 62n2, 211, 212, 219, 220
Pantheon Society (1773), 12, 18, 19, 107, 167
Paton, Robert, 91
patronage, 5, 14, 19, 20, 55, 59, 75, 92, 97, 217; female patrons, 14, 210, 212, 214, 215, 217, 219, 220; literary patrons, 11, 147, 156
Peddie, James, 207, 208
Peebles, 58, 65n52
periodicals, 7, 10, 35, 49, 56, 129; and clubs and societies, 21, 161–162, 163–166, 168, 169–170, 174, 176–177, 180–182; medical, 72, 75, 76, 81. *See also* newspapers; print culture
Perth, 51, 52, 55, 58–59, 60, 61, 62n2, 64n32, 64n38, 65n57; female societies of, 214, 215
Perth Antiquarian Society (1784), 15
Peterhead, 52
philanthropy. *See* club and society types; women
Phillipson, Nicholas, 3–4, 88, 198, 199
Philosophical Society of Edinburgh (1737), 4, 9–10, 34, 38, 72–75, 77, 169, 177, 198; *Essays and Observations: Physical and Literary*, 74, 75
Pittock, Murray, 6, 26n36
Playfair, James, 53
Poker Club (1762), 9, 38, 104, 106, 121, 169, 175, 177, 179; as elite club, 104, 106, 127–129, 133–134; and Scottish militia, 4, 9, 175
polite culture, 2, 4, 6–9, 33, 37, 103–104, 116, 121–122, 199, 204n33; and conversation, 1, 4, 7, 37, 169, 176, 196; and education, 15, 35, 41; and England, 3, 7, 11, 38–39; and gender, 5, 15, 23, 105, 191–202; and Ireland, 11, 23, 163; in print, 161, 162, 163, 169, 176–177, 181, 182; and religion, 93, 204n33
political economy, 10, 86–89, 94, 169, 207–208
Political Economy Club (c. 1743), 10, 86–89, 94
politicization of clubs and societies, 5, 23, 24, 138–140, 141, 172–173
politics, 5–6, 10, 16–17, 35–36, 38–46, 57, 138–140, 165, 171–176, 179–180; as a career, 8, 11, 174; loyalism, 5, 6, 16–17, 22, 156, 164, 172, 175, 182; radicalism, 16–17, 34, 41, 155–156, 164, 172, 175–176, 181–182, 210, 213; reform, 5–6, 16, 45, 160n76, 164, 172, 175, 207, 213, 221; republicanism, 155–156, 177–178; Whigs, 10, 17, 22, 34, 35, 45, 87, 107, 109, 171, 174, 178; Tories, 20, 22, 162. *See also* club and society types; political economy; politicization of clubs and societies
Prendergast, Amy, 167
Presbyterianism, 7, 8, 93, 161, 193, 199, 202, 221. *See also* Church of Scotland; seceding churches
Press, The (Dublin), 164
print culture, 10–11, 61, 70–72, 73, 74–75, 81, 86, 121, 161, 163; booksellers, 11, 50, 51, 164, 171; printers, 50, 130, 134, 148, 164–165, 168, 170, 174, 175; publishers, 11, 75, 82n26, 176. *See also* newspapers; periodicals
Prochaska, F. K., 206
Protestant Association (1778), 164, 174. *See also* Gordon Riots; sectarianism
provincial towns, clubs in, 4–5, 6–7, 12, 13–16, 23–24, 49–62, 130, 164, 214, 219, 220. *See also* burghs
public sphere, 103, 105, 155, 161–163, 165, 167–168, 171, 181–182, 196, 198. *See also* Habermas, Jürgen; sociability

Quakers, 218

radicalism. *See* politics
Raeburn, Henry, 134
Ramsay, Allan, 1, 36
Ramsay, John, of Ochtertyre, 33–35, 36, 37
Rankenian Club (1716/17), 8, 37, 169, 176
Reader, Nicola Sian, 210
reading rooms: in burghs, 23, 50, 51, 52, 53, 56–57, 64n32, 64n38, 64n40, 64n44; Glasgow, 56. *See also* libraries
Reid, Thomas, 10, 11, 93–94
Relief Church, 221. *See also* seceding churches
religion, 54, 85, 93, 156, 193; church buildings, 51, 54; and education, 7, 96, 215–216, 217; missionary activity, 13, 14, 206, 207, 218, 220–221; moral reform, 7, 13, 119, 207–208, 216; religious publishing, 13, 15, 218; theology, 15, 85, 90, 91, 93, 96. *See also* club and society types; sectarianism; women; *and individual denominations*

republicanism. *See* politics
Richardson, Samuel, 169
Richardson, William, 94, 95
rituals, 5, 6, 24, 129, 131, 136, 161, 172, 175, 176; in Freemasonry, 7, 13, 17, 19, 144, 152–153, 154, 157n3; in friendly societies, 2; and initiations, 7, 17, 18, 19, 129, 132–133, 137, 140, 144, 153. *See also* admission procedures
Roberts, Marie Mulvey, 165, 175
Robertson, William, 9, 104, 198–199
Rose, George, 209
Ross, Alexander, 89
Ross, Ian Simpson, 89
Rothery, Mark, 192–193, 200, 201
Royal Company of Archers (1676), 6
Royal Medical Society (1737), 11, 78–80, 81, 204n38
Royal Physical Society (1771), 79
Royal Society of Edinburgh (1783), 10, 15, 73, 75, 198
Royal St. Crispin Society (1817), 6, 19
rules and regulations, 19–20, 77, 92, 93–94, 106, 153, 179, 196, 198; in female societies, 209–212, 214, 218; in print culture, 164, 174, 176; and satire, 162, 168. *See also* Cape Club (1764)
Runciman, Alexander, 130, 133, 134, 135
Ruthwell, 212

satires, 171; on clubs and societies, 21, 22, 161–163, 166, 171–172, 173–175, 177, 178, 180–182; on Freemasons, 152–153, 154; on women, 166, 167–169
Schetky, J.G.C., 134, 142n33
schools, 50, 51, 53, 54, 192, 195, 208; academies, 53, 54; charity schools, 7, 13, 208, 215, 216–217; Gaelic schools, 13, 14, 20, 218, 220, 221; girls' schools, 195, 206, 214–215, 216, 217; industrial schools, 216. *See also* club and society types; Lancastrian school movement
Scotland: distinctiveness of, 2, 5, 8, 52, 69, 75, 103–104, 162; egalitarianism of, 42, 128, 129; history of, 2, 5, 6, 15, 38–39, 40–41, 46, 60, 104, 129; origins of Freemasonry in, 5, 7, 143; and Union of 1707, 3, 6, 7, 35, 36, 37, 46; universities of, 8, 40, 85, 169, 191, 194, 197, 199; women's distinctive experiences in, 18, 209–210, 219, 221
Scott, Sir Walter, 14, 15, 21–22
Scott, W. R., 88
Scottish Enlightenment, 3, 5, 11, 14, 15, 104, 116, 169, 208; and associationalism, 2–9, 22–23, 33–46, 49, 104–106, 127, 180; culture of, 2, 5, 7, 13, 103, 106, 129, 152, 193, 197–199; and the formation of character, 192, 202; ideas of, 4, 38–46, 104, 191–192, 197–198, 202; and medicine, 69, 70–71, 72, 75–76, 79–81; print culture of, 10, 162. *See also* periodicals; print culture
Scottish Missionary and Philanthropic Register, 218, 220
seceding churches, 207, 220. *See also* New Light Burgher Church; Relief Church
sectarianism, 22, 38–9, 40, 46, 178, 221. *See also* factionalism
Select Society (1754), 4, 8, 18, 38, 91, 107, 119, 169, 194, 202; as elite club, 3, 34, 104–105, 106, 116, 128, 134, 191, 200
Select Society for Promoting the Reading and Speaking of the English Language in Scotland (1761), 8, 108
Selkirk, 14–15, 58, 59
Selkirk, Earl of. *See* Hamilton, John
Shaftesbury, third Earl of. *See* Cooper, Antony Ashley
Shakespeare, William, 135
Shapin, Steven, 69, 72–73
Shepard, Alexandra, 191
Sher, Richard B., 4, 88
Sheridan, Thomas, 116
Sibbald, Sir Robert, 3, 6
Simeon, Charles, 208
Simson, Robert, 89–90, 91, 93, 94, 198
Slavery and the slave trade, 158n44, 193; anti-slavery societies, 6, 13, 218; defenders of, 6; hostility to, 176
Smellie, William, 21, 75, 127
Smith, Adam, 44, 46, 93, 94, 95, 197, 201, 202; criticisms of clubs, 40, 47n23, 105–106, 194; membership of clubs, 3, 9, 94, 169, 194; and the Political Economy Club (1743), 86, 87–89, 94; *Lectures on Rhetoric and Belles Lettres*, 98n35; *The Theory of Moral Sentiments*, 105–106; *The Wealth of Nations*, 86, 87–88
Smollett, Tobias, 21, 85, 91, 98n38, 114, 182; *The Adventures of Peregrine Pickle*, 90, 173; *The Expedition of Humphrey Clinker*, 166, 173, 178; *Ferdinand Count Fathom*, 173; *Roderick Random*, 90, 92
"soaping" and "shaving", 109–122
Soaping Club (c. 1760), 12, 23, 105–122, 174, 200

sociability, 6, 119, 144; and associationalism, 2, 3–5, 18, 33–46, 49–50, 61–62, 86, 104–107, 127, 161–163; changing patterns of, 4, 23, 35, 56, 61; and character, 35, 192; and civil society, 3–4, 24, 35–46, 57, 86, 93, 103–107, 206, 222; and education, 202; and improvement, 9; philosophical ideas about, 4, 8–9, 22, 24, 35, 37–46, 103–106, 195; and polite culture, 4, 15, 37–39, 193; undesirable forms of, 23, 39–41, 105–106, 121, 173, 179–180, 193–194, 199–200; and women, 15, 18, 167–168, 196. *See also* character, formation of; conviviality; polite culture; public sphere; taverns
Society for Constitutional Information (1780), 16
Society for Propagating the Gospel at Home (1797), 14
Society for the Reformation of Manners in Scotland (1699), 7
Society in Scotland for Propagating Christian Knowledge (1709), 7, 13
Society of Antiquaries of Scotland (1780), 10, 15, 21
Society of the Friends of the People (1792), 22, 34, 160n76, 176
Society of United Irishmen (1791), 16, 164, 168, 172–173
Society of United Scotsmen (1797), 16, 34
Somerville, Thomas, 192–193, 197, 199–200, 201, 202
Spectator, The, 7, 10, 21, 35, 36–37, 161–162, 165–166, 168, 179, 181
Speculative Society (1764), 2, 11, 20, 21, 79, 161, 169, 176, 192, 194–199
St. Andrews, 34, 63n20; University of, 133
Statistical Account of Scotland, The (1793), 13
Steele, Richard, 7, 8, 35, 162, 165
Stevenson, Alexander, 92
Stevenson, David, 5, 7, 143, 144, 147
Stevenson, John, 8
Stevenston, 219
Stewart, Dugald, 11, 12, 22, 88, 89, 95, 143, 149, 198
Stewart, George, 58
Stewart, Matthew, 89
Stewart Watson, William, 142n33, 159n60
Stirling, 52, 53, 55, 59, 62n2
Strang, John, 2, 12, 90, 94
Stuart, Charles, 206–207, 222
students. *See* club and society types; youth culture
Surtees, Robert Smith, 112
Sutherland, Elizabeth, nineteenth Countess of Sutherland, 18
Sweet, Rosemary, 208
Swift, Jonathan, 168, 174, 177, 179

Tain, 221
Tarbolton, 153; Masonic lodges of, 23, 144–148, 152, 153, 154
Tarbolton Bachelors Club (1780), 20
Tatler, The, 10, 21, 35, 162, 168, 177, 181
taverns, 12, 20, 23, 105, 111, 191, 196, 200–201; in burghs, 23, 50, 56, 57, 60–61; in Dublin, 166, 174, 175, 181; in Edinburgh, 9, 22, 107, 110, 128, 131, 136, 177, 199; figurative, 121; in Glasgow, 12, 90, 198. *See also* inns
Thackeray, William Makepeace, 129
Theological Society (1759), 9, 193
Thom, William, 85–86
Thomas Ruddiman's Club (1718), 8
Thomson, Andrew, 218
Thomson, James, 135–136
toasting, 21, 92, 134, 136, 149–150, 164, 173, 177–179; criticisms of, 174, 177–179, 180, 182; political, 139, 161, 167, 176, 177–179. *See also* conviviality
Tocqueville, Alexis de, 45
Tories. *See* politics
Turnbull, George, 8, 37

Ulster, 38, 161

Voltaire (François-Marie Arouet), 111
Volunteer Evening Post, 164, 165, 172
Volunteer's Journal, 164, 165

Wallace, Mark C., 12, 17, 143, 155, 157n3
Ward, Edward, 162, 166, 168, 171, 174, 177–178, 182
Watt, James, 89
West Indies, 54, 80, 92. *See also* British empire; Jamaica
Whig Club of Dundee (1789), 16, 34
Whigs. *See* politics
Whitefoord, Sir John, 145–146, 147–148
Wig Club (1775), 12
Wight, William, 87
Wilberforce, Samuel, 112
Wilkes, John, 105, 164, 171
Wilson, Alexander, 94
Wilson, John ("Christopher North"), 22
Wilson, John (Tarbolton), 153
Wishart, William, 8

women: in coffee houses, 167; and education, 195, 206, 208, 211, 212, 214–215, 217–218, 221; exclusion from male societies, 1, 5, 17, 92, 163, 167, 181–182, 206, 208–209, 219; in female clubs and societies, 17–18, 23–24, 167–169, 206–222; in friendly societies, 1, 16, 18, 66n77, 207, 208–213, 221; on ladies' committees, 20, 208, 210–11, 214, 215, 216–217, 220–221; in mixed clubs and societies, 14–15, 18, 20, 167–168, 170, 206, 209–211, 214–215, 217, 222; in mixed public spaces, 12, 42, 61, 86, 168, 180, 196, 197; opposition to, in societies, 23, 163, 167–169, 180, 206, 210, 212–213, 219, 221–222; and philanthropy, 18, 23, 206–208, 209, 210, 211, 213–218, 221; and prison reform, 217; public processions of, 1, 212–213; in religious societies, 218–221; in salons, 105, 167, 168, 181; satires on, 21, 166, 167–169; and sex work, 113, 200; and the term "coterie", 167, 181; toasting of, 92, 179. *See also* gender

youth culture, 107, 114–116, 118–119, 191–202. *See also* club and society types